RICKOVER

Francis Duncan

RICKOVER

☀ *The Struggle for Excellence* ☀

Naval Institute Press
Annapolis, Maryland

First Naval Institute Press paperback edition, 2011

Naval Institute Press
291 Wood Road
Annapolis, MD 21402

Library of Congress Cataloging-in-Publication Data
Duncan, Francis, 1922-
    Rickover : the struggle for excellence / Francis Duncan.
    p. cm.
    Includes bibliographical references and index.
    ISBN 978-1-59114-221-8 (alk. paper)
    1. Rickover, Hyman George. 2. Admirals—United States—Biography.
3. United States. Navy—Biography. 4. Nuclear engineers—United States—
Biography. 5. Nuclear warships—United States—History—20th century.
6. Nuclear submarines—United States—History—20th century. I. Title.
    V63.R63 D86 2001
    359'.0092—dc21
    [B]   2001030793

Printed in the United States of America on acid-free paper ∞
16 15 14 13 12   9 8 7 6 5 4 3 2

Title page photo courtesy of Eleonore B. Rickover

For Frances—forever

CONTENTS

FOREWORD

IN 1954, as a newly commissioned ensign in the Navy Nurse Corps, I was under indoctrination into the Navy at St. Albans Naval Hospital on Long Island, New York. On a free weekend I traveled by train with a friend in order to tour Washington, D.C. While on the bus tour we passed the U.S. National Naval Medical Center in Bethesda, Maryland. I vividly recall telling my friend that I hoped I never would receive orders there since I did not want to be around all that brass. Little did I know what the future held in store.

I was delighted when my orders to report to the U.S. Naval Hospital, Oakland, California, arrived. At my third duty station I was one of four nurses at the U.S. Naval Ammunition Depot in Hawthorne, Nevada. Since it was considered an isolated area, we were led to believe that we would choose our next assignment. I requested the Naval Hospital in Bremerton, Washington, or any place on the West Coast. I was disappointed when I received orders directing me to report to the U.S. National Naval Medical Center in Bethesda, Maryland. I thought perhaps they had confused Bremerton with Bethesda. After some consideration I decided to comply with the orders since I had enjoyed all my previous duty stations. I was a Reserve officer, so if I disliked duty in Bethesda, I was not obligated to remain in the Navy.

After about a year and a half at Bethesda, I was assigned to Tower 16, where the patients were all VIPs—admirals, senators, congressmen, foreign diplomats—but I was reluctant to go because I had enjoyed the positive and professional working relationship we had developed with our medical officer and Hospital Corpsmen. Nevertheless, as a young lieutenant relieving a commander, I had no choice but to accept the assignment.

On the day I reported for duty on Tower 16, Vice Adm. Hyman G. Rickover was admitted to my floor. He did not arrive until my shift was over, so I met him for the first time the following morning. The duration of his hospital stay was twelve weeks, followed by frequent appointments with his doctor, whose office was on Tower 16. During that time I was privileged to get to know Admiral Rickover to some extent. Later, as I furthered my education, he became my friend and my mentor.

In January 1974, Admiral and I were married. I was still a commander on active duty at Great Lakes Naval Hospital in Waukegan; he had been promoted to four-star admiral a month earlier. So much for not wanting to be around all that brass. However, Admiral Rickover was not a typical admiral. He did not wear his uniform, had no military aide, and worked in frugal surroundings.

Admiral and I were sent orders from the secretary of the Navy, who at that time was John Warner, to attend the dedication of Rickover Hall, the engineering building at the Naval Academy, and it specifically stated we were to wear our uniforms. We did. The day of my retirement from the Navy, Admiral appeared in my office wearing his uniform. I was quite surprised and pleased at the same time. He said, "I thought you would like it."

Shortly after we were married, I found a quotation from an ancient Sanskrit text that I thought described my husband very well, and I would like to share it with you: "Softer than the flowers where kindness is concerned / Louder than the thunder where principles are at stake." Those who knew my husband well could relate to the first part; however, most of the men told me they were more familiar with the latter. He was a very sensitive, caring, kind, funny, and principled man.

I would like to leave the reader with a paragraph from the last letter I received from my husband while at sea on 24 January 1982. Knowing that his retirement would take place on 30 January, he was thinking about his life in a philosophical way: "As I have amply known in the course of a long life—'success' in one's work is not and never has been the major object of my life. It seems to have come naturally to me to work hard and to complete whatever work I have undertaken. This feeling and attitude of full personal responsibility is what has made it possible for me to accomplish every working duty I have ever been assigned—and to improve the previous status of the work."

Admiral Rickover was most grateful to this country for the opportunity that made it possible for him to do what he wanted to do. He knew that had his parents not emigrated to the United States, he would have become a victim of the Holocaust. Years later he learned that no one from his home town in Makow, Poland, had survived.

In this well-written, factual, and readable book, Francis Duncan tells the story, in as concise a manner as possible, of a complex man who dedicated his life to his country for sixty-three years while demonstrating that through discipline, determination, and hard work, great accomplishments are possible.

I enjoyed reading *Rickover: The Struggle for Excellence,* and I hope you will too.

ELEONORE BEDNOWICZ RICKOVER

PREFACE

THE ORIGINS of this biography go back to 1969, when Adm. Hyman G. Rickover requested that the Atomic Energy Commission assign its chief historian, Richard G. Hewlett, and me to his office to write historical studies of the joint Atomic Energy Commission–Department of the Navy naval nuclear propulsion program. As a result, we wrote *Nuclear Navy, 1946–1962*, published by the University of Chicago Press in 1974. Afterward, Hewlett returned to his task of writing the history of the commission, but I continued in Admiral Rickover's office, where I wrote *Rickover and the Nuclear Navy: The Discipline of Technology*, published by the Naval Institute Press in 1990. The purpose of the book was to show how the admiral ran a technical program that had gained worldwide recognition for its excellence.

To that end he made sure that I visited his laboratories, attended some technical meetings, talked to his engineers, and went on the initial sea trials of some of the nuclear-powered attack and missile submarines as well as attack carriers and cruisers. When he was in Washington he frequently came into my office, located a few doors down from his own. He spoke of the books he was reading, usually histories and biographies, and sometimes about episodes in his career. He did not intend by these brief conversations to furnish material for his biography: indeed, he declared vehemently that he did not want a biography and would not help anyone to write one. He rejected with even greater force the suggestion that he write an autobiography. From his own wide reading he had decided that such books were self-serving and of limited value.

While his view on an autobiography remained adamant, his opinion on a biography shifted. I believe he changed his stand for two reasons. The first was the appearance of a volume that showed little understanding or interest in the nuclear technology that he had done so much to develop and that had revolutionized naval operations. Unless he cooperated with a biographer, however, history would see him through works of this kind. The second reason was his rediscovery of the letters that he and his first wife, Ruth Masters Rickover, had written to each other. Their prolific correspondence, beginning in 1929, continued until he reported for duty in Washington in 1939. At the time of her death in May 1972 she had begun destroying her letters. He reread their correspondence, finding in it a rich record of their lives.

When he decided to make himself and his papers available for a biography, it was almost inevitable that he should turn to me. He was aware that I admired his achievements, that I had some understanding of his program, and that, although my technical knowledge was weak, I knew whom to ask for help.

Admiral Rickover died before the biography amounted to more than preliminary research and a rough outline. Eleonore B. Rickover, the admiral's second wife, made available to me his correspondence, his fitness reports, and other material. Without her patience, understanding, encouragement, and delightful sense of humor, this book would not have been possible. I owe a great debt to her and to many others. Several officers gave me their perspective on Admiral Rickover and the program he led for more than three decades. Among them are Adm. James D. Watkins, former chief of naval operations; the three successors of Admiral Rickover in leading the program, Adm. Kinnaird R. McKee, Adm. Bruce DeMars, and Adm. Frank L. Bowman; and a former commanding officer of the *Hyman G. Rickover* (SSN 709), Rear Adm. Jay Cohen.

Many individuals, now retired, who worked closely with Admiral Rickover in the program were unstinting in their help. They are William Wegner, James W. Vaughan Jr., and Carl H. Schmitt, who were deputy directors; David T. Leighton, program manager for surface ships and the water-cooled breeder; Thomas L. Foster, director, fiscal, acquisition, and logistics management; William M. Hewitt, director, secondary components division; and Joseph P. Zimmer, director, reactor safety and computation.

I also owe much to the understanding and perception of others who knew Admiral Rickover and the program. Robert M. Rickover, the admiral's son, spoke of his life with his parents; John T. Conway and Edward J. Bauser, successively executive staff directors of the Joint Committee on Atomic Energy, explained the committee's importance and its influence on the admiral's career; George Norris, formerly chief counsel for the

Subcommittee on Seapower of the House Committee on Armed Services, spoke of the special role it played in the congressional authorization process.

I particularly want to express my deep appreciation to John M. Maloney, director, commissioned submarine systems division. In addition to his sharp insight into technical and organizational problems, he brought keen logic, skill in research, cheerful candor in pointing out flaws of grammar, and great zeal in his quest for facts.

Responsibility for the biography is, of course, mine.

It is my hope that *Rickover: The Struggle for Excellence* will cast fresh light on the remarkable life of a remarkable man and encourage others to study the many aspects of that life. He was a superb engineer, an advocate of high standards in education, a contributor to the history of the United States, a skilled leader of a major defense program, and a philosopher of personal responsibility in a technical age.

CHRONOLOGY

Jan. 1900	Born in Makow, Russian Poland
Mar. 1906	Arrived in America
1911	Settled in Chicago
Feb. 1918	Graduated from high school
June 1918	Entered Naval Academy
June 1922	Graduated Naval Academy, commissioned ensign
Sept. 1922–Dec. 1924	Served in destroyer *La Vallette*
Jan. 1925–Apr. 1927	Served in battleship *Nevada*
June 1925	Promoted to lieutenant (jg)
July 1927–Oct. 1929	Attended postgraduate school
June 1928	Promoted to lieutenant
May 1929	Received master's degree in electrical engineering from Columbia University
Oct. 1929–Jan. 1930	Served in submarine *S-9*
Jan.–June 1930	Attended submarine school
June 1930–June 1933	Served in submarine *S-48*
Aug. 1931	Qualified to command submarines
Oct. 1931	Married Ruth D. Masters
July 1933–Mar. 1935	Assigned to Inspector of Naval Material, Philadelphia
Apr. 1935–June 1937	Served in battleship *New Mexico*
July 1937–Oct. 1937	Commanded minesweeper *Finch*
July 1937	Promoted to lieutenant commander
Oct. 1937	Transferred to engineering duty
Oct. 1937–May 1939	Served at the Cavite Navy Yard
Aug. 1939–Mar. 1945	Assigned to electrical section, Bureau of Ships
Oct. 1940	Birth of son, Robert M. Rickover
Dec. 1940	Became head of electrical section
Jan. 1942	Promoted to commander

June 1943	Promoted to captain
Mar.–Nov. 1945	Commanded Naval Repair Base, Okinawa
Dec. 1945–May 1946	Assigned to 19th Fleet, Western Sea Frontier, mothballing ships
June 1946	Assigned to Oak Ridge, Tenn, atomic energy facility
Jan. 1947	Atomic Energy Commission established
Sept. 1947	Ended duty at Oak Ridge
Feb. 1949	Assigned as head of joint AEC-Navy program for naval nuclear propulsion
May 1953	Mark I plant, prototype for *Nautilus*, produced first substantial usable power from atomic energy
July 1953	Promoted to rear admiral; commission assigned Rickover to head the first full-scale civilian power plant, the Shippingport Atomic Power Station
Jan. 1955	Sea trials of *Nautilus*
Dec. 1957	Shippingport operated at full power
Aug. 1958	*Nautilus* crossed the North Pole
Oct. 1958	Promoted to vice admiral
Apr. 1959	Awarded Congressional gold medal
July 1959	Traveled to Soviet Union with Vice President Nixon
May 1960	*Triton* completed first circumnavigation of the world submerged
July 1961	Sea trials of cruiser *Long Beach*, first American nuclear surface ship; suffered heart attack
Oct. 1961	Sea trials of *Enterprise*, first nuclear aircraft carrier
Apr. 1963	Loss of submarine *Thresher*
May 1972	Death of Ruth M. Rickover
Nov. 1972	Suffered second heart attack
Dec. 1973	Promoted to admiral
Jan. 1974	Married Eleonore A. Bednowicz
June 1976	Sea trials of high-speed submarine *Los Angeles*
Dec. 1977	Shippingport at full power with light water breeder reactor
June 1980	Awarded Presidential Medal of Freedom
June 1981	Sea trials of *Ohio*, first Trident submarine
Jan. 1982	Retired from leading propulsion program
Aug. 1983	Submarine *Hyman G. Rickover* launched
Nov. 1983	Awarded second Congressional gold medal
July 1986	Died in Arlington, Virginia

RICKOVER

Introduction   *Forever Skeptical, yet Questioning*

ARLINGTON NATIONAL CEMETERY in the early afternoon of 10 July 1986 was bright, windy, and hot. In an area cordoned off by sailors, a small group of mourners—most were civilians, but a few were naval officers in spotless white uniforms—gathered in silence. Eleonore B. Rickover, escorted by Vice Adm. Bruce DeMars, deputy chief of naval operations for submarine warfare, approached the grave. A small figure dressed in navy blue, she knelt, bowed her head, kissed a small box containing her husband's remains, and placed it into the earth. Then, following a Jewish tradition, she placed a handful of earth over it. Cdr. Bruce E. Kahn and Rear Adm. John R. McNamara of the Chaplain Corps spoke briefly. At the end of the committal service came the sharp sound of three rifle volleys, the haunting call of taps, and the solemn words of benediction.

In time a stone would mark the grave. Incised on its face would appear the words:

H. G. RICKOVER

ADMIRAL

UNITED STATES NAVY

"FATHER OF THE NUCLEAR NAVY"

63 YEARS ACTIVE DUTY

JANUARY 27, 1900   JULY 8, 1986

More than one person present must have reflected upon the contrast between the shaded site at the cemetery and the man just laid to rest.

For more than three decades—from 1949 to the beginning of 1982—he headed the joint naval nuclear propulsion program established by the Atomic Energy Commission (AEC) and the Department of the Navy. During these years he served under eight presidents of the United States, fifteen secretaries of defense, sixteen secretaries of the Navy, eleven chiefs of naval operations, seven commission chairmen, two administrators of energy research and development, and three secretaries of energy. He dealt with countless industrial organizations, ranging from giant conglomerates to small manufacturers. They could all agree on one thing: he was an exceedingly hard man to deal with.

From his first introduction to atomic energy in 1946, he was convinced that the usual institutional procedures, organizations, and management systems were inadequate for its safe development and use. That realization thrust him into countless battles and controversies. When he left the program, the technology he developed had transformed naval operations and powered more than 40 percent of the Navy's major combatant ships: eighty-eight attack submarines, thirty-three ballistic-missile submarines, one deep submergence research vehicle, four aircraft carriers, and nine guided missile cruisers. He and the organization he created had also designed and developed the world's first full-scale civilian atomic power station (which was an AEC, not a Navy, project).[1] The discipline he demanded paid off. The propulsion plants and the power station met their design objectives, and there has been neither an accident involving a program reactor nor a release of radioactivity that has adversely affected the environment.

These achievements themselves are magnificent, but Rickover also left a legacy of engineering principles, applicable to both military and civilian technology, which are essential in a world growing ever more closely together. He frequently used aphorisms to illustrate his philosophy. "Technology will not obey an order" was one; "You cannot decree a technology" was another. They sounded like platitudes, but they were not. He demanded detailed knowledge, not leadership or management systems. He required strict adherence to technical standards. He insisted on training his own personnel. His engineering principles brought him into conflict with the Navy, the Atomic Energy Commission, and industry, but over the years they proved themselves. Those same principles were the key to his career.

Some time after he left the joint program, those who had worked for him were asked to list the adjectives that best described him. Considering his stormy reputation, some were to be expected: abrasive, acerbic, demanding, implacable, intolerant, irascible, obnoxious, and "son of a bitch." Those less caustic included elfin, impish, and puckish, as well as brilliant, quick-witted, insightful, and dedicated. A few individuals who knew him well, usually outside of working hours, described him as well-read, a good conversationalist and good company, compassionate, and possessed of an active, restless, and inquiring mind. All agreed he was complex and unpredictable.

But beneath the surface of conflicting impressions were strong, unchanging currents. Rickover was exceedingly ambitious and filled with driving energy. He was patriotic. He was profoundly grateful to the United States for giving him, a Jewish boy coming to America at the age of six, opportunities that would have been denied him elsewhere. He was convinced of the virtue of hard work, investing it with an almost spiritual meaning. He believed in excellence in technology and in the professions. He sought standards not only for technical matters but also for ethical issues. He was certain that the cause of the failures of society was the refusal of individuals to take responsibility. Institutions, management systems, and bureaucracies could not solve problems—only men and women accepting responsibility could do that. He saw no end to the search and definition of that obligation in a world that was growing more and more complex. That was why, in an address entitled "Thoughts on Man's Purpose in Life," he declared, "Our minds must be forever skeptical, yet questioning."[2]

The mourners quietly departed from Arlington. They had attended a private ceremony, paying their respects to an individual they knew. In a few days at the Washington National Cathedral, the nation would pay its tribute to Admiral Rickover.

Becoming an Officer

UNTIL HE was eighteen years old Rickover thought he was born on 1 January 1900. Only when filling out forms to enter the U.S. Naval Academy did he discover the date was actually 27 January 1900. There was no doubt about his place of birth. It was Makow, an old town located on a windswept plain about fifty miles north of Warsaw in what was then Russian Poland. His father was Abraham Rickover, a deserter from the Russian army who had become a tailor. His mother was Rachel, the youngest daughter of Abraham Unger, owner of a prosperous clothing store. In June 1897 their first child, a daughter (whose Americanized name was Fannie), was born. Life was harsh and they were poor.

Because of virulent anti-Semitism, many Jews were fleeing Russia. Abraham Rickover, leaving his family behind him, made his way to New York, arriving in November 1897. He lived in desperate poverty. Sometime after February 1898 he returned to Makow. In January 1900 his only son Chaim (from the Hebrew word meaning "life," a name his parents later changed to Hyman) was born. Abraham returned to New York; when is not known. Within a few years he had saved enough money to send for his family.[1]

In the early months of 1906, Rachel bundled up their possessions: a mortar and pestle, brass pans, candlesticks, serving spoons, bedding, and a six weeks' supply of kosher food. With her two children she joined a small group of Jews traveling in a covered wagon to the German frontier. They were almost there when a band of dreaded Cossacks surrounded them, shouting and jeering, lashing the horse and rocking the wagon. Finally they left, and the fugitives slipped across the border at night.

With other Jewish refugees, the Rickover family crossed Germany by train, arriving on 16 March 1906 at the Belgian port of Antwerp. Their ship was the *Finland*, a Belgian steamer of the Red Star Line. Before board-

ing, all immigrants had to provide information for the American authorities in New York. Rachel attested she was married and thirty-two years
old, her daughter Fannie was eight, and her son Chaim was six. Whoever
filled out the form noted that none of the three could read or write (here
there was a misunderstanding, for Rachel knew Yiddish and Polish), that
New York was their destination, that Rachel's husband had paid their passage and was the father of the children and lived at "214 Attorne [sic]
Street," that their physical condition was good, and that the mother and
her two children were not paupers, polygamists, or anarchists.[2]

Rachel had given her son the tickets to hold. At the top of the gangway
she asked for them. He said he lost them. For one terrifying moment
she believed him, but, spinning him around, she found them in his back
pocket.

The ship sailed on 17 March. The crowded steerage, with its noise,
stench, and lack of privacy, did not bother the two children. While Rachel
sat guarding her possessions, the boy and his sister explored and played.
When the weather was good her children darted out on deck. If there it
was crowded and cold, at least the air was fresh. From the decks above,
first- and second-class passengers looked down with idle curiosity. A few
tossed candy or fruit.

Anxiety swept through steerage as the *Finland* neared New York. The
immigrants had to pass an examination to enter America. Those who
failed would be sent back, and, if they had sold everything to get money
for their passage, they would return to dire poverty. Many listened to a
man moving importantly among them. He declared that regulations
required messages be sent to relatives or sponsors in the United States: his
job was to collect the money. Rachel gave him all she had and her husband's address.

On 26 March the *Finland* reached New York. The immigrants were
promptly shepherded onto small steamers for the short trip to Ellis Island
and the dreaded examination. Rachel and the children passed the medical
part unscathed but were detained because she had no money and her husband had not come to meet her. Watching over her belongings, she waited
for Abraham as one day stretched into another, bringing closer the
moment when they would be sent back. Opposite their names on the list
of detained aliens, an official had already stamped "Deported."[3]

With only a few hours to spare, Abraham Rickover finally appeared. He
had never received the message from Rachel and would never have known
she was on the island if a friend, coming to pick up a relative, had not seen

her name on a list. The man on the ship had cheated her, a fraud, they learned, that was not uncommon. In the record of detained aliens under the heading "Disposition" someone entered an illegible scrawl, perhaps the abbreviation for the Hebrew Immigrant Aid Society, a private organization that did so much to help unfortunate Jewish immigrants. The notation "3/31" suggests the family was reunited on the last day of March 1906.

On 6 September of that year Abraham Rickover became an American citizen, an act conferring the same status on his family. Legally he was not qualified. The law required him to have lived continuously in the United States for the preceding five years. According to the sworn affidavit he and his witness signed, Abraham Rickover had lived continuously in the state of New York since 1896 or, as declared in another part of the document, since November 1897. Apparently no one noticed or cared about the discrepancy.[4] In 1908 Augusta, Abraham and Rachel's third and last child, was born.

Hyman loved school. He learned English rapidly, for his mind was at that fortunate stage where it could quickly absorb a new language. But New York was a place of failure for Abraham. He had finally acquired a small apartment building—or was about to—when he lost everything to a swindler who came from his own village. In 1909 or 1910 Abraham left for Chicago, once again leaving his family behind.

He found a place to live in Lawndale, on Chicago's West Side. Located a few miles from the business and commercial center of the city, the area was made up of small houses, apartments, shops, and a few larger businesses. Although poor, the neighborhood did not have the shattering poverty of Chicago's notorious Maxwell Street. In 1911 Rachel and the children joined him, riding the day coach with their goods once again in bundles.

Their new address was 3243 Grenshaw Street, a small, two-story building with two apartments on each floor. Abraham Rickover chose one on the second floor facing the rear. It had three rooms, two for living in and one for renting out. It also had a back porch on which his son was to sleep during the stifling summer nights. One room contained a big wood-burning stove for cooking and heating. Family life centered around a large table covered with oil cloth, cheap and easily wiped clean. Here they ate, Rachel holding back her portion in order to give it to her husband and children if they did not have enough. A back yard ended in an alley, while a vacant lot on the east side of the building gave space for growing vegetables.

In September 1911 the two older children entered the Victor F. Lawson Grammar School, Fannie in the eighth grade, Hyman in the sixth. Through books he was discovering a world of fascination and wonder, and, far more crucial to his future, a way to provide the stimulation and nourishment his mind craved. Each day after leaving grammar school he went to Hebrew school in the basement of a nearby synagogue. At thirteen he celebrated his bar mitzvah.

In every possible way Hyman helped his family. In his manual training class at Lawson he made a reading stand, an ironing board, and bookcases. When Augusta outgrew her baby buggy, he used it to scavenge alleys and railway tracks for coal. He found things. One day he brought home an old doll that became Augusta's cherished companion for years.

After school he worked. He was nine when he got his first job: he was paid three cents an hour for holding a kerosene lantern for a neighbor who had a machine in the basement for shaping pieces of galvanized iron used in decorating buildings. When a little older, he worked in a small fruit and vegetable store and drove a horse and wagon to make deliveries. In some jobs he ran into religious prejudice. Once in a while other kids, mainly Irish Catholics shouting, "Christ killer! Christ killer!" beat him up. Frail and slight, he was a poor fighter.

Rickover graduated from grammar school on 26 June 1914. For him and for most of his classmates formal schooling was over. They were fourteen, the minimum age Illinois set for working full time. Fannie was already a stenographer in an office and helping to support the family. Rickover's earnings were also needed, but because the country was sliding into a depression, work was hard to find. His break came just a few blocks from home. The Western Union Telegraph Company, which had set up a temporary office in a nearby bank, needed boys to deliver telegrams. Rickover was one of the boys who got a job. Because he was paid by the hour, he worked every day as long as he could. He saved money on clothing by wearing his uniform, and he took his meals at home.

At the end of that summer Western Union decided to make the temporary office permanent. At once Rickover saw his chance. He would combine work with attendance at the nearby John Marshall High School. It took some arranging because his hours at Western Union were from three in the afternoon until eleven at night. That meant he would have to leave school a little early. The school, to his delight, was willing to help. Only one obstacle remained: state law declared anyone working at night had to be at least sixteen. He solved that problem by changing his birthday from

1 January 1900 to 24 August 1898 for school records.[5] In none of these steps had he consulted his parents.

High school students expecting to enter the business world could take commercial courses emphasizing office skills; those preparing for higher education could take general courses. Without hesitation Rickover chose the latter. Excellent teachers instilled in him an interest in history that he never lost; in an English class he discovered in himself a love of literature and a fascination with the nuances and rhythms of words. Vast quantities of the poetry he memorized remained with him throughout his life. He was an exuberant student. "It was in our third year that Rickover began to entertain us with humor well suited to what our ideas of humor were," wrote one classmate at graduation. "Certain students of our class are likely never to forget Miss Bennett's English class of that and the following year."[6] He fell in love with Jeanette Goldstein, having a depth of feeling for her that was greater than the usual high school romance. She was planning to go to the University of Wisconsin and, therefore, was probably from a better-off family.

At Western Union, Rickover was always busy. Other messengers skylarked and horsed around, but he took his school books to the office to read and memorize while waiting for telegrams to deliver. He also found time to master Morse code. By reading messages as they came over the teletype, he could pick out those to deliver that offered the best chance of tips. He recited school assignments to himself while delivering telegrams. For nearby addresses he used a bicycle; when the secondhand girl's bike he owned was stolen, he had enough money saved to buy a boy's bike. He made more distant deliveries by streetcar, frequently saving fares by using transfers that had been tossed away at busy intersections. The hours at Western Union were long and the work often hard. At times he could barely keep awake at school.

Through Western Union he made his first contact with politics. When the Republican Party chose Chicago as the site of its 1916 presidential convention, Rickover volunteered to be a messenger boy. He would miss school, but the semester was nearly over and he could not resist the fascination of seeing politics in action. The morning of 7 June Rickover made his way through a torrential downpour to the Chicago Coliseum. While the Western Union operators and messenger boys were stationed beneath the speaker's platform, Rickover created a position for himself between the politicians and the messengers. He could see everything and collect most of the tips.

Three days later, after the Republicans had nominated Charles Evans Hughes, Rickover went back to school. His history teacher asked him where he had been. "Sick," he replied, handing her an excuse he had signed with his mother's name. Smiling broadly, she held up a copy of the *Chicago Evening American*. On the front page was a photograph showing the convention's political leaders, with Rickover in the foreground, easily recognizable in his Western Union uniform.[7]

On 6 April 1917, the United States entered the First World War. On 18 May Congress passed the Selective Service Act, calling for men between the ages of twenty-one and thirty-one to register for the draft. If the age limit were to be lowered, young men just graduating from high school might be called up. To give them some preparation, they were drilled a part of one day each week in the gym. Under the direction of an army sergeant, Rickover and his classmates marched and learned the manual of arms.

Rickover's class graduated in February 1918. Chosen as mantle bearer at the ceremony, Rickover wore a scarlet cloak embroidered with the word "Knowledge" in gold, and before classmates, their parents, and his own family, who watched with deep emotion and great pride, he made a brief speech and then transferred the mantle to the next class, which he called "large in number but small in brain."

Although Rickover did not know what he would do after graduation, about one thing he was determined: somehow he would continue his education. The war and the possibility of being drafted shadowed Rickover's hopes to go to college, but as was to happen so often in his life, the unexpected intervened. Joseph Rothstein, the uncle of a cousin, was renting a room from the Rickovers. Rothstein was on the draft board. A local wealthy man with political pull had a son he did not want drafted. Quickly Rothstein struck a bargain. In return for deferring the boy, the father asked Congressman Adolph J. Sabath, who represented the West Side, to nominate Rickover to the Naval Academy. In normal times each congressman and senator could nominate only two men to the academy, but because of the war, the number had been increased to five. Only that fact and Rothstein's political maneuver opened a naval career to Rickover. Early in February 1918 he learned that his nomination had been accepted.[8]

In filling out the forms, Rickover discovered that 1 January was not his birthday. His mother had been following the Jewish lunar calendar at the time of his birth and remembered the phase of the moon. His curiosity aroused, he went to the library. The moon on 1 January 1900 did not match her memory, but its phase on 27 January 1900 did. That was the date he filled in, and that was the date that became his birthday.

Nomination to the academy did not mean acceptance, only the right to take the entrance examinations. Rickover was not worried about the physical; his health was good and from information the Navy had sent him, he knew he met the qualifications for height and weight. The academic examination was another matter. Scheduled for 16 April, it took place in several cities and towns across the country, lasted three days, and consisted of three-hour sessions each in arithmetic, algebra, and geometry; two hours each in grammar, geography, and American history; and twenty minutes in spelling. Grading was on the 4-point system with 4.0 the highest possible score. One fact was crucial: less than 2.5 in any subject meant failing the entire examination.[9]

Rickover knew he had to have help. His interests were literature, history, biography, and current events, not the technical and engineering subjects required of a naval officer. He had received brochures from schools preparing young men for entrance examinations to military academies. The one from the U.S. Naval Academy Preparatory School in Annapolis impressed him most. Although tuition and transportation would take a huge bite out of his savings, Rickover saw no alternative. He applied and was accepted.

He quickly realized that the lessons and lectures at the school were geared for young men with far better backgrounds than his. While the school had a good record and had done well for its students, it was not the place for him.

He had no one to turn to. His parents would not have understood. He had no friends to talk to and he knew no one in the Navy to advise him. The chance of a lifetime was fast slipping away. He dropped out of the school.

On the Annapolis waterfront he found a place to stay in the house of a scrap-metal dealer. For a few dollars a week he roomed in the attic and ate with the family. Using his books from the school, he spent hour after hour memorizing, breaking his isolation only for meals and a brief evening walk along the water's edge, where he watched small schooners loading scrap metal for the steel mills of Baltimore. A few times he went back to the school for help on some problems, as his tuition entitled him to do.

Finally the grind ended. On 16 April Rickover checked into a hotel in Baltimore and walked to the customs house. Along with a number of other hopeful young men, he sat down in a large room and listened to the instructions. At the end of three days and tense with anxiety, he returned to Chicago. On 13 June 1918 the academy sent him the results:[10]

English	3.4
Geography	3.0
History	2.7
Arithmetic	3.8
Algebra	2.5
Geometry	2.6

He had just made it. Anything less in algebra and he would have failed. Leaving the preparatory school to study on his own was one of the most important decisions he ever made. He thought the grading system saved him. To prevent favoritism and discrimination, examinations were identified by numbers so that individuals doing the marking could not know the name of the man whose paper they were scrutinizing. Had they seen his Jewish name, he believed they would have shaved the 2.5 in algebra to a 2.4.

He was elated. In boys' magazines he had read stories about Annapolis and West Point—how they took young men from all walks of life (none, however, like his) and transformed them into officers and gentlemen dedicated to the service of their country. Mixed with his exhilaration was the realization he would be moving into a society and an institution of which he knew nothing.

Rickover reported to the Naval Academy on 29 June 1918. Not until he had passed his physical examination, taken his oath of office, and paid $350 for uniforms, books, and other supplies, would he be a midshipman. Delivering telegrams in all kinds of weather apparently had been good for him: the medical board found him in excellent health.

He and his future classmates reported for swearing in to the superintendent of the academy, Rear Adm. Edward W. Eberle, a vigorous, gray-haired officer with a neatly trimmed beard and mustache. The mechanics of the ceremony were simple. The oath was printed on a form containing blanks for name, age, state from which appointed, and signature. Another blank gave the superintendent space to sign as witness. One after another the young men signed a register. Rickover received a shock when his turn came—all his classmates had a first, middle, and last name. His middle name was Godalia, Yiddish for "God is great," but he never used it. Promptly he chose the name "George" and, as Hyman George Rickover, swore to "support and defend the Constitution of the United States against all enemies, foreign and domestic."

The deposit for uniforms, books, and other supplies stripped him of all his money. Now in uniform, he and his classmates marched to lunch in Bancroft Hall. Philippine waiters scurried around bearing heaping platters and dishes of food—never had he seen so much food. The meat looked like pork, which was forbidden to Orthodox Jews. Before him lay a bewildering array of knives, forks, and spoons. Carefully he watched other plebes to see which utensil they picked up and how they held it. He did what they did and began to eat.

In the space of a few hours he had chosen a name, spent all his money, and ignored the dietary prohibitions with which he had been brought up. At the age of eighteen Rickover was nothing if not a realist. Determined to stay at the Naval Academy (he would always use the word "survive"), he quickly assessed his position. He saw poor academic background and anti-Semitism as his greatest dangers. The first he determined to overcome by study, the second by not calling attention to himself. He would accept those procedures, traditions, and customs that helped; he would circumvent those that did not.

Fourteen months of war had left an imprint on the academy. The class of 1922 (to which Rickover belonged) numbered 963, more than the entire prewar regiment.

Rickover's class was quartered in the Marine barracks, a large, red-roofed, sand-colored brick building separated from the main grounds by Dorsey Creek. The barracks had its drawbacks. It was noisy, for one thing. Screens partitioned large spaces into smaller rooms but could not keep out the sound of voices and the bustle of movement. Knowing he had to make good grades, Rickover often studied in the lavatory.

Promptly Rickover and his classmates were caught up in plebe summer. During these months, while the upperclassmen were away on a training cruise, plebes drilled, marched, sailed, and practiced shooting on the rifle range—activities that introduced them to military life, toughened them, and instilled a class spirit.

Autumn destroyed the confidence summer had given. On 17 September, near the beginning of the academic year, he and about fourteen other midshipmen were quarantined in the basement of the hospital on suspicion that they had been exposed to diphtheria. Largely ignored and forgotten, most idled away their time. In contrast, Rickover snatched up his books and studied as best he could.

He was still immured when the great influenza epidemic of 1918, sweeping across the country, struck the academy. Eberle restricted the regiment to the grounds, closed the library, and banned all activities except classes. At recitation midshipman officers found it easier to report those present than those absent. Despite all precautions, more than a thousand men, including midshipmen and others at the academy, were stricken and eight died.

After forty-five days Rickover finally got out of the hospital. Seizing every possible moment to catch up on his class work, he bitterly resented any intrusion on his time. Not even the arrival of the Armistice on 11 November 1918 broke his concentration. Looking back, he was puzzled that so historic an event had left almost no impression on him. He thought the reason was hearing that some classmates who had been with him in quarantine were failing—perhaps as many as twelve of the fifteen. Discharged from the hospital only ten days before the Armistice and convinced he was in jeopardy, he dared not leave his books.

Moving into Bancroft Hall near the end of the year did not change his self-discipline. At night, when his three roommates slept, he sat in the shower stall, having rigged a blanket to hide the light, and prepared for the morrow's classes. The technique of memorizing he had practiced in Chicago while delivering telegrams stood him in good stead. To the cadence of marching to class he recited to himself formulas he had just learned. Occasionally he was lucky. One night before a trigonometry class he had time to memorize only one of three formulas he might need. To his great relief, the one he had chosen was the one he needed.

Rickover had little interest in athletics, probably because Chicago had given him no experience in sports. Briefly he took up fencing, but he soon discovered he lacked coordination. Well aware of the need for exercise, he swam and ran.

He detested hazing but did not find it too bad. One afternoon, when Rickover and others of his class were hoisting boats out of the river, an upperclassman ordered Rickover to place himself on report for having his hands in his pockets, an offense carrying a number of demerits and therefore affecting class standing. The charge was obviously false because the plebes' pockets were sewn shut. Seething with anger, Rickover reported without comment to Myron A. Baber, class of 1920, the midshipman officer who dealt with such infractions. Furious at the injustice, for he could see the sewn pockets, Baber wanted to take formal action against the upperclassman. Rickover persuaded him to drop the matter. Asking for official redress would only make the situation worse. Hazing, after all, lasted only a year, but to be a major figure in some incident might be remembered during his entire career.

In June 1919, the end of his first year, Rickover had done more than "survive." His grades were respectable:

Mechanical drawing	2.73
Descriptive geometry	2.77
Solid geometry	2.72
Analytic geometry	2.87
Composition and literature	3.23
Modern history	3.42
Spanish	3.40

In his class of 820 he stood 357.[11]

No longer a plebe and no longer subject to hazing, Rickover still had to be careful about anti-Semitism. In his years at the academy, bigotry was particularly bad in all parts of American society. It was the time of the "Red Scare," "100 percent Americanism," and the powerful resurgence of the Ku Klux Klan. Anti-Semitism was no worse in the academy than outside, but that was scant consolation for those who had to endure it.

Rickover did not recall any anti-Semitism in the classroom or in grading, but he found it elsewhere in the academy. At one meal he took the last piece of bread. Someone exclaimed, "What can you expect from a Jew!" Flaring up, Rickover issued a challenge. The next morning at 5:30 in the gym, in the presence of their seconds, he and the other man fought. No boxer, Rickover "got the hell beat out of me," but the matter was closed.

It is impossible to discuss anti-Semitism during Rickover's time at the academy without referring to the Leonard Kaplan episode. A brilliant scholar, Kaplan did not fit into midshipman life, a fact that became evident in the academy yearbook, the *Lucky Bag*, for 1922. The section devoted to graduating midshipmen was arranged so that each page contained photographs and brief, lighthearted biographical sketches of two midshipmen. The midshipman editor for 1922 inserted a page (perforated so it could be torn out) containing a photograph of Kaplan and his biography, along with a gross cartoon and a cruel biographical sketch that were transparent disguises of Kaplan.

Tearing out the page obliterated any trace of Kaplan in the yearbook. Because no similar incident had ever occurred and because the episode attracted newspaper attention, it became part of academy history, but with one significant change: over the years Rickover became identified as the midshipman of the perforated page. The reason was clear. The future would see Rickover having well-publicized arguments with the Naval Academy, charging it with failing to inculcate good study habits in the midshipmen. Because of the tone of his remarks (frequently appearing in congressional hearings), it was easy to assume that he hated the academy because of its treatment of him and jump to the erroneous conclusion that he was the man on the perforated page.

Rickover thought the practice cruise the best part of academy life. On a June morning the regiment, except for the plebes, with hammocks, sea bags, and buckets, lined up on the pier and eagerly awaited the boats that were to take them to a squadron of battleships anchored out on the bay. During the cruise the midshipmen, under the direction of the ships' officers and petty officers, rotated from one job to another, gaining experience in the environment that was to play such a great part in their lives. Ships competed against each other, especially in seamanship and in the "smartness" in such evolutions as lowering, hoisting, and manning boats. Life was vigorous, with pranks and horseplay leavening the routine. Best of all, practice cruises had none of the pettiness and irritations that marked existence in Bancroft Hall.

Rickover found ways to make life easier during the practice cruises. On his first cruise he discovered a small compartment filled with coffins for use in case of death at sea. Sleeping in one was more comfortable than in a hammock. On another cruise he and Henri Smith-Hutton, a classmate, found a compartment used for storing coal chutes. The space was grimy, but figuring no one would look for them there, they moved in. At midnight, when the watches changed and the water was turned on (fresh water was always in short supply) one of the two would take their buckets, fill them, and bring them back. For other midshipmen the day began at 5:30, followed by two hours of swabbing decks and polishing bright work before breakfast. By that time Rickover and Smith-Hutton, awake and washed up, joined the others. Once the two of them manned the ash whip, a job of hoisting heavy buckets of ashes from below and emptying them into the sea. Smith-Hutton found Rickover "a very good man on that ash whip."[12]

Travel abroad was not yet a common experience for most Americans, and the slogan "Join the Navy and See the World" was a call to adventure. In 1919 the squadron went to the Caribbean, the next year to Hawaii, and in Rickover's final year, Europe. By washing hammocks and bedding, he earned money to go ashore. His most vivid memory was steaming up a fjord to Oslo, Norway, through the colorful fishing fleet, and walking through the forest that came right to the edge of town.

Rickover had a few friends, although he was not to maintain close contact with them. Two were William J. Sebald and Smith-Hutton, both of the class of 1922 and both to leave the Navy for distinguished careers in diplomacy. To Smith-Hutton, who wrote a letter in 1973 beginning "Dear Ricky," Rickover replied, "I have often thought of our friendship, not only during our Naval Academy days, but also later on. . . . It is not easy for me to make friends, and it meant a great deal to me to know you. I well remember our midshipmen's cruise . . ."[13]

Although he had no desire to hold rank in the regiment, in the academic year 1920–21 Rickover was second petty officer, 4th Battalion, largely because the superintendent had decided that all midshipmen insofar as possible would receive some training in the handling of men.[14]

By the time Rickover became a first classman he qualified for graduation, but whether he would be able to make the Navy his career was in doubt. Under the naval armaments limitation treaty signed at Washington in February 1922, the United States would have to scrap several ships under construction. Obviously the Navy would not need the number of officers it had sought so eagerly as late as 1918. As a hedge against the future, many midshipmen looked for jobs in industry. For its part, the Navy made resigning easy. Rickover was accepted by the Commonwealth Edison Company, an Illinois utility. By the late spring of 1922 the situation had eased; all who wanted and qualified for commissions would get them.

A few weeks before graduation, a list of billets was posted in smoke hall, a part of Bancroft Hall set aside for smoking. The midshipmen took their choice of assignments in order of class standing. Rickover asked for destroyer duty in the Pacific and got it. He was ordered to report to commander, Destroyer Squadrons, U.S. Pacific Fleet. In Dahlgren Hall on the rainy Friday of 2 June 1922, Rickover received his commission. Out of a class of 540 (the largest so far to graduate from the academy) Ens. H. G. Rickover was 107.[15]

He was grateful to the academy. It had given him an education and opened a career. He also found that being a loner and an outsider had its advantages: it had given a perspective, enabling him to look into an institution and determine what was essential to its operation and what was not. In years to come, superintendent after superintendent would receive blistering telephone calls in which Rickover accused the academy of not preparing midshipmen for a Navy undergoing a technological revolution—a revolution he had done much to bring about. He thought the academy had done well for him, however, and for midshipmen of his era. He would make the Navy his life.

Sea Duty, Shore Duty, and Love

AFTER SPENDING some time on leave in Chicago, Rickover took the train to New York, at his own expense because the Navy did not provide travel money. At the Brooklyn Navy Yard he and seventy-five newly minted ensigns, as well as a number of nurses and enlisted men, boarded the transport *Argonne* for the West Coast; she arrived at San Diego on 13 August 1922. Commander, Destroyer Squadrons, was in the cruiser *Charleston*. Rickover was ordered to the destroyer *La Vallette*, which was operating off the coast of Washington.

Learning that the *La Vallette* would be in San Francisco in early September, Rickover arranged for his passage in the *Arctic*, a Navy freighter. Late in the morning of 5 September 1922, Rickover watched Destroyer Squadron 12, to which the *La Vallette* belonged, escort the battleships *California, New Mexico, Tennessee, Arizona,* and *New York* through the Golden Gate and into San Francisco Bay. By early afternoon all were at anchor. Later that day he reported to his ship. Lt. Cdr. Philip Seymour assigned his new ensign the duties of assistant torpedo officer, commissary, supply, and watch officer.

On 13 September the squadron arrived at San Diego. In the routine of harbor drills, broken occasionally to take part in tactical formations, short- and long-range battle practice, and target runs, Rickover found himself fitting in. Seymour liked him. An easygoing man, the captain did not care how his officers did their work as long as they got results. Rickover got along well with the other officers. Ens. Benton W. Decker, who had graduated from the academy a year ahead of Rickover, became a friend and had a home where Rickover was always welcome. No one cared about Rickover's religious beliefs or background. Life in *La Vallette* had none of the unpleasantness that had marred his years at Annapolis.

On 6 February 1923 the *La Vallette* left San Diego as one of many ships taking part in a fleet problem, the first of several the Navy conducted in the interwar years to gain experience in planning and carrying out fleet operations. The main objective of the first effort was to test the defenses of the Panama Canal. For that purpose, the Navy divided twelve battleships, sixty-three destroyers, and twenty-five submarines, as well as twenty-two hundred officers and thirty-seven thousand men, into a Black Fleet (to which the *La Vallette* belonged) to attack and a Blue Fleet to defend. The exercise revealed that the locks and dams of the canal were vulnerable to air attack, the fleet needed destroyers and cruisers, communications were faulty, and many ships were in poor material condition.[1]

The fleet problem and the maneuvers that followed, when both forces were combined into the United States Fleet, were exciting for a young officer. All the evolutions—screening battleships, laying down smoke screens, changing from one formation to another—were demanding, and the stress on competition and smartness forced officers and men into tightly knit, high-spirited teams. And there was the beauty of the tropics that Rickover was always to find fascinating: the intense blue skies, azure seas, dazzling white clouds, sudden rain squalls, magnificent sunsets and dawns, and the breathtaking loveliness of the nights.

A heavy blow struck Rickover in the spring of 1923. Jeanette Goldstein, seriously ill, had returned to Chicago from the University of Wisconsin. Near the end of April he took emergency leave and sped to her side. Seeing her in the hospital, he could tell the end was near. At her death he gave the letters she had written him to her parents; they gave him his letters to her. Having no place to keep them, he burned them.

He was not sure they would have married. His sister Augusta, attending the university with his help, had written him that Jeanette was dating someone else. She was his first love, however, and he felt her loss deeply. Looking back from decades, Decker remembered that the whole ship sympathized. Lonelier than ever, Rickover turned in upon himself and sought solace in work.

He was doing well: that was Seymour's verdict after observing his new ensign for six months. In a fitness report, the means by which a senior officer periodically evaluated a junior, Seymour noted that Rickover was hardworking, efficient, and spent much of his leisure time in studying. When a routine transfer left the engineer billet open, Seymour put Rickover in the position.

Rickover's new domain consisted of two main turbines, four boilers, auxiliary machinery, fuel tanks, and a "blackgang" of thirty-six men—machinist's mates, enginemen, water tenders, boiler men, and firemen. He also got a room to himself. In his new quarters he could hear any change in the sound of the machinery and could be summoned by a voice tube to the engine room. He liked the privacy, partly because it had been so rare in his life, and partly because it was easier for him to study his naval war college correspondence course on policy, command, strategy, and tactics.

Almost at once his men tested him. Shortly before the ship was to get under way, the chief machinist's mate reported a crack in a condenser tube. It would take a few hours to repair. Rickover was in a foul mood when he entered the wardroom for lunch. Not leaving on schedule was a black mark against the ship, the captain, and himself. A picture flashed across his mind. Most of the blackgang had returned to the ship drunk. Heedless of wardroom etiquette, which called for him to ask the captain to excuse him from the table, he abruptly got up and strode down into the engine room. He discovered the "crack" was only a heavy pencil mark: the men had hoped to take advantage of his inexperience to get a few hours of sleep. After reporting the ship could get under way, a furious Rickover cursed out the chief and others, warning them never again to try a trick like that.

He never forgot the incident. He would never be at the mercy of subordinates. He would always check up. He would always inspect.[2]

Most of his time he spent in the engine room, learning to detect out of all the noise the one false note that betrayed a component out of adjustment, to touch a steel casing with his fingernail and feel from the vibration whether the machinery inside was running true, to taste boiler water to see if it was pure, and to dip his finger into the lubricating oil to find out if a bearing was running hot.

In the summer of 1923 the *La Vallette* entered the Mare Island Navy Yard for boiler work. Either Rickover or his men found a lathe in an unguarded machine shop. At night they quietly disassembled it and brought the parts on board. Discovering its loss in the morning, the yard immediately suspected the ships in overhaul, most especially the destroyers, because their officers and crews were notoriously light-fingered. A long and painstaking search uncovered no clue. In due time the *La Vallette* left the yard. Once through the Golden Gate, the blackgang assembled the lathe. They had stored its parts in an empty fuel tank and covered the theft nicely by pumping oil into the tank.

Rickover considered the lathe a valuable acquisition, as it enabled him to do work that otherwise would have taken the time and effort of a destroyer tender. The philosophy that a ship should be able to maintain its machinery and make its own repairs as far as possible was another belief he brought to his later career.

At San Diego on 24 October 1923, Seymour turned his ship over to Cdr. Herbert E. Kays. Rickover was sorry to see the change; Seymour was easy to approach, whereas Kays proved to have a taste for formality and a tendency to get into detail.

Rickover was driving his men hard and was justly proud that his ship stood first among all destroyers in the competition for engineering excellence.[3] He became even more intense as the *La Vallette* steamed south in early 1924 to take part in the new fleet problem and maneuvers. Decker thought it would be good for all hands to get Rickover off the ship, even if only for a short time. When the fleet anchored off Panama, Decker finally persuaded Rickover to go ashore for an afternoon at the officers club. Maybe conviviality would loosen things up.

They found a table at which another *La Vallette* officer was sitting. Before him was a shot of bourbon. Although he had never before had a drink, Rickover was certain that a strong mind was more than a match for strong drink. He ordered the number of shots the other man had already consumed, downing them one after the other. Then he ordered more. Staring at each other in consternation, Decker and the other officer quickly decided to get Rickover back to the ship. With Rickover between them, they walked down to the dock. Rickover was a trifle unsteady, but his speech was clear. Seeing the senior executive officer of the squadron in the shore boat, a man who had been one of the dullest of instructors at the Naval Academy, Rickover freely and candidly gave his opinion of the other's teaching ability. That night a very sick young engineer was put to bed.

In the morning his fellow officers gathered around, telling him the terrible things he had said to the senior executive officer and generously adding things even more terrible he hadn't said. He had to apologize, they told him, or his career was ruined. Sprucing him up, they sent him across the nest of destroyers to the former instructor's ship. That officer was startled as Rickover drew himself up and offered a formal apology. Possibly a poor instructor but possessing a sense of humor and a knowledge of destroyer life, he recognized at once what had happened and, breaking into laughter, waved the incident aside.

Rickover's time in the *La Vallette* would end in 1924. Kays thought he needed duty in a large ship and more experience as deck officer. Rickover wanted a change but not necessarily more sea duty. In April of that year he applied for postgraduate work in civil engineering, which, in the Navy, meant the construction, upkeep, and repair of shore facilities. Nothing came of the request, but it was evidence of his intent to obtain additional formal education.[4] Suffering from a kidney infection and chronic appendicitis, Rickover was transferred on 11 July 1924 to the Mare Island Naval Hospital. On 28 October he applied again for postgraduate instruction in civil engineering, a request Kays approved, but again without result. He was still in the hospital on 3 December 1924 when he was detached from the *La Vallette*. He asked to be ordered to the *Colorado*, a new battleship that had recently arrived on the West Coast. Instead he was assigned to the much older *Nevada*.

On 21 January 1925 Rickover reported to the *Nevada*, Capt. David W. Todd commanding, 3d Battleship Division, United States Battle Fleet, at the Puget Sound Navy Yard. After twenty-six months of the rough-and-ready life in a destroyer, Rickover was entering the world of the large warship, in which successful operation demanded formality, organization, protocol, etiquette, and tradition—qualities he disdained. In a ship with an overall length of 583 feet and a beam of 95 feet, 1,275 officers and men lived, their lives dominated by the ten 14-inch guns making up the main battery. The course of history could be determined in a single day or night by how well the guns were served; consequently, officers and men in the gunnery department were selected with special care. Rickover had every reason to be pleased with his assignment to the Fire Control Division of the department.[5]

On 3 February 1925, Todd announced to the ship's company, as was his custom on such occasions, "The *Nevada* is putting to sea on the nation's business." Rickover liked the statement; it expressed the purpose of the naval profession. Five days later the ship arrived at San Pedro, California, since 1919 the operating base for the heavy ships of the fleet. There she took up the routine of constant drills in port, broken once in a while by short exercises at sea for target practice, night battle practice using star shells for illumination, and full-power runs to test propulsion plants.

One of thirty-five ensigns in the ship, Rickover was sufficiently senior to escape being quartered in the "guinea Pullman," a large compartment in which a score or more ensigns lived and skylarked. He had his own room, a "blind tiger," which got its name from the lack of a porthole. He kept to himself, usually returning to his room after meals, refusing to join the social life of the wardroom, with its pleasant games of acey-deucy and bridge and its general conversation. Only talk on gunnery could draw him out. Rickover was soon making his mark as an extremely able, though taciturn and uncongenial, young officer.

Todd, a dignified and efficient officer of the old school, was impressed with Rickover. The captain found his new officer mature, forceful, industrious, and reliable. Furthermore, Rickover had completed the naval war college correspondence course on strategy and tactics, something not many officers began and far fewer completed. Todd asked him to give a series of lectures. Afterward, Todd observed, twenty-three line officers and one staff officer enrolled for the course.[6]

Todd might have been trying to interest his officers in tactics and strategy because of the operations scheduled for mid-1925. After completing the annual problem, the fleet would concentrate on the West Coast and cruise to Hawaii; major elements would then go on to Australia and New Zealand.[7] The fleet sortied through the Golden Gate on 15 April. On the following days and nights the ships were deployed in various tactical formations and prepared to recapture Hawaii from the "enemy." The islands braced themselves. The *Honolulu Advertiser* warned, "Honolulu Likely to See Period of Debauchery." On 26 April the fleet "seized" Maui and Lanai, and three days later the umpire declared the maneuvers ended. Off the beach at Waikiki, ships anchored in an array that seemed to stretch endlessly.

Three years an ensign, it was time for Rickover to take his physical and professional examinations for lieutenant (jg). For months he had studied military and international law, seamanship, ordnance and gunnery, strategy and tactics, navigation and piloting, communications, marine engineering, and electricity. Under the watchful eye of a higher-ranking officer, Rickover and a few other ensigns were taking the examination in the wardroom when a loud, rumbling noise suddenly broke their concentration.

At that moment Rickover was describing the correct way to anchor a ship in deep water. Proper procedure called for letting the anchor out slowly, otherwise it might gain such momentum that anchor and chain would pull out of the ship and plummet to the bottom of the sea. He and the other ensigns rushed to the portholes: a nearby battleship in deep water had let go her anchor too fast and had lost it. Returning to his paper, he embellished his answer with a description of the event he had just witnessed.

He passed the written tests with high marks, although his grade in engineering was lower than he expected. Some years later in Washington he looked up his paper: he had been marked down for spelling "sulphur" as "sulfur."

His physical examination, however, was ominous. In early May, after a long walk, he discovered a bulge on the right side of his abdomen. With consternation he heard the ship's doctor diagnose a hernia that, he flatly predicted, would end Rickover's naval career. On 20 May 1925 Rickover was transferred to the hospital ship *Relief* and later to the hospital at Pearl Harbor. At his urgent request he was sent to Mare Island for an operation. The hospital discharged him toward the end of June. Because the *Nevada* would not return from the far Pacific until fall, he was granted permission to attend the torpedo school at the naval air station on North Island, San Diego.

Rickover returned to the *Nevada* at San Pedro on 7 October 1925. A lieutenant (jg) since 3 June, he assumed the duties of engineer watch officer and headed the Electrical Division. Aware that the ship was about to leave for an overhaul at Puget Sound, he checked over the work that had to be done. He already knew from his duty in the gunnery department that the fire-control electrical system was in bad shape. With quickening interest he studied a circular from Washington describing a fire-control system intended for a new battleship that, under the naval limitation treaties, would not be completed. Any battleship could have the system—provided the ship's force installed it, a formidable stipulation probably dictated by a shortage of yard funds.

Rickover thought he could do it. Todd agreed to let him go ahead. The fire-control system was waiting when the *Nevada* arrived at Puget Sound. Before she left in February, Rickover had to install several switchboards and several hundred telephones as well as the wiring linking the fore and main mast stations, gun directors, range finders, plotting room, magazines, fire-control stations, and turrets.

He and his men turned to at once, ripping out old wiring and switchboards and putting in the new equipment. Although working day and night, they began to fall behind: the job was bigger than Rickover had thought. He worried that when the ship was scheduled to leave, she would not be able to use her guns. The executive officer gave him all recruits reporting on board. While that helped, it was not enough.

Civilians in the yard came to his rescue. Amusement that a young officer should be so brash as to undertake such a huge job turned to admiration as they saw him constantly working and driving himself as hard as he drove his men. The man in charge of the shipyard's electrical shop quietly stepped in and gave Rickover assistance. Having worked in the yard for years, he knew all the ways to circumvent rules and regulations. As a result the *Nevada* left Puget Sound on schedule with the fire-control system completely installed and tested. Rickover learned another lesson that was to stand him in good stead: in Navy yards longtime civilians, not the officers, were really in charge.

Secure in the knowledge that his work was respected, Rickover flaunted his contempt for etiquette. He was almost always in dungarees, even on the quarterdeck when exercising by himself. Caring little for the insignia of rank, he neglected for several weeks after his promotion to get the half stripe of a lieutenant (jg) sewed on his uniform. When Todd refused to excuse him from attending a reception given on another battleship, Rickover boarded the ship on one side, crossed the quarterdeck, shook hands with the admiral, continued to the other side, and went down the ladder where, by prearrangement, a boat was ready to take him back to the *Nevada*.

In fitness reports Todd praised Rickover's initiative and responsibility, found his judgment far above average, thought him well-read professionally, and described him as forceful and persistent. And yet, Rickover puzzled Todd, who, in one report, wrote that Rickover got results with his men despite "having no outward signs of qualities of leadership."[8]

Capt. Clarence S. Kempff relieved Todd on 11 June 1926. Able but unorthodox, "Pluvy" Kempff also had a puckish sense of humor. (Writing an article about some practical points of seamanship with an electric-drive ship, for example, he concluded with the warning, "Do not anchor in the flagship's berth.")[9] Rickover got along very well with Kempff, each man sensing in the other an outlook similar to his own. Other commanding officers had praised him, but Kempff was the first to offer friendship.

Rickover did not serve long under Kempff. Eligible for shore duty in 1927, Rickover preferred for his next assignment either a billet on the West Coast or instruction in Japanese at the embassy in Tokyo. He applied for training in aviation (a step he was to repeat in the fall of 1928), but failed the medical examination because of defective vision and muscular imbalance. His mind turned to engineering. On 13 November 1926, with the strong endorsements of Seymour, now stationed at the Cavite Navy Yard, and Kempff (who thought the move was a mistake), Rickover asked for postgraduate instruction in electrical engineering, agreeing to remain three years in the Navy after completing the courses. On 22 January 1927 his request was approved. He was to report to Annapolis on 1 July.[10]

In February 1927 the ship left San Pedro, steaming south with the fleet for annual maneuvers in the Caribbean and on to a major overhaul at the Norfolk Navy Yard. Rickover left the ship on 28 April, receiving a fine fitness report from Kempff: "An exceptionally able and capable officer. High sense of duty and devoted to it. Excellent mind, a student and always improving himself. Has [word illegible] initiative and industry. Trains his electrical force and educates them well. Has done excellent work in keeping a worn out plant in operating condition. An excellent character. Thoroughly honest and painstaking in all his work. Would be glad to have him with me again."[11]

Judging from his recollections, Rickover liked sea duty. He mixed his memories of light-hearted escapades with accounts of the steps he took to learn in detail the propulsion plant of the *La Vallette* and his "brashness" (the word he used) in deciding he could install the fire-control system on the *Nevada*.

Nevertheless, he was looking forward to postgraduate school, although he worried whether he could make the grade. Aware that the change from sea duty to academic life was not easy for most officers, the Navy divided the postgraduate program into two parts. The first year was spent at the Naval Academy learning engineering fundamentals, the second at a major engineering school. Because Rickover had chosen electrical engineering for his field, he would spend his last year at Columbia University.

Eager to get a head start, he arrived in Annapolis some time before classes began. He and another officer had decided to share expenses by rooming together. A house on Maryland Avenue near the academy's main gate offered two tiny bedrooms and a small living room. Promptly he moved in, squeezing into the living room two desks facing away from each other. Although preferring to read widely, he began studying only technical books.

He took courses in mathematics, mechanics, physics, hydraulics, engineering measurements, metallurgy, and chemistry in Halligan Hall, once the Marine barracks where he had lived when a plebe. As he had done when a midshipman, he memorized, stopping only for meals and a daily walk of a mile and a half. On 26 June 1928 Rickover completed his first year of postgraduate work. He was pleased with one other event: on 3 June he was promoted to full lieutenant.

He had welcomed one interruption: Kempff visited him. All that night the two men stayed up, exchanging views and ideas, the differences in their rank and age meaning nothing.

At Columbia, Rickover would be attending a major university, an ambition he had held since high school. In addition, he would be living as a civilian for the first time since entering the Naval Academy ten years earlier. Some of his Navy classmates were choosing apartments near the university, but he wanted something different. A room at the International House, located on Riverside Drive, suited him perfectly. More than half the several hundred students at the house were foreign-born. Men and women lived in separate wings but shared a lounge, cafeteria, and recreational rooms in which they discussed world affairs in many accents and languages.

He found Columbia's School of Engineering every bit as good as he had hoped. Its faculty, most of whom could season their teaching with practical experience gained in the Navy and in industry, was demanding but fair. He took particular pride when Morton Arendt, an expert in storage batteries, accepted his help in performing battery experiments and revising his textbook. Professor Charles E. Lucke probably summed up the views of most of his colleagues when he observed that the officers the Navy sent to Columbia were fine and intelligent but excessively prone to memorization.[12] The words described Rickover perfectly, but at Columbia he began to understand and appreciate the logic and philosophy of engineering, qualities upon which he was to depend so heavily.

Rickover liked living in the International House. Shortly after moving in, he went to the first meeting of a foreign relations group at the house. During a discussion on tariffs he observed a lovely young woman who was offering perceptive comments in excellent English flavored with a German accent. A few days later—he was to remember it was 9:30 on a Monday morning—she was seated on a sofa near the information desk. He found someone to introduce him to her. She was Ruth D. Masters, a recently arrived graduate student majoring in international law.

They began to see each other often. Her accent had misled him: she was not German but American. Although born in Washington, D.C., on 22 January 1903 of German parents, she had lived most of her life in Germany. After the death of both parents in an automobile accident in southern France, she was brought up by relatives in Germany, one of whom loved her as a daughter and whom she called "Mother." Her home was in Freiburg, an old town near the Black Forest. There she had lived through four years of war, hearing the sound of guns, watching aircraft overhead, seeing hospital trains carrying wounded from the front, and witnessing the grim consequences of the blockade. Passionately she wanted to help create an age of peace, fervently she hoped international law could solve disputes between nations.[13]

Rickover had never met anyone like her. Speaking English, German, and French fluently and able to read Italian and Spanish, she was well versed in history, art, and literature. She loved music, especially opera, and played the piano. In spite of these accomplishments she had a very practical outlook; she had to get along on very little money, a condition Rickover knew well. Occasionally they went to the theater, once seeing the classic French play *Cyrano de Bergerac.* That evening they reached an understanding, and the play became a symbol of an event to be cherished and remembered.

Yet he was troubled. Her background was Protestant; his was Jewish. She was from highly cultivated European society; he was from Chicago's West Side. Her profession demanded concentrated thought, large libraries, and the intellectual stimulation of cosmopolitan cities. His career moved him every few years from place to place, some certain to be remote and far from the resources she needed. She would win her master's degree in June 1929 and, if she got a fellowship, remain at Columbia to work on her doctorate. He would get his master's degree in engineering in May 1929 and then spend some months visiting industries in which electric power played a great part. Then it was back to sea.

He was not looking forward to it. He liked the cultural and intellectual atmosphere of Columbia, especially the discussions on foreign affairs, a subject that had always attracted him. He felt out of place and knew that her friends looked down on him as an engineer and as a naval officer. He was driven to show her that he could share her interests.

He had already thought about his next duty. In the fall of 1928 he applied for flight training but failed the medical examination. He considered submarines. They offered a chance for an early command, so important to his career. While he spent two years in postgraduate school, his academy classmates were moving ahead in the mainstream of the Navy. In April 1929 he asked for submarine duty, a request Captain Todd and Capt. Albert T. Church, in charge of the postgraduate program, strongly endorsed.[14]

His later letters to Ruth suggest additional reasons for his request. He was twenty-nine years old and deeply in love. If his application was accepted, he would go to submarine school at New London, Connecticut, which was in easy distance of New York. The first class he could attend would start in January 1930 and last about six months. After that he stood a good chance of being sent to a submarine operating out of New London. If all these pieces fell into place, he and Ruth could be together, or at least not too far apart, for more than a year.

Some weeks separated the end of the postgraduate program in October and the beginning of the January class at the school. If, during that period, he was assigned to a submarine operating out of New London, he could get some practical experience. A physical examination threatened these plans. He had another hernia, and until it was corrected, the Navy would not consider him for submarine duty. As if this was not enough, he received orders to report to the battleship *California*, flagship of the Pacific Fleet, on completing his postgraduate work. He hated the idea. He had already had battleship duty; it would not offer the chance of early command and, most of all, it meant an earlier separation from Ruth. But he might get his orders changed if he had an operation.[15]

In May 1929 he graduated from Columbia with distinction and a master's degree in engineering; in June he entered the hospital at the Brooklyn Navy Yard. Fully recovered and having passed the physical examination, he promptly asked that his orders to the *California* be revoked. To his dismay, his request was denied.

A trip to the Navy Department in Washington revealed that at twenty-nine and a full lieutenant, he was considered too old and too senior to begin submarine duty. Discouraged and disconsolate, he happened to run into Kempff, who promised to see what he could do. Kempff was successful. In July 1929 Rickover received orders to report early in October to Submarine Division 12 at New London. The orders said nothing about submarine school, but he was sure he would attend the January class.[16]

He still had to tour several industrial facilities, among them the plants of the General Electric Company in Schenectady, New York, and the Westinghouse Electric and Manufacturing Company at East Pittsburgh, Pennsylvania. In the course of his travels he discovered an opportunity to see the Electric Storage Battery Company in Philadelphia, a major manufacturer of submarine batteries. Because the plant was not on his list to visit, he had to get permission. He turned to Arendt, who endorsed his request with a handwritten note: "This young officer is one of the most earnest of men whom I have met in 37 years of engineering work."[17]

On 3 October Rickover saw the plant. The visit, though professionally rewarding, had a dark side. In many parts of the facility acid fumes contaminated the atmosphere. In one section men had to wear gas masks all day long. At another place a man was working an automatic machine as fast as he could over ladles of molten lead; he looked as if he had not much longer to live.

To lessen the differences between his background and that of Ruth, he decided to learn German. While riding the subways, eating lunch, or simply walking, he studied a textbook, trying to acquire an extensive vocabulary and to master the complicated grammar. In August he fell into a black mood, unable to concentrate or study. Disturbed, she wrote to him on 30 August 1929: "I shall never be able to follow you all the way in your engineering problems and you will never be quite able to share German art and literature completely with me." A few days later, on 3 September, she wondered whether the cause of his despair was that "when you met me, you were not very happy and not overly enthusiastic with your work."

Although Ruth had written to her adopted mother of her intent to marry, Rickover had not yet corresponded with her. Ruth suggested, emphasizing it was only a suggestion, that he do so:

> Don't write Mother that I am beautiful, or she will be afraid you are blind, nor that I am an angel, or Mother will reverse things and believe I roped you in. And then nothing could prevent her to try and open your eyes and tell you what a horrible person I am and of course, this would result in your sending a good-bye letter! When I wrote about telling of your professional plans, I meant you might tell how you plan to combine your work with my work, and Mother would like to hear about that. I think it would be nice if you told her that you want me to make good in my work. She is proud of it, you know. I am sure you will write such a lovely letter that in the future Mother will like you better than me, and I shall be jealous.[18]

Her phrase "combine your work with my work" referred to Rickover's belief that the difference in their professions could be a source of strength. He thought any result of their collaboration in international law could not be considered militaristic because of her well-known hatred of war; on the other hand, it could not be considered pacifistic because of his profession.

Before reporting to New London he had a chance to spend a few days with Ruth. They walked and talked; she was pleased he could act "silly." He tried to explain his philosophy. "I realize," he wrote, "that success in this world is in great measure due to 'self advertising,' etc.—still my nature is such that aside from what you think of me, I value my own self-approval far more than I do the approval of others. I cannot create false impressions, even in small matters; such would have a devastating effect upon my character with the consequence that my individuality would be submerged. These many years I have refused to conform, combating continually the natural tendency to become engulfed in the ordinary."[19]

Submarines and Marriage

AT 11:00 A.M. on 12 October 1929 Rickover boarded the *S-9*, moored to a target raft on the north side of Pier B at the New London submarine base. Meeting the four other officers didn't take long. Lt. Burton G. Lake commanded; the others were junior grade lieutenants. Because Rickover was to be in the ship for such a short time before reporting to submarine school, Lake gave him no special duties.

After lunch on his first day aboard, one of the officers began reading aloud. "You couldn't guess in a million years what it was—Cyrano de Bergerac by Rostand," Rickover wrote to Ruth.[1] That was the play they saw the night they realized the depth of their feeling for each other. It was a good omen.

To a destroyer or battleship man, the *S-9* was not much to look at. She measured only 231 feet in overall length and 21 feet 10 inches in extreme beam. Her most prominent features topside were a conning tower fairwater, fitted with an open bridge for surface operation, and, forward of it, a 4-inch, 50-caliber deck gun. Below decks the four officers and thirty-four men lived, jammed in among the torpedoes, engines, motors, valves, and piping.

Like all submarines at this time—as would be the case until the advent of nuclear power—she had two propulsion plants. For surface operation and long voyages she depended upon diesel engines that, if all went well, could drive her at a maximum speed of fifteen knots. For running submerged, her electric motors, drawing power from 120 lead-acid batteries, could propel her at eleven knots. At that speed she quickly exhausted her batteries, but by creeping along very slowly she could stay submerged for hours. Two hundred feet was the greatest depth at which she could operate safely, but she seldom ventured so far down.[2]

Lake offered Rickover the choice of an upper or lower bunk. Both were cramped, but the lower was best. Not only was it easier to slide into, but it had a locker at its foot. Whoever had the bottom bunk could open the locker, put his feet into it, and stretch out. Although entitled by his higher rank to the lower, Rickover took the upper because the other officer was taller.

The discomforts of living in a submarine disappeared when he thought of the future. He and Ruth would marry in May 1930, only about half a year away. A month later he would graduate from submarine school. Then they would separate—she back to Columbia to study international law and he to a submarine division attached to the Asiatic Fleet. She would take her examinations and get another fellowship to do research in Paris on her doctorate. After a year in Europe she would join him in the Far East, where they would travel as much as possible.

Although he was happy, she was troubled. She would have to study up to the last minute before the ceremony and even during the brief time they were together afterward. Otherwise she might fail her examinations and not receive the fellowship she needed to go to Europe. And, unless she studied abroad, she would lose all that she had worked for. If all this was not enough, she had to face the reproaches of her mother. Not once, her mother chided her, had Ruth returned to Germany; why did she not come home to visit? If the time between mid-December and mid-January would interrupt her studies least, why not come then? Why did Ruth want to marry in May if she and her husband were going to separate almost immediately? And (echoing Ruth's concern) was she not risking all that she was working for?

Ruth felt the justice of her mother's criticisms. She was, after all, marrying a man her mother had never met. Ruth also felt guilty because she had toured the United States the previous summer instead of going back to Germany. Was her mother right? Should they postpone their wedding until Ruth finished her year in Europe? Suppose they did delay their marriage, perhaps until after his graduation from submarine school, and suppose he got duty in New London instead of the Far East. Then, at least, they could be together on weekends.

Convinced that her mother was opposed to the marriage, Rickover worried but did not put pressure on Ruth, and he even offered to pay for her trip. Later he wrote, "At that time I decided that it was all up to you— if there were anything or anybody which could shake your connection with me, it were better that we went no further."[3]

Ruth and her mother worked out a compromise. The marriage would be postponed, but Ruth would not return to Germany over Christmas. Instead, she would go to Europe in the summer, still unmarried, for research on her doctorate and for a lengthy visit with her mother.

In long letters to Ruth, Rickover described his life on the S-9. In November, on her way back from Charleston, South Carolina, the submarine ran into a strong winter gale. Green seas coming over the bow swept aft, drenching the few men on the bridge. Below decks the retching of seasick men fouled the air. Finally wind and seas fell, but all the dishes had been broken and fresh water was running low. Cold penetrated all areas of the submarine because there was no way to heat them.[4]

When the S-9 was in New London, Rickover lived in the officers barracks and at night worked on an article about the submarine and international law. The lack of material in the base library slowed him down, and he worried whether someone else might be working on the same topic and beat him to publication. He sounded out the views of other officers on submarine warfare. Without hesitation nearly all assumed that the United States would not be bound by treaties or laws restricting undersea operations. "I should be disappointed in my country if it adopted such an attitude," he wrote Ruth. "I trust our statesmen will have the strength of character to stand by our solemn treaty obligations." If civilian authorities placed restrictions on warfare, he had no doubt they would be obeyed. "I do know this about the mentality of naval officers—that they will always carry out their orders exactly—no matter what their personal opinions may be."[5]

Rickover reported to the submarine school on 5 January 1930. In his class of thirty-seven officers, he was one of two senior lieutenants; the rest of the class consisted of twenty-three junior grade lieutenants and twelve ensigns.[6] The class spent about half its time in classrooms and half in submarines attached to the school.

Rickover thought too much time in classes went into studying and memorizing publications, a type of instruction that no longer satisfied him after Columbia. Most of the training devices were old and in bad shape, having come from decommissioned submarines. Wanting to work on his article, Rickover resented the approach of an officer instructor who, finding Rickover had a postgraduate degree in electrical engineering, wanted his help in revising the course.

The training in the submarines, however, was invaluable. In them students learned the duties of the officer of the deck and the diving officer and gained detailed technical knowledge by tracing out water and air lines, sketching the arrangements of components, and operating equipment and machinery blindfolded. Students were also taught the mechanism and operation of the torpedo tubes as well as how to make minor repairs and adjustments to the torpedoes. Each officer got a chance to fire two.

Rickover could not get Ruth out of his mind. Certain she did not understand the impact that marriage to him would have on her career, he agonized and, determined to build a common ground between them, continued to study German and international law.

She was dismayed. Love was strengthening her and enriching her life, but it was devastating him by destroying his interest in his profession and eroding his ambition. On 16 January she wrote, "It has worried me for quite some time (and you remember long ago I wrote you on the subject) that your love is such an exclusive power, almost intolerant of any other interest." He had to learn to take misunderstandings more calmly, she wrote, and their love for granted. Should she curb her ambition and her hopes for success? She could, but she would be miserable, and therefore he would be miserable. His own self-interests, not what he thought best for her, should guide him in considering his next assignment.

Seeming to understand, he returned to his work with renewed spirit. After regular school hours he "dived bilges," which meant crawling around in the muck and oil to trace piping and locate valves. Each week every student had to sketch one or more pipe systems. Although most of his classmates merely copied blueprints, he insisted on seeing things for himself. On 20 January he was the diving officer for the first time, giving all the orders to submerge, level off, and surface.

One moment he was on the height of happiness, the next in the abyss of misery. Uneasy over their relationship, Rickover wrote Ruth on 25 January that he planned to come to Columbia soon to strip away the "shadowy veil of misunderstanding which has arisen between us and which can only be torn asunder by communion." The next day he wrote, "Let this letter constitute complete reassurance about my feelings, and permit it to dispel the fogs of misunderstanding." On the following day, he declared, "Now that the shadows of last week are gone I feel like a new person and can work much better." On Saturday, 1 February, he went to New York.

He was shocked. Here was no "shadowy veil" but substantial differences—ones he had created. He had completely failed to grasp how she was trapped between her need to study and his emotional demands. Back in New London he bitterly censured himself, writing in anguish, "It is clear to me now that I have been draining the store of our love and bringing about situations unbearably trying to you and always placing you in the position of maintaining our relationship—preventing it from being broken." He promised never again to be jealous of her work or to interfere with her choice of friends. He agreed that they should not try to balance their love by some formula of equality. "In our love," he wrote, "I want you to be dependent upon me and rely upon me for everything."[7]

Uncertainty regarding her future at Columbia was driving Ruth into despair. A professor, not realizing Ruth's need for the fellowship offered by the Carnegie Foundation for International Peace, was recommending another candidate for study in Paris. She could not help but wonder if the reason was that, because of love, she had fallen down in her work. "It is not the fellowship but the fear that I have failed. I don't know what I would do if I could not turn to you," she wrote Rickover. "You are the only one who does not care whether I am a failure professionally. You don't, do you?"[8] He tried his best to calm, encourage, and reassure her. "Fame and fortune I cannot give you; understanding I can," he replied. She needed to have no fears about going to Paris the next year, for "whatever is mine is yours."[9]

In letter after letter he suggested how she might approach her professors to obtain their backing. And he tried to cheer her up. From New London he wrote, "I shall now tell you something which will make you proud. We are about to redesign our submarine storage batteries and make them ultra-modern—that is, copy the German U-boat submarine design as used in 1917!!" And from Columbia, "Your attempts to get the U.S. submarines into shape have gone down like honey (I am afraid this isn't good English, but you'll probably get the drift of my thought). It is very fortunate for you that the Versailles Treaty prohibits Germany to build subs!!!!!"[10]

On 18 March 1930 she had wonderful news: she was Columbia's first choice for the Carnegie Fellowship. "I am less interested in the fellowship than in this obvious refutation of my recent fears that I have been slackening." The following day Rickover replied, "It has been a long time since I have been so genuinely happy as I am right now." And later that same day he wrote, "All day I have been sharing your happiness; I am so glad that your good work is not going unnoticed."[11]

If her immediate future was settled, his was not. Arranging to be assigned to a submarine operating out of New London did not appear difficult, but nothing was certain. He could be sent to the West Coast,

Hawaii, or the Far East. If he could not get New London, she should consider her profession first. "I don't want you to compromise too much for my sake," he stated. "I am strong enough to bear a long absence from you."[12]

In May an officer telephoned Washington to find out the assignments of everyone in the class. Rickover, he said, was to go to the V-4—the Argonaut—at San Diego. "Can you imagine how I felt?" he asked Ruth. "I was ready to write and tell you that we must break off and not become married because this would interfere with all your hopes." To his vast relief he found he was instead to be sent to "Div. 4," based in New London.[13]

He graduated submarine school on 6 June 1930, standing fourth in his class. The school had not impressed him; the instructors were inexperienced and gave frequent examinations that demanded time to memorize—time that might be better spent in learning. Rickover was disturbed, too, by the closed minds of his classmates; they thought of nothing but their careers. "Certainly there is something woefully wrong with our system of education which brings about a condition such as this," he thought.[14] He believed his classmates and instructors regarded him as an interloper, partly because he was Jewish and partly because he was senior to so many. He was certain they didn't like him.

After graduation Rickover hurried to New York and Ruth. He was disconcerted to learn that she intended that they plunge immediately into the study of international law. Surely, he thought, on their first day together they could do something else. They did fill his leave with study, but, following his plans, they also read poetry from Palgrave's *Golden Treasury* and, as a high point, saw the popular musical play *Green Pastures*. On the evening of 20 June he was reluctantly on his way back to New London. At 10:10 the next morning he reported as the new engineer and electrical officer on board the *S-48*, Lt. William J. Lorenz commanding.[15]

The *S-48* had a bad reputation. Built by the Lake Torpedo Boat Company of Bridgeport, Connecticut, she was nearly lost in December 1921 on her first dive. Four years later she ran aground twice in a heavy snowstorm while on her way to the Navy yard at Portsmouth, New Hampshire. No lives were lost, although the ship was heavily damaged. Over the next few years the yard worked on her and, as funds became available, installed German-designed diesels and lengthened her hull by inserting a twenty-five-foot six-inch section to give her greater operating range and better habitability. The modifications did little good, and she kept her reputation for getting into trouble.

Portsmouth had also installed pneumatically controlled vent valves in the *S-48*, another feature that led to trouble. The purpose of the valves was to let air leave the ballast tanks so that water could enter them and cause the submarine to submerge. The lives of everyone in the ship depended upon the proper working of the valves. On the *S-48* it was impossible to synchronize them; valves on one side operated faster than those on the other. Consequently, when beginning a dive, she lurched to one side or the other, frequently by as much as twelve degrees. In time one became accustomed to it, but no one, Rickover remembered with a grin, ever warned a new man or visitor of this trick.

On 7 July 1930 the *S-48* slipped down the Thames River toward Long Island Sound. As engineer officer, Rickover was anxious. The big test was whether her diesels could drive her at full power for four hours. In the future he would preside over many full-power runs, but none like this. He wrote Ruth the next day:

> On the way out of the Thames River the electrical controller for one of the motors became inoperative, necessitating stopping of the ship. In an hour repairs had been effected and we were underway again. I thought—"Well, I'm glad this is over." Just about then the gyro compass repeater went "haywire" so that it was impossible to steer a correct course. When this had been repaired I said fervently to myself, "I hope there will be no more trouble."
>
> So we steamed out past the light-house. Then the Chief Machinist's Mate . . . came up and reported that a stem on one of the exhaust valves of the diesel engine was cracked, and that at least an hour would be required for repairs. Well—there was nothing to be done but stop once more. Finally, when we were chugging away again and I had begun to lose my dour expression . . . the word came up that the new valve stem was heating up. So we stopped once more.
>
> By this time I was completely downhearted. . . . We started off once more . . . and I was about to inform the Captain that I was ready to commence the run when three of the cylinder jackets of the port engine developed leaks. This meant that there was a possibility of getting salt water into the lubricating oil system—which is dangerous. This casualty was the result of a poor feature of design in the original German engines. . . .
>
> I made a quick decision: Probably the Captain would become disgusted if I kept on reporting casualty after casualty, so I decided to take the chance and run with the leaky cylinder jackets. I really didn't expect the engines to hold out . . . and I knew that if anything serious should happen there would be a Board of Investigation and I would be held responsible for not having informed the Captain of the state of affairs.
>
> I had become tired running around from the bridge to the engine room and

back and then I had the 8–12 evening watch. . . . Each minute I was expecting the engines to break down. . . . I could almost imagine something was wrong with them. At this time the electrician reported that something was wrong with one of the main motors. . . .

By now I had become philosophical. I went below, and crawled into the bilges and inspected . . . and could see nothing wrong. So we started up again. . . .

I had the 8–12 watch this morning. . . .

About 11 I heard a jangling in the bow—the anchor chain was coming loose and the anchor started dropping out in the open sea in about 200 fathoms of water! We immediately stopped the ship and found that the control panel for the anchor windlass had become grounded and the motor had started running of its own accord. Well, this was soon remedied.

Never in all my experience in the Navy have I had such a multitude of ill-starred events befall me. I am surprised that I am acting like an ordinary human being and not overwhelmed by all of this.

Sharing his thoughts with Ruth had become a necessity. He believed constant practice was producing an American submarine force as good as or even better than the best the Germans had during the war. But he was disturbed that the officers showed no intellectual interests—a trait he had noticed at the submarine school. They were petty in their treatment of the enlisted men and discouraged initiative. With a little consideration, he believed, the crew would have worked with much more enthusiasm.

Visions Ruth had of their married life continued to trouble him. She wrote of having a summer home where they could get away for a month each year, but he knew it would be very hard for him to get that much time. They talked of going to Washington for his next shore duty, but he could be sent to Guam or the Virgin Islands. "I would like to do ever so many things for you in the way of your comfort and pleasure, but I know it will be impossible," he wrote.[16]

He never hid from her the dangers of submarine duty. On Monday evening, 15 September 1930, the S-48 had surfaced after completing a submerged run on Long Island Sound. She had finished charging her batteries at 7:45 P.M. Half an hour later smoke was discovered escaping from the casing of a blower (ventilator fan). A quick check showed the blower was not at fault—the smoke was coming from the battery compartment itself. When it was opened, black smoke billowed out. Lieutenant Lorenz ordered all personnel out of the living and work spaces above the batteries and had the blowers stopped and the watertight doors closed.

Wearing a gas mask and trailing a lifeline, Rickover opened the forward hatch to the battery compartment at 11:00 P.M. This was the moment of danger—when the mixture of air and hydrogen gas might explode. He waited an instant, then climbed down into the compartment. He saw no flames but found plenty of smoke curling out from beneath the battery flooring. He felt the flooring: it was warm but not hot. Eyes aching and breathing with difficulty, he made his way back out. He had an emergency ventilating system rigged and lime placed in the compartment to remove carbon dioxide. By 1:00 A.M. the air was good enough to work without gas masks. Examination showed that some of the floor boards were charred to a half-inch depth; the worst of the fire had occurred where connections from several batteries came together.

At 2:30 A.M. a short circuit among the charred battery connections started another fire. Seizing carbon tetrachloride extinguishers, he and two electricians tried to put out the flames. The chlorine gas choked them and hurt their eyes while the growing fire increased the chance of an explosion. Rickover suddenly remembered the ship had an instruction book describing the best extinguishers to use for various types of fire. He thumbed through its pages, only to find it recommended the very type of extinguisher they were using with so little effect. Almost at his wits' end, he sprinkled lime over the fire. With great relief, he saw the flames die. It was later discovered that old and deteriorating insulation had caused the fire.

He wasn't afraid of death; it was the horror of being maimed. "I could not bear to live like that," he wrote Ruth. Later he saw the humorous aspect of the situation: in searching through the instruction book he was like a cook with a cookbook in one hand and a pot in the other. Ruth saw nothing funny about it: he must promise to get other duty as soon as possible. "It is so terrible to have the constant fear with me that you may be in danger."[17]

On 20 February 1931 the *S-48* left Portsmouth for Coco Solo, the submarine base on the Atlantic side of the Panama Canal. Usually the submarines spent two weeks at the base and six weeks maneuvering in the Gulf of Panama on the Pacific side. The Pacific stint began on a Monday, when the ships, accompanied by a tender, would leave Coco Solo and pass through the canal. At the end of each week they tied up at Balboa, the harbor on the Pacific end of the canal. The *S-48* kept her reputation. Because of engine trouble she usually took off early on Friday for Balboa, and because of engine trouble she was usually the last to arrive.[18]

Rickover was discontented. The climate, boredom, his absence from

Ruth, cramped quarters, lack of privacy, and his growing dislike of sub-marine duty were all factors. In the tropics, temperatures soared well over one hundred degrees and humidity reached 100 percent. With water drip-ping on bunks, sleep was almost impossible. During the rainy season the daily downpour made surface navigation a miserable chore; every few minutes he had to pour water off the chart. Lorenz was constantly carp-ing, criticizing, and treating officers and men as servants.

On 6 July 1931, Lt. Olton R. Bennehoff took command and Rickover moved up from engineer to executive officer, which put him in charge of the ship's organization. He was also the navigator. To Rickover's deep dis-appointment, Bennehoff, while intelligent, was doctrinaire and hard to get along with.

Even doing well at long-range battle practice brought him little satisfac-tion. In this exercise the submarine would be driven at full speed to the surface from a given depth at a "hell of a steep angle." The conning tower had glass ports: as soon as the first hint of light showed through them, Rickover knew the conning tower hatch and the bow were above the sur-face. The gun crew opened the hatch, sped to the gun through water still swirling across the deck, removed the devices that protected the gun from water, got the range, fired sixteen rounds, replaced the devices, secured the gun, then raced for the hatch across the deck, already awash as the ship had begun her dive. Accuracy and time on the surface were the two most important measures of success. Because Rickover was the diving officer, much depended upon him. "Well—we did rather well," he told Ruth. "Nevertheless, I find myself unable to become enthusiastic."[19]

At least he was advancing toward command. He passed his physical on 29 June 1931. Later a board of officers, all commanding submarines, quizzed him and set problems demanding rapid responses and quick solu-tions. They were with him when, in a submarine not his own, he got under way, dove, made approaches on a target, surfaced, and returned to the base. On 4 August he qualified for command.[20]

"If it were not that I have you I don't believe I could keep on going along as I do," he wrote on 29 July to Ruth, now studying in Europe. He thought constantly of the coming fall and marriage. In letter after letter he poured out his emotion: "I can feel ours will be a great happiness." "In two more months!" "You are not going to confine yourself to menial tasks in any household which boasts of me as the master!" "I respect and admire your independence and your integrity. I shall never encroach upon those." "The time *is* getting shorter." "You are the only one I can write to freely. The only one I can tell what I think. . . . I will so want to forget this terrible year."[21]

At long last, on 27 September, he sailed to New York. In a simple ceremony in a church in Litchfield, Connecticut, in the presence of a few witnesses, he and Ruth were married on 8 October 1931. After their honeymoon at a friend's summer home near Northfield, Massachusetts, he started back to Coco Solo and the *S-48*. Sometime in January Ruth would join him for a few weeks.

She had some misgivings about how she would get along where "everybody plays bridge and gossips all the time! Honestly, I am afraid of them. I wish we could stay away entirely, but it would not be the wise thing to do; in the end we would not like to be outsiders either."[22]

At Coco Solo Rickover learned that the *S-48* had been in trouble again. On 16 November she began a dive to make an approach for a practice torpedo attack. Immediately she took a twelve-degree list and a sharp downward angle. At seventy feet below the surface she was out of control, but by blowing tanks, Bennehoff brought her up. Investigation showed a vent valve had failed to open.[23]

Learning about the near-disaster was bad enough, but Rickover was also upset by risks to his personal plans. In the first part of February, or even earlier, the *S-48* would begin taking part in a scientific expedition to measure the earth's gravity. As Ruth was not to arrive until 15 January, their time together would be short. That disappointment was lessened somewhat when she arranged to leave New York earlier.

Eagerly he sought for a place for them to live. Wives of other officers helped; one found a suitable apartment, another lent him curtains and a carpet. To see the countryside he bought a car. The crew cleaned the engine, drained the crankcase, put in new oil, overhauled and charged the battery, and checked the radio.

Then she was with him. They explored the country, went on picnics, spent quiet evenings at Gatun Locks, and, in sampling the night life, glanced at "wicked things." Their month together was idyllic and parting was difficult. He waited silently on the dock until the ship left, but her emotion was too deep for her to appear at the rail. On 30 January 1932, she wrote, "I want you to know that we cannot stay separated for all this long time until you get shore duty. If you cannot come North, I will come to you. It is more important to be happy than to save or to have a career."

With Ruth gone, Rickover turned his attention to the scientific expedition. Because the earth is not a perfect sphere of uniform composition, its gravity varies from place to place. The Caribbean region, with its mountainous islands and ocean deeps, its history of volcanic activity, and its earthquakes, was an excellent place to study anomalies in the earth's crust. On 4 February 1932, F. A. Vening Meinesz, a professor at the University of Utrecht in the Netherlands, Harry Hess from Princeton, and a Navy technician boarded the *S-48* at Guantánamo, Cuba. The Dutch scientist had earned an international reputation by his measurements of the earth's gravity, and Hess was on his way to becoming a pioneer in developing the theory of plate tectonics and sea floor spreading.

Meinesz had devised an instrument consisting of three carefully arranged pendulums. Local features in the earth's terrain would affect the oscillation of one pendulum more than the others. Successful measurements over a wide area, however, depended upon having a stable and mobile platform. A submarine met the requirements perfectly: she was mobile, she was stable when operating far enough beneath the surface to be unaffected by waves, and her position could be determined by navigation.

Accompanied by the submarine rescue vessel *Chewink* to provide navigational and sounding checks, the expedition departed on 7 February. The next day the *S-48* acted up. After submerging erratically off the easternmost point of Jamaica, she lay on the surface for five hours to make temporary repairs to the valves. On her dive at 11:00 P.M. on 9 February, she took a sudden downward angle of twenty degrees but recovered. "It was scary," Rickover recalled.

He turned in to catch a few minutes sleep. At midnight he was called to the wardroom. In that small space the other officers, nervous and tired, had drawn up a message to Washington for all to sign, stating that the ship was unsafe and could not complete her assignment. Rickover argued them out of it, declaring that it would be bad for the reputation of all concerned and that he could work out a new procedure for diving.

His method took longer to submerge, but it worked. "The way I feel about it," he wrote on 10 February to Ruth, "if we are assigned a duty to perform, it is up to us to accomplish it, no matter how much extra effort, lack of sleep, etc. it may involve." He added, "I am cheering Dr. Meinesz up. He became gloomy at developments, and now I have turned out to be a veritable optimist (aren't you sincerely surprised)."

Rickover was thriving, even though the ship was dirty and stank, the water was so scarce that no one showered or washed, the fresh food was gone, all the bread had been eaten, and the cook's biscuits were terrible.

But he was getting excellent experience in navigation, in one day taking eighteen sights and finding it gratifying to see how well the lines of position from several stars converged to a single point on his chart. But conversations with Meinesz and Hess were the main reason for his new spirit—they gave him the intellectual companionship he craved.

The Dutch scientist was unassuming and highly intelligent. He and Rickover discussed the lack of moral strength in intellectuals, Darwin's theory of evolution, and mutation against natural selection as the cause of change. With Hess he talked about geology. "I enjoy these friends," Rickover wrote enthusiastically. "They are so different from the officers in the ship in whose heads a philosophical thought never enters." Most of all, he was taking part in important scientific work. He would far rather be contributing to its success than doing what he considered useless tasks alongside some dock.[24]

The expedition finally ended in Miami. Meinesz on 24 March gave a dinner party for the S-48 officers and the next day left the ship. In an interview with the press, the scientist furnished a few facts: the voyage had lasted a month and a half, had covered five thousand miles, and had included fifty-four dives. It was, he thought (without doubt choosing his words carefully), the most strenuous expedition he had ever been on. Finding a new depth of twenty-four thousand feet for the Bartlett Deep was among the data the expedition had gathered.[25] Rickover hated to see Meinesz and Hess go: there would be no more stimulating conversations.

On 5 April 1932 Rickover applied for command. He preferred an R-class submarine operating out of New London. The R class was older than the S class (in which he was serving), but some were attached to the submarine school at New London. If his request was granted, he would have the best of all possible worlds: command for himself and a chance for him and Ruth to establish their first home, which, because it would be in the New York area, would allow her to continue her work in international law. She was about to receive her doctorate and was preparing her thesis for publication; furthermore, she had been appointed a research assistant at Columbia. Everything looked bright.

Although strongly endorsing Rickover's request, Bennehoff observed that the S-48 was about to go into overhaul and to lose two officers to postgraduate school. With this turnover Rickover could not yet be spared. The commander of Submarine Division 5 concurred in Rickover's request, observing that he was qualified to command and would perform his duties excellently. The commander of Submarine Squadron 3 agreed, noting that Rickover was senior to two officers of the squadron who had been ordered to command submarines. On 28 May, however, the Bureau of Navigation informed Rickover that it was not practicable to assign him command at that time.[26]

Both Rickover and Ruth had recognized the possibility that their plans for New London might fail. Still, Ruth thought she could get a job in Washington or New York and on 6 October 1932 wrote, "Please try not to let yourself get annoyed—everything will be over soon and there will not ever be another S-48 in your life."

Rickover still clashed with Bennehoff, although after one particular blowup they got along better. "One thing I am determined upon—as soon as I am detached from the S-48, I shall cast her and her troubles out of my mind completely," he wrote on 19 December 1932. "I hope that never again in my naval service will I ever be subject to conditions such as these." But there were bright spots. On 9 January 1933, while Bennehoff was on leave, Rear Adm. John W. Greenslade, commander, Submarine Force, U.S. Fleet, witnessing the performance of the *S-48* under way, commended Rickover for the excellent state of training of the crew.[27]

Rickover still did not know what his next assignment would be. With no submarine command available, he thought of Washington, where Ruth might find work in the State Department. Citing his postgraduate work in electrical engineering and his interest in doing research on submarine electric propulsion, he had asked on 5 January for duty at the Naval Research Laboratory, located on the outskirts of the city. His endorsements were good. Greenslade stated that Rickover had an excellent professional reputation, that his judgment on electrical problems, particularly those on submarine storage batteries, was often sought, and that he would do well in research.[28]

On 20 January the Bureau of Navigation informed Rickover that his request would be considered, but on 25 February he received bad news: he had been assigned to the office of inspector of naval material in Philadelphia. Immediately, but without much hope, he asked for a change of orders. Anything in Washington would be acceptable, but he preferred some phase of engineering. His wife, he pointed out, was a doctor of philosophy in international law, was actively engaged in that profession, held a research fellowship at Columbia, and had written a book, *International Law in National Courts*, which had just been published. She had a chance at a position in the State Department, and even if that did not materialize, she could still do research. Since their marriage they had been separated most of the time because he had been stationed in a place where she could not work. "I feel I have no right to ask her to give up her profession," he wrote, "insomuch as she is accomplishing a worthwhile object, and her work is as important to her as my profession is to me."[29]

If it were not for its impact on Ruth, the assignment to Philadelphia would not be so bad. It was a billet in which he would operate almost independently, he would have a good deal of time to himself, and he would be working with the Exide Storage Battery Company, a leading manufacturer of submarine batteries. Ruth was soon reconciled. "Don't you think I am beginning to learn the Navy way of making the best of the inevitable?" she asked.[30] She liked the idea of his being his own boss, having some free time, and becoming an expert on storage batteries—that should help him in his career, she thought. But most of all, she longed for them to have a home. On 22 March he wrote her that his request for Washington had been turned down; they would go to Philadelphia.

The S-48, with four other submarines, left Coco Solo in April and, after a stop of some days in Miami, departed for Baltimore. On 15 May at 5:01 in the afternoon, the S-48 moored at the Broadway Pier. Finally, on 5 June 1933, he was detached from the ship.

Was Rickover just in his appraisal of Lieutenants Lorenz and Bennehoff? Rear Adm. William D. Irvin, who won the Navy Cross and the Bronze Star while commanding the submarine *Nautilus* during World War II, was an ensign in the S-48 and remembered the ship and Rickover well. Irvin recalled that anything that could go wrong on the S-48 did go wrong, and that the ship had the "damnedest line up of skippers." He thought Bennehoff and Rickover were brilliant, but, he said, they argued constantly, with Rickover taking the part of the other officers and the men. Irvin would wrangle with Rickover over some engineering matter only to hear, "Now look, Bill, I've heard what you have to say but shut up and do what I said." In these instances Irvin found Rickover was right. It was possible to get "as mad as hell at him" and still come away with respect. Rickover was, Irvin concluded, a fine shipmate.[31]

Rickover reported to Rear Adm. Richard M. Watt, inspector of naval material, on 5 July 1933 in Philadelphia. Rickover liked what he saw. Watt's office examined equipment and goods ordered from private industry in one of the most important manufacturing areas of the country. Watt gave his officers a great deal of responsibility and expected them to exercise initiative. He assigned his new assistant inspector of naval material those matters dealing with submarines.

While Rickover was in the *S-48*, he and Ruth wrote to each other of their intense longing to set up their own home. They were exhilarated at the thought of bringing their dreams into reality. He did not want the flat 15 percent reduction in pay—an economy measure instituted by the Navy because of the Great Depression—to affect their two years in Philadelphia: "Let us make them the most enjoyable ones each of us has ever had. I wish to get lots and lots of clothes, and neckties, and shirts, etc., etc., and you also must have decent clothes—or I'll be ashamed to go out with you!"[32] Because she had to remain in New York for a while, it fell to him to find a place to live.

Ruth often came down from Columbia to visit, and when she could not, he wrote to her of his adventures. Eventually they found an apartment at 5060 City Line Avenue, where they lived from August 1933 to March 1935. Exuberantly he began furnishing it, "buying two glasses (drinking) for five cents . . . most beautiful to behold, manufactured by Woolworth and Company." Tired of not having a single chair in the house, he bought one for sixty-nine cents.[33] "Tomorrow I believe I'll go looking for bookcases (second-hand) because you doubt my capacity to manufacture suitable ones. I'll never forgive you for that. (Evidently you are not aware that 23 years ago I had a course in manual training in grammar school and that I actually made a stand which was used at home for a number of years—not to mention an ironing board and other sundry items). Wait until you see the shelves I make and you will be utterly apologetic and sorry."

To add to his happiness, he found his work was important. German submarines acquired at the end of the world war had revealed the startling inferiority of American submarines. There were two major reasons for the poor quality: disputes between the Navy and the private shipbuilders, particularly with Electric Boat, over legal and technical matters and the inability of the two parties to understand the importance of both profit and good technical quality, which led to "vessels with poorly designed engines, terrible habitability, and numerous other defects." The years since the end of the war, however, had seen improvement in the technology and in the relationship between the Navy and Electric Boat. Moreover, several outstanding Navy officers were working on the design and development of submarines.[34] What was needed was impetus.

It came on 16 June 1933. On that date President Franklin D. Roosevelt signed the National Industrial Recovery Act as one major weapon to fight the Great Depression. He apportioned $238 million under the act to construct thirty-two ships for the Navy, among them four submarines.

Rickover felt the effect of the legislation. He spent much of July and August at the facilities of battery manufacturers, among them the Electric Storage Battery Company. On the last day of August he attended a meeting at the Bureau of Engineering in Washington. "From the standpoint of accomplishing what I set out to do my trip was highly successful," he wrote jubilantly to Ruth the next day. "Practically every one of the ideas I advanced was adopted, and I more than saved the U.S. my salary for this year by these two days work. However, I now have a great deal of work in prospect and one item—the attempt to cut-down the weight of the batteries for the new sub is of such great importance that I must let everything else go tomorrow and tackle it immediately." The following day he wrote, "I was at the Exide plant all afternoon discussing the saving of weights for the new submarine and we managed so far to save 4 tons—which I am sure will be a pleasure to the Navy Department."

In his letter to Ruth, Rickover did not mention the name of the "new sub." Probably it was the design for the four submarines the National Industrial Recovery Act provided. These were the *Porpoise, Pike, Shark,* and *Tarpon,* all laid down late in 1933, the first two by Portsmouth, the last two by Electric Boat.

As Rickover knew from firsthand experience, American diesels were poor and were one of the major problems the Navy faced in building a first-rate submarine force. Maschinenfabrik-Augsburg-Nürnberg (MAN), a German organization, led diesel technology. In the immediate postwar years, MAN designs and engines were sold to several nations, including the United States, both for propulsion and as the basis for further development. Nonetheless, MAN diesels maintained their superiority, partly in design and partly in materials. As the 1930s began, the Navy in its effort to build improved submarines faced the prospect of relying on German technology.

Getting American companies to develop and manufacture diesels for submarines was the best solution, but the Navy could not offer a big enough market to attract manufacturers. American railroads, however, were beginning to offer a tremendous market for lightweight diesel engines. Best of all, from the Navy's perspective, the technical requirements for locomotive engines did not differ too radically from those for submarines. In 1932 Rear Adm. Samuel M. Robinson, chief of the Bureau of Engineering, invited proposals for engines from manufacturers. At the end of the year he had five responses. General Motors, which was developing the Winton engine, made the best offer, but the other companies were not far behind.[35]

On 24 October 1934, Rickover received orders to go to Cleveland to see the design and witness the operation of the Winton diesel. From there he was to go to Hamilton, Ohio, to inspect the Hooven-Owens-Rentschler Company engine, and then on to Washington to attend a conference at the Bureau of Engineering. Two days later he wrote to Ruth from Cleveland:

> I arrived here early this morning and have been on the go ever since. I was at the Winton Engine Co. about 9 A.M. and an engineer was detailed to stay with me all day—as long as I cared to have him. It was extremely interesting to see how many engines they have here. Evidently General Motors has gone into this on a large scale—they expect to get a good deal of railroad business. In fact, they have some orders already.
>
> I had a brilliant idea: I called the Navy Department by long distance telephone and asked them if it would be all right to also go to see the engine being built by Fairbanks Morse Co. at Beloit, Wisconsin. So I am now at the station (10 P.M.) waiting to catch the train for Chicago. It will arrive there early in the morning and the Fairbanks Morse people will drive me to Beloit. . . .
>
> I wish you could see some of these things. It is remarkable what progress is being made in mechanical lines. Yesterday a Union Pacific train (with a Winton engine) ran from Los Angeles to New York in 57 hours at a cost in fuel oil of about $957!! You can see the possibilities.

Winton engines, as well as new and more powerful batteries, drove the *Porpoise*, the *Pike*, commissioned in 1935, and the *Shark* and *Tarpon*, commissioned in 1936.[36] All were to see combat in World War II, and all except the *Shark* were to survive. They were not the final stage in the evolution of the fleet submarine, which played such a great part in the defeat of Japan, but were a major stride toward that goal.

In the demands of his work and in the excitement of having his first home, Rickover had delayed meeting one obligation: he had not visited his parents since his marriage. He and Ruth had considered the matter while he was still in the *S-48*. Knowing his family, especially his father, had not accepted his marrying out of the Jewish faith, he would go to Chicago alone. Ruth was reluctant to see him go, possibly worried that a visit to his parents might subject him to unpleasantness at a time when such marriages were rare; she might even have thought that, back in the environment in which he had been brought up, he himself might regret the marriage. Toward the end of September 1933, he took the train to Chicago.

The nearer he got to his destination, the more he longed for Philadelphia. "If you ever had any doubt that my visit here would change my attitude, you can certainly dispel it," he declared. Staying with his family did not change his feelings. "As you must realize, these days I am spending here are no time of pleasure. It is very clear to me that I have outgrown much that is here—and I feel a great deal out of place." He added in another letter, "This is the last time I shall write you before I leave . . . and I am very happy that this is so." "It seems as though I have been away for a year already. I didn't think it would be so hard—but it is. Thank you for writing me so often."[37] Visits to the Chicago World's Fair were the only bright spots during his stay.

He never broke with his parents or his sisters, although he saw them rarely and then by himself. He always spoke highly of his father and of his love for his mother. He referred to both of them with pride, but he believed the gulf between their life and the one he had chosen was too great to bridge.

While in the S-48 Rickover had come across a reference in a publication of the Office of Naval Intelligence to a book by a German naval officer. Adm. Herman Bauer's *The Submarine. Its importance as part of a fleet. Its importance in international law. Its employment in war. Its future* was published in Berlin by E. S. Mittles and Son in 1931. Rickover decided to translate it. Before the war Bauer was chief of staff, 1st Submarine Flotilla, and during the war until the summer of 1917 was commander, Submarine Flotillas. Proud of the technical superiority of German submarines and of their achievements, he saw their operations, regarded as a violation of international law, as just reprisal against the way in which the British were breaching international law by their blockade. The naval war college issued Rickover's translation in July 1936.[38]

Conditions at Philadelphia were better than in the S-48 for writing. He sent a letter, titled "Quarterly Marks and the Promotion of Enlisted Personnel," to the United States Naval Institute *Proceedings*. Calling for the adoption of standard procedures, it appeared in the March 1934 issue.[39] He also found time to revise a poorly organized chapter on batteries in the Bureau of Engineering manual. He freely consulted Ruth on the chapter; even if knowing nothing of the technology, she had a keen sense of logic.

They decided that a chronological approach was best, beginning with the tests and inspections and proceeding through packing for shipment, preparations for installation, installing, operation, and upkeep and repair.

Ruth had earlier suggested that they work together on articles dealing with the submarine and international law. Their interest in the subject went back to their days at Columbia, but until they were together, they had never found it possible to undertake the project. Their analysis pointed out the rapidly growing gulf between international law and military technology. Submarine attacks on merchant shipping during the world war dramatically illustrated one aspect of the issue, and the employment of military aviation was another. Yet nothing had been done to revise international law. The Rickovers argued that an international conference, similar to those held at The Hague in 1899 and 1907, and in London in 1909, was urgently needed.

Behind the meticulous footnotes, citations, and quotations was the conviction that international law, frail and flawed though it was, remained a great and precious achievement of mankind. The article was submitted to the United States Naval Institute for its annual prize. Rickover was disgusted that it failed to win, but "International Law and the Submarine" by Lt. H. G. Rickover appeared in the September 1935 *Proceedings*.[40]

On 23 March 1935, Rickover was detached from the office of inspector of naval material. Rear Admiral Watt praised him highly in fitness reports. For his next assignment at sea, Rickover wanted either the command of a submarine or duty in a heavy cruiser; in each case he preferred the Asiatic Fleet, a preference no doubt motivated by the plans he and Ruth had discussed years earlier to travel in the Orient. If he were to be assigned to shore duty, he wanted to attend the Naval War College at Newport, Rhode Island.[41] Instead, he was ordered to the battleship *New Mexico* operating out of San Pedro, California.

On 16 March 1933, when his time in the *S-48* was almost at its end, he wrote to Ruth about the world's supply of energy. Observing that the sudden increase in industrialization had coincided with the introduction of oil, he thought it might be a blessing if cheap and abundant fuels were exhausted, slowing down industrialization and forcing mankind to return to a sane life. "To offset the possible decline in the available supplies of fuel, scientists are attempting to obtain sub-atomic energy," he continued. "I sincerely hope they fail in this. It reminds me of Pandora's Box; where a great deal of misery was let loose by learning too much."

In January 1933 the *New York Times* carried a number of stories on atomic research. Possibly he had come across one appearing almost at the end of the month titled "Predicts Utilizing of Atomic Energy," in which Karl T. Compton (destined to play an important role in the development of the atomic bomb), a professor at the Massachusetts Institute of Technology (MIT), had declared that science was ready to harness the atom.[42]

Preparing to join the *New Mexico*, Rickover had no reason to think that submarines or "sub-atomic energy" would ever play a great part in his life.

Engineering Duty Only

Lt. H. G. Rickover reported on board the battleship *New Mexico*, Capt. Charles C. Soule commanding, off San Pedro, California, on 13 April 1935. With her graceful clipper bow and her main battery of twelve 14-inch guns, the ship looked handsome and powerful. She had a good reputation, and Rickover found the officers friendly. His quarters were spacious, even luxurious, compared with those he had on the *S-48*.

Rickover was assistant engineer, but his responsibilities were far greater than his title. The chief engineer had never had engineering duty before and was willing to leave everything to Rickover. He was in charge of a propulsion plant with geared turbines that could drive the ship at a top speed of twenty-three knots. A loose-leaf notebook on the ship's engineering organization gave some idea of the magnitude of his job. More than 280 men were divided among four divisions: A was in charge of the shops and auxiliaries; B, the four boilers; M, the starboard, center, and port engine rooms; and E, the production and distribution of electric power.[1]

On the night of 29 April 1935, the *New Mexico*, along with other ships of the battle force division, got under way for San Francisco to take part in Fleet Problem XVI, which would extend from the West Coast to Hawaii and beyond. The mood was grimmer than it had been during previous fleet problems. In December 1934 Japan, already embroiled in China, had given the two-year notice required by the Washington and London Treaties limiting naval armaments that it would no longer be bound by them.[2]

Under war conditions the ships advanced—by day, frequently changing formations while planes from the aircraft carriers *Lexington* and *Saratoga* scouted ahead for "enemy" cruisers and submarines; by night, maneuvering in close quarters with darkened ships. Rickover found battleships refueling destroyers a "pretty sight." On 8 May he described it to Ruth:

"We go along at about ten knots, the destroyer comes alongside and keeps with us at this speed. Meanwhile, we run an oil hose over to her. Today we broke all records—supplying oil to the destroyer at the rate of over 70,000 gallons per hour!"

Having so much to learn, Rickover rarely had a free moment. In the mornings he took care of paper work; in the afternoons he roamed about the engineering plant, spending hours climbing through bilges and studying the various steam, oil, salt-water, and air systems. He was also teaching young officers just out of the academy who had been assigned to the Engineering Department. "They are working like the devil trying to learn, and to such an extent that all the rest of the Ensigns on the ship are razzing them for working so much," he wrote. "Nevertheless, all the others are trying to get into the Engineer Department because they realize that instead of treating them like school boys (as they are frequently treated elsewhere on the ship) I give them responsible duties to perform. . . . I get great pleasure out of seeing these youngsters suddenly becoming interested in their work."[3]

About once a month Rickover gave his ensigns assignments dealing with approved engineering practices, casualty procedures, and exercise evaluations. Usually they had to crawl into bilges, boilers, tanks, and double bottoms. Frequently they had to sketch piping systems—as Rickover had done in the La Vallette and at submarine school—and, as he had discovered at New London, most ensigns preferred to copy blueprints. On the New Mexico there was none of that: he kept the plans locked up.

Ensigns not meeting his standards were promptly transferred, but those passing his scrutiny were given jobs with more responsibility. They might find themselves standing key engine-room watches, even when the ship was darkened and maneuvering at night. ("I never told anybody I was doing that," Rickover recalled.) In port they stood "top watch"—they were in charge.

Not all admired Rickover's methods of training, but all agreed he taught the need for knowing a job thoroughly, for ascertaining facts and not hesitating to state them. Occasionally he and some of the ensigns went ashore together: almost always the talk was of engineering. Rickover was to look back with pride upon the ensigns he trained who reached flag rank, among them Edgar H. Batcheller, William A. Brockett, Charles A. Curtze, and Charles E. Loughlin.

Brockett worked for more than twenty-four hours with a group of men to repair an engineering casualty so that the ship could get under way on schedule. At one point he glanced up to find Rickover looking over his shoulder.

"Anything I can do for you?" asked Rickover.

"Yes, sir."

"What?"

"Please get your ass off the floor plates. I'll call you if we need your help."

"Very well."

As that was not the way ensigns addressed senior lieutenants, Brockett expected trouble. Consequently it was with some trepidation that he reported when the job was done. Never saying a word about the lapse in etiquette, Rickover offered congratulations to him and to the men for a job well done.[4]

Rickover also trained his petty officers thoroughly, a task probably made easier because the Great Depression was bringing men of high caliber into the enlisted ranks of the Navy. Rickover arranged to see the list of those about to report to the ship and have those with the best records assigned to him. Whether they were new in the department or veterans of years' standing, Rickover insisted that they know their jobs. He would not, for example, accept any requisition for spare parts unless the need was proven and forms were properly made out. He would make no correction nor permit other officers to do so: the man had to prove his case.

When Rickover reported to the *New Mexico*, she ranked eighth out of fifteen battleships in the annual competition for engineering.[5] The contest was carried out under elaborate rules and formulas developed over decades so that ships built at different times and operating under different schedules had an equal chance to place the coveted red *E* on the stack. To be at the top of the list was a major achievement, comparable to winning the award for accuracy in gunnery.

Because the operation of a ship's machinery and equipment depended upon energy produced from fuel the ship carried, its economical use was the chief yardstick for measuring efficiency. Many practices had grown up to save oil; some were legitimate, some were not. Rickover knew them all.

The steps he took were not unusual: it was the lengths to which he carried them that became legendary. Operation of every part of the main propulsion plant and every piece of auxiliary machinery was analyzed, adjusted, and carefully tuned; all steam lines were inspected and all leaks stopped. He scrutinized records to find places for additional fuel savings.

He took new officers reporting to the department on deck and over to the side and had them look down and see fresh water used by the ship returning to the sea. Vigorously he lectured them on the number of gallons of oil that were burned to make and pump that water.

He carried the drive to save fuel beyond the machinery compartments. He slashed the amenities of living. Rules for showers were promulgated: get in shower, turn on water to wet body, turn off water, then soap, turn on water to rinse, turn off water, dry off. Turning faucets on as far as they would go produced only a thin trickle. He cut back on heating. Stateroom radiators stopped working, and requests for repairs got lost. Once, in protest, officers bundled up in winter coats and swathed in scarves ostentatiously bustled into breakfast. When they claimed they were catching colds, Rickover turned to the medical officer, who found that there were fewer colds on the *New Mexico* than on other battleships. The rank of an offender did not matter. Once Rickover admonished the captain for turning on the heat in his cabin, pointing out he was setting a bad example and risking the chance of gaining credit for commanding a ship that stood first in engineering. The commanding officer accepted the rebuke.

Rickover drastically reduced the use of electricity. He and his men turned off lights, replaced some bulbs with those of lower wattage, or simply removed them entirely. Most ships in port festooned the gangway with a number of lights. Not the *New Mexico*. She had one light at the bottom and one at the top. In Rickover's words—and others echoed them—the ship was "as dark as hell." Looking back on those days from the rank of rear admiral, Charles Loughlin observed that the assistant engineer was liked by his ensigns but not by other officers.[6]

Rickover believed that every ship had lessons to teach—practices to follow and practices to avoid. To learn what these might be, he sent his men visiting other ships. No one came to the *New Mexico* for new ideas, he observed, even though monthly reports showed the ship was compiling an outstanding record. Rickover described the effort to Ruth on 27 July 1935: "I have all the officers in the Engineering Department extremely enthusiastic over the competition and they are working harder than any group of officers I have ever seen. The Captain is due for selection to Admiral next Spring; the Chief Engineer for Commander; and yours truly for Lieutenant Commander, so if we stand near the top it will be a big help all around."

For the first time in his career, his future, as well as those of other senior lieutenants, was in the hands of a selection board, a group of officers temporarily gathered in Washington to choose those to be promoted to the next rank. Selection boards had been operating since 1916, but at that time their use was limited to promotions from captain to rear admiral and from commander to captain. In 1931 the boards' scope was broadened to include promotions from lieutenant commander to commander, and in 1934 from lieutenant to lieutenant commander. The last change affected Rickover, a lieutenant since 3 June 1928.

If not selected for advancement within a time "zone" of a few years, officers could serve a little longer but then had to retire. Men who had given years to the Navy might find themselves in early middle age trying to build a new career in civilian life. A number of officers, some of very high rank, sent articles criticizing the system to the Naval Institute, which published them in its *Proceedings*. "Only a handful of us in each [naval academy] class can complete our careers, the cards are inevitably stacked against us, most of us inevitably face a forced retirement of some sort," wrote one officer. Another officer had heard that some boards proceeded alphabetically and disbanded when the number of vacancies was filled. If this was so, those whose names came toward the end of the alphabet were never even considered.[7]

Rickover pretended to Ruth an optimism he did not feel, claiming that in any case he was too busy to dwell on the matter. Retirement wouldn't be so bad, he assured her, since the law provided an adequate pension for those who had served in the Navy for twenty-one years. "All of my friends say I have nothing to worry about—but you know how it is," he wrote. "At any rate, I am working hard and I will not feel bad if I know that I am not selected—despite that I have done the best I know how."[8]

By the summer of 1935 Ruth was back in Europe. By letters and newspaper clippings he did his best to keep her informed of national happenings. He was enthusiastic over New Deal legislation that aimed at protecting unions, regulating banking, and levying high taxes on the wealthy. "I hope the Depression keeps up a little longer. We shall have a fine country, if it does," he declared. One opinion he had maintained for years and was to continue to hold: "I believe that business men are, as a rule, the most stupid group, from a large viewpoint. Money apparently warps people's judgment and causes them to have an unreal attitude."[9]

In October 1935 Ruth joined him in Bremerton, Washington, while the *New Mexico* was in the Puget Sound Navy Yard. Valuing their privacy, the Rickovers kept to themselves. By working on board ship he avoided some of the social claims on his time, but as a Navy wife she could not always do so. Ruth was pressured to become involved in an organization of officers' wives that tried to help the lot of enlisted personnel and raise their morale. The group's meetings opened with the ship's song, the words of which were sung to the tune of "Pony Boy, Pony Boy." Not every undertaking of the group was successful: presenting maternity clothing to the pregnant wife of an enlisted man only to find she was not pregnant was one such instance. Reacting against the attempts to involve Ruth, Rickover ridiculed the group's efforts.

In his view, wives disrupted the ship's work. They wanted to be with their husbands as much as possible. To get time off, married officers prevailed upon bachelor officers to trade watches. To check abuses in the practice, Rickover allowed an officer to take the watch of another but did not permit them to trade watches. Not only did that cut down on the practice, but he discovered some married officers welcomed the opportunity to stay on board to get their work done. That technique of controlling watch swapping Rickover was to carry over into the nuclear propulsion program.

In November Ruth left for New York and the *New Mexico* departed for San Pedro. Again separation was hard to bear. He wrote to her of whatever crossed his mind. A chance remark by a newspaperman led Rickover to consider what it meant to be a Jew. The writer had observed that Jews were Jewish by race and therefore unlike other minorities. In one of Rickover's rare references to the subject, he wrote,

> Among other things he said that the Jews, as opposed to other minorities, such as the Irish, were international from a *racial* standpoint. I thought this over a great deal later on, because on the face of it this appears to be true, and under present conditions is a just criticism. But—I do believe [here Rickover was probably referring to the persecution of Jews in Europe] that if the Irish were placed in the same position as the Jews, or if any other people were—they would become equally international racially. There is very little to distinguish the Irishman from other people where he generally settles—whereas the average Jew does appear different. The American or English Jew feels a great responsibility towards the German or Polish Jew because he knows that debilities imposed on the German or Polish Jew can easily be emulated in other countries. Thus he helps the unfortunate for (largely) a selfish reason. For example, I am exasperated that the Orthodox Jews of Poland make a tremendous issue of the manner of slaughtering cattle, and thereby create anti-semitic feeling in Poland. And I think that many of them are a rather poor type and that much of the sentiment expend[ed] on their "beautiful" home life is nonsense.

Of course, if people could see clearly, as I do, that a great deal of the difficulty is being brought about by the impact of 20th century progress upon an alien medieval people—the problem could be understood better.[10]

On 12 March 1936, a friend on watch in the radio room brought him good news: he had been selected for promotion to lieutenant commander. Now, he thought, maybe he and Ruth did not have to worry so much about finances.[11] He felt no elation. Too many people he knew had failed to be selected and would have to leave the Navy. "That took all the joy away," he stated. "It is all a horrible mess and I think the Navy is making a big mistake. . . . I am afraid the people at the top are not aware of the human suffering they are causing. As a rather interesting point, I noted that the three Jews in my class who were among those considered—were all selected. This is encouraging in that it showed that only merit counted."[12]

At the end of 1935, after six months of competition, the *New Mexico* was standing first in engineering, but the effort was taking a lot out of her assistant engineer: "It has been quite a strain—carefully watching all sorts of little things for every hour of the day and night, day in and day out—but I wouldn't feel right unless I was doing my work to the best of my ability. I tend to become impatient with officers who do not take their duties seriously and who do not use all their efforts to keep their machinery in the best possible condition. . . . In all our inspection reports, the Engineering Department has been rated as 'outstanding.'"[13]

But the competition was not over and some unforeseen event could yet cost the ship her prize. On 17 May 1936, it looked as if the blow had come. While on maneuvers off the west coast of Central America, one of the main turbines began vibrating violently. Rickover immediately shut it down. Investigation showed that a few blade segments had broken loose and damaged the turbine. The ship could operate only on three of her four propellers. For the *New Mexico* the maneuvers were over.

It seemed as if the chances of winning the competition were over as well. If the damage was caused by human error, the ship would be penalized heavily. The next day, however, the battleship *Mississippi* suffered the same casualty, which seemed to reduce the likelihood that personnel were at fault.

At slow speed the two battleships, accompanied by a few smaller vessels, limped toward the Puget Sound yard. By shrewd and careful engineering, Rickover rigged the propulsion plant so that the useless propeller was allowed to rotate freely as the ship moved through the water. For technical reasons it would have been easier and perhaps more prudent to have locked the shaft so the propeller could not turn, but dragging the immobile propeller would have increased the resistance that had to be overcome. Thus, it would have taken more fuel to reach the shipyard.

He also wanted an unchanging demand on the propulsion plant; in that way he could fine tune its operation to be as economical as possible. He obtained an agreement from Captain Soule: unless there was an emergency, there would be no orders from the bridge to the engine room. In addition, Soule agreed to use the rudder as little as possible.

The entire blackgang, not just those on watch, saw the New Mexico slowly build up speed and the idled propeller shaft begin to rotate. To the relief of everyone, the temporary measures were working. As soon as the ship reached the speed agreed upon by Soule, Rickover set the turbine throttles and did not touch them, except on 22 May, when the ship backed down to avoid colliding with a steamer.[14]

From San Pedro on 2 June Rickover wrote to Ruth, "On the way up from Panama there were two battleships in column, the New Mexico and the Mississippi. We consistently burned about 20 percent less fuel than they did—every day. Over a period of two weeks, this amounted to a difference of about 50,000 gallons of oil."

Investigation ultimately disclosed that the turbine casualty had been caused by a material failure. Consequently, the ship's standing in the competition was not affected. At the end of June the results were in—the New Mexico was first.[15] After turbine repairs at Puget Sound, the ship rejoined the battle force.

One family problem arose to disturb him. In November 1936 he learned from one of his sisters that the bank holding the mortgage on his parents' home had been closed in 1933 and that its affairs were being liquidated. Although the details are not clear, money was needed to save the home. His father and sisters were doing what they could but needed his help.

The request came at a bad time. Some years earlier he and Ruth had purchased a farm near Sherman, Connecticut, partly as an investment and partly to take up farming if, because of the Depression, Rickover should have to leave the Navy. He and Ruth also thought that her mother, finding life in Nazi Germany increasingly uncomfortable, could live at the farm for a while. Unfortunately, it needed a lot of work, which had reduced his available funds.

To meet the family emergency Rickover borrowed from his bank and cashed in some government bonds. He hated to go into debt, but he saw no alternative. He seems to have paid off his loan by the first quarter of 1937.[16] His parents' home was saved, and Rickover kept the farm for a few years.

In January 1937 the *New Mexico* steamed to Bremerton and the Puget Sound Navy Yard through some of the roughest weather Rickover had seen. Ruth came out from New York to join him, and they worked together on some writing. On 21 April 1937, as a part of Fleet Problem XVIII, the *New Mexico* sailed with a few destroyers and the cruisers *Cincinnati* and *Concord* for Dutch Harbor, Alaska, to reconnoiter and establish a seaplane base.[17]

After a rough passage of six days, the *New Mexico* anchored and the *Concord* came alongside for fuel. Assured by the fueling officer that the hose was properly rigged and ready, Rickover gave the order to start pumping. A plug in the hose gave way, spewing a huge geyser of oil that filled lifeboats, barges, and gigs to the brim, streamed over the once immaculate teak deck, and showered a furious executive officer. The engineer of the *Concord* rushed his men onto the *New Mexico* with buckets, mops, and squeegees. Oil recovered had flowed through the *New Mexico*'s meter but not that of the *Concord*. In the engineering competition the unmetered oil was a windfall to the cruiser, but, having passed through the meter of the battleship, would be charged against her. A now-angry Rickover ordered the cruiser's men off the battleship and got his own men to saving the oil. As for the fueling officer, he apparently had worked hard and had established a good record, because Rickover never mentioned the incident again (except years later when the two were reminiscing) and gave him a good fitness report. Still, despite holy-stoning and scouring, the teak deck of the *New Mexico* never looked the same.[18]

It was a relief to leave the foul weather of Dutch Harbor for the tropic calm of Pearl Harbor as a continuation of the fleet problem. However, by the time the *New Mexico* reached Hawaiian waters, the forces to which she belonged had been defeated. In San Francisco he rejoined Ruth, and on 2 June 1937 he was detached from the ship.

Rickover's record was outstanding. Capt. Frank Jack Fletcher (who had succeeded Soule and as rear admiral was to play important parts in the battles of the Coral Sea and Midway in World War II) thought very highly of him. When the lieutenant commander who was the engineer officer was transferred, Fletcher was willing to move Rickover (still a lieutenant because all the procedures for promotion had not yet been completed) into the position. That, however, Washington would not accept. Fletcher in his last fitness report on Rickover wrote,[19] "This officer is more than any one man responsible for the *New Mexico* winning the engineering competition two years in succession. Has untiring energy, unusually keen intelligence and is devoted to his profession. I consider he is exceptionally well qualified for engineering duty only."

The words "engineering duty only" referred to a special group of officers, usually known as EDOs. They provided the Navy with the indispensable engineering knowledge and skills it needed. Because of their specialization, such officers were barred from commanding ships or fleets and would spend most of their time ashore.

Rickover had requested engineering duty on 14 September 1936, but it would be some time before he would know if he had been accepted. It would be a major change in his career, one he was reluctant to make because he preferred to command a destroyer, but he saw little chance of that.[20] On the other hand, he liked the discipline of engineering and his superb record on the *New Mexico* had won him strong support among the EDOs.

Rickover remembered no celebration when the red *E* was painted on the stack, for periodic reports showed the ship was going to win. One of his ensigns, probably Brockett (years later he was chief of the Bureau of Ships and Rickover's superior), believed the event deserved commemoration. In an "Ode to a Senior Assistant Engineer," he wrote,

> The fire main pressure's down to naught
>   In the scuppers we must pee
> These Arctic nights
>   Sans heat and lights
> Will help us win the "E"
>
> At last we've won the pennant
>   And Rick is filled with glee
> With a forlorn screech
>   And a bath on the beach
> We're off for the next year's "E"[21]

On a March evening in 1937, while the *New Mexico* was at Puget Sound, the Rickovers were entertaining a small group of guests. During a pause in the conversation, he announced, "By the way, darling, we are going to China in June." It was, Ruth thought, one of the nicest surprises she had ever received. She even had a kind word for the Navy. "Where else," she wrote a friend, "could you stay on one job for one, two, three years and just when you were beginning to get tired of it find another waiting for you somewhere else?"[22]

Rickover was eager to leave the New Mexico and the constant strain of competing to win the red E. In the Far East he would be facing the challenge of his first command. He would not know which ship it would be until he reported to Adm. Harry E. Yarnell, commander in chief, United States Asiatic Fleet, who was flying his flag from the cruiser Augusta. On 5 June 1937, Rickover, Ruth, and Ruth's mother sailed from San Francisco on the passenger liner President Monroe for Shanghai. Her mother, with whom Rickover and Ruth got along well, would stay with them and eventually go on to Germany.

They stopped in Japan on their way to China. In the cities they encountered heavy-handed surveillance, clumsy spying, and frustrating bureaucracy; in the country they met courtesy, curiosity, and neatness. Even away from the cities, however, they could see the impact of the fighting in China. Following simple ceremonies, young men were leaving their villages for service in the army.

The Augusta was at Tsingtao, about two hundred miles north of Shanghai. For years the Asiatic Fleet had sought relief from the sweltering heat of Shanghai and Manila by spending the worst part of the summers in the delightful climate of Tsingtao. Rickover learned he was to command the minesweeper Finch. "George . . . swore terribly," Ruth recorded. With his record and rank—he was to be promoted to lieutenant commander on 1 July 1937—he thought he deserved better. He was only slightly mollified by the explanation that, for reasons of prestige, the Navy assigned officers to its ships who outranked their foreign counterparts in similar assignments. On the other hand, he found it good to make contact with his classmate Henri Smith-Hutton, serving on Yarnell's staff as fleet intelligence officer.[23]

Early in the morning of 17 July 1937, Rickover stepped into the Finch's boat, which was to take him out to the ship. A swift glance about the boat was an eye-opener. Dirt and banana and orange peels washed about in the bilge, and the crew was out of uniform. The minesweeper itself made no better impression; everywhere he could see the ravages of years of neglect. Inspection revealed serious corrosion—rust on the decks, in the compartments, and along the side of the ship. Disheartened but determined to improve his first command, he relieved Lt. Joseph P. Rockwell at 1:30 in the afternoon.[24]

The length of the *Finch* was only a little over 187 feet, her beam slightly more than 35 feet, her draft about 10 feet, her top speed fourteen knots. Built by the Standard Shipbuilding Company of New York, she was commissioned in 1918, a few weeks before the end of the First World War. Since 1921 she had served in the Asiatic Fleet, mainly towing targets and undertaking minor salvage jobs. Two inspections before Rickover took command pointed out her poor state.[25] Further confirmation, if he needed such, came when he got the *Finch* under way for the first time and her engines broke down as she was leaving the harbor.

Immediately Rickover took drastic steps to raise the ship to the standards he had known in the Pacific Fleet. His executive officer, Lt. (jg) Frederic S. Steinke, the only other commissioned officer on board, acknowledged the bad condition and the need for improvement but thought the new captain was moving too fast. So did Paul E. Dignan, chief machinist's mate, whom Rickover quickly recognized as very able and efficient, and whom he was to call upon more than once in future years. To Steinke and Dignan, the *Finch* wasn't so bad for the Asiatic Fleet, but bringing her up to the level Rickover wanted was an enormous, almost quixotic, task.

The crew quickly resented the new strong hand. They especially hated working on deck in the hot sun, chipping away the rust with a hammer and scraper; it was sweaty, dirty, and monotonous drudgery in which the noisy rhythm of the pounding reverberated throughout the ship. Over the exposed metal the crew spread a coat of protective red lead paint. Until it dried and navy gray could be applied, the *Finch* looked terrible, with splotches of red standing in gaudy contrast against the gray. To make matters worse, the duty was dull, consisting mainly of towing targets for other ships. For this purpose she left port early in the morning to get on station and returned when the other ships were already back.

Events in Shanghai shattered the monotony. Fighting in the city had flared to new heights after two Japanese marines were killed at a nearby airfield on 8 August. Three days later, against fierce resistance, the Japanese landed a naval force. To protect the interests of their governments, warships from the French, British, American, and Italian navies anchored in the Whangpoo River, which flowed by the city. Yarnell ordered the *Finch* to join his force at Shanghai to perform the myriad of odd tasks that only a small ship could do.

Eager to see action, Rickover welcomed his orders. In looking over dispatches from Shanghai, he read that gasoline was in short supply. Seizing the chance to show initiative, he took on board fifteen hundred gallons in five-gallon cans. He had no place to store them except on the open deck. On Thursday night, 19 August, the *Finch* got under way.

He exercised his men at the two 3-inch guns and machine guns. He also kept the crew busy chipping paint. At midnight Friday, he picked up the lights for the Yangtze channel. In the brightness of the full moon he sighted two Japanese aircraft carriers, a squadron of destroyers, and a large supply vessel. None had their navigation lights on and all apparently were at anchor. He could even see eight planes on one carrier being prepared for takeoff. Knowing the intelligence would be welcome in the *Augusta*, Rickover made every effort to locate and identify all the ships he saw.[26]

At five in the morning he picked up a pilot and steamed up the Whangpoo. The outskirts of the city were heavily damaged, but the nearer the *Finch* approached the European section of the city, with its banks, business houses, and hotels, the fewer the signs of conflict. Many buildings were flying huge British, French, and American flags, creating a holiday air that the deserted streets denied by their silence.

At 11:30 A.M. the *Finch* was ready to go alongside the *Augusta*. The *Augusta*, however, was not ready for the *Finch*. While waiting in the crowded river, Rickover narrowly avoided colliding with another ship. Finally, he was able to go alongside the cruiser. He thought to receive praise; instead, he caught hell. He explained the situation to Ruth: "The presence of this gasoline (which is really liquid dynamite) on deck was disconcerting . . . and a stray bullet might explode it, with disastrous results."[27] The danger was real. Only the day before, an antiaircraft shell had landed amidships on the *Augusta*, killing one man and wounding eighteen. Even as unloading the *Finch* began at 1:00 P.M., eight Japanese planes were bombing the Chinese section of Shanghai. As the Chinese opened fire with their few antiaircraft guns, the *Augusta* blew her whistle—the signal to take cover. When the unloading was completed at 4:30 P.M., the *Finch* moved upstream and moored alongside the *Isabel*, a converted yacht that was serving as the flagship of the famous Yangtze patrol, and the gunboat *Sacramento*.

During the day the *Finch* performed various tasks, among them carrying dignitaries and newspapermen along the waterfront for a good view of the fighting, taking marines from the transport *Gold Star* to Shanghai, and bringing a deckload of American civilians out of a danger zone—an exploit that won Rickover a few paragraphs in the *Chicago Tribune*.[28] Nights the *Finch* usually spent moored alongside another Navy ship that showed movies. As officers and crew watched the stars of Hollywood, big green balls of fire—tracer shells fired from Japanese ships shelling the city—arched across the sky. Because of the heat and humidity, sleeping on deck was better than sleeping below. There were risks, however: erratic fire from the Japanese and Chinese often forced the men on deck to take cover. Once a fragment of a shell came close to Rickover. He kept it as a memento.

Although his duty was interesting, even if it took place against scenes of appalling misery, Rickover was in trouble professionally. A signal from the *Augusta* criticized the appearance of the *Finch*. In the presence of ships from many nations, appearances were important. In that respect his ship, with its blotches of red lead paint, did not measure up. He resented the stricture and felt humiliated. On 4 September 1937, he renewed his request for engineering duty. Finally, on 2 October he learned his application had been accepted. His designation would become effective on 5 October 1937.[29]

On that date Lt. Donald S. Evans, an academy classmate, took over the ship, but Rickover remained on board for a few weeks. It was not an easy situation for either man. In Rickover's presence and before men he once commanded, coats of navy gray were slapped over the red lead paint—and the rust. ("You can imagine how I felt about that," he recalled.) Believing he had improved the *Finch* in the two months of his command, he would have liked to have stayed another five months to see the results of his efforts. He had taught the ship's company how to analyze their duties, organize their work, inspect properly, and anticipate the ship's requirements. "In a few months the Finch, from being the ship in worst material condition in the Asiatic Fleet, will be much further up," he wrote Ruth.

When he took command of the *Finch*, he was told that the Navy assigned officers higher in rank than those officers in foreign navies with similar assignments. Yet he relieved a lieutenant and was relieved by a lieutenant. It is difficult to interpret the two events as anything but evidence that Rickover's career as an unrestricted line officer was, for some reason, in trouble.

His fitness report for the period ending 5 October 1937 was not as good as those earlier in his career and was markedly different from those he received while in the *New Mexico*. His highest marks were in loyalty and perseverance, but they were not the highest that could be awarded in these categories. In other areas he did less well. His "judgment" was fair in "normal and routine things"; his ability to achieve results was effective "under normal and routine circumstances," and he led "fairly well." The report could be summarized by a statement that he "performed his duties satisfactorily."[30]

He was to be assigned to the Cavite Navy Yard, near Manila in the Philippines, with the understanding that in a few months he would be sent to the Bureau of Engineering in Washington. Still, he was learning not to expect too much. "All we can do is hope," he philosophically wrote to Ruth. "Otherwise we will have to make the best of Manila." In a sentence that revealed his disappointment with the Asiatic Fleet, he continued, "It will not be so bad, after all, no matter how things turn out."

On 24 October the submarine tender *Canopus*, carrying American dependents leaving the war zone, anchored in the Whangpoo. Soon the *Finch* came alongside. Ruth observed, "George looks very well and is full of exciting and amusing stories of his experiences in and around Shanghai. He seems to have got to know everybody worth knowing."[31]

In his recollections, Rickover had little good to say about the *Finch* or the Asiatic Fleet. In his view the job of the captain of a Navy ship was to prepare and keep that ship ready for combat. He did not think he had been wrong in striving to do so, but the Asiatic Fleet was mainly interested in appearances. He thought if he had been able to see Yarnell he might have gotten things straightened out. Seeing no future as a line officer, he thought he had been fortunate to be accepted for engineering duty only.

He and Ruth arrived at Cavite on 30 October 1937. The yard did not have a good reputation and was best known as a final place of duty for officers about to retire after lackluster careers. As a married officer and a lieutenant commander since 1 July 1937, he rated a large house on the base and two servants. He and Ruth settled in; he to work, and she to observe life around her. Expecting to leave for Washington in February 1938, they intended to travel at every opportunity.[32]

Rickover was assigned the job of assistant to the production officer for engineering, charged with carrying out repairs and maintenance. At first he had little to do. Ruth observed in a letter to a friend that in a few months some personnel shifts might change things, but "it's a long time waiting until then, if one is George." He found it hard to get things done. In early December, Ruth recorded, "George blew up" because he had trouble getting funds for testing the engines of the destroyer tender *Blackhawk*, which was undergoing an overhaul.[33]

He was gaining a reputation. Before a ship arrived for scheduled yard work he scrutinized previous records. To his surprise he found the requests submitted by the ship were much the same year after year. His curiosity aroused, he boarded the ship as soon as it arrived and required the ship to get under way and the officers to operate the equipment that was to be repaired. He suspected the officers were padding the list of work so they could spend more time ashore in nearby Manila, the capital of the Philippines. He was right. By canceling several requests, he saved money, time, labor, and material.[34]

Decades later, when Vice Adm. William P. Mack, at the end of a distinguished career, was interviewed for his reminiscences, he recalled that, when a very young officer, he was in a destroyer that entered Cavite for some work:

> The last overhaul done on the *John D. Ford* was done under the supervision of the ship inspector, one Lieutenant [*sic*] Rickover—that was a very good overhaul. We couldn't figure out why he was giving us so much trouble when we had our overhaul but as the years progressed after that overhaul, we soon found out that whatever he did he did well and the ship functioned as she was supposed to. . . .
>
> It had been two years out of overhaul when the war began and it never once broke down. It made every commitment.[35]

At times, because of petty intrigues and jealousies, life at Cavite seemed like a comic opera, but outside the theater the skies were lowering. Turmoil in China was often changing ships' schedules while dependents arriving from Tsingtao and elsewhere brought lurid accounts of the fighting. Although American sympathies were with the Chinese, there was little sentiment for military involvement, and it seemed most unlikely that the Japanese, deeply entangled in China, wanted a war with the Americans. The Japanese shattered that comfortable assumption on 12 December 1937, when they bombed and sank the American gunboat *Panay* in broad daylight as she was anchored in the Yangtze River. No one could tell whether the event was an isolated incident or the beginning of serious trouble.

Determined to see as much of the Far East as they could, the Rickovers traveled through the Dutch East Indies and Malaysia, avoiding as much as possible colonial officials, businessmen, and planters.[36] Only delay in getting orders for Washington made the extent of their trips possible.

Once his orders were canceled because eighteen ships of the Asiatic

Fleet were to be inspected by a board of which he was a member. Another effort to get orders failed, with wording that implied he should serve a normal tour of duty at Cavite. He went outside channels by writing an airmail letter to an engineering duty officer in Washington asking for help. Sometime, probably in February 1939, he learned they would leave Cavite the following May.[37]

At once they began to plan their return to the United States. Recrossing the Pacific held no interest, but going back by way of Russia and the trans-Siberian railroad, Europe, and the Atlantic was attractive. Washington had no objection, but the Russians were a problem. Application for a visa might take six weeks or even three months, and even then it might be rejected. Because he had to report in Washington on 15 August, Rickover could not risk a delay.

They drew up other plans. Ruth would leave Cavite while he remained until 26 May. She would visit Japan, Korea, and North China. When he got free of Cavite, he would travel over much the same route and go down the coast of China until he reached Haiphong in French Indochina; there he would turn inland to reach the China end of the Burma Road. After going down the road they would meet and complete the journey to the United States together.[38]

Their paths crossed in Shanghai. Although ill and tired, she persuaded him to continue his trip: they would meet in Calcutta. He went on but, because her illness grew worse, she returned to the Philippines for a convalescence that lasted a few weeks.

The trip down the Burma Road was the high point of his journey. Blocked by Japanese control of the sea coasts, the Chinese had begun building the road in 1937 between Kunming and Lashio in Burma to gain access to western nations and military supplies. By straight line about 230 miles separated the two cities; by the road the distance was 717 miles. The climate was hot and humid and the country was mountainous.

Having a semiofficial status and a demanding attitude, Rickover managed to get a government truck assigned to him. At every step he ran into inertia and delay. Travel was rough. More than once the front springs broke and had to be repaired, landslides had to be cleared before he could go on, and at times the road was blocked by trucks caught in deep and soggy ruts. Often he was on the road for ten or twelve hours at a time, and usually he got only five or six hours of sleep, but the scenery was magnificent. Never, however, had he encountered such bureaucracy, never had he seen humans so dirty, so ragged, and so diseased. Some, he heard, had never seen a white man. On 2 July, tired and exhausted, he finally reached Lashio. "Believe me," he wrote, "to carry out a schedule in China—as I have insisted this past week—is a major job and required overcoming endless difficulties."

He promptly began turning his penciled notes into a report to the director of Naval Intelligence. Its sixteen single-spaced, typewritten pages detailed weaknesses in the control and maintenance of transportation, listing the stations that had gasoline and oil and asterisking those having repair facilities. He enumerated the trucks, noted their manufacturers, and pointed out those that performed best. About 75 percent of the ammunition entering China, he was told, came over the road. He sent the report to Naval Intelligence on 28 August 1939, shortly after returning to the United States. On 9 October the office replied that his report was of marked value to the office.[39]

He and Ruth did not meet again until they reached the United States. Crossing India by rail, he flew across the Mideast and, after making some stops along the way, finally landed in Athens. His trip across Europe to London by air was uneventful, except over Germany, where authorities forced the plane to fly low because of German air force and army maneuvers. At London he took the opportunity to see the Tower of London and the British Museum, which, he commented, was "a remarkable place." On 4 August he sailed for the United States.[40] On her way home, Ruth entered Germany and saw her mother. Alarmed by the swift approach of war, they went to Basle, Switzerland, where they were when the Germans invaded Poland on 1 September 1939. Ruth's mother returned to Germany, where she lived throughout the war and until her death sometime in the 1950s. Fortunately, Ruth had already made reservations for her passage to New York on the American liner *Excaliber*, which left from Marseilles. She probably arrived at the end of September.

Rickover was glad to be in Washington, but he worried about the future. In the Bureau of Engineering he would be part of a highly skilled group of officers. He did not know, he said, how he would "make out."

The Electrical Section and the War

RICKOVER WAS nervous when he reported to the Bureau of Engineering on 15 August 1939. He would be working with officers and civilian engineers far more experienced than he in naval engineering and naval bureaucracy. He decided to begin by working hard, learning, and observing. It was the same strategy he had followed in his plebe year at Annapolis, another time when the course of his life changed drastically.

He and Ruth found a one-bedroom apartment at 4801 Connecticut Avenue in Washington. Although small, it had wonderful compensations, including air conditioning and a magnificent view over Rock Creek Park, an extensive stretch of woodland running through the northwest part of the city. For more than thirty years he and Ruth were to live there quietly, avoiding social life except for an occasional dinner party to which they invited only small numbers of guests, all chosen for their ability to talk well.

Rickover's office was in Main Navy, a sprawling three-story building located on Constitution Avenue between Seventeenth and Nineteenth Streets. Main Navy also held the offices of the secretary of the Navy and the chief of naval operations as well as those of several bureau chiefs. At its front were huge and gracious elm trees, which shaded Constitution Avenue, while at its back was the Mall with its reflecting basin. The Washington Monument and Lincoln Memorial were nearby. Built during World War I as temporary quarters for a growing Navy establishment, Main Navy had somehow escaped demolition and had become a Washington landmark. If its temporary construction made it difficult to maintain, it also fostered flexibility and informality, valuable qualities that might have been lost in more dignified surroundings.

Rickover arranged to get morning rides to his office by asking John C. Niedermair, a well-known civilian naval architect who drove down

Connecticut Avenue to Main Navy, to pick him up. Niedermair was willing and was intrigued by one stipulation upon which Rickover insisted: if Rickover was not on the appointed street corner at the appointed time, Niedermair was to drive on, even if Rickover was running across the street.[1]

The Navy was undergoing a major reorganization. Because the Bureau of Engineering and the Bureau of Construction and Repair, both having responsibilities in building and maintaining ships, had not worked well together, they were being merged to form the Bureau of Ships. The new entity would come into existence officially in June 1940 and, with a roster of 117 officers and about 1,000 civilians, would become by far the largest of the Navy's bureaus. Some of the finest warships the world would ever see would be built under its supervision.

Assigned to the Electrical Section as assistant chief, Rickover had been brought in to succeed Lt. Cdr. Louis Dreller. The section was responsible for the generation, distribution, control, and use of electric power needed to operate shipboard equipment. More specifically, the section handled the development, design, and procurement of electrical systems, lighting, electric cable, electric motors and generators, motor controllers and circuit breakers, switchboards and panels, as well as miscellaneous equipment.[2] The work was vital: no warship could operate, fight, or long survive without electric power.

The section was an excellent place in which to learn how to deal with major electrical suppliers as well as both Navy and private shipyards. The section had only two or three officers and about eighteen civilian engineers, making it easy to know what was going on.

Rickover could count on being busy. Because Europe was on the verge of war and the Far East was already the scene of fighting, the Navy was expanding rapidly. Between 1934 and 1938 Congress had passed legislation providing for ten battleships and three aircraft carriers (none of which had been commissioned when Rickover arrived) as well as several cruisers, destroyers, and submarines.[3] Without doubt more ships would be built.

Rickover first attracted notice in the bureau by undertaking, on his own initiative, the development of a system to explode magnetic mines. He did not devise the technique: the British did that in 1939 and 1940, after suffering heavy shipping losses in coastal waters from magnetic mines laid by German aircraft. The British had worked out a system in which a small ship towed two floating cables, through which pulses of high-energy current produced a field similar to that of a passing ship. Details, however, the British would not provide. Through the American naval attaché in London, Rickover obtained a piece of the cable to analyze.[4]

He worked closely with Schuyler N. Pyne, an officer in the Minesweeping Section of the bureau, on the design and specifications of diesel-electric generators to power the magnetic field. They went to General Motors and General Electric in the summer of 1940 to get a prototype manufactured. The companies were reluctant, possibly because of patent and licensing problems, possibly because they were not sure how much authority the two officers had. Pyne recalled, "Rickover just stood up and said, 'Listen, you boys are going to do this. You're going to develop these generators and if you hurry we have got a big order here for you. If you don't get to work on it we will have to find ways to force you to do it.'"[5]

Rickover committed the bureau to a $12 million contract with General Electric for a special high-current generator. Having ignored the elaborate procurement procedures established in a time of peace and tight budgets, he wondered if he would "survive" (a word he also used to describe his uncertainty when entering Annapolis). Suddenly recognizing the magnitude of the minesweeping problem, senior officers in the bureau praised his initiative. Rear Adm. Samuel M. Robinson, chief of the Bureau of Ships, gave him fine fitness reports and, for one covering the six months ending on 30 September 1940, recommended his promotion. "This officer not only possesses exceptional technical ability but has the resourcefulness to accomplish unusual tasks," he observed. In December 1940, no longer having the slightest doubt of his own abilities, Rickover became head of the section.

To discover the effects of combat on electrical equipment and components, he inspected every damaged warship he could. Most belonged to the British and had been sent to the United States for repair because their own yards were receiving a pounding from the Germans. He learned that shock from combat operations resulted in far more damage than anyone had expected. Most ships he boarded were designed to withstand the type of shock experienced in World War I, which came from either a ship's own gunfire or direct hits. Equipment nearby might be heavily damaged, but that which was only a short distance away might escape unharmed. The effects he was seeing now were far different. Explosions from mines and depth charges, and near-misses from projectiles and bombs, transmitted shock through the water with terrific force against a hull. Often the entire ship would "whip" violently, displacing some part of the hull as much as a foot, jarring machinery off its footings, breaking and shattering equipment, and disrupting electrical systems. The ship might remain afloat, her hull even watertight, but without power she was dead in the water. Lessons from the British were soon confirmed by the experiences of the Americans.

The attack on Pearl Harbor on 7 December 1941 startled Rickover as it did most Americans. The Japanese had badly damaged eight battleships. The *Arizona* and the *Oklahoma* would never fight again, and although the other six ships could be repaired, the magnitude of the task required the aid of yards and facilities on the distant mainland. With Herculean effort, Pearl Harbor got the *Pennsylvania, Maryland,* and *Tennessee* in shape to steam to the West Coast. Accompanied by four destroyers, they departed on 20 December. That left the *Nevada, California,* and *West Virginia* at Pearl Harbor.

The *California* and *West Virginia* were equipped with electric-drive propulsion plants (steam from their boilers went to the turbine generators, which drove huge electric motors). The *West Virginia* had settled on hard bottom, and the *California,* after lingering afloat for several days, sank into the soft muddy bottom, her quarterdeck about seventeen feet beneath the surface. The motors of both ships were covered with filthy harbor water.

Immediately after the attack, Rickover hurried to the General Electric works at Schenectady, New York, to see what the possibilities were for repairing the electric drive propulsion plants. He was excited to learn from Charles E. Wilson, a company engineer, that some essential equipment used in fabricating the motors still existed—therefore, it might be possible to rebuild them. That, however, could be done only at a major yard, probably Puget Sound.

Work on the *Nevada* suddenly raised a new possibility. Unlike the other two battleships, she had geared turbines and therefore did not require the same extensive reconditioning of her propulsion plant. Many of her compartments were flooded with seawater and oil. Electric motors and other electrical equipment taken off the ship were rushed to the yard facilities for "washing out and drying out" (shorthand for a much more complicated procedure). Most of the reconditioned electrical equipment operated successfully on test.

Capt. Homer N. Wallin, in charge of the salvage operations at Pearl Harbor, reported on 5 February 1942, "Based on the results experienced at the Yard in salvaging and reconditioning electric motors and generators there is a feeling of optimism that the electric drive machinery of the *California* may possibly be reconditioned and put in operation. Such reconditioning would be done in place by suitable arrangements for washing out the electrical machinery and drying out by some means within the machinery spaces themselves."

Rickover scrutinized the message with astonishment. He was certain washing and drying out would never provide reliable operation. Dirty saltwater had covered the electric propulsion plants for over two months. He was sure the insulation was ruined and the pressure from several feet of water had forced contaminants into it and other parts of the motors. He saw a different way to get the ships to the West Coast under their own power: he proposed to rewind the motors at Pearl Harbor and restore them to the degree necessary for the voyage to Puget Sound.

Major electrical installations had been reconstructed before, but never under these circumstances. In other instances the machinery had been in utility plants, had not been submerged for weeks, had not been in crowded spaces in which every surface was covered with oil and slime, and had not been far from industrial support. Because Pearl Harbor did not have the required facilities, the mainland would have to furnish special equipment, tools, and highly skilled personnel, and many organizations thousands of miles away would have to receive small but essential components for reconditioning and return them on a tight schedule. Every step would require careful coordination.

In the section and in the bureau, officers and civilians argued over the scheme. From the vividness of Rickover's recollections, technical differences swelled into bitter personal disputes. In his mind, the issue had become one involving his own prestige—even his own career.

From Pearl Harbor to the bureau on 19 March: "We expect to begin unwatering the main machinery of the USS California befor [*sic*] the 25th of March. Yard will proceed wash and dry out electrical units and instruments preliminary to efforts towards reconditioning. Arrangement should be made by you for arrival G.E. representatives as near to March 25th as is possible."[6] On 24 March the *California* rose off the bottom, almost on an even keel. On the morning of 9 April, with the assistance of four tugs, she was carefully moved across the harbor to Dry Dock Number 2 and at 12:20 was resting on the blocks on the dry dock floor.[7]

Rickover had been mobilizing his resources. At Schenectady on 16 March he met with General Electric engineers who would take a major part in the effort. He arranged for the company to coordinate with the

Puget Sound Navy Yard to send special tools to Pearl Harbor, and he worked with contractors, especially those on the West Coast, on the part they would play.[8]

He flew into Pearl Harbor on 10 April, the day after the *California* entered dry dock. The war news was grim. The Japanese had taken Singapore, won the battle of the Java Sea, and had nearly completed the conquest of Java. In the Philippines, American forces on the Bataan Peninsula could not resist much longer. Corregidor was still holding out, but its fall was only a matter of time. He saw the heartbreaking devastation of 7 December, but also the signs of a determined recovery. The *West Virginia* was showing signs of life as men struggled to get her afloat; a few weeks would see the *Nevada* depart for Puget Sound, and other ships were in various stages of salvage.

The log of the *California* recorded that at 1:35 on the afternoon of 11 April, "Commander H. G. Rickover, U.S. Navy, from Bureau of Ships, came on board to inspect progress of salvage work." He made his way down into the dark, dirty, and damp compartments containing the electric motors and ran his hand along the insulation. It was like putty. "I cannot describe the utterly hopeless appearance of the electrical machinery," he later wrote.[9]

At 3:30 that same afternoon, Rickover outlined his plan to Wallin and to several other officers. After much consideration and consultation, he said, the bureau had concluded that "the washing out process, as recommended by most sources, is not a safe procedure. Although the washing out process might prove to be successful, there is no assurance of this, and since certainty must be had that these vessels could return to the mainland under their own power, it had been decided that part of the main propulsion equipment must be thoroughly reconditioned." Rickover went on to say the bureau did not object to the yard's washing out the Number 4 main motor, providing there was no delay or interference with rewinding the other motors.

Rickover turned to organizing the effort, arranging for engineers from the mainland to remain as long as they were needed, appointing contact men in each group to funnel requests and information to others, and confirming the tasks that Mare Island, Puget Sound, and private contractors would undertake. Every piece of work, every item, every component, every shipment had to be clearly marked; lost or strayed shipments could cause serious delays.[10] The session finished, Rickover flew back to Washington.

Four days after the meeting, Pearl Harbor stated in a periodic report that washing down the electrical units would have worked had there been sufficient manpower. Rickover was always to disagree. No amount of manpower could have restored the high-voltage propulsion components. Later reports showed the insulation was soft and spongy, penetrated by salt and showing traces of oil; some small equipment, apparently restored to good condition, proved contaminated. One washed-down motor showed that, in all probability, salt remained deep within the machinery.[11]

In Washington Rickover resumed his work but kept a close eye on Pearl Harbor. On 7 June 1942, six months to the day after the attack that had nearly destroyed her, the *California* sailed for Puget Sound under her own power. The washed-down motor, which had been worked on shortly before the war and was in reasonably good condition, was put in operation for the last four days of the voyage and did well. At the yard the motor was disassembled: parts were badly rusted and considerable dirt and oil had penetrated into the more inaccessible places.[12] Whether washing out would have worked on the other motors was at best doubtful.

It was an important addition to the fighting force when the vastly improved *California* left the yard on the last day of January 1944 for a shakedown cruise and the remaining campaigns in the Pacific. The *West Virginia* came afloat on 17 May 1942. Some months later she sailed under her own power for Puget Sound. After extensive modernization, she left the West Coast in September 1944 for the invasion of the Philippines and, with the *California*, took part in the Battle of Leyte Gulf, the last major fleet engagement of the war.

With the Navy now a combatant, the Electrical Section moved into high gear. On the mechanics of shock, for example, Rickover needed data. To get it, he established a testing program in which several organizations took part, among them the research laboratories at Westinghouse and General Electric, the Navy's David Taylor Model Basin at Carderock, Maryland, and the Naval Engineering Experiment Station at Annapolis.

They analyzed the nature of shock and developed test devices to measure it. Rickover had a hammer built that, by hitting an anvil with two thousand foot-pounds of energy, delivered a shock to equipment mounted on the underside of the anvil. Learning from the British that electric switchboards were not shockproof, he had an 8-inch shell fired against an eight-inch steel armor plate on which a switchboard had been mounted. The switchboard almost completely disintegrated, but after a year's work, a redesigned switchboard passed the identical test with flying colors. In some tests depth charges were carefully positioned and detonated beneath fully instrumented ships. By the end of the war generators, motors, controllers, circuit breakers, voltage regulators, and switchboards passed realistically simulated shipboard shock conditions.[13]

Rickover had his own method of testing small components, advertised as unbreakable, that arrived at his office. They had to pass the "radiator test": he hurled the item against the radiator on the other side of his office.

These and other efforts showed that neither the Navy nor industry had set standards and specifications high enough to meet the test of battle. The Navy set its requirements too low; industry considered specifications as goals at which to aim but not necessarily to achieve. Neither the Navy nor industry had adequate tests or practices, which, in a later day, would become known as "quality control." To meet the demands of battle Rickover set the Electrical Section to redesigning equipment, investigating new mountings, and eliminating some materials, particularly those that were inflammable.

He could take such actions because circumstances were creating the opportunity. The nation had launched a "Two Ocean Navy" building program, and the magnitude of that effort was swamping procedures and practices that had once been adequate. Other bureau sections, unable to cope with the demands upon them, left technical decisions to industry and concentrated on contract administration and budget matters. In contrast, the Electrical Section saw itself as representing the United States Navy, which, as the customer, had the right to set the specifications of the product it purchased and to demand that the producer meet the specifications. Under Rickover, the Electrical Section undertook engineering leadership.

In order to exercise that leadership, Rickover had to have technically trained people. He did not find them in naval personnel because their duty moved them from one billet to another, and he did not find them in the government because most personnel from this source could not adapt to the burdens he placed upon them. He turned to industry and "borrowed," to use the word in the official history of the Electrical Section, young engineers. He interviewed them to make sure they had a good scholastic background and some practical experience and were not marginal performers that a company was trying to cast off. Under the guidance of the best engineers in the section, the newcomers soon were able to assume responsibilities in specialized fields.

I. Harry Mandil, a freshly commissioned Reserve officer, came through the bureau and was interviewed by Rickover. Rickover asked what he did, and Mandil replied that he was an engineer.

"What do you wear at work?" Rickover asked.

"A suit."

"Engineers work in overalls!" Rickover exploded.

Mandil was to become a key figure in the nuclear propulsion program and stay with Rickover until 1964.

The section developed equipment that had increased fire resistance. It developed waterproof cable so that water did not leak from a flooded to a dry compartment through the cables and their connections. Based on British experience, the section developed the casualty power system, which consisted of portable cable and fittings, allowing a ship's crew to bypass a damaged permanent cable installation and restore power to pumps, antiaircraft guns, steering gear, and essential lighting—all needed to keep a badly wounded ship afloat and fighting. The section developed shockproof fluorescent lighting to replace incandescent lighting and thereby save power; phosphorescent devices to mark walkways, deck obstructions, valves, levers, instruments, and hatches; hand lanterns that, when fixed to bulkheads, would light up when usual lighting failed; and waterproof flashlights that could be clipped to headbands for doctors and nurses operating near a combat area when power went out. The section met the demands of amphibious warfare for beachmarker lights, portable signal lights, and portable high-intensity flood lamps.[14]

The Electrical Section continued research and development, among other things working with General Electric to devise a system for locating underwater mines and getting into the development of infrared equipment. Early in 1942 Rickover witnessed a demonstration of silicone insulation that, if further developed, could reduce the size and weight of certain electrical equipment. He gave crucial support by getting materials limited by priorities, arranging for supporting services, and obtaining draft deferments for key personnel. The war ended as the material was undergoing extensive testing. In later years silicone insulation added greatly to the efficiency of electric motors, generators, and transformers.[15]

The section grew in personnel as its responsibilities increased. In 1939 it had a handful of officers and a score of engineers; in May 1945 (the month Germany surrendered) the section had a total of 341 people: 18 officers, 185 professional personnel (most from industry but placed in positions established by the Civil Service), 34 professional personnel under contract, 75 civilian clerical or stenographic personnel, and 29 women in uniform. It was the largest section in the bureau.[16]

Rickover devised his own techniques for managing the section. Under the ever-increasing workload, Rickover saw jobs overlapping, responsibilities blurring, and difficulties of control increasing. He created new sections rather than shoehorn a growing problem into an existing organization. Looking back on those days, he recalled studying books on management with their diagrams with arrows showing steps to keep informed and to make decisions. Finding them useless, he tossed them aside. They were far too abstract and academic.

On first reporting to the bureau, he recalled, "I found that one man was in charge of design, another of production, a third handled maintenance, while a fourth dealt with fiscal matters. The entire Bureau operated that way. It didn't make sense to me. Design problems showed up in production; production errors showed up in maintenance; and financial matters reached into all areas. I changed the system. I made one man responsible for his entire area of equipment—for design, production, maintenance, and contracting. If anything went wrong, I knew exactly at whom to point."[17]

He could not know at whom to point without knowing what was going on. To keep informed he devised the "pinks" system. The name came from one sheet of a sheaf of multicolored typing paper that had carbon paper beneath each sheet. The usual procedure called for certain offices and files to receive routinely a carbon copy of outgoing correspondence on paper of a certain color; chronological files, for example, were usually green. In the Electrical Section Rickover got the pink copy. He received it at the end of every working day, whether the original was complete or in draft. If he had questions, he called the writer into his office the next morning.

He found the pinks invaluable. He could see matters that might be going wrong, clear up misunderstandings, glimpse policy implications, and—what he considered priceless—spot a person who might be in the lower reaches of the organization but who should be watched and brought along. He recalled that Robert Panoff, who had recently joined the section, had an idea that his immediate supervisor tossed aside. Through the pinks Rickover saw the suggestion and not only recognized its merits but the potential of Panoff to assume more responsibility. Panoff, too, was to have an important role in the naval nuclear propulsion program, and remain with Rickover for many years.[18]

Relationships between engineers in the Electrical Section and their counterparts in the bureau were usually good, but that could not be said of those between Rickover and the officers and civilians holding administrative positions in other parts of the bureau. Never considering his work confined to that outlined in an organization manual or job description, Rickover without hesitation plunged into matters outside his purview if he considered they were not being handled properly. While inspecting a battleship under construction, possibly the *Washington* at the Philadelphia Navy Yard or the *North Carolina* at the New York Navy Yard, he noticed that the reading lights in the enlisted men's quarters were poorly placed, that a gyro was not shock-mounted and could tumble under vibration, and that some medical cabinets were installed in such a way that glass bottles would shatter if the ship were hit. Back in Washington he had the lights changed and wrote letters to the sections having cognizance over the other items. He received replies that these items were none of his business.

Rickover was hard to deal with, but he got results. Rear Adm. Earle W. Mills, assistant chief of the Bureau of Ships, observed Rickover closely. Mills, a shrewd, blunt, and tough officer, had graduated from the academy in 1917 and had served in destroyers and battleships before taking postgraduate work in electrical engineering. In 1933 he was designated "engineering duty only," and the fall of 1940 saw him in England, where, as assistant naval attaché, he studied battle damage suffered by ships of the Royal Navy. Two years later he was back in Washington in the Bureau of Ships.

Recognizing Rickover's talents as a troubleshooter, Mills summoned him to his office one day in early December 1944. Not knowing why he had been summoned, Rickover entered Mills's office, finding it filled with a number of senior officers, some from the office of the chief of naval operations, others from the office of the chief of the Bureau of Supplies and Accounts. They were in the final stages of a conference on the situation at the recently established Naval Supply Depot at Mechanicsburg, Pennsylvania. The depot, which reported to both bureaus, supplied diesel engine spare parts. The depot was in serious trouble, unable to meet the demands upon it, and apparently upon the verge of collapse.

It was hard to overestimate the gravity of the situation. The production of diesel engines was going well; it was the supply of spare parts that was the problem. The Navy was facing the landing on Okinawa and, after that, the invasion of Japan. The landing craft of the amphibious forces were almost completely powered by diesel engines, most of which received hard usage.

Mills turned to Rickover: "Rick, why don't you go up and see what this is all about?" He left for Mechanicsburg on the night of 13 December, taking with him four other officers, among them Dause A. Bibby, an articulate young junior grade lieutenant in the Bureau of Supplies and Accounts.

The next morning the group from Washington began their investigation. Liking the young and intelligent officer, Rickover kept Bibby with him, partly to train him and partly to get his perspective. At the end of the day, Rickover, to find out how he had done, turned to Bibby. Too tough, came the reply. Rickover had left a trail of weeping women who were doing their best to get the data he demanded from the files. Rickover looked thoughtful; the next day his manner with the clerical force was just as insistent but much less imperious.

Rickover found Mechanicsburg in terrible shape. On his return to Washington he declared that a detailed analysis of the operation of the depot was essential, and for that purpose he needed the help of industrial experts and specialists. Some of the largest and most important companies of the country—including American Steel and Wire Company, the Chevrolet Division of General Motors, the General Electric Company, International Business Machines Corporation, and the Sears and Roebuck Company—lent him experts.

While the demand for spare parts was skyrocketing, the time it took from the receipt of a requisition until the item was issued, for one category of engine components, was 48.7 days if the request was routine, 15.5 days if it was urgent. Another statistic showed an equally dismal record. On the average, it took eighteen days from the time an item was received at Mechanicsburg until it could be issued. The depot had been given more and more personnel, but numbers only made matters worse. It was drastic reform that was needed.

On 1 March 1945, Rickover submitted a report almost two inches thick to the chief of the Bureau of Ships. It contained a number of general and specific recommendations, accompanied by charts, tables, and figures. Defining authority and responsibility at the depot and in Washington was common to them all. The last fitness report he received while heading the Electrical Section said that he "has been assigned to a duty in which he acts directly for the Chief of the Bureau in reorganizing the whole spare parts program, the most important single problem in keeping our ships in action at sea."[19]

Rickover was restless. He had served in the Electrical Section since mid-1939 and been its chief since the end of 1940. He had become a commander on 1 January 1942 and captain on 22 June 1943.[20] He wanted an overseas assignment, not so much to help his career as to avoid someday having to tell his son, Robert Masters Rickover, born on 11 October 1940, that he had spent the entire war in Washington. Mills gave him his choice. The campaign for Okinawa was just beginning. Because the island would play a great part in the final assault on Japan, Rickover asked to command the ship repair base. On 24 March 1945 he was detached from the bureau in Washington to become industrial manager, Naval Operating Base, Okinawa, commanding the Naval Repair Base.

He had learned a great deal in the Electrical Section. He had seen the strengths and weaknesses of the Bureau of Ships as well as those of industry. He knew the leaders in the electrical industry and had worked with some of their ablest young engineers. He was tough, abusive, and abrasive. While his superiors in the bureau admired his work, engineer officers who were his contemporaries and rivals for promotion would not forget or forgive his high-handed ways or his insulting manners. He made enemies among contractors, too, at least one of which three times asked Mills to get rid of him. On leaving the section, Rickover received several letters of the type usually sent by company executives to a departing officer: they were sorry to see him go and wished him well. He tossed them aside with contempt. "If I were on fire they wouldn't piss on me."

His final fitness report summed up his record in the bureau: "Forceful and fearless. An organizer & leader of outstanding ability. One of the country's foremost engineers. Equally capable in production matters. As head of the Electrical Sec. of BuShips since before Pearl Harbor, he has performed this highly responsible duty with distinction. It is considered that he has made as great a contribution to the successful preparation for the carrying on the war as any officer of the Navy's Shore Establishment. The value of his contributions to the improvement of our ships is inestimable."[21]

It was unlikely that events would ever arrange themselves again so that he would have a assignment similar to the one he was leaving. Exhausted by six years in the Bureau of Ships, Rickover boarded the train for San Francisco in late March 1945. At last he was away from the endless pressure of the Electrical Section. Becoming the industrial manager and commander of the Repair Base at Okinawa would be a different challenge, and one that he was looking forward to.

On 1 April 1945 more than seventy-five thousand American troops landed on Okinawa, an island about 50 miles long and 3 to 10 miles wide, which gave ample space for airfields and other military installations. Kyushu, the most southern of the Japanese home islands, was only 360 miles to the north; the Chinese mainland, occupied by a powerful Japanese army, about 400 miles to the west; and the large island of Formosa, held by strong Japanese forces, a little over 330 miles to the southwest.[22]

The repair base would be located on Nakagusuku Wan (later renamed Buckner Bay for Lt. Gen. Simon B. Buckner, killed in fighting for the island) on the southeast coast and the only large fleet anchorage between Kyushu and Formosa. The Japanese had done little to develop the bay, but along its shores the Americans planned to build facilities to supply major fleet units and occupation forces and to repair ships.

Plans dated April 1945 called for Rickover to have under him twenty-five hundred repair personnel, facilities the equivalent of two repair ships, and special tools found on destroyer and submarine tenders. About forty-five hundred feet of repair docks would front on water having a depth between twenty and thirty feet. Possibly there would be a sectional floating dry dock. Finally, the base would have the small boats and landing craft indispensable for harbor operations. Rickover's command was important: ships that Okinawa could not repair would have to steam fourteen hundred miles to Guam, or even to Pearl Harbor or to the West Coast. Finally, he had to have the base operating by 1 November 1945, when the Americans would land on Kyushu. By that date the base should be able to handle all repairs to the amphibious ships and 80 percent of all other repairs.[23]

Japanese resistance on Okinawa, at first light, soon stiffened. It quickly became clear that the struggle on land would be long and bloody. At sea the fleet was already suffering from kamikaze attacks. Those ships that were hit and survived, their hulls and upperworks twisted, torn, and charred, limped back or were towed to a temporary anchorage at Kerama Retto, a group of small islands off Okinawa, for patching and makeshift repairs. If they were any indication, storming the home islands meant heavy casualties in men and damage to ships.

Rickover had a lot to do to get ready for his new assignment. He selected Lt. Cdr. James S. Bethea as assistant industrial manager. The two immediately set out to gather information, stopping first at San Bruno, a few miles south of San Francisco, where about fifteen thousand men were undergoing six weeks of intensive training before shipping out to an advance base. Rickover gained an idea of the type of men he would command and the skills they possessed. He planned a tour of major Pacific bases to determine the spare parts and shop equipment Okinawa would need. Furthermore, he wanted to learn from the experiences encountered at these bases. On 12 April he and Bethea flew to Honolulu. Rickover learned he would have great freedom in laying out the repair base and would get additional equipment. Even so, meetings and conferences seemed endless. "I will be glad when I am finally on Okinawa—actually watching the buildings go up and getting into the swing of things," he wrote Ruth.

He was still at Pearl Harbor when the radio announced the death of President Roosevelt. Rickover and Ruth thought the loss was tragic, far more serious than most people realized. The outcome of the war would not be affected, for the end was clear, but hopes for establishing an international agency to keep peace had dimmed. Ruth wondered whether their son Robert, now almost five, would be caught up in a future war.[24]

On 18 April Rickover and Bethea left for Guam, the site of a major repair facility. The island was a startling revelation of American power. From his work in Washington, Rickover knew the immensity of American industrial might and had helped harness that strength; nonetheless, he was unprepared for the tremendous airfields, huge camps, and well-equipped repair facilities. His personal quarters, a Quonset hut with running water, were excellent. The food was good, and laundry and haircuts were free.

He had several long conferences with Vice Adm. William W. Smith, commander of the service force (which handled logistics for the Pacific Fleet), and with Capt. Schuyler N. Pyne, with whom Rickover had worked on degaussing early in the war. As industrial manager of the naval operating base on Guam, Pyne had put into operation shops and facilities capable of repairing even large units of the fleet. Rickover thought it an impressive accomplishment from which he could learn much.[25]

He flew to Okinawa to inspect the proposed site of the repair base and to meet Commodore Fred D. Kirtland, commanding the naval operating base. Still fighting tenaciously, the Japanese were penned up in the southern part of the island. Elsewhere the Americans were already leveling the ground for immense airfields and rushing other facilities to completion. Rickover thought the location of the repair base looked good. Most facilities would be at Baten Ko, a part of Buckner Bay where deep water was nearest to shore. Finding good footing for heavy structures, however, might be a problem. Against all the activity, he found it surprisingly easy to get used to the sound of the guns during the day and the light of their flashes during the night.

In quick trips away from the bay, Rickover encountered natives tilling their fields and could not help but wonder what they thought. He sympathized with them, knowing their land would probably be seized for airfields. Their lot might be greatly improved if the United States kept Okinawa after the war and introduced modern hygiene and a proper school system.[26]

Reflecting on what he had seen, Rickover flew back to Guam for further conferences with Smith and Pyne. On 5 May he sent a long letter to Capt. Henry C. Eccles, a classmate making a distinguished name for himself in the complicated field of logistics. Stationed at Pearl Harbor and on the staff of the commander of the service force, Eccles was deeply involved in planning and outfitting advance bases.

The Okinawa repair base, Rickover wrote, would include a ship repair yard as well as landing craft and small boat repair units. He wanted more track for the marine railway than had been planned; he needed more equipment, such as portable, gasoline-driven floodlight units, generators, and portable air compressors. He had already made detailed plans for the layout of equipment in the buildings. Most of the material and supplies had been ordered, but he needed more fire-fighting equipment, and medical and dental dispensaries. Guam, he learned, never had enough welders or welding sets, and to meet peak demands the base had to scrounge personnel and other equipment from wherever it could. Guam never had enough boats assigned to its industrial facility and repair base, which hindered working on ships at anchor. He did not want the base saddled with jobs such as outfitting buildings or making office furniture. "By including these important items *now* in the Base Development Plan," he wrote, "we will be able to devote all of our energies to the constructive work of repairing ships, instead of engaging in fruitless conferences, arguments, and letter writing, official and personal."[27]

By 22 May, after hurried visits to other repair bases, Rickover and Bethea were back at Pearl Harbor. At last he had mail from home. He eagerly welcomed the arrival of Ruth's latest book, *Handbook of International Organizations in the Americas*, published by the Carnegie Endowment for International Peace. Proudly he turned its pages; her writing was good and strong, its only fault was too many qualifying words such as "in general."

Every day, from eight in the morning until ten at night, he and fifteen other officers worked on preparations for the base. Anything not done, any agreement not reached, any arrangement not made were opportunities lost that might never come again. But at Pearl Harbor, so far from the fighting, Rickover found no sense of urgency; the red tape was endless, the required concurrences numerous, the organization inefficient, and the administration poor. And yet, he was happy in fighting the bureaucracy and getting things done. He succeeded in doubling the number of buildings allowed him and in getting more men.

He did not have much time. It was already the end of May; the first of November was only five months off. "During this time," he explained to Ruth, "we must prepare an 85 acre site, put up some 50 large buildings, install hundreds of machine tools, and have everyone ready to work—because we will be depended on to perform most of the urgent repairs to ships which are damaged in the next operation."[28]

To his delight, Rickover had to go to Washington for a few days to expedite the flow of personnel and the shipment of material as well as to make some last minute arrangements. In contrast to Pearl Harbor, everyone was exceedingly helpful and cooperative. From Guam, Vice Admiral Smith had added his voice on the importance of the Okinawa repair base by taking unusual steps to speed the flow of material and equipment and declaring that delays in Washington could upset the schedule. Rickover was pleased: "There is practically nothing I have thought of that has not been approved, and knowing what an active mind I have I know you can realize how unusual this is."[29] With so much to do, he had little time for his family.

He reported to Kirtland on Okinawa on 20 July. The commodore saw the island as the "England of the Pacific," playing the same role in the invasion of Japan as England had played in the invasion of Normandy. At least England had facilities to support a landing force; Okinawa had none. Everything had to be built from scratch. Kirtland pressed hard to speed up construction.[30]

Rickover found mud the ever-present enemy. Rain from low-lying, heavy gray clouds drenched the island almost daily. By destroying rice paddies and ancient drainage systems in order to lay out airfields and construct other installations, the Americans had created a treacherous terrain. Trucks often slid off the slippery roads. Bethea, who had arrived before Rickover, learned that foundations at Baten Ko had to be driven through eighty feet of mud.[31]

Rickover was exhilarated—even if living conditions were poor, even if he had little of his cherished privacy (for he was living in a tent with three other officers), even if it was always damp, even if it took forever for laundry to dry. "I enjoy the work very much, because there is an unlimited scope for my ideas," he remarked. "I look at a place, decide what buildings are to be put there, etc. etc. I am so tired at night that I cannot help sleeping well. The days go by without my knowing it and I cannot even remember what day of the week this is."[32]

Finding the Seabees, who were responsible for constructing the base, were moving too slowly, Rickover began using his own personnel and equipment. He soon recognized his mistakes in earlier planning. Arranging for the shipment of materials before he had sufficient men to use and care for them was one of the worst. On the other hand, no matter how detailed his scheduling, men often arrived without notice, thereby making preliminary planning and construction difficult. Most of his officers were inexperienced and had to be taught a great deal before they could act independently. But with everyone working twelve-hour days and seven-day weeks, the base was taking shape. By the end of July living conditions were improving: men were no longer sleeping in the mud and eating K rations. Furthermore, sections of the Quonset buildings that would house the industrial shops, tools, and equipment were coming ashore.[33]

On 3 August he wrote proudly to Ruth, "I am the Commanding Officer of the Naval Repair Base; this includes not only the Ship Repair area, but also the camp for about 5,000 men. We will have all sorts of things such as laundries, bakeries, Red Cross facilities, chapels, etc. etc." But three straight days of rain had stopped nearly all traffic and construction.

He had two outstanding men in his command. John F. O'Grady came from civilian life and had no intention of making the Navy a career. A big man, a shrewd judge of character, highly intelligent, and possessing tremendous charm, O'Grady excelled in getting scarce supplies. Filling the back of his jeep with coolers of beer, he would lead a truck to a Seabee camp. Stopped by sentries, O'Grady joked and talked with them, soon leaving with whatever he had come for. When commanding the *Finch* in the Asiatic Fleet, Rickover met Paul E. Dignan. Rickover brought him (now a commissioned officer) to Okinawa to take charge of the boat pool, a job demanding toughness and efficiency.[34]

Kirtland had his own man for the job. Rickover had learned on Guam the importance of the boat pool to the smooth running of a repair base. He was determined to have Dignan. In a violent disagreement, which apparently took place at a staff meeting before a large number of officers, Rickover prevailed, but at the cost of poor relations with Kirtland.

Everything suddenly and drastically changed—not just on Okinawa but throughout the world. The Army Air Force dropped two atomic bombs, the first on Hiroshima on 6 August 1945, the second on Nagasaki three days later. On the latter date, Rickover wrote Ruth, "We learned today of Russia's declaration of war and of the atomic bomb. We have very little news here; furthermore we are too busy to worry too much about it."[35]

On 10 August the radio announced the Japanese offer to accept peace terms. That night discipline collapsed: ships in the harbor fired machine guns in all directions, Army antiaircraft batteries fired tracers, and several men and officers on the naval base fired rifles and pistols into the air. "It was the most disgraceful episode I have ever witnessed or heard of," Rickover declared. A large number of people were wounded, some fatally. One of Rickover's men at Baten Ko received a bullet through a lung.[36]

Rickover did his best to keep his command busy, but it was not easy. Plans for the base drawn up before the war's end were useless. In September a directive canceled the shipment of material from the United States to all repair bases and announced a study to determine the future of each. That same month word came that the Okinawa base was to have facilities to maintain and repair all ships up to and including cruisers. Rickover prepared a list of needed installations and equipment and, to get further guidance, flew to Pearl Harbor.

On his trip back he contrasted the civilized amenities of Pearl Harbor and Guam to the crudeness of Okinawa, with its poor roads, its mud when it was raining, and its clouds of dust when it was dry. There was no escape, no change of scene, no place to go. Worst of all was its lack of privacy: "I find it hard to live 24 hours a day, every day, without being alone one moment." Did the Navy need the repair base? Rickover thought not— unless there was some political reason he did not know.[37]

Heavy rain in August, a typhoon in September, and another a month later swept away almost all the progress he had made. The October typhoon was the worst: 120 mile-an-hour winds blew buildings to pieces, spun huge sheets of metal across the ground, and drove ships ashore. Fortunately, there was enough warning to evacuate most men to the hills and for those who remained to find shelter. When wind and rain gave a chance, the men searched the beach for survivors. They found seventy unharmed, thirty injured, and seven dead. Rickover got a lacerated hand when the wind knocked him down as he warned a truckload of men that they were entering an area where flying metal was dangerous. In two days the storm had almost leveled the base, leaving only one building of seventy still standing.

Rickover started rebuilding immediately. For a brief time he lived in a merchant ship that had been driven ashore; it was the only dry place he could find. In a few days everyone had at least some shelter, a typhoon-proof mess hall was under construction, and hundreds of tons of wreckage had been cleared away. In two weeks there was good food and the living quarters had some semblance of order and cleanliness. But it was uphill work, as most officers and men were interested only in going home.[38]

Washington was now convinced that a temporary fleet anchorage was all that was needed at Okinawa—that and what little was necessary to support local small craft. There would be no ship repair facilities, no floating dry dock, no supply depot.[39] Rickover's job was to decide what was essential and close out everything else. "Exactly what will happen to me . . . I do not yet know," he wrote to Ruth on 1 November.

When possible he explored the island, once going into a camp run by the military government for thirteen thousand Okinawans. He saw children naked and starving, and the mentally retarded and the elderly crowded into filthy huts. The condition of the children upset him most. To the Army captain in charge he offered to send food and clothing, only to be told the children would not eat the food. He offered to send ice cream, only to be told that the military police would be angry because they were not getting any. Because children were sleeping naked on floors he sent blankets and cots; two days later he found they had not been issued. "Don't think I am exaggerating on the subject," he wrote Ruth. "I kept thinking of Robert and of how well he is taken care of—and here were poor naked kids 3 and 4 years old. So apathetic and dull that their attention could hardly be attracted—crying and no one paying any attention to them." Elsewhere he saw some geisha girls. "They were all in sleek, healthy condition—so you can guess where the food is going."[40]

He did all he could to relieve the suffering. A leper colony among the hills in the northwestern part of the island, mistaken for a military installation, had been bombed and its facilities ruined. There was no electricity, no medicine, no bandages; its inhabitants clothed only in rags. He sent food, bedding, clothing, medicine, and a small generator. In another instance he helped villagers near his own quarters. As the scope of the repair base was scaled back, his orders called for the destruction of unneeded stores. Instead he placed them in a central location and told the headmen of the villages to help themselves.[41]

Finally he had a place of his own: half a Quonset hut. He had designed a suite consisting of a living room, kitchen, bedroom, and bathroom, all fitting into an area of twenty by twenty-eight feet. He had hot and cold running water, a large shower, electric lights with concealed wiring, glass windows, linoleum floors, and even curtains. He could understand why officers liked to command bases: a jeep and driver, guards, and all sorts of amenities were his just for the asking.

Closing the repair base gave him time for reflecting. He unburdened himself in a long letter to Ruth on 18 November. Roughly speaking, his thoughts fell into three categories. One dealt with the quality of officers assigned to the base, a second with his inability to advance enlisted men to officer rank, and a third with his belief that reputations of high-ranking officers in the Pacific were inflated beyond their merits.

Although nearly all the officers reporting to him came from good families and had formal college education, he found only about 10 percent worthwhile. His use of the words "formal college education" meant he was thinking not of academy graduates but of men taken from civilian life, hurriedly indoctrinated into the Navy, quickly and superficially trained, and swiftly sent overseas. They were not men whom he had interviewed and chosen, as was the case for engineers whom he had selected for the Electrical Section. Possibly he was expecting too much.

It irked him that he could not do much about increasing the 10 percent: "I have found many enlisted men whom I would like to make officers in place of those who do not come up to officer standards—but this is impossible under our system. I never realized how little opportunity an enlisted man has in our Navy until I came out here." But there was no immediate action Rickover could take. An individual who possessed *reliability* and *initiative* (Rickover underlined both words) should have the proper rank and responsibility.

"Most of the stories and articles of the great officers of the Pacific war are a lot of rot if Okinawa is any example," he wrote in the same letter. What was behind this observation he did not say, except that he was referring to operations in the combat areas. "I am not too impressed and I believe that if we were fighting an enemy who had equal material resources it would go hard with us."

Kirtland gave Rickover an unfavorable fitness report for the period from 1 September to 25 November 1945. One section of the report placed the officer under consideration in the top 10 percent, in the top 20 percent, in the middle 40 percent, in the lower 20 percent, and in the bottom 10 percent in several categories. Kirtland put Rickover in the top 10 percent in only three categories: "Assume responsibilities when specific instructions are lacking," "Follow through despite obstacles in carrying out responsibilities," and "Maintain discipline." His lowest marks fell in the 40 percent category: "Ability to command," "Give frank opinions when asked or volunteer when necessary to avoid mistakes," "Use of ideas and suggestions of others," and "Effectively delegate responsibility." Rickover's chances of reaching flag rank were seriously damaged.[42]

What had gone wrong? Rickover later remembered fighting with Kirtland over the assignment of Dignan to run the boat pool. He also recalled a dispute over the initiative he took after one typhoon: when the Seabees were busy elsewhere, Rickover rushed to complete quarters for the Red Cross women and received criticism for his initiative. Doubtless there were other differences.

Rickover's orders came in the first half of November. He was to report to San Francisco to help lay up surplus ships. It was temporary duty; he did not know what would come next. O'Grady remarked that with modern methods of preserving equipment, mothballing ships shouldn't be too difficult. Silently Rickover filed the remark in his mind. On 27 November he left Okinawa.

Atomic Energy

ON 16 DECEMBER 1945, Rickover left Washington, D.C., for San Francisco to report for temporary duty to Rear Adm. Walter E. Kilpatrick, deputy commander, Western Sea Frontier. The admiral was in charge of the Nineteenth Fleet, which was decommissioning and preparing ships for mothballing.

Two days earlier the *New York Times* had run a story under the heading "Atom Power Held Boon for the Navy." It quoted from the testimony of Ross Gunn before a Senate special committee considering legislation to place the new source of energy into the national life. A senior physicist at the Naval Research Laboratory, Gunn had declared that "the main job of nuclear energy is to turn the world's wheels and run its ships."

Gunn had seen that possibility in late January 1939, when the discovery of atomic fission was announced at the Washington Conference on Theoretical Physics. Energy from a single fissioning atom was minuscule, but if fission continued as a "chain reaction," the amount of energy released could be tremendous. In its fundamentals, submarine propulsion had changed little since Rickover left the *S-48*. Diesel engines drove the ship on the surface; batteries propelled her when submerged. Diesel engines needed air to operate, and although batteries did not, their endurance was short. But energy from atomic fission was different: it did not need oxygen. An atomic submarine would be capable of long, submerged voyages. But what had been announced in 1939 were the results of an experiment; no one could tell whether getting energy from the atom was feasible, whether atomic energy could be used to drive machinery, or whether the technical problems could be solved. Indeed, no one even knew what the technical problems were.

A close reader of the *New York Times*, Rickover must have seen the story, but he had other things on his mind during the long and tedious flight.

Ruth was not well. Winter was hard on her, and their son Robert, exuberantly exploring the world around him, was imposing heavy demands upon her. In a few weeks Rickover would be forty-six years old, and he did not know what his future in the Navy would be. In his nearly six years as head of the Electrical Section he had made many enemies in the Bureau of Ships and knew of no one in industry who would hire him.

His mood was not improved by finding out that Kilpatrick didn't know what to do with him. The admiral made him inspector general, a job that required traveling up and down the West Coast visiting shipyards and inspecting their work. He soon found their officers had neither the administrative experience nor the technical knowledge for their jobs. Because most of the personnel were naval reservists waiting impatiently for discharge, it was a struggle to get things done. No one cared. Even when he entered a yard and signed in as "Captain A. Lincoln," "Captain G. Washington," or even "Captain J. Christ," no one cared.

To get help, he arranged for Paul E. Dignan and John F. O'Grady, who had proved themselves on Okinawa, to be assigned to him. Because Dignan was a Navy career officer, getting him was no problem, but O'Grady was a different matter. He was a noncommissioned officer eager to get back to civilian life and resume a promising business career. His ship had barely entered San Diego when a boat pulled alongside: Rickover had sent it to take O'Grady off the ship before he could be sent to other duty for the remainder of his time in the Navy.

At every yard Rickover insisted that officers wear dungarees and personally direct the work. His inspections were rigorous and often stormy: no compartment was too small for him to squeeze into; no trick to hide rust or conceal poor work could fool him. He required written reports at the end of the day. Those inaccurate or in poor English he shot back, demanding that they be redone and on his desk first thing in the morning. To his surprise, he found his recommendations and reports were having an effect. Initial resentment and resistance to his methods and principles often gave way to requests for help in changing procedures and organizations. Kilpatrick appreciated his work. Rickover was "Flag officer material as EDO officer" and "Definitely of Flag Officer caliber."[1]

Rickover was eager to get back to Washington. In mid-March Kilpatrick relieved him of one anxiety—the admiral was willing to release him around 1 May. While that banished Rickover's fears that his temporary duty might be extended, he still did not know what he would do next. Finally word came. From Astoria, Oregon, on 19 April 1946, he wrote to

Ruth, "I received word from the Bureau today that I am to take one year's course in 'nuclear energy' at the Massachusetts Institute of Technology, Boston, starting in June. They asked me how soon I can be detached. I talked it over with my Admiral, of the 19th Fleet, and I'll probably be able to be detached early in May."

Ruth was pleased. Hard at work on a manual on international affairs for the Carnegie Endowment for International Peace, she saw his new duty as a fine opportunity for him to plunge into a new and promising field as well as evidence that the Navy appreciated his work. But then something changed. He learned on 3 May that "the plan now is not to send me to school but to be engaged actively in some project connected with the matter, somewhere in the U.S. I don't know what that means and will not be able to find out until I reach the Bureau."[2]

He arrived in Washington a few days later to learn that he was to be sent to Oak Ridge, Tennessee, one of the major installations of the Manhattan Engineer District, the Army organization that had built the atomic bomb. In March 1946 the district, still in charge of the nation's atomic energy program until a civilian agency could take control, had invited a few engineers from industry and the Bureau of Ships to Oak Ridge to take part in developing an experimental power reactor proposed by Farrington Daniels, a leading chemist in the Manhattan project. Behind the wall of secrecy these individuals would gain practical experience in the esoteric field of reactor technology. Accepting the invitation, the bureau promised to send five officers and three civilians.

Capt. Albert G. Mumma had drawn up a list for Vice Adm. Earle W. Mills, assistant chief of the bureau. As head of the Machinery Design Division, Mumma had cognizance of nuclear propulsion. He had already placed two research contracts on materials looking toward the application of nuclear propulsion. Moreover, he had some background in atomic energy. In World War II he had been a member of a team of engineers and scientists who had followed on the heels of the retreating Germans to see how far they had gotten in the development of an atomic bomb. Extremely able, articulate, and personable, he was well along in a career that would see him become chief of the Bureau of Ships in 1955.

The caliber of men Mumma selected showed he recognized the importance of the assignment. Three were lieutenant commanders. Louis H. Roddis Jr. and James M. Dunford, both of the class of 1939, and Miles A. Libbey, class of 1940, had done exceedingly well at the Naval Academy and at MIT. The background of the fourth man was very different. Not an academy man, Lt. Raymond H. Dick had an outstanding combat record, and his graduate work in metallurgy at Ohio State University gave him a specialty that was unusual in the bureau. To lead the group, Mumma chose Capt. Harry Burris, who had solved with dispatch and diplomacy tough problems blocking the rapid construction of steam propulsion plants for destroyer escorts during the war. Mills made only one change to the list: he substituted Rickover for Burris.

It was not an easy decision for Mills. Mumma argued that Rickover was not the man for the Oak Ridge assignment, that his selection would raise a storm of protest. Mumma was right; many senior bureau officers had dealt with Rickover when he was head of the Electrical Section and disliked him intensely. Furthermore, he had shown a drive to control and dominate any job assigned him, qualities hardly conducive to heading a project that had to be folded into the bureau organization. He got results, but Oak Ridge required someone who could work with the Army and had a sense of tact and diplomacy. As if all this was not enough, Mills had to persuade Rickover that sending him to Oak Ridge was not a move to ease him out of Washington.

From seeing Rickover at work in the Electrical Section, Mills knew he could take part in a rough-and-tumble fight for the Navy's place in an Army installation should that be necessary. Not able to ignore the men whose support he needed to create a postwar Navy, Mills made one concession: Rickover would have no authority over the other officers going to Oak Ridge. Deeply resenting the arrangement, Rickover felt angry and humiliated but could do nothing about it. If anything, the affront only gave him additional determination to succeed.

Rickover did not find much in the bureau files to prepare him for his new assignment. A report issued by the Naval Research Laboratory in March 1946 was probably the most interesting item. Its authors, Philip H. Abelson, a young physicist, and two associates, believed that a nuclear-powered submarine could be in operation in only two years once the decision had been made to build it, providing the effort had high priority and the Navy and the Manhattan District worked closely together. Rickover found the report vague and lacking in technical data.

He was also finding out that Oak Ridge was not the only center, perhaps not even the major site, of reactor development. An astute observer could well have concluded that the General Electric Company at Schenectady, New York, would take the lead in nuclear ship propulsion. For decades the company had provided propulsion equipment for submarines and surface ships and had close ties to the Navy. Moreover, it was clear that the company, having important contracts to operate key installations producing nuclear material, would play a major role in the future atomic energy program. At a briefing on 13 May, Rickover heard company scientists and engineers present design studies on a power reactor and a propulsion reactor based on the same technology.[3] Even if preliminary, the studies were impressive.

Before Mills could send the five officers to Oak Ridge, he had to assure Brig. Gen. Kenneth D. Nichols, second only to Maj. Gen. Leslie R. Groves in the district's organization, that the man directing the Navy group could handle the job. Mills gave six references from industry for Nichols to call, but diplomatically omitted to state that Rickover would have no authority over the group. Nichols promptly called all six. Three described Rickover as outstanding, imaginative, and difficult; three declared him absolutely impossible to deal with. On 4 June, about to leave for Oak Ridge, Nichols asked Mills to send Rickover to the Washington National Airport. No sooner had Rickover climbed into the plane than it took off for Knoxville, Tennessee, the location of the nearest sizable airport to Oak Ridge.

The hours of intense study of bureau files and books from the technical library paid off as, during the flight, Rickover described his goal, philosophy, and experiences with the bureau and contractors. In the course of his work Nichols had seen countless officers, engineers, and scientists and was a good judge of their capabilities. From Oak Ridge he called Mills. "Rickover will do, so start the ball rolling," he said. "It will be interesting to see what happens."[4]

During his career Rickover had seen some strange places, but none like Oak Ridge. Five years earlier he would have seen a series of desolate pine ridges, the tiny hamlet of Elza, and a few farms reached by rough roads. Choosing the area for its isolation and the availability of power from the Tennessee Valley Authority, the Army had carved out an immense area for a huge installation to produce enriched uranium, a sophisticated laboratory, and a town that soon became one of the largest in the state. For reasons of security, the entire complex, including the town, was behind barriers and off limits. About thirty thousand people made up the population, which included highly educated men and women with advanced degrees in many scientific fields, skilled technicians, people from the surrounding hills, and a tough construction force drawn from across the nation.

Headquarters were in the "castle," a long, rambling wooden structure also known from its five wings as the "wooden Pentagon." Here Rickover reported to Col. Walter J. Williams, responsible for the facilities producing uranium. The two men got along well from the first. Immediately understanding Rickover's assignment, Williams made him a deputy and gave him a desk in his office. Such recognition opened all doors to Rickover: he could see any part of the vast installation he wished.

Promptly he began educating himself. He found it hard to know where to begin. A month and some days after his arrival he wrote to Ruth, "It is very difficult for some one with my temperament to do nothing but study—particularly when there is no set course and when I have to figure out myself just what to study."[5]

Libbey and Dunford arrived in June and Roddis and Dick in September. Rickover found they were exceptional individuals. Roddis, Dunford, and Libbey were highly motivated young career officers of the best type. Dunford was exceedingly perceptive, whereas Roddis possessed an uncanny ability to write fast and well. Libbey had a deep interest in research, which, in a few years, would lead him to leave the Navy for academic life. Nervous, deeply troubled, and resenting any hint of condescension because he was not an academy man, Dick was possessed by an intense drive that was to center on Rickover instead of the program or the Navy. Rickover knew these men had an educational advantage over him, but he had far more years of practical engineering. That, he thought, helped balance things.

They, in turn, found in Rickover inexhaustible energy, an insatiable appetite for work, an unswerving determination to define and reach his goal, a sense of humor, and a gift for mordant, trenchant, and ironic appraisals of his surroundings. Widely read and possessing a superb memory, he had no hesitation about expressing an opinion on any subject. Dunford noticed something else, something hard to interpret: Rickover wore his uniform casually, almost as if he was distancing himself from the Navy.

Before they left Washington, Dunford, Roddis, Libbey, and Dick had been carefully briefed that they were not to report to Rickover but to the Army officers who headed the organizations to which the newcomers were assigned. That meant that Army officers would be making out their fitness reports. One day Rickover called them all together and told them he knew that they were not to report to him. "That is alright with me," he said, "but I just thought you might be interested to know that Col. Williams has asked me to prepare your fitness reports." His small audience immediately understood: good fitness reports were indispensable to pro-motion. They were now working for Rickover.[6] Looking back, he saw the incident as his first step in gaining control of the naval nuclear propulsion program.

He organized them into a team that soon became known as the "Naval Group." Its members attended lectures and classes. To cut through poor instruction, Rickover in class demanded clear definitions and explana-tions. Soon there were evening sessions, which he and many others, who had been less candid in admitting their difficulties, eagerly attended. In addition, the group witnessed the operation of the X-10, the research reac-tor in Oak Ridge, discussed reactor technology with anyone who seemed knowledgeable, and exchanged ideas and impressions among themselves. Under Rickover's guidance the Naval Group divided areas of responsibili-ty. Roddis followed weight and space requirements, Dunford took power generation, Libbey studied new designs, and Dick handled fuels, metallur-gy, and chemical processing. They got to know engineers from industry who had come to work on the Daniels reactor. Some had been with Rick-over in the Electrical Section, and some he would call upon in the days ahead.[7]

The Naval Group had a thin technical base upon which to build. The Manhattan Project had constructed huge reactors to produce plutonium as well as smaller research reactors to provide nuclear data and, although both types produced heat and therefore energy, neither was meant to gen-erate power to drive machinery. During the war many scientists and engi-neers in the project had considered various types of reactors for civilian electric power plants to be built when peace arrived. They had gathered and analyzed the nuclear properties of several metals and materials but much had yet to be discovered.

Roughly speaking, all reactors had certain features in common: a core of nuclear fuel (usually uranium), systems for starting up, controlling, and shutting down the reactor, a coolant to transfer heat from the core to some medium that would impart energy to machinery, and shielding to protect personnel and equipment from radiation. Rickover and his group found three promising technical approaches: pressurized water, sodium-cooled, and gas-cooled.

Each approach carried its own set of technical problems. The metallur-gy, shielding, and methods of control for the water-cooled approach, for example, were not the same as those for the other two approaches. No one knew how various materials would actually behave under prolonged and intense radiation. No one knew how to fabricate components that could operate reliably for long periods of time in such an environment. The obstacles might be daunting, but there was the optimism that was the legacy of the technical accomplishments achieved by the Manhattan Project in the war.

In addition, submarine propulsion levied a host of constraints on Rickover that scientists and engineers developing civilian power plants did not face. The reactor had to produce enough energy to propel a ship at significant speeds. It had to operate reliably for sustained periods of time, and it had to be manned by highly skilled Navy enlisted men. Placing the reactor and the steam plant with its steam generators, turbines, and associated systems within the confines of a submarine presented severe challenges. Moreover, the propulsion system had to withstand the shock and motion that were part of the life of any combatant ship. Later Rickover would maintain that developing nuclear propulsion was more difficult than developing the atomic bomb. A bomb had to go off once; a propulsion reactor had to operate reliably and safely for years.

Rickover and the Naval Group were reaching some important conclusions. Developing a naval propulsion plant was a job for engineers, not scientists. Rickover's initial impression of scientists had been one of awe, but he soon discovered their views on engineering were dangerously naïve. Nuclear propulsion demanded standards far above those the bureau had encountered in the past. From his own experience in the Electrical Section, he knew that industry would have to be forced to reach and adhere to the new standards. To sum up, an engineer should be in charge of the program: he would have to raise the engineering standards in the Navy and in industry. Whether this was the course of his reasoning and whether he phrased it so starkly to himself, his actions make clear that he saw being in charge was a goal worth scheming and fighting for.

Mumma, however, headed the bureau's effort in nuclear propulsion. Accompanied by Burris, the bureau's liaison officer with General Electric, Mumma visited Oak Ridge, probably in October 1946. Rickover and the Naval Group had already begun sending detailed reports to the bureau on such technical matters as shielding, reactor materials, and reactor control.[8] For the visitors the group put on its "dog and pony show," an elaborate presentation of their work.

Mumma declared that the reports Rickover was sending to Mills should come to him. Burris was reporting to him on the General Electric work at Schenectady, and the organizational structure called for Rickover to report to him from Oak Ridge. Angrily, Rickover rejected the change. It would, after all, have meant acknowledging Mumma was in charge. Rickover argued that Mills had assigned him to the Army and through the Army he reported to Mills. If Mumma wanted to change the arrangement he would have to go through official channels. What Rickover did next is not clear. He had planned to go to Washington on 20 October.[9] Probably he did so and saw Mills. Nothing seems to have changed; reports continued to flow as they had and Rickover was still not the head of the program.

Not much could be done until Congress decided how the new source of energy, with its tremendous destructive power and its potential uses for peaceful application, should take its place in the nation's social and political fabric. The law President Truman signed on 1 August 1946 created the Atomic Energy Commission, with the responsibility for developing atomic energy for military and peaceful uses. Put in other terms, the Navy had to work with the commission on a nuclear propulsion program. The commission would assume its authority on the first day of January 1947.

As part of its effort to prepare the commission for its new task, the Manhattan Engineer District had to summarize the status of its various programs, among them the naval propulsion program. In November 1946 Nichols asked Rickover to draft the paper. Rickover was at the Bethesda Naval Hospital, outside Washington, being prepared for a hernia operation. Immediately he summoned Roddis from Oak Ridge. The younger man was thoroughly familiar with nuclear technology and the problems of nuclear propulsion. Furthermore, he was the son of a senior naval medical officer and knew from childhood men who now held high rank. The senior Roddis got office space at the hospital while Mills provided secretarial help.

Working as fast as they could, Rickover and Roddis prepared the statement. Assuming availability of skilled and trained personnel, sufficient funds, and proper resources, they thought a shipboard plant might be in operation in five to eight years. The technical problems, however, were immense. The document, "Nuclear Energy Propulsion for Naval Vessels," completed, Rickover was wheeled toward the operating room. Just before disappearing behind the swinging doors, he charged Roddis with the urgent task of getting it into the proper hands, including those of Admiral Nimitz, chief of naval operations.

By going outside channels, Roddis did so. Mills forwarded "A Discussion of the Navy's Interest in Nuclear Energy Applications" on

12 November to Nichols by way of the chief of naval operations, observing that the chief of naval research had also reviewed the paper. Stating that the document was an excellent summary and a reasonable evaluation of the Navy's position, Mills cautioned that it had to be considered as the view of two individuals.[10]

The paper had little impact on the commission. In the last days, hours, and minutes of 1946, it was struggling to get organized. Nuclear propulsion for the Navy was hardly its most urgent problem. The effect on the Navy was far stronger, for by its title the document was stating the Navy position. Furthermore, it was giving the Naval Group and its leader a reputation and status they would not otherwise have had—and it also led to a shouting match in a dining hall where bureau officers told Rickover that he was not in charge of the program and had no business writing the paper and forwarding it directly to Mills and Nimitz.

Much had to be done to bring a joint commission-Navy program to life. Still, toward the end of 1946 one thing had become certain: Rear Adm. Thorvald A. Solberg, a highly regarded officer in the Bureau of Ships, would head the program.[11] He was probably more familiar with the technical aspects of atomic energy than other senior officers. In 1944 he and Mills were members of a special policy committee that considered postwar applications of atomic energy, among them ship propulsion. With the Navy and the commission regarding the head of the joint program as a liaison position, Solberg was an excellent choice.

In Oak Ridge, Rickover was restless and anxious about his future. By continuing to learn the reactor technology and defining, in so far as possible, the engineering problems that had to be faced, he was gaining a reputation as a leading figure in reactor development and in naval nuclear propulsion. But program decisions were made in Washington.

On the other hand, the time in Oak Ridge was still valuable. In April 1947 the Naval Group attended a lecture by Hermann J. Muller of the University of Indiana. A geneticist, Muller had won the Nobel prize in 1946 for his studies of the hereditary effects of X-rays. His audience listened closely, for X-rays were a form of radiation, an inherent part of nuclear fission and reactor operation. Muller spoke well and knew what he was talking about, characteristics that Rickover rarely found and always welcomed.

Muller strengthened Rickover's conviction that no one in the naval program or associated with it should receive more radiation than the civilian authorities established for civilian projects. By meeting civilian standards, the Navy and its contractors would be able to recruit personnel for nuclear-powered ships, shipyards, contractors, and other support facilities on the same basis as industry would employ personnel in civilian nuclear enterprises. In 1947 some officers in the Air Force and the Navy were facing difficult technical problems that might be eased if military personnel received higher radiation levels than civilians. Aircraft nuclear propulsion, for example, might gain feasibility if the weight of shielding was reduced. The increased radiation dosage to personnel would be justified as required by national defense.

Whether Rickover would have a voice on establishing radiation levels was anything but certain. His time and that of the Naval Group at Oak Ridge was drawing to an end. For most of July and August he, Roddis, Dunford, Libbey, and Dick would be crossing the country, visiting one laboratory and installation after another to see what was going on that might be of use to naval propulsion. Perhaps, in the process, they might even drum up support from the individuals they would see, some of whom had been important in the Manhattan Project and had good connections in Washington.

Not knowing what their status would be when they returned, Rickover urged Mills to take advantage of the Naval Group. On 4 June, before they left on their tour, he sent a long memorandum to Mills, now chief of the Bureau of Ships, stating that he saw no evidence that the commission had either the time or the personnel to develop nuclear propulsion. Consequently, the Navy had to be the driving force, and for that purpose the bureau had at its disposal in the Naval Group a cadre of engineers, each an expert in some aspect of reactor technology. By keeping the group together, the bureau could have an effective agent to act with the commission. Mills did not accept the proposal, possibly thinking the time was not right, or possibly thinking the opposition was too strong to give Rickover such a role.

Even though their future was unsettled, the five officers found it good to get away and gain a fresh perspective, one not dominated by Oak Ridge, Schenectady, and Washington. Their itinerary included major facilities such as the AEC's Argonne National Laboratory outside Chicago, the Los Alamos Scientific Laboratory in New Mexico, the Radiation Laboratory at Berkeley, California, and the Brookhaven National Laboratory on Long Island, New York, as well as several industrial facilities.

Having a clear goal in mind, knowing reactor technology, and asking the right questions, the group made an excellent impression. In Berkeley they talked to Glenn T. Seaborg, a brilliant young chemist who had won an outstanding reputation in the wartime program, and was already an influential member in the scientific community. Never had Seaborg encountered "a more enthusiastic, dedicated and persistent individual." He was certain Rickover would prevail over Navy opposition.[12] At Los Alamos the five officers obtained a strong endorsement of their efforts from Edward Teller, already at work on the hydrogen bomb.

The trip bore out Rickover's assessment of the status of nuclear propulsion. Everyone to whom the group talked agreed that a propulsion reactor was feasible but would be expensive. The project would require nuclear engineers, but as yet there were no nuclear engineers. Finally, the group had not met anyone who had been assigned the specific task of developing a propulsion reactor. As Rickover had written Mills, it was up to the Navy to take the initiative.

To get started, Rickover wrote Mills on 20 August, the Navy should send men to the commission laboratories for training and for evaluating the various technical approaches. The Naval Group, he pointed out, had the technical background to take charge. As Mills did not reply, Rickover on 28 August offered a more modest proposal. The group should be assigned part time to the commission and part time to the bureau. In September Mills acted. He broke up the group. Roddis now reported to Mumma; Dunford to the commission's Division of Military Application, which dealt with the design, development, and production of atomic weapons; Libbey to the staff of the military liaison committee, which handled relations between the armed services and the commission; and Dick to the bureau's Research Division. Mills left Rickover dangling.[13]

It was possible to see Mills's position. Rickover's proposals would have upset the organization led by Mumma and have caused controversy in the bureau. Mills might have felt such decisions should be made by Solberg. Gossip swept through the bureau that Rickover would be sent back to Oak Ridge, where he would determine the classification of atomic energy documents. If the rumor was true, it meant the end of his career in nuclear propulsion.

In the event, Mills decided to make Rickover an assistant for nuclear propulsion. He gave Rickover an office: a former ladies' room that had not yet been completely refurbished. Fresh plaster marked where the fixtures had been removed but the tiles still ran halfway up the walls. Rickover was mortified, and he never forgot it. He could take some consolation that

Mills had not cut him off from nuclear propulsion. Rickover could know what was going on, and he could occasionally borrow other members of the group for an assignment.

He visited the major reactor development sites. General Electric at Schenectady was working on its sodium-cooled reactor approach. The company was firmly in control of the effort and there was little Rickover could do. The situation at Oak Ridge was different. Because the Daniels reactor was facing insurmountable technical difficulties, Rickover easily persuaded its engineers to study a water-cooled reactor, a concept proposed by Alvin M. Weinberg, the research director at the laboratory. That the redirection was accomplished so smoothly was a tribute to the reputation Rickover had acquired at Oak Ridge.

Little could be done on nuclear propulsion until the Navy and the commission settled how the joint program would operate. The Navy wanted to develop the sodium-cooled, pressurized-water, and gas-cooled approaches. General Electric was undertaking the first, the Westinghouse Electric Corporation, which, like General Electric, had a long history of providing propulsion equipment to the Navy, would take up the second, and the Allis-Chalmers Manufacturing Company would investigate the third. The AEC, however, was struggling to convert the facilities hurriedly built during the war for the Manhattan District to permanent installations and to expand the production of nuclear weapons as relations with the Soviet Union grew more tense. Furthermore, the commission was finding it hard to get organized. Given these circumstances, it did not consider developing naval nuclear propulsion an urgent matter.

The Navy, however, could take certain necessary administrative steps. Rickover and Dick, with Mills's approval, began the long and tedious bureaucratic process of drafting letters for Nimitz and John L. Sullivan, secretary of the Navy, stating that the Navy required a nuclear-propelled submarine and calling for its prompt development, design, and construction. It should be operational sometime in the mid-1950s.

Writing the letters was not difficult; it was getting them through the naval hierarchy that an impatient Rickover found so frustrating. Each level demanded petty revisions before giving the required endorsements. Rickover and Dick got valuable support from Cdr. Edward L. Beach, a submarine commander during World War II, who had been assigned to the Nuclear Propulsion Section of an office that Nimitz had set up for nuclear matters. In the course of his work Beach frequently visited Oak

Ridge and had gotten to know and assess Rickover and the Naval Group. Impressed by their drive and competence, Beach believed that operation of a nuclear-propelled submarine was not a distant goal. Immediately grasping the possibilities of the program, he became Rickover's contact and advocate in the office of the chief of naval operations and among other submariners. Moreover, the time was right. American submarines had done very well in the Pacific war and German submarines had been a serious threat in the Atlantic. The postwar Navy was considering a number of new missions for submarines and investigating various designs and propulsion systems to give greater speed and submerged endurance.[14]

On 5 December 1947, almost as soon as the letter reached his desk, Nimitz signed it. He himself was a submariner, having commanded submarines and submarine flotillas before World War I. On 8 December Sullivan signed his letter and, that same day, designated the Bureau of Ships as that part of the Navy to work with the commission. With that issue settled, Rickover and Roddis drafted a letter for Mills to send to the commission. Dispatched on 20 January 1948, it proposed that the bureau, acting for the commission, set up an organization to take charge of the program and report to both parent agencies.[15]

The AEC gave the plan a cool reception, but out of several meetings among various committees, the outline of a joint program began to emerge. Under a compromise Solberg drafted, the commission would make a nuclear submarine a formal project and the Navy would be responsible for building the submarine. Rickover was to work out the details.

He delayed. He disliked the arrangement because it lacked the sharp focus needed to develop a propulsion reactor and it left to the commission the task of making the technical decisions. They would, therefore, be made by individuals more inclined to scientific research than to practical engineering. He did want the commission to give formal recognition to submarine nuclear propulsion—that would be an important administrative step forward. The commission, still beset by serious organizational difficulties, saw no reason to hurry.

Rickover saw a chance to force the commission's hand. He, along with Mills and Mumma, were to speak before the annual symposium on undersea warfare. Attended by scientists, engineers, and naval personnel, it would meet in Washington on 12 April 1948. In going over the drafts of the speeches, Rickover realized that it would be far more effective if Mills was the sole speaker for the bureau and if he was the one who presented the

Navy's case for a nuclear submarine. Rickover wrote a fighting speech and in Mills he had the right man to deliver it.

The bureau chief had a fine reputation, was an excellent speaker, and was not afraid to depart from a text. After a brief history of the Navy's interest in nuclear propulsion, Mills launched his blistering attack. Not even 1 percent of the work had been done to design a nuclear submarine, he declared—and that was the AEC's fault. It had not made the submarine reactor an official project; it had not given the effort any priority; it had not established an organization to carry out the program.

It was a rousing speech, but its impact was hard to measure. Rear Adm. Paul F. Lee, of the office of naval research, thought it was important because it gained support for the Navy. Looking back, Rickover considered the influence of the speech could be overemphasized; the commission still showed little interest in a naval propulsion program. At least it had agreed to establish a submarine reactor as a formal project. It did so grudgingly with a statement that was not hard to interpret: the project would have "the high priority commensurate with the importance of this project."[16]

One new element added to the confusion. The commission and the Navy had understood that Solberg would head the joint program. That agreement collapsed on 17 June when the Senate confirmed Solberg to be chief of naval research, a position he would take on 1 July. Under the Atomic Energy Act, he could no longer be part of the atomic energy program. Mills had to find someone else. Facing more signs of commission delay, Mills, after some hesitation, acted. On 16 July 1948, he chose Rickover for the job.

Mills really had no other choice. No officer had a better background than Rickover, had worked harder to understand the technology, and was more widely recognized among those expert in reactor technology. He had certainly proved he could maneuver, scheme, and fight. By title, Rickover was the liaison officer between the Bureau of Ships and the AEC; by dictionary definition, a liaison was a link or a means of communication between two organizations. That was not how he saw his position. He would be in charge. "Every job I ever had," he remarked more than once, "I ran as if I owned it."

He did not own much beyond his title. He knew what he wanted. It was an organization that he—not a contractor—would run. He would set the technical standards and specifications that industry and the Navy would have to follow.

For his system to work he had to have engineers trained in nuclear technology. Soon he had reporting to him Dunford, Roddis, Libbey, and Dick. Others he had to recruit and train. He persuaded some engineers who had been with him in the Electrical Section to join him, among them I. Harry Mandil, Robert Panoff, and G. Wesley Faurot. By mid-February 1949 Rickover had a professional staff of twenty. No matter how badly he needed them, he sent them first to school for advanced training in reactor technology; some went to the Oak Ridge School of Reactor Technology, which he had been instrumental in founding, or to MIT, where he had played a major role in setting the curriculum. Including himself and those who had been with him in Oak Ridge, half of the twenty were naval officers.

The joint organization was taking shape. On 4 August 1948 Mills set up a Nuclear Power Branch under Rickover in the Research Division. Rickover's situation was different in the commission. It was still undergoing the reorganization that had begun in late 1947. Nonetheless, an impatient Rickover could see some signs of progress. In November 1948 the commission approved a plan to establish the Division of Reactor Development in Washington. It proved unexpectedly difficult to recruit a director, but, mainly at the urging of Mills, Lawrence R. Hafstad, executive director of the Research and Development Board in the Department of Defense, accepted the position. Hafstad took up his responsibilities on 1 February 1949.

Rickover received orders on 15 February from the Bureau of Naval Personnel. In the usual Navy phrasing, "on or about 20 February 1949" he would report for duty with the Division of Reactor Development in the Atomic Energy Commission and to the chief of the Bureau of Ships for additional duty.[17] He now had what he wanted—primary duty with the commission and secondary duty with the bureau.

The arrangement was not unusual. In Rickover's case, however, the legend grew that as an official of one agency he could make a request to the other and, as an official of the second agency, approve that request. Put into the jargon of the bureaucracy, he wore "two hats." Reality was more complicated, but he could prepare one agency for an action he was taking in the other, make sure that the actions of the two agencies were consistent, and make decisions affecting both agencies within the scope of his authority. He could also play the Navy and the commission against each other, but it was a tactic he had to use skillfully.

Rickover's organization was soon known as "Naval Reactors." It was housed in T-3, one of a number of temporary buildings run up during

World War II. Located on the Washington Monument grounds near Main Navy, it was, like all the temporaries, a ramshackle structure that was hot and humid in summer and cold and drafty in winter.[18] Rickover had a penchant for unpretentious offices; in this respect T-3 could not be beaten.

Because studies were showing that the gas-cooled approach held the least potential for ship propulsion, Rickover's program consisted of the sodium-cooled and pressurized-water projects. His problem was to get control of them both.

General Electric was in a particularly strong position. As an incentive to operate a major facility to produce material for nuclear weapons, the AEC was building the Knolls Atomic Power Laboratory just outside Schenectady. Owned by the commission but operated by the company, the laboratory had among its activities developing a sodium-cooled civilian power reactor as well as a propulsion reactor. Civilian power was an important commission objective—more important in the eyes of many than submarine propulsion. The basic difficulty Rickover faced was the attitude of the company and laboratory officers. Their view, one Naval Reactors engineer recalled, was "give us the money and we will do the job." Rickover liked and admired many of the company's engineers, but he would make the technical decisions. There was no easy or quick solution to the situation.

Rickover faced different complications in getting control of the pressurized-water project. Westinghouse had already been selected to be the industrial contractor, occupying a position similar to that of General Electric with the sodium-cooled Navy project. As the Knolls laboratory was commission-owned but General Electric–operated, Westinghouse would have Bettis Atomic Power Laboratory, named after a former airport outside of Pittsburgh. It would be commission-owned but Westinghouse-operated. Westinghouse did not have a major contract with the commission and, to gain entry into the promising field of nuclear power, needed a reactor project. Consequently Rickover could lay down stiff terms. He wanted to deal directly with senior officers; he wanted the company to set up a separate division; and he wanted that division manned by the company's best people. All of its assignments would come through Rickover.

Rickover's problem was not so much Westinghouse but Walter H. Zinn, director of the Argonne National Laboratory and perhaps the nation's leading expert on reactor development. The commission had assigned

Zinn the task of deciding when research on the pressurized-water approach was sufficiently advanced that the focus should be on engineering. He made that determination, under pressure from Rickover, on 21 March 1949. Argonne would transfer various areas of pressurized-water technology when Zinn believed Bettis was ready. Rickover found the pace of the transfer of work agonizingly slow. To urge greater speed he frequently went to the laboratory to meet with Zinn. Because both were determined men, the meetings between Rickover and Zinn were usually loud and stormy, Rickover arguing that Bettis was ready to assume more responsibility, Zinn asserting that Bettis had much to learn.

The technical difficulties of developing a propulsion reactor, whether sodium-cooled or pressurized-water, were daunting. Theodore Rockwell, an engineer Rickover had recruited early in the program, remembered that "almost none of the necessary technology was available; it all had to be created by his program. This included the development of fuel materials and construction materials such as zirconium and zircaloy, beryllium, reactor grade uranium oxide, hafnium, and stainless steels. It also involved radiochemistry of liquid metals and of high temperature water, reactor physics, radiation protection and safety, heat transfer, fluid flow and a wide range of basic component and system development. These subjects were all classified in the early 1950s."[19]

One battle Rickover remembered was with the commission over the development and procurement of zirconium for pressurized-water reactors. Zirconium was one of several metals under investigation in the immediate postwar period for use as a reactor structural material. First results were not promising, but at Oak Ridge in December 1947 Rickover learned that if the chemically similar element hafnium was removed, zirconium might meet the requirements for pressurized-water reactors. Then and there he decided to use zirconium for the pressurized-water naval reactor.

At the time he did not know where he would get it, how much he would need, whether there was any known or conceivable process that could produce the required amount, or what specifications for the nuclear, mechanical, or corrosion qualities the metal had to meet. It was also possible that removing the hafnium could destroy the other qualities that had made zirconium worth investigating in the first place. He did know zirconium was not available in large quantities. In 1945 only a few hundred pounds were produced in the United States, and the cost was more than three hundred dollars a pound. Furthermore, the production method yielded metal of uneven quality. He was going to need about thirty thousand pounds of reactor grade zirconium for just one reactor.[20]

Rickover wanted the commission to authorize Bettis to procure zirconium, pointing out that otherwise he could not meet his schedule. The commission would not go that far. The staff argued that Rickover was moving too fast and further research should be carried out on the metal and its methods of production before launching into a major procurement effort. The issue remained unresolved and contentious.

Rickover had some fierce arguments with Hafstad, some over zirconium, others stemming from Rickover's single-minded zeal to reach his goal and Hafstad's responsibilities for the other projects in the division. At times Rickover would return to his office, shaking with anger. Despite their differences, Rickover could not deny that under Hafstad reactor development took on a coherence that had been conspicuously lacking.

Rickover argued that he needed large quantities of zirconium to meet his schedule. On 19 August 1949, Adm. Louis E. Denfeld, who had succeeded Nimitz as chief of naval operations, signed a memorandum giving nuclear propulsion the formal status of a development project in the Navy. Furthermore, the memorandum called for a nuclear propulsion plant ready for operational evaluation and installation in a submarine by 1955. The document, which Rickover helped draft, followed the recommendations of the conference of submarine officers, which had analyzed several potential propulsion systems and found nuclear propulsion the most promising.

The memorandum had little influence on the AEC but gave further recognition to the propulsion program in the Navy. It was very important for another reason: Rickover told a few of his men he was shooting not for 1955 but for 1 January 1955. That was the date he set and that was the one for which he planned and worked. Five years and 134 days from the date of Denfeld's signature, Rickover planned to have a nuclear submarine ready to go to sea. Within that time he would have to resolve all the technical uncertainties; develop the fuel elements, control rods, coolant pumps, and auxiliary systems; and coordinate design, fabrication, and installation of a multitude of components and systems among the laboratory, the equipment manufacturers, and the shipbuilder.

The propulsion program became one of the defense efforts gaining additional momentum on 3 September 1949. On that date Air Force planes flying over the North Pacific Ocean detected signs that the Soviet Union had

detonated its first atomic device. Because it took time to gather and analyze additional evidence as well as to inform congressional leaders and
American allies, President Truman did not issue a public statement until
twenty days later. There was no panic, but it could not be ignored that the
American monopoly in nuclear weapons had been shattered and that the
detonation occurred about two years ahead of most predictions. The president, Congress, the Department of Defense, and the AEC began weighing
the possibility of developing the hydrogen bomb as well as further military applications of atomic energy.

Within the Division of Reactor Development, Rickover argued for making the pressurized-water reactor an Argonne priority, strengthening Bettis, and focussing Knolls on developing a naval sodium-cooled reactor.
Hafstad hesitated. Neither Hafstad nor Zinn was convinced that Bettis
was yet able to take over more of the Argonne work. Zinn had not been
persuaded of the importance of naval nuclear propulsion. The question of
Knolls was even more complicated. In November 1949 the commission set
new priorities for General Electric. They were assisting Hanford, the huge
facility on the banks of the Columbia River in Washington, continuing the
development of the civilian reactor and, in last place, working on the
Navy reactor.[21]

On 31 January 1950, Truman announced that the United States would
develop the hydrogen bomb. On Capitol Hill, the Joint Committee on
Atomic Energy, under the chairmanship of Sen. Brien McMahon of Connecticut, was pushing hard for the new bomb and a huge stockpile of
atomic weapons. The joint committee, established under the Atomic
Energy Act, was a very powerful body. All bills and legislation introduced
in either house of Congress dealing with the commission or atomic energy had to be referred to it. Wanting to know the impact of the massive
hydrogen bomb effort on the commission's other activities, the committee's subcommittee on reactor development, consisting of Congressmen
Carl T. Durham, Melvin Price, Henry M. Jackson, and Carl Hinshaw,
called for a hearing on the Navy program.

At 10:00 A.M. on 9 February 1950, Rickover, as sole witness, described
the program to a small but intensely interested audience. He declared that
the Soviets were making huge strides in atomic energy and without doubt
knew that nuclear submarines could inflict heavy damage on the United
States and its allies. Consequently, the Navy needed two nuclear submarines to prepare countermeasures. Maybe more time would allow better design and construction, but he thought it was unwise to wait.

If the Navy got funds for the two ships, the committee asked, would it take skilled manpower from other important atomic energy projects needed for defense?

"In this game," Rickover replied, "you must create your own talent."

Jackson wanted to know if Rickover could move faster—if he could have a nuclear submarine in 1954.

"If you got a higher-powered guy than myself in there you could probably do it," Rickover replied.

"It seems like you are doing a real job," Jackson declared.[22]

Rickover had made an excellent impression on the joint committee members. He, in turn, had become convinced that the committee was important, that it was under strong leadership, and that its members took their responsibilities seriously.

Rickover saw progress in two other areas that had been stubborn problems. One was zirconium; the other was priorities for Knolls. In March 1950 he had again asked the AEC to let him deal directly with zirconium producers. Again he faced arguments that he was too eager, that further research and development could give less expensive and better production methods. In August, however, he won the authority he sought. As for Knolls, on 17 March the commission decided that the laboratory should not go ahead with the sodium-cooled civilian reactor project. For some time reports coming out of the laboratory were showing that the nuclear data no longer looked promising. Negotiations among the commission, General Electric, and the Bureau of Ships ended on 12 April 1950 with agreement that the laboratory would split its effort between supporting Hanford and developing a sodium-cooled naval reactor prototype. At last Rickover had two technical approaches to naval propulsion.

He already had a shipbuilder. The history of American submarine construction suggested a pattern. For years Westinghouse had provided propulsion equipment for submarines built at the Navy's shipyard at Portsmouth, New Hampshire, while General Electric had furnished propulsion equipment for submarines built by Electric Boat, the private yard located at Groton, Connecticut.

On 6 December 1949, Rickover talked with O. Pomeroy Robinson, general manager of Electric Boat. During World War II the yard had built up its production to the point where it launched a submarine every two weeks. But now the shops were idle, the building ways silent, and the future bleak. Robinson welcomed the prospect of working with Rickover and General Electric.

On 12 January 1950, Rickover, Dunford, and Roddis, along with Charles H. Weaver, the general manager of Bettis, were at Portsmouth to explore the possibility of Westinghouse and the yard pairing up. Capt. Ralph E. McShane, the yard commander, and his staff listened to Rickover explain that at this stage Portsmouth participation would hardly be demanding or extensive. McShane was inclined to participate and so were his senior staff. But one key officer, perhaps influenced by Rickover's reputation for taking over a job, strongly demurred, arguing that Portsmouth was too busy modernizing World War II submarines. McShane accepted his advice.

Promptly Rickover reached across McShane's desk and telephoned Robinson, asking him if he was willing to build a second nuclear submarine. Robinson was. The Rickover group left at once for Groton. During the drive down Dunford more than once questioned the wisdom of placing both ships at one yard. Rickover brushed the argument aside. That evening Robinson's home saw an informal agreement. Official negotiations would follow, but Robinson had committed Electric Boat for both ships.

Later Rickover was to castigate Portsmouth for failing to grasp the opportunity he had offered. The quickness with which he called Robinson, however, and the speed with which he made an agreement for the two submarines, could be interpreted as welcoming the turndown and wanting to give McShane no second chance. Electric Boat was, after all, a private yard and hungry for work. As Electric Boat's only major customer, Rickover could enforce his demands.

If a nuclear submarine was to be operating in 1955, it had to be in the Navy's 1952 construction program, which had to be submitted to Congress in 1950 for authorization and appropriation of funds. Putting the ship into the program required the approval of the chief of naval operations and the secretary of the Navy. They, in turn, depended upon the recommendations of the ship characteristics board, which reported to the office of the chief of naval operations, and the general board, which advised the secretary of the Navy on such matters.

Rickover appeared before the general board on 28 March. He warned that the Navy had to go ahead. The commission had given the project a high priority. If now the Navy said, "We are sorry, we don't have the submarine to put it in," the commission would turn its attention and resources elsewhere. Never again, he declared, would the Navy be in so strong a position with the commission.

Some skirmishing occurred over whether the first nuclear submarine would be a test vehicle or a combatant ship. Rickover was convinced that the Navy would never recognize the revolutionary impact of nuclear propulsion unless it was powering a submarine that could operate as a unit of the fleet. That position, too, he won.[23]

The 1952 construction program contained a nuclear-powered submarine as the fourth in a list of twenty-six ships. Congress passed the legislation, which Truman signed on 8 August 1950.

By mid-1950 Rickover had made tremendous strides in getting control of the program and in attacking the technical problems. By the end of that year he had recruited thirty-seven professional personnel. Seven of these had left the program in 1950 or earlier; of the remaining thirty, fifteen were officers and fifteen were civilians. Of the fifteen officers, twelve were Naval Academy graduates.[24]

Circumstances were to draw some more than others into prominent roles in the program. Dunford, Roddis, Dick, and Libbey (who left in 1950) were in the program from its beginning. John W. Crawford Jr. and Edwin E. Kintner, both academy graduates, joined in 1950. As for the civilians, I. Harry Mandil and Theodore Rockwell entered the program in 1949, Robert Panoff and Milton Shaw in 1950.

It was possible to say by mid-1950 that the naval nuclear propulsion program had taken shape. Rickover had a place in both the Bureau of Ships and the AEC. He had two laboratories, two technical approaches, a shipyard, and a ship in the construction program. He had also won the respect of the Joint Committee on Atomic Energy. Although accomplishing much he had far to go. Some technical problems he could clearly see, others were taking shape, and some had not yet emerged. No energy from the atom had yet been generated in the amount and with the reliability needed to propel a submarine.

The Soviet Union detonated its first atomic device in 1949, and its communist satellite, North Korea, launched an attack on South Korean and American forces in the summer of the following year. In a dangerous world, the development and application of naval nuclear propulsion was part of the American response to the Soviet threat—it would become and remain an important weapon in the arsenal with which the nation fought the cold war.

Promotion

BY MID-1950 Rickover's driving pace had brought the naval nuclear propulsion program to a new stage. On 1 July 1950 the Atomic Energy Commission authorized Westinghouse to construct the pressurized-water reactor prototype, called the Mark I, at the commission's national reactor testing station in Idaho. The prototype was a vital element in Rickover's goal of getting the *Nautilus,* the first nuclear-powered submarine, to sea by 1 January 1955. Before that event, he expected to be selected for promotion to rear admiral, and perhaps become assistant chief of the Bureau of Ships.

Probably few things epitomized Rickover's engineering genius more than his concept of a land prototype. He would not use an older procedure in which plant components were spread out so that they could be operated and modified if necessary. The Idaho prototype would consist of an operating reactor and its steam plant in spaces that were the same as those in the ship. By the prototype Rickover would save time and exert engineering discipline by demanding early decisions that were fundamental and were based on long-range forethought. Furthermore, improvements in the Mark I could be factored into the Mark II, the *Nautilus* plant.

It was a risky strategy. Not all development had been completed, not every technical problem had been solved, and the ship for the propulsion system was not yet under construction. It also laid heavy demands upon Rickover: he "owned the job."[1]

On the Idaho desert floor, now scarred with machinery tracks, and against a background of stark mountains, men from several contractors, including Westinghouse and Electric Boat, along with naval officers and enlisted men, found themselves working side by side, rushing to get as much done as possible on the Mark I site before the bitter winter closed in.

Rickover would be considered for promotion to rear admiral in July 1951, and, if failing that year, in July 1952. An officer came up for promotion in two consecutive years. Under the provisions of the Naval Personnel Act of 1916 and the Officer Personnel Act of 1947, failure both times meant he could serve a year longer but then had to retire.

He did not expect to fail in 1951. He was, after all, in charge of a major program. Nevertheless, he knew he had enemies in the bureau. "Of course, you don't expect to make admiral," he remembered one bureau chief casually remarking. "Jesus, I was so God-damned mad," Rickover recalled. To make the transition to a new leader as smooth as possible, he hand-picked his successor. He was Capt. Robert L. Moore, who had been his deputy in the Electrical Section, where they had gotten along well. In June 1950 Rickover sent Moore to the Massachusetts Institute of Technology to audit a course in nuclear physics. Rickover also arranged for Moore to visit several installations taking part in the program.

Only so many officers in each grade could be advanced each year. A board of nine officers, assigned to it for temporary duty, reviewed the records of officers eligible for promotion. Members on the board were of higher grade than those they evaluated. The composition of the board changed when engineering duty officers were considered. Then three engineering duty officers, replacing three line officers, selected the engineers for promotion. At least two of the three had to vote for the selection. Because the board met behind closed doors and kept no records, it was impossible to know why some officers were selected and others were not.[2] On 11 July 1951 the Navy announced the promotion of thirty-two captains to rear admiral. Rickover was not one of them.[3] He decided to stay on for one more year and for his last chance to be selected.

Devastated and bitter, Rickover continued to meet his commitments, one of which was a classified lecture to submarine officers at New London. Rear Adm. Stuart S. Murray, commander of the Atlantic submarine force, was present. While serving in the S-48 Rickover had met Murray, who was commanding the S-44. Of more immediate importance, Murray had been on the selection board that had passed over Rickover. When the two were alone Rickover asked why he had not been selected. Murray replied that he was not a member of the board when it considered engineers and therefore did not know. Furthermore, Rickover should be aware of one thing: he could not get along with people. In the just-finished lecture, Murray pointed out, Rickover had angered his audience by talking down to them and calling them stupid. After a moment's silence Rickover stood up. "Thank you very much, I'm going back to Washington."[4]

Moore returned to Naval Reactors in September 1951. While away from Washington, he had spoken incautiously on how he would change things when he took over. Inevitably such comments got back to Rickover and to Rickover's senior engineers, who realized that Rickover's engineering philosophy and his methods, if not his style, were the only way to run the program. Moore no longer had a place in the section. Rickover gave him nothing to do and made no effort to prepare him to take charge.[5] Moore was to leave and go on to a successful career in which he would become a rear admiral and an assistant chief of the Bureau of Ships. An animosity, eventually to become legendary, sprang up between the two men.

The failure of the Navy to promote Rickover occurred at a time when the nuclear propulsion program was gaining public and congressional recognition. In August 1951 the Navy announced that it was letting a contract to build a nuclear-powered submarine. Clay Blair Jr., a *Time-Life* correspondent, promptly began gathering material for a story. Young (only twenty-five), ambitious, and imaginative, he had been an enlisted man in a submarine and had made two war patrols. He was fascinated by the idea of an atomic submarine and by the officer in charge of the program.

Blair's stories appeared in both magazines on 3 September 1951. *Life* illustrated its article with an artist's rendering of a nuclear submarine, a photograph of Rickover in civilian clothes, and an aerial view of Electric Boat. The story followed a "slim, sparrow-faced Navy Captain" from Washington's Union Station to Groton, where, the account continued, behind closed doors officers and civilians scrutinized blueprints. Blair wrote that Rickover thought Navy officers were more interested in "catching their breath from the last war than preparing for a new one" and that he "had declared war on naval indifference." In Blair's mind there was no doubt who was the hero and who were the villains of the propulsion program.

Rickover stood high in the opinion of the Joint Committee on Atomic Energy. On 18 September its chairman, Brien McMahon, spoke in the Senate urging even further expansion of the military uses of atomic energy. He called for the views of the armed services. Dan A. Kimball, secretary of the Navy, testified on 27 September. The committee welcomed his remarks on Rickover. "This fellow Rickover is a tremendous fellow," declared McMahon. Congressman Melvin Price of the committee agreed: "It is tremendous that we had some one like that because he was interested in it and he pushed it himself and he did a lot of pushing." McMahon summed it up: "He stepped on a lot of toes over there and I think he has made some enemies but I think he is a tremendous little guy."[6]

President Truman, who followed atomic energy matters closely, wanted a briefing. On 9 February 1952 Rickover appeared at the White House with a cutaway model of a nuclear submarine and a small bar of zirconium. The man who had ordered the bombing of Hiroshima and Nagasaki at last could see evidence that atomic energy was being developed to power machinery. Responding to the relaxed and informal atmosphere, Rickover pointed out that the value of the zirconium he had brought with him was enough to pay off the debts of the Democratic Party. The session over, Truman walked Rickover to the door of the oval office. It was an election year and the press was filled with speculation about Truman's intentions: would he run for a second term?

"Mr. President," Rickover said, "the reporters outside are going to ask me if you are going to run again."

Truman grinned and answered briskly, "Tell them you don't know."

The meeting had gone so well that Rickover thought Truman might be persuaded to speak at the keel laying of the *Nautilus*. Because he could hardly approach the president directly, Rickover turned to McMahon. The senator willingly asked Truman to preside. He accepted, and Flag Day, 14 June 1952, was scheduled for the event.

A few days before the keel laying, Robert Panoff and Ray Dick went to Electric Boat. They discovered that Rickover was not included in the list of guests to be seated in the stands for dignitaries. Outraged, Panoff and Dick protested to Navy officers assigned to the yard. Finding they refused to get involved, the two engineers strode into the offices of Electric Boat. Company officials shrugged off the matter, claiming it was for the Navy to decide. Vehemently the two engineers argued that Electric Boat was the host. On 8 June Rickover got a telegram from O. Pomeroy Robinson, general manager of Electric Boat, cordially inviting Rickover and his wife to attend the keel laying and the luncheon that would follow. The invitation was addressed to Rickover as chief of the Naval Reactors branch of the Atomic Energy Commission, not as the naval officer heading the Nuclear Power Division in the Bureau of Ships.[7]

By noon on a warm and sunny 14 June, more than ten thousand people had gathered in the south yard of Electric Boat. Several individuals stood on the platform at the head of the building ways: senior officials from the host company, Westinghouse, Bettis, and General Electric, as well as

Chairman Gordon E. Dean, the most prominent figure from the AEC. The Navy was well represented by Kimball and several flag officers. Rickover (in civilian clothes), was also on the platform. Ruth and their son Robert were nearby in the audience.

Kimball addressed the crowd, telling it that nuclear power was "the greatest advance in propulsion since the Navy shifted from sail to steam." Dean declared that many people had played a role, but if one person were to be singled out, "such an honor should go to Captain H. G. Rickover."

Truman spoke of the "wonderful thing" that had been accomplished, and said that he prayed the day would never come when the atomic bomb would have to be used again and that the *Nautilus* would never have an enemy to fight. At his signal a crane picked up a bright yellow curved plate that was a part of the hull and placed it on the building ways. The president walked down to the plate and chalked his initials on it. A welder came forward and burned them into the plate. Truman stepped back: "I declare this keel well and truly laid."

At the luncheon at the officers club a relaxed Truman, obviously enjoying himself, said that "this will be what you might call a milestone today in the historical setup of the discovery of the breaking of the atom and using it for energy for peaceful purposes."[8]

Possibly during the ceremony Rickover had given thought to another issue. The Navy had announced on 3 June that it was convening a selection board that would meet on 8 July to recommend captains for promotion to rear admiral. Rickover underlined one sentence in the announcement: "Each eligible officer and reporting senior should insure fitness reports covering regular reporting periods are submitted promptly." Believing his official files were incomplete, on 2 July he submitted additional information dealing with his work in the Electrical Section.[9]

On 7 July Rickover got a telephone call asking him to report to Kimball's office. As Rickover recalled, he did not know why he had been summoned but, just in case, snatched up an exceedingly simplified model of a nuclear-powered submarine with a section cut away to show the propulsion plant. He was ushered into a room crowded with civilian officials and photographers but not, he noticed, with many officers. When silence fell, Kimball announced that on behalf of the president he was presenting Rickover with a gold star in place of a second Legion of Merit. The accompanying citation praised Rickover for having "held tenaciously to a single important goal through discouraging frustration and opposition" and for advancing the Mark I and the keel laying of the first nuclear-powered ship well ahead of schedule. The photographers snapped pictures of Kimball and Rickover leaning over the model.[10]

The next day the selection board met. On 19 July the Navy announced the names of those selected for rear admiral. The list contained thirty names, four of which were engineer officers. Rickover was not one of them.[11]

Nothing more could be done. He could serve until he had completed thirty-one years of active duty. Because he graduated from the Naval Academy in 1922, his final year would end in mid-1953. The Navy's partner in the program, the AEC, was deeply concerned about Rickover's promotion. The commission had spoken up for him in 1951 and even more strongly in 1952. Dean had praised Rickover by name at the *Nautilus* keel laying; Lawrence R. Hafstad, director of reactor development, had written to Vice Adm. Lawrence T. DuBose, chief of naval personnel, that the Navy was to be congratulated on having a man of Rickover's caliber in charge of the program. "It seems to me that such an outstanding record cannot fail to be recognized by the Navy awarding Captain Rickover due recognition in the form of a promotion to the rank of Admiral," he declared. Hafstad felt that it was technically unwise as well as unjust to Rickover to remove him from the program at a time when it was moving ahead so fast.[12]

Hafstad was worried. There was no conceivable way in which a new man could take over without disrupting the program. In addition, there was the strong possibility that the engineers Rickover had so carefully gathered and trained would go elsewhere. Hafstad considered having Rickover become a civilian in charge of the commission's part of the joint program. If nothing else, the scheme was a measure of the straits to which Hafstad was reduced: it must have been extraordinarily difficult to think of Rickover as a commission official working with the officer who would be in charge of the Navy's part of the effort.[13]

Still, the law was the law. Ray Dick thought there had to be a way out. Ill and troubled, he turned to Blair. On 4 August 1952, *Time* magazine carried a story headed "Brazen Prejudice," which hinted at anti-Semitism but also charged that the Navy was unwilling to accept technical specialists, an attitude that "promises to cost it a brilliant officer who developed the most important new weapon since World War II."[14]

Rep. Carl T. Durham of North Carolina, who had succeeded McMahon as chairman of the joint committee, was disturbed by the decision not to promote an officer whom the committee had praised so highly. He wrote to Kimball on 16 December that he did not look forward to the day when a nuclear submarine was operating and he would have to explain why the man who had been responsible for its success had been passed over. "It may be that the Navy has someone else who could carry on the job just as effectively," he remarked. "If so I do not know him."[15]

Kimball, too, was troubled. On 15 January 1953, just a few days from the end of the Truman administration, he held a press conference. He was certain that the United States would have an atomic-powered fleet. He wanted to see Rickover promoted but would not interfere with the selection process. "The system calls for officers to be judged by fellow officers who know them, and I am against any change in that," he said.[16]

Rickover was exerting every effort to reach his goal of getting nuclear-propelled ships to sea. He went to Bettis, to the Mark I, to Knolls, and to West Milton, a small town outside Schenectady where General Electric was constructing the Mark A, the land prototype for the sodium-cooled propulsion system. In all the urgency he refused to compromise technical standards, specifications, and engineering practices. If anything had to give way, it was in the lives of those people who worked for him and their families.

One officer found himself ordered to Idaho the day before he was to be the best man at a friend's wedding. Rickover called back Paul E. Dignan and John F. O'Grady, who had served with him on Okinawa. A former enlisted man, Dignan was about to reach the summit of his career—command of a ship. "Only Rickover would do this to me," he said. O'Grady, in the midst of a prosperous business career, refused to return. Knowing O'Grady was deeply devoted to his mother, Rickover persuaded her that her son could do an important job for the country. Dignan went to Bettis; O'Grady went to Washington. They served as expediters, tracking down shipments from contractors that had gone astray or were lost. The pace was terrific. O'Grady remembered time after time returning to T-3 building, taking a "handkerchief shower" in the men's room, and then charging out again on a new mission.

In early 1953 the pressurized-water approach, on which the Mark I and the Mark II were based, fell into serious trouble. To make sure that the zirconium-clad fuel elements and stainless steel piping would keep their integrity while in prolonged contact with hot, flowing radioactive cooling water, Rickover had sent test samples to the research reactor at Chalk River, Ontario, Canada. It was the only facility available that could provide the necessary nuclear environment. The elements were placed in a loop of piping that passed through the reactor core.

As time went by, instruments revealed that the amount of water flowing through the pipe was dropping. Clearly, deposits were building up and blocking the flow. At the end of several months the elements were moved to a pool of deep water. Even as observers watched, the water near the elements turned cloudy. Investigation revealed that the elements had not corroded—it was the piping, the type of piping that was being installed in the Mark I and Mark II.

Rickover thought that the pressurized-water approach was finished. (The deposits, inelegantly called "crud," could block heat transfer and lead to temperatures that could melt the reactor core.) He sought facts, raised questions, and consulted authorities and launched an investigation. Work continued at its usual high pace at Bettis and in Idaho. To his intense relief, data from the research efforts soon provided the solution: it was largely one of adjusting chemicals in the cooling water.[17]

In January 1953 a new administration took office. The election of Dwight D. Eisenhower ushered in a Republican president and a Republican Congress. One consequence, apparently insignificant, was that the promotions recommended by the selection board in 1952 had not been completed.

After a selection board finished its work, it sent its selections to the secretary of the Navy, who sent them to the president for approval. The president then sent the list to the Senate for confirmation. In practice the Senate's Committee on Armed Services sent the list to the Senate floor and recommended approval. The process had become cut and dried, and only rarely had it been challenged. The Senate committee, however, had not yet confirmed the promotions that the outgoing Democratic administration had approved. Presumably as a matter of courtesy, the committee had sent them back to the White House. The action did not change Rickover's status; it simply meant the promotion process had not been completed for those who had been approved.[18]

Early in 1953 a few individuals in Rickover's own organization determined to rescue him. How, they did not know. The chronology of their actions and the effect of their efforts is impossible to determine. Efforts to overcome his first failure to be selected had failed, and there was no reason to think a new attempt would be different.

Panoff, I. Harry Mandil, and Theodore Rockwell—all civilians—took the initiative. Panoff had the idea of contacting Rep. Sydney Yates, who represented the district in Chicago where Rickover had grown up and where his family still lived. Rockwell telephoned Yates's office and asked for an appointment. They got one for two o'clock that afternoon. To Rockwell it all smacked of the Jimmy Stewart–Jean Arthur movie, *Mr. Smith Goes to Washington,* in which a young man with no experience but armed with idealism triumphantly fights for justice.

A Democrat elected in 1948, Yates had succeeded Adolph J. Sabath, the congressman who had nominated Rickover to the Naval Academy thirty years earlier. (Yates was still in Congress when Rickover left the program in 1982.) Yates explained he could do little: the Senate Armed Services Committee was the place for them to go. He set up an appointment with Henry M. Jackson, recently elected from the House to the Senate, who was also a member of the Joint Committee on Atomic Energy. Jackson was an admirable choice. Highly intelligent and greatly interested in defense, he knew and was deeply impressed with Rickover. Jackson discussed strategy with his visitors. He arranged for them to talk with other members of the Armed Services Committee.

In the following days, Mandil, Panoff, and Rockwell saw several members of the committee. Rickover knew what the three of them were doing, but not in detail. They thought Rickover should not be seen as taking part in their efforts, for it was politically dangerous for him, an officer on active duty, to lobby for himself. Furthermore, he was toying with the idea of staying on as a member of the commission staff; becoming too deeply involved with Congress could ruin that chance. For her part, Ruth Rickover, a trained legal scholar, did research in the Library of Congress on laws, regulations, and procedures governing promotion.

If talks with members of the Armed Services Committee drew various responses, at least none was hostile to Rickover. Three were particularly important. James H. Duff, former governor of Pennsylvania and a power in the Republican Party, wanted facts. Estes Kefauver, a Democrat from Tennessee who had presidential ambitions, was interested in the matter. Committee chairman Leverett Saltonstall, former governor of Massachusetts and also an important figure in the Republican Party, recognized that there was an issue, but, he said, the committee's schedule was heavy. Besides, how could he justify taking up the cause of one Navy captain to his constituents? That point bothered Rockwell.

Rockwell was convinced that the press was the best way to reach the public. None of the three engineers knew any newspaper reporters. Rockwell remembered that, while at Oak Ridge, he had met Michael Amrine, formerly managing editor of the periodical *Bulletin of Atomic Scientists* but now a newspaper reporter. Having no idea of where Amrine was, Rockwell called the National Press Club, hoping at least for an address. By good fortune Amrine happened to be strolling by the phone and answered the shout of the man who had taken the call.

Getting the story Rockwell wanted was not easy. With the approval of the AEC and the Navy, Rickover gave Amrine an interview. But it took time and effort to get the two organizations to clear the story. Finally it appeared in three installments in the first week in February under the title "Intraservice Row May Imperil Immediate Future of America's First Atomic Powered Submarine." The story attracted attention and, best of all from Rockwell's point of view, was picked up by Massachusetts newspapers. Now he had something to show Saltonstall.[19]

Yates had swung into action. On 22 January 1953 he asked permission of the House to speak for one minute and extend his remarks in the *Congressional Record*. In its pages he declared that, in the age of the atom, service politics should not dictate discarding a man whose knowledge was essential to the nation's well-being. Pointing out that Rickover had been praised by the secretary of the Navy on one day and rejected by the Navy on the next, Yates suggested that the Senate Committee on Armed Services investigate.[20]

In the House on 12 February Yates opened fire. Waste in military procurement was bad enough, but what about the appalling waste of men of ability "in which the admirals disposed of a naval officer who would not conform, an officer who is perhaps the Navy's outstanding specialist in the field of atomic energy." Yates proposed to reform the promotion system. First, engineer officers eligible for promotion should be considered by a board consisting of three line officers, three engineering duty officers, and three civilians selected by the president from outstanding engineers and scientists. Second, appoint as chairman of the board an assistant secretary of the Navy. Third, keep a stenographic record of the proceedings to be forwarded, with minority views, if any, to the secretary of the Navy, the secretary of defense, the president of the United States, and the chairman of the Senate Committee on Armed Services. Finally, the two secretaries and the president could reject the finding of the selection board in whole or in part and reconvene the board.[21]

His proposals were so radical that they had little chance of acceptance, but Yates had done something else: he had written Saltonstall suggesting that the Senate committee withhold confirming the board's July 1952 selections.[22] That proposal was a powerful threat, and it could not be ignored because Yates had gotten the publicity he wanted. On 13 February the *Washington Post* headed its story "Refusal to Promote Rickover Assailed," the *Washington Times-Herald* reported "Yates Blasts Navy Again on Capt. Rickover," the *New York Times* declared "Navy Rules Scored in High Promotions," the *Boston Herald* announced "Forced Retirement of Expert on Atomic Subs Held 'Shocking,'" and the *Daily World* in far-off Tulsa, Oklahoma, under the heading "Naval Scientist's Retirement Brings Charges of 'Waste,'" quoted a Yates press release stating that because of the secrecy surrounding the selection process, "Only God and the nine admirals on the board" knew why Rickover had been rejected. The widely read Bob Considine began his 17 February column, "The Navy's upper brass has never looked worse than during its deplorable treatment of Capt. H. G. Rickover."[23]

On 18 February Yates announced to the House that he had received a letter from Saltonstall: the committee would consider the Rickover case.[24] Late in the morning of Thursday, the twenty-sixth, Saltonstall opened the committee meeting. The number of nominations from all services for officers of all grades came to 5,887. All were routine. The committee quickly approved all nominations except for Navy captains to rear admirals. It could not act on these because doing so would fill all vacancies and hence be a decision against Rickover. The newspaper coverage had been effective. W. Stuart Symington had received quite a lot of mail on "a Captain Rickover. I do not know him. I have been impressed by some of the things that have been written to me." Kefauver announced that he, too, had gotten plenty of mail on Rickover. The committee decided to hold up confirmation of thirty-nine captains to rear admiral while it investigated the Navy's promotion system. Hearings would begin on 3 March.[25]

Mandil, Panoff, Rockwell, and Yates agreed one more speech was necessary, a speech that would describe how Rickover worked, the commission-Navy organization, and the nuclear propulsion program philosophy. Working day and night, Panoff drew the material together. On 2 March Yates was recognized before the House for ninety minutes. In one part of his speech, he offered a superb summary of Rickover's personal role in the nuclear program:

> Training, scope of program, time scale—these are functions that could come out of any administration. But people in the program say this was only a small part of Rickover's operations. He traveled frequently, often times spending every day in his office and every night in some plant away from Washington. He

was not content with reading reports, or receiving glowing accounts of progress from company officials. He went out into the plants, watched equipment on test, picked out design soft spots and continually brought his naval engineering experience to bear on equipment designs. Where he saw danger in depending on one source of supply, he pushed parallel efforts. He was never satisfied with satisfactory performance. He was always seeking excellence. He would personally check to satisfy himself that the equipment could be maintained by sailors and did not require doctors of philosophy to nurse it. The design and performance standards were Rickover's. His influence was felt right down to the drawing boards where people were working on pumps, boilers, control equipment and other items too numerous to mention.[26]

The committee met in executive session at 4:00 P.M. on 3 March to hear Rear Adm. Homer N. Wallin, chief of the Bureau of Ships. (Rickover had earlier been to see Wallin, warning him that he could be getting into trouble.)[27] The committee was ready. The Naval Reactors men had met with different members several times, briefing them on how to get behind superficial replies that might be offered to their questions. Mandil, Panoff, and Rockwell were helped by having a copy of Wallin's statement, slipped to them from Wallin's office.

Wallin took the position that there was no issue. The selection board had already decided that Rickover should be retired. That being so, all Wallin wanted to do was to assure the committee that the Navy had officers who were qualified to lead the program. From its beginning, he went on, the effort had moved rapidly with many people and organizations taking part. Certainly Rickover deserved great credit but his role was principally that of project manager and expeditor. The heart of Wallin's statement was that "the nuclear power billet in the Bureau of Ships is presently a Captain's billet, and we now have on hand a number of Engineering Duty Captains who are well qualified to assume this post."[28] The Navy was willing to invite Rickover to submit a request to continue to serve on active duty after his retirement. That, Yates thought, was like pushing Rickover out the front door and pulling him in at the back door.

Yates and Jackson were to testify before the committee on 5 March. On the preceding day Jackson called Rickover. Although the context of the conversation is not completely clear, Jackson apparently asked Rickover to meet with some members of the committee. Rickover drew back. "I stated I did not think this was the thing to do as I could not get up there and put this thing on an 'I,' 'I,' 'I,' basis."[29]

Jackson, as a member of the Armed Services Committee as well as the Joint Committee on Atomic Energy, was an extremely effective witness. On 5 March he declared that the program was on the threshold of realizing its objectives, "and I am sure that it is the drive, the energy and leadership of Captain Rickover that has put us there." He continued, "If Captain Rickover hadn't stuck his neck out, we wouldn't have this program, and I can cite chapter and verse over a long, long period of time in that connection."

Wallin had declared the nuclear power billet in the Bureau of Ships was a captain's billet, but Vice Adm. James L. Holloway Jr., who had succeeded DuBose as chief of naval personnel, made an important comment at the 5 March session: there was no statutory reason why the program could not be headed by an admiral instead of a captain. That observation opened a way out: Rickover could be promoted to rear admiral *and* remain in charge of naval nuclear propulsion.[30] Furthermore, the selection process would be preserved.

A letter from Robert B. Anderson, secretary of the Navy, to Saltonstall on 6 March followed through on the idea. Nothing, of course, could change the fact that Rickover had been passed over and would have to retire in June 1953. The secretary, however, would convene a new board to recommend retaining engineering duty captains for one year. He would cast the precept of the board so that it would have to select an officer who was experienced and qualified for atomic propulsion of ships. Selection by the board (and under the precept they could not select anyone else) would carry Rickover past his scheduled retirement date of 30 June 1953. He would then be eligible to be considered by a board meeting in July of that year, which would be required to select an engineering duty captain experienced and qualified in nuclear propulsion to the grade of rear admiral.[31]

On 10 March the Navy announced a board would consider engineer officers for retention. A week later the Navy stated that Rickover and five other captains would be retained for one year. He would be considered for promotion in July 1953. At last his future looked secure. In fact, it looked better than it had in 1951, when promotion would have removed him from the propulsion program.

At the end of March, Rickover was at the Mark I, which was to reach criticality, the stage at which a self-sustained chain reaction was achieved. Criticality was not to generate power (less than one-hundredth of a horsepower would be reached) but to provide data that would verify theory, calculations, and experiments that would indicate that the reactor would operate as planned, at least from the reactor physics standpoint. It took time to check procedures and instrumentation, but at 11:17 P.M. on 30 March 1953, the Mark I reached criticality.

But only operation at high power could prove whether the Mark I could produce energy at the levels, reliability, and duration for ship propulsion. As the reactor underwent low-power tests, physicists gathered their data, engineers checked and rechecked plant components and tested them over and over again, and operating crews practiced and repracticed procedures. For safety considerations, early plans had called for starting up the Mark I from over a mile away. Rickover vetoed the idea because it was too complicated; he also rejected a plan to begin operation from a balcony overlooking the hull. He decided the Mark I should be started up from inside the hull. Special circuits, however, had been installed so the plant could be shut down in a fraction of a second.

On 31 May Rickover was at the Mark I. He had brought with him an unexpected visitor from the Atomic Energy Commission, Thomas E. Murray, whom Truman had appointed commissioner in 1950. The first professional engineer to hold that office and strongly interested in defense and in developing atomic energy for civilian use, Murray became Rickover's ally. Rickover told Cdr. Edwin E. Kintner, his representative at the site, that Murray would have the honor of turning the valve that would release to the turbine the first large amount of steam ever generated by atomic energy.

Kintner argued strongly against the idea. For endless days and nights he had watched and taken part in the detailed preparations of equipment, men, and machinery for the first power run. No one could tell how the Mark I would react as it began to feed steam to the turbine. It was not the time, Kintner asserted, for a man unfamiliar with the plant to turn the valve. Rickover would not budge.

Rickover, Murray, Kintner, and a few others climbed into the hull that housed the Mark I and made their way to the maneuvering room, the designation of that small space from which the propulsion plant was controlled. Kintner stationed himself directly behind Murray, ready to intervene immediately. All eyes focussed on the dials and gauges as the power was slowly increased. The failure of an emergency circuit shut down the reactor, and again came the laborious and painstaking process of bringing the Mark I back into operation. At the proper moment, Murray carefully turned the valve. The whining sound of the accelerating turbine filled the building.[32]

When the Mark I was operating at several thousand horsepower, Rickover and Murray climbed out of the hull, descended to the floor, and walked aft. A red-and-white candy-striped propeller shaft ran from the hull to a load absorber, a large boxlike structure containing the mechanism that took up the power. In silence the two men watched the shaft rotate.

Rickover was awed. He could see before him the result of so many efforts: the fruition of daring and courageous decisions, the search for materials that would withstand radiation and a corrosive environment, the establishment of production lines to provide materials never before needed on such scale, and the development of components that had to operate reliably in unprecedented conditions. He could also see the results of countless debates and disputes that forced technical decisions by his own organization, the laboratories, and the contractors. He would never again find anything to equal the exhilaration of that moment.

The Mark I was not the first reactor to produce power; that honor belonged to Walter H. Zinn's experimental breeder reactor, which, on 20 December 1951 at the national reactor testing station, produced 410 kilowatts of energy from the atom. The Mark I, however, was the first to generate substantial amounts of power.

Another important test remained—that of bringing the Mark I up to full power and operating at that level for some length of time. On 25 June 1953 Rickover was again at the site. He had authorized a forty-eight-hour power run, enough time to get technical data. After only twenty-four hours the engineers had the measurements they needed and were ready to end the run. Rickover ordered operation to continue. After forty-eight hours had passed he still refused to shut down the reactor.

Many of his engineers at the site, in Washington, and at Bettis thought he was foolhardy. Rickover, however, did call some of his top engineers, and a few, including Mandil, agreed with his decision for a long run. Rickover had calculated the speed at which the Mark I could propel a submarine. Unrolling a chart of the Atlantic, he had progress of a hypothetical submarine marked as it crossed the ocean. At the ninety-sixth hour the track reached Fastnet, Ireland. Toward the end of the run several problems had emerged, and it was with a sigh of relief that the Mark I was shut down.

Rickover knew that if he had ruined the Mark I he would have ruined his career in the Navy, but for two main reasons he had thrust aside the advice of most of his engineers to stop the run. First, if anything was going to go wrong he wanted to know about it then. And second, he wanted to show the "Navy bastards" in Washington what nuclear propulsion could do. The chart of the Atlantic was evidence they could not sweep aside.

By any standard, bringing the Mark I to full power on 25 June 1953 was a magnificent accomplishment. Time is one measure of achievement. Although it is hard to pick a point at which to mark the beginning of the effort, perhaps December 1947 is a good choice. In that month at Oak Ridge, Rickover decided to use zirconium for the pressurized-water approach, even though the technical, developmental, and procurement problems were recognized as formidable and could not be clearly defined. At that time the Navy and the AEC had not even established a joint program, let alone placed Rickover in charge. Five and a half years later he and the organization he created began the power run and a nuclear submarine was under construction. Moreover, during these years he was driving ahead with the sodium-cooled approach at Knolls and West Milton, the naval propulsion program was expanding, and he had begun to take a role in the development of civilian nuclear power.

In the second or third week of July the selection board that would consider Rickover for promotion to rear admiral met. As was customary, it consisted of six line and three engineer officers. As was also customary, the three engineers would select the engineers for promotion and the six line officers would accept their choice. One engineer to be promoted to rear admiral had to be experienced in nuclear propulsion. Unbelievably, the engineers did not select Rickover but another engineer, a gesture that showed the engineer officers' implacable hostility toward Rickover. Aware of the outrage that would break out in Congress, the press, and the Navy itself, the six line officers broke tradition and cast their votes for Rickover.

On 24 July 1953, the Navy announced the names of the officers selected to the grade of rear admiral. The first name on the list was Hyman George Rickover.

Nautilus

POWER OPERATION of the Mark I in June 1953 was a brilliant engineering triumph and a tremendous stride toward the operation of the *Nautilus*, now under construction by Electric Boat at Groton, Connecticut. Rickover had aimed at having her ready for sea on 1 January 1955; it looked now as if he might better that target.[1] He had begun selecting and training the officers and enlisted men for the *Nautilus* long before the power operation of the Mark I. They spent a year at the Bettis laboratory, receiving intensive schooling in mathematics, physics, and reactor engineering, courses not intended to make reactor design specialists of either officers or crew, but to make them specialists in the reactor they were to operate. They went from Bettis to Idaho to acquire practical experience by working on the Mark I alongside men from Westinghouse, Electric Boat, and other contractors. They helped bring the reactor to power in May 1953 and to full power the following month. Later they were at Electric Boat and helped install the Mark II.

Rickover, who had followed personally every phase of their instruction, gave them high praise for their role in writing plant operating and maintenance manuals. Those that had been drawn up by vendors and fabricators of components, as well as those by Naval Reactors, Bettis, and Electric Boat, were so confused and poorly organized that they were impossible to use.[2]

Although the ship's company had been selected, its commanding officer had not been chosen. Rickover observed with wry amusement the cordial greetings he received from the submarine officers he encountered in the corridors of Main Navy and the Pentagon. Command of the first nuclear-powered submarine could be a powerful lever to open the door to advancement and even to fame. Many officers, coveting the assignment, realized Rickover could help them get it.

Rickover already knew whom he wanted. Cdr. Eugene P. Wilkinson was highly intelligent, imaginative, and free from the deadly embrace of tradition. Born in California in 1918, he had graduated from the University of Southern California in 1938, where he had been awarded a bachelor of science degree in physics. After a brief spell teaching chemistry and mathematics in a high school, he joined the Navy in 1940 as an ensign in the Naval Reserve. Transferring to submarines after serving a year in a heavy cruiser, he had made eight war patrols, had become an executive officer, and had risen to the grade of lieutenant commander. When the war was over he decided to remain in the Navy.

His first contact with Rickover came as the result of an interview by Cdr. Edward L. Beach in the office of the chief of naval operations. Beach was seeking a submariner for duty at the Atomic Energy Commission's installation at Oak Ridge, Tennessee. From there he would keep the office informed of the developments in atomic energy. During their conversation the thought crossed Beach's mind that he might well be sending to Oak Ridge the officer who would command the first nuclear submarine— an assignment Beach himself wanted.

Wilkinson impressed Rickover and the Naval Group at Oak Ridge. Later he worked at Bettis, where he proved his value in helping to get the laboratory organized. In 1950 he returned to submarine duty. Probably he and Rickover had already reached an understanding that he would command the *Nautilus*.

He was captain of the *Wahoo* when Rickover wrote him on 25 March 1953 that competition to command the *Nautilus* was intense and he should submit his request quickly:

> For Christ's sake, don't be as lazy as you always are; *act* on this *at once*.
>
> Of course, it is also at a great personal sacrifice that I will have to put up with you for another period of time but I will do this "for the cause."!!!!!
>
> With kindest personal regards,
>
> [adding in his own hand] To the Wilkinson family.[3]

Many in the submarine force opposed Wilkinson. Possibly the resistance stemmed from several factors: he was not a Naval Academy graduate, he had not commanded a submarine during the war, and (perhaps worst of all) he had been picked by Rickover. For years the headquarters of the Atlantic submarine force had assigned officers to submarines. Rickover, an engineer, was challenging that practice. Echoes of opposition reached the press in August 1953 when the *Washington Times-Herald* reported that

Wilkinson had been selected because he was "trained as a scientist" and represented the "technical view." Some officers, the story continued, fought the selection, asserting that an atomic propulsion plant was "just a steam plant" and "you can't command a submarine if you've got your mind in the engine room." Many officers thought Beach should have been chosen because he was the "nation's No. 1 submarine commander."[4]

Beach was naval aide to President Eisenhower when the Washington press reported the squabble. Wanting no part of what promised to be an ugly fight and recognizing that Wilkinson by his work at the laboratories had better technical qualifications, Beach quashed the effort to make him the first captain of the *Nautilus*. Nonetheless, hostility in the submarine force against Rickover soon surfaced again as the time approached to launch the submarine.

The Navy had long been eager to have First Lady Mamie Eisenhower christen a ship. Beach had recommended to her and to her husband that she wait for the launching of the *Nautilus*, certain to be an important and famous ship. Mrs. Eisenhower accepted, and 21 January 1954 was settled as the date.

Without question the event would receive broad publicity. Henry Holt and Company, a well-known publishing house, advertised in the *New York Times* on 28 December 1953 that the book *The Atomic Submarine and Admiral Rickover* by Clay Blair Jr. would appear on 18 January 1954. In other advertisements Holt declared, "WARNING! The Navy will not like this book."

To gather data for his book Blair had gone to the Office of Naval Information, headed by Rear Adm. Lewis S. Parks, a submariner who had compiled a superb combat record. Blair saw Cdr. Slade D. Cutter, director of public information, a part of the Office of Naval Information. Cutter, too, had been an outstanding submarine commander. Blair received a very cold reception and very little help.

Blair sent a portion of his manuscript to Rickover, who, with his senior engineers, went over the draft. It was well-written but far too flamboyant, and the emphasis on anti-Semitism far too strong. Still, they agreed, there was a story to be told. Rickover gave Blair office space, allowed him access to unclassified material, and assigned Louis H. Roddis, who had belonged to the Naval Group at Oak Ridge, to explain naval organization and procedures. Rickover, finding a sympathetic listener in Blair, freely unburdened himself of all the slights and insults he had received in his fight for nuclear propulsion. Pleased with the manuscript, Rickover showed it to Ruth.

She was horrified, certain that its intemperate language would ruin her husband's career. Insisting that it be toned down, she worked with Blair to do so. Even after these changes the manuscript was a severe indictment of the Navy. Early in January advance copies were circulating throughout the Pentagon.

As the day for the launching approached, John W. Finney, a respected and well-informed writer on military affairs for the *Washington Post*, decided to write an article on the *Nautilus*. Suspecting that the revolutionary importance of the submarine had been exaggerated, he believed a comparison of the capabilities of the nuclear ship and the latest diesel-electric submarine would make his point. Finney went to the director of public information. Cutter welcomed him and informed him that there was no great difference between the two types of submarines. Although the nuclear submarine would be larger than its conventional counterpart, that difference was a disadvantage in combat. Finney also learned that the primary purpose of the *Nautilus* was to test nuclear propulsion.

The *Washington Post* published his story, "A Submarine Held Unfit for Battle Now," on 4 January. Its readers learned that high-ranking naval officers believed the United States was years away from having an atomic submarine with offensive capabilities. The *Nautilus* was too large, her torpedo tubes had been added as an afterthought, and, in the words of an unidentified officer, she "is strictly a test vehicle. I doubt if she will ever fire a shot in anger." The *Washington News* headed its story "Nautilus Already Obsolete."

An outraged President of the United States telephoned Charles E. Wilson, secretary of defense, wanting to know why his wife should christen a test vehicle. Upset and angry, Wilson promptly summoned Roger M. Kyes, deputy secretary of defense; Robert LeBaron, assistant secretary of defense (atomic energy); Robert B. Anderson, secretary of the Navy; Thomas S. Gates, undersecretary of the Navy; Parks; and Cutter to a meeting. Wilson received two other telephone calls: one from Congressman W. Sterling Cole, chairman of the Joint Committee on Atomic Energy, who was unhappy over the Finney article, and one from Lewis L. Strauss, chairman of the AEC, who suggested a news conference to straighten matters out.[5]

Wilson didn't want to talk to the press: classified information might be revealed. Perhaps canceling the launching was the thing to do. Papers brought to the meeting revealed that some wording in the *Post* story was identical to that in memorandums Cutter had written to Parks and that

Parks had written for the files. While there was no breach of security, there was no doubt that Finney was repeating what he had been told. The discussion turned to Rickover. He was doing a good job, LeBaron declared, but had definitely aroused antagonism. Kyes asked if Rickover was working for the Navy or for Westinghouse. For the Navy and the Atomic Energy Commission, replied LeBaron. Wilson wanted to know if the money for the *Nautilus* was being spent properly. It was, LeBaron answered. One thing was settled: the launching would go ahead as planned.

On 6 January the *Washington Evening Star* reported the meeting and the White House annoyance. Drew Pearson, a widely read columnist, wrote in the *Washington Post* of 26 January that the episode was evidence of an anti-Rickover conspiracy. It was, indeed, a plausible interpretation.

Thursday morning, 21 January 1954 at Groton was cold, wet, and foggy. Workmen at Electric Boat scurried around the bleachers and viewing stands, trying to sop up the heavy moisture with huge rags. Guests—the total would reach fifteen thousand—were thronging into the yard. Most visitors could just make out a shadowy mass looming through the mist; only those closest could see that the ship was painted olive green above the waterline and black below.

Timing was critical. The *Nautilus* had to be launched at high tide, which was about 11:00 A.M. At 10:30 a gentle breeze suddenly swept away the fog. Flags and bunting, once damp and limp, now shone in the sun and began to wave and ripple in the fresh breeze. A train slowly backed into the yard, stopping a short distance from the building ways. The first lady, escorted by Beach, descended and climbed the steps to the stands where senior company officials and high-ranking officers waited. Graciously she listened to the self-congratulatory speeches that were inevitable on such occasions.

A few minutes before 11:00, she ascended the stairs to the small platform from which she would break a bottle of champagne over the bow of the submarine. There was an unexpected and nerve-racking delay, but finally a yardman stationed far below on the floor of the building ways released the trigger that had kept the ship poised for launching. Her voice firm and clear, the first lady declared, "I christen thee *Nautilus*." The champagne bottle broke nicely. Among cheers, whistles, and loud brassy music, the first atomic submarine slid stern foremost into the river, where four tugs caught her and moved her slowly to a pier. There she would remain for almost a year as further work was done on her.[6]

One reporter observed, "Not a word and scarcely a smile came from a small slender man in the uniform of a rear admiral who sat quietly at one end of the first row of the guests of honor and stood quietly in the last row of the smaller group behind Mrs. Eisenhower for the christening."[7] Beach had made sure of the seating arrangement for the guests of honor, and of who should be included in the small group behind the first lady. Otherwise, he was certain, Rickover would have been in the last row of the guests of honor and not at all in the small group.

Work on the *Nautilus* continued at a grueling pace of three-shift days and six-day weeks. Many of the officers and crew, as well as the yardmen, were also coming in on Sundays to test components or to recover lost time. It looked as if the ship would be ready for initial sea trials late in 1954.

On the night of 16 September, men in the engine room were using steam from shore facilities to test various parts of the propulsion system. Just before midnight a small pipe burst, filling the reactor compartment with steam. The pipe was in the steam system, not in the nuclear portion of the plant. Prompt action prevented serious damage and injuries were confined to one man who suffered slight burns. Investigation quickly revealed far-reaching ramifications. Rickover had two approaches to nuclear propulsion under construction: the pressurized-water concept being developed by Bettis and Westinghouse for the *Nautilus* and the sodium-cooled concept being developed by Knolls and General Electric for the *Seawolf*, the second nuclear submarine authorized by Congress. Each approach had its prototype and shipboard plant. Electric Boat had installed piping of the wrong specifications in all four steam plants. Experts Rickover brought in from government and industry could not devise a test that could tell whether the piping already installed in that part of the propulsion systems was good or bad. Seeing no alternative, he had all suspect piping ripped out and replaced. By October he knew that the schedule of the *Nautilus* would be delayed three months.[8] His chance of getting the ship to sea before the end of the year was gone.

The *Nautilus*'s reactor reached criticality on 30 December 1954 and, on the second day of the new year, generated steam for the electrical system and then for the propulsion turbines. Slowly the propellers rotated, roiling the frigid, placid, and murky waters along the dock.

At this point Rickover decided to run the plant at full power. His engineers, those from Electric Boat, and other contractors and the ship's officers protested vigorously. Steam propulsion plants were not designed to operate at full power when a ship was not under way. Doing so placed a tremendous strain on the propulsion system. Rickover, they argued, was endangering the plant when sea trials were only a week or two away. But Rickover would not yield, declaring that if anything could go wrong he wanted to know about it before sea trials. On 3 January the Mark II reached full power. Once Rickover climbed out on deck. Hot water from the plant turned to steam when it met the cold air: he could scarcely see the dock or the river through the billowing clouds. The plant worked perfectly.

The Navy wanted plenty of news coverage of the sea trials. For several months newspapers and magazines had carried accounts, carefully crafted to avoid disclosing classified data, of the submarine as well as biographical information on its officers and men. The Navy had even released a few photographs of the ship under construction, carefully taken to reveal little more than a massive shape, most of which was obscured by scaffolding.

The five members of the Atomic Energy Commission disagreed. A reactor was a complex mechanism; no one could be certain how it would operate in a ship that was rolling and pitching. The commissioners had understood that no news would be released until the ship was at sea because "if anything happens to it the AEC will get a terrible black eye." Rickover agreed, but the Navy was going ahead with its plans to give notice of the event a few days ahead of time.[9]

There was no chance of avoiding news coverage. Everyone in the shipyard could see the last-minute preparations; all Groton and the surrounding area knew that the *Nautilus* would soon leave the yard. The Department of Defense dispelled all uncertainty by announcing on 14 January that the trials would take place on 17 January.[10] Plans divided the trials into two parts. In the first phase the *Nautilus* would operate on the surface at various speeds and return briefly to the yard. In the second phase she would go back to sea to operate submerged.

The seventeenth of January dawned clear and cold. Rickover, who had been in the ship the preceding night, came on board at 8:00 A.M. At 10:00 A.M. the ship was alive with preparations to leave the yard. A few men, clad in heavy clothing and wearing bright orange life jackets, began singling up the lines. Wilkinson, Rickover, and a few others were crowded together on the bridge. At 11:00 A.M. Wilkinson ordered the last line cast off. With a long blast on her whistle and with a surge of white water at her stern, the *Nautilus* backed into the Thames River.[11]

Yardmen crowded the waterfront, and thousands of spectators lined the riverbanks. An Air Force helicopter hovered overhead, and a small private plane circled slowly. The submarine rescue vessel *Skylark*, carrying several newspapermen and photographers invited by the Navy, waited on the river. Once clear of the pier, Wilkinson ordered the engines "All back full."

Then it happened.

The scream of metal scraping on metal filled the engine room. It came from the starboard reduction gear—not part of the nuclear plant but vital to the operation of the starboard propeller. Quickly informing Wilkinson, the chief engineer shifted to electric propulsion. The ship was fitted with electric motors for emergency use. They ran off turbogenerators driven by steam from the reactor plant, so the *Nautilus* was still operating on nuclear power.

Prudence required returning to the pier, but Rickover refused. Everyone watching from the waterfront, every person lining the riverbanks, and every reporter scanning each move of the ship would realize something had gone wrong. And soon the entire nation would know. He proposed, once the ship was safely headed downstream, to start the port main turbine and steam with the port propeller, leaving the starboard propeller free to spin. While Wilkinson maneuvered the ship, Rickover sped below. The trouble had already been found: it was a loose screw scraping against the metal casing. It was easily fixed. When the submarine was at the mouth of the Thames and about to enter Long Island Sound, Wilkinson sent a message to the commander of the Submarine Force, Atlantic Fleet: "Underway on nuclear power," words that became part of naval history.

Submarines were notoriously uncomfortable on the surface. Because of the shape of their hull, they rolled in the presence of the slightest sea. The first nuclear submarine was no exception. Twelve-foot seas tore off some of the teak decking and also damaged some light metal plating around the bridge. Many of the eleven officers, the eighty-five enlisted men, and the sixty civilian engineers and technicians became violently seasick. Robert Panoff and Theodore Rockwell, the only members of Naval Reactors that Rickover took on the trials, moved from compartment to compartment and found that everyone on watch, even if miserably sick, was conducting tests, taking measurements, and recording data.

The trials were going so well that Wilkinson radioed for permission to dive. That request was refused: submerged operations were scheduled for the second part of the trials. On Wednesday morning, 19 January, the

Nautilus reentered the Thames River and, disdaining any assistance from tugs sent to meet her, swept proudly upstream and at 1:00 P.M. moored at Pier Charlie at Electric Boat.

The next day she again encountered poor weather at sea. Wilkinson could not get permission to submerge, where she would ride much more smoothly, because the schedule called for a helicopter to take photographs. When it did not show up, Rickover refused to wait any longer. At 1332 Navy time, 1:32 in the afternoon in civilian time, the *Nautilus* began, in words later typed into her smooth log, "FIRST DIVE EVER MADE ON NUCLEAR POWER."

She submerged slowly and cautiously, disappearing completely beneath the surface seven minutes from the beginning of her dive. After fifty-six minutes she surfaced. She performed well and handled beautifully in this and subsequent dives. Some things went wrong, including two minor leaks and two small electrical fires, but there were fewer problems than usual on initial trials.

The ease with which *Nautilus* submerged fascinated everyone on board. Almost in a state of exultation, one man after another dove the ship— Rickover was the forty-first to have the honor. Someone remembered a voyage in which a submarine had made fifty dives. To break that record the *Nautilus* made fifty-one.

Rickover showed no emotion of personal triumph, as he had when he was nominated for the Naval Academy and when he saw energy from the Mark I turn a propeller shaft. He did remember officers coming to him on the last day of the trials, confessing that they had been wrong in doubting him. Some, he recalled, were in tears.

Although soon setting record after record for high-speed submerged voyages, the *Nautilus* was not without problems. She was noisy and her hull vibrated badly when she was moving quickly beneath the surface.[12] But exercises with the Navy and participation in the North Atlantic Treaty Organization (NATO) maneuvers made it clear to all: naval operations would never be the same after 17 January 1955.

Shippingport Atomic Power Station

THE SEA TRIALS of the *Nautilus* in January 1955 made an already well-known Rickover into a public figure. Most people, having followed the event by scanning newspapers, listening to the radio, or watching television, probably had no idea that he also led a civilian power reactor project, carrying it out under the auspices of the Atomic Energy Commission, not as part of the AEC-Navy nuclear propulsion program.

In August 1950, when the Korean War was less than two months old, Adm. Forrest P. Sherman, chief of naval operations, asked for a feasibility study of a nuclear-powered aircraft carrier. While in Oak Ridge Rickover and the Naval Group had considered that use but decided against it, mainly because the new energy source would have a greater impact on submarine operations than on those of surface ships. Because it would take years to develop the propulsion plant for a carrier as well as to build the ship, Sherman's request reflected his interest as a naval aviator, not his concern over the conflict in Korea.

Rickover did his best to interest the Navy and the AEC in the project, but neither had any enthusiasm for it. The war in Asia had set higher priorities on more urgent defense demands. Nonetheless, some planning and development continued on what was named the "large ship reactor," or LSR.

From one aspect the large ship reactor threatened Rickover's plans for himself and Naval Reactors. Nuclear propulsion for an aircraft carrier would require several large reactors, but even one of these might have a power rating great enough for electric power utilities to see it as a step toward the civilian use of atomic energy. Consequently, Lawrence R. Hafstad, director of reactor development, considered assigning it to that part of his division charged with developing nuclear power for industrial use. If Hafstad did so, Rickover would no longer have the sole responsibility for naval propulsion reactors.[1] The future of the large ship reactor, how-ever, would not be determined until after the presidential election of 1952.

The election held a special interest for Robert Rickover. He and his father, when the latter was in town, took long walks in Rock Creek Park on Sundays, usually to some construction site where Robert would collect pop bottles he would then take to the grocery store for the deposit—two cents for the small ones and five cents for the large. They talked about whatever interested them, but often the subject was politics. His father thought Eisenhower would lose; Robert thought he would win. Naturally, they bet on the outcome in each state. Robert won a few dollars.

Taking office on 20 January 1953, Dwight D. Eisenhower was deter-mined to cut the federal budget, foster business, and find some way to halt the world on its way to a nuclear Armageddon. He named Lewis L. Strauss his special assistant on atomic energy matters. A conservative Republican and one of the five original AEC commissioners, Strauss had resigned from the commission in April 1950 to resume his financial career in New York. Scrutinizing the commission's budget for savings, he recommended cutting several projects, among them the large ship reactor. As yet it re-quired no great sums, but that would soon change. Rickover was furious. He had assigned its development to Bettis. Morale at the laboratory sank rapidly as the press reported the effort might be canceled.[2]

The Department of Defense did not want the reactor. Before the Na-tional Security Council on 22 April, Roger M. Kyes, deputy secretary of defense, urged its cancellation. Gordon E. Dean, chairman of the AEC, offered a different proposal. Stripped of its military features, the large ship reactor could be an important step toward civilian nuclear power. Interested in the idea, Eisenhower asked for a recommendation.

Dean's proposal held no attraction for Rickover. He might head a large ship reactor project, but not a reactor directed at civilian application. In a final attempt to save the reactor as a Navy project, Rickover saw Kyes and Robert LeBaron, chairman of the Military Liaison Committee, on the last day of April. It was not an easy meeting. Kyes, who had won a reputation at General Motors as an able and tough executive, refused to change his mind. As if that was not enough, he declared the commission should not build a civilian reactor. Private industry could do the job—and do it faster and better than the government. LeBaron agreed; industry could do it.[3]

Kyes and LeBaron were reflecting a philosophy that private industry was ready to take a major part in developing civilian nuclear power, pro-vided that government restraints imposed by the atomic energy act of

1946 were eased. Rickover disagreed: reactor technology demanded an engineering and technical discipline unknown to industry or, except for his own organization, to government.

Thomas E. Murray, the first professional engineer to become a commissioner, agreed with Rickover. A successful businessman and a powerful Democratic figure in New York City politics, Murray took his place on the commission in May 1950. Focusing on civilian nuclear power, he explored the views of industry executives. More realistic than Kyes and LeBaron, they convinced Murray that the technical uncertainties were as yet too great for private investment. From these talks Murray concluded that if the United States was to take the lead in developing nuclear power for civilian use—a most important national objective—the government had to demonstrate its technical feasibility. He saw converting the large ship reactor to civilian use as an opportunity to meet that goal: he was, indeed, the source of the suggestion that Dean had made at the National Security Council meeting on 22 April.

Certain conclusions flowed from Murray's conviction that the United States should move fast. Only the pressurized-water technology was far enough advanced for a civilian power reactor, although some research and development would be necessary. Only Rickover had the organization and resources that could be mobilized quickly. But before Rickover could be assigned the project, it had to have presidential approval and the support of Congress. Moreover, the opposition to Rickover within the commission and industry had to be overcome.

By mid-May 1953 Murray had gotten the approval of the president and the Joint Committee on Atomic Energy, which, as its title implied, spoke for Congress on such issues. Putting Rickover in charge was more difficult. Many on the commission staff disliked his abrasiveness and the skill and ruthless tactics he sometimes used to gain his ends. Others thought it incongruous that a civilian project should be based on military technology and directed by a naval officer. In addition, a decision had to be made between two approaches—one proposed by Rickover and another by Robert P. Peterson, chief of the industrial power branch.

Rickover had much to offer. He had built a skilled and trained group of engineers in Naval Reactors, Bettis, and the various contractors. They were producing results: in mid-May the Mark I was just weeks away from its first power run. On the other hand, his approach had drawbacks. For technical reasons the electrical power rating of his proposed reactor would be about sixty thousand kilowatts, and the power it generated would cost far more than it would from fossil fuel. Furthermore, Rickover would run the project as he did his others. Other commission laboratories as well as industry would have no opportunity to participate in directing the effort.

Peterson and many others favored a much broader approach. With more time and the active participation of industry and the several laboratories, they would explore ways to improve the pressurized-water technology. By building a reactor of greater capacity, they would come closer to generating power at competitive costs to that from fossil fuels and, therefore, of more interest to the utilities.

Emotions ran so high that on 16 June the commissioners took the unusual step of meeting in executive session, excluding the staff and even the general manager. Finally a decision emerged: the civilian project would be assigned to Rickover. Yet even then the issue was not closed. Strauss, becoming chairman on 2 July, had to hear the arguments and take part in the decision.

On the morning of 9 July the new chairman, his colleagues, and the staff met in the commissioners' conference room. Again the arguments for both sides were presented and reviewed; again the issue came down to which was the quickest way to advance civilian reactor technology. The tension was heightened when the door to the room opened and a letter was handed in. It was from Rep. W. Sterling Cole, chairman of the joint committee. Writing that he had succeeded in getting congressional funds for the project, Cole declared that his action meant that Congress had initiated the project and could impose certain conditions. Demonstration of peaceful application of atomic energy might be impaired "from Navy direction, extensive Navy specifications, and the inevitable 'leaked' news articles referring to aircraft carrier reactor prototypes."[4] Cole's letter was a maladroit maneuver to snatch the project away from Rickover, and Murray had little difficulty in convincing his colleagues that the commission could not yield to the committee.

Nevertheless, intrigues within the Division of Reactor Development continued, as did attempts by the laboratories and industry to overturn the assignment to Rickover. More than once Murray had to step in to keep the project on track. Emotions still ran high. Rickover attended a social occasion at which several members of the commission and the staff were present. One man from the division was standing near a lady whom he did not know. Gesturing across the room to Rickover, he declared, "The scum always rises to the top." He was speaking to Ruth Rickover.

Murray announced the enterprise to a group of utility executives in Chicago on 22 October, telling them that although Rickover would be in charge, "the only Navy aspect which the Admiral will bring to this work is his title."[5] Arrangements for building the project soon took shape. The commission would build the reactor and a utility would provide a site and a power network. On 11 March 1954 the commission accepted the offer from the Duquesne Light Company of Pittsburgh. It included a site at Shippingport, a small village outside Pittsburgh on the Ohio River. Furthermore, Duquesne agreed to build the generating facility and make a financial contribution to the reactor plant. The offer could hardly have been better from Rickover's view, as Bettis and Westinghouse were in easy reach.

Rickover was deeply aware that he was setting precedents for a civilian industry. In many respects he was treating Shippingport as if it were a Navy project, trying to see every contingency, taking every measure to protect personnel and the environment from radiation, and planning to make sure the plant's personnel were thoroughly trained. He and his senior engineers chose a conservative design philosophy in which safety was the main principle. In addition, Rickover decided to use as much as possible steam and electrical equipment already familiar to industry.

Very early in his planning he decided to place the reactor containment system underground as one further addition to the number of barriers keeping radioactivity from the environment. The system was made up of four parts: a sphere for the reactor; two cylinders, each containing two boilers; and a third cylinder for auxiliary equipment.

Shippingport was not yet under construction in August 1954 when Eisenhower decided to use the groundbreaking ceremony for the plant to show the American commitment to the peaceful uses of atomic energy. At the United Nations on 8 December 1953, he had announced the "Atoms for Peace" program, in which the major powers, primarily the United States and the Soviet Union, would donate nuclear materials from their stockpiles to an agency that would use the materials to help other nations develop atomic power for peaceful purposes, among them electrical energy for those areas of the world that badly needed it. He chose Labor Day, 6 September, for the Shippingport ceremony.

He would speak over radio and television from Denver, where he was on vacation. At the end of his remarks he would pick up a wand containing a neutron source and, by waving it over a neutron counter, flash an electronic signal that would start up an unmanned bulldozer at the Shippingport site.

Maj. Gen. Kenneth D. Nichols, who eight years earlier had introduced Rickover to Oak Ridge, was now the commission's general manager. "You are in complete control of all our responsibilities," he told Rickover, "and if the bulldozer doesn't push ahead and move dirt when Ike waves his wand, you are fired."

"Don't worry, I'll still be here after the event," Rickover replied.

Rickover took his son Robert with him to Shippingport while Ruth, detesting large gatherings, remained at home. As part of a large audience they heard Eisenhower declare that even though cynicism had stopped progress toward the goal he had set at the United Nations, the United States was moving ahead and opening new avenues of constructive employment and respite from burdensome toil, obligatory references since it was Labor Day. He waved his wand and the bulldozer roared into action.

Discussing the ceremony later with Rickover, Nichols said that as a young man he had operated a bulldozer and found that it stalled if its blade dug too deep. Rickover replied that he had thought of that and had placed two railroad rails about six inches below the surface for the blade of the bulldozer to ride upon. "It pays to pick the right man and give him full responsibility," concluded Nichols.

John W. Simpson of Westinghouse, assistant general manager at Bettis for all technical activities, remembered the ceremony differently: he was in charge, he had the idea of placing the rails beneath the surface, and he had a man ready to trigger the bulldozer to start if the wand didn't work.[6]

The origins of Shippingport had shown how effectively Rickover and Murray could work together. Both were united in their belief that the AEC's reactor development program needed the same hard-headed discipline that naval propulsion was receiving. Toward the end of 1954 Hafstad announced his intention of leaving the commission. Murray and Rickover saw their chance: Rickover would become the next director of reactor development.

Rickover's credentials were impressive. Shippingport was the centerpiece of the American civilian power program; at Electric Boat the *Nautilus* sea trials were not far off, and the *Seawolf*, which would be powered by a sodium-cooled reactor, was under construction. These were the products of Rickover's vigorous efforts, the same efforts with which he was pressing ahead to increase the application of nuclear power to the Navy. For several reasons, some technical, some organizational, and some political, the commission's other reactor projects could not show such progress or match such achievements.

Murray and Rickover apparently did not commit much of their actions to paper, but the outline is clear enough. On the morning of 22 November 1954 Murray asked Nichols to come to his office to discuss candidates to replace Hafstad. Leaving no doubt that he strongly favored Rickover, Murray declared his intention of bringing the matter up before the commissioners that afternoon. Nichols demurred: a military officer in charge of a major civilian program was a bad idea. That afternoon Murray proposed Rickover to his fellow commissioners. They were noticeably cool. Still, they asked Nichols to get the reaction of leading individuals and organizations working in the field. If there was no opposition they would favor naming Rickover to the position. Considering the recent struggle to get Shippingport assigned to Rickover, there could have been little doubt what the survey would find.

Nichols found no support for Rickover. Furthermore, according to the recollection of one individual close to the struggle, major contractors, among them General Electric, were dead set against Rickover. Nichols sounded out Walter H. Zinn, a leading figure in reactor development, on taking the post Hafstad had left, even going so far as to state that Rickover would be kept where he was and under control. Even so, after thinking about the offer for a few days, Zinn declined.

Murray continued to fight, even going behind closed doors. Strauss was opposed (he and Murray were already at swords' points on many issues), and so were the other commissioners. On 23 February 1955 the commissioners decided to offer the directorship to W. Kenneth Davis. A few days later Strauss wrote to Murray, "As I have repeatedly stated, my reluctance to consider him [Rickover] for the directorship of the Reactor Development Division is the unanimity and vigor with which our most trusted and disinterested advisors have urged us to avoid his selection, and the attitude of the laboratory directors and others upon whose morale we must depend."

A chemical engineer by profession, Davis had served half a year as Hafstad's deputy and had played a major role in framing a cooperative program with industry. Admittedly he was young (he would turn thirty-seven in 1955), but he would grow into the job. Murray scorned the argument. Why wait for someone to grow into the job when there was a man on the job getting the desired results?[7]

It was fortunate for Rickover that he did not become director of reactor development. He could not have counted upon the support of the majority of the commissioners. He would not have commanded the loyalty of the division, the laboratories, or the contractors to the technical discipline he intended to exercise. He would inevitably have been drawn into the public versus private power dispute, an issue that had vexed politics for decades and would have split the unanimity of the joint committee that supported him. And yet, had he somehow succeeded, he might have instilled discipline and technical standards into the civilian power program that would have made a great difference in the history of atomic energy in the United States.

Murray was to leave the commission in 1957 and become a consultant to the joint committee. Rickover owed him a great deal. Thanks to Murray, Rickover had Shippingport and, therefore, a voice in the civilian power program. It was also because of Murray that the naval nuclear propulsion program would develop all the naval reactors—none would be turned over to another part of the division.

When announcing the commission decision to build the Shippingport power plant, Murray had declared that the only naval aspect that the admiral would bring to the project was his title. Rickover ran the venture as much as if it were part of the Navy program. His goal was to have the plant operating by 15 March 1957. But steel shortages, strikes at plants manufacturing components, and bad weather took their toll of progress. Additional pressure to complete the plant came from an announcement that the British were also building an atomic power plant of sixty thousand kilowatts, a rating that seemed more than a coincidence. Their plant, however, had a dual purpose because it was to provide electric power and to produce nuclear materials for their weapons program. Shippingport would still be the only full-scale atomic power station built solely for civilian application and would be another badge of leadership for the United States.

In October 1956 the 153-ton pressure vessel that would contain the reactor core was lowered into place. The same month of the next year saw the installation of the 58-ton core. It took eight nerve-racking hours until it was positioned precisely in the pressure vessel. Start-up was only a month and some weeks away. Duquesne personnel, some of whom had been training for over two years, were eager to assume their responsibilities. That time was not far off. Criticality was achieved on 2 December 1957.

The date was significant. Fifteen years earlier to the day a small number of scientists at Chicago had achieved the world's first self-sustained nuclear chain reaction. It was an event that was accepted as the beginning of the atomic age. Rickover "thought it would be nice" if criticality of the first civilian atomic power reactor occurred on the anniversary of that milestone. Lawton D. Geiger, a tower of strength to Rickover and the program and manager of the commission's Pittsburgh area office, was present at the event. He recalled that everyone was so busy that no one remembered that the date marked an anniversary.

Duquesne was to begin operating Shippingport when its reactor produced enough steam to bring the turbine up to speed and to the point where the generator could be synchronized so that the electric power produced could be fed into the utility's network. Although the point of turnover was in the contract with Duquesne, Rickover decided not to accept it. The commission owned the reactor plant, and it, through Rickover, was responsible for its safe operation. After synchronization the reactor still had to be tested at various power levels and operating conditions; the plant, therefore, could not yet be turned over to the company.

Philip A. Fleger, chairman of the Duquesne Board of Directors, fought back. The commission under Rickover had trained his men for the jobs they were to assume and had found no fault in their training. Furthermore, Rickover's action was undermining the trust and cooperation that had governed the relationship between the commission and Duquesne. A compromise, mainly on Rickover's terms, was reached on 9 December. It established joint procedures that the commission, Duquesne, and Westinghouse would exercise during test operations.

On 17 December Rickover arrived for power operation. He still did not think he had sufficient authority to meet his responsibility for safe operation. That night as steam was flowing to the turbine and the generator was ready for synchronization, he called a halt. He wanted a personal representative in the plant at all times. That person would report directly to him and would have authority to shut the plant down if, in his view, it was not in a safe condition. His representative was to make certain that plant personnel did not allow routine and familiarity to erode standards and procedures. Again Rickover had to overcome the resistance of Duquesne. On 18 December 1957 power from the plant first flowed over the Duquesne lines and five days later it reached its full power of sixty thousand kilowatts.

The first full-scale atomic power station demonstrated its ability to operate on a utility network, meeting base and swing load demands.

Furthermore, a decision Rickover made in April 1955 to develop and use uranium dioxide for the reactor fuel was widely adopted in the civilian power industry. Shippingport soon began offering classes to employees of other organizations, both American and foreign. In addition the power plant became a major source of technical information. Reports, some periodic, others dealing with a single subject, were widely distributed to those individuals and organizations having professional interest but were also available to the public. Rickover's personal representative showed that he could fulfill his demanding responsibilities; only twice, and then in the early years of operation, did he have to shut the plant down. Later Rickover was to use Shippingport to investigate the feasibility of breeding by converting thorium into fissionable uranium 233 with pressurized-water reactors.[8]

Not all the lessons Shippingport offered were followed. Whether industry would accept the demands nuclear technology made on operators and managers was a question that troubled Rickover and Murray.

Initial operation was overshadowed by another event. The Soviet Union had become first in another technology: on 4 October it had launched the first manmade earth satellite, a triumph it followed on 3 November with another satellite, which carried an even heavier payload than the first. Nonetheless the atomic power plant on the Ohio River was an important engineering achievement. It also became a showpiece on the itinerary of foreign dignitaries to visit, and it was to bring Rickover into the field of international relations.

A National Figure

SINCE THE END of World War II, Americans had taken their technological supremacy for granted. Soviet *Sputnik* satellites shattered that complacency. Rockets launching the satellites had the potential to become intercontinental missiles. As never before the United States was vulnerable to sudden and devastating attack. The American response was swift. In two of its many elements—national defense and strengthening ties with Great Britain—Rickover had a role to play. These and other events during the remainder of the Eisenhower administration made him a national figure.

He must have listened with interest to President Eisenhower's radio and television address on 7 November 1957. The nation was still strong, Eisenhower declared. As one piece of evidence of that strength he pointed out that "atomic submarines have been developed. One ran almost sixteen days without resurfacing; another cruised under the polar ice cap for over five days." He did not name the ships, but he was speaking of the *Nautilus* under Cdr. William R. Anderson, which had operated beneath the ice, and the *Seawolf* under Cdr. Richard B. Laning, which had remained submerged for over two weeks.[1]

On 6 January 1958 Rickover appeared before Sen. Lyndon B. Johnson's Preparedness Investigating Subcommittee of the Committee on Armed Services, which was examining the nation's missile program. That day the Polaris submarine missile system was the subject. Originating in 1955, the Polaris concept called for a sea-based ballistic missile having a range of about fifteen hundred miles. The sudden appearance of the *Sputnik*s led to the decision in December 1957 to accelerate the effort and to schedule the first two ships to go to sea in October and December 1960 and the third in March 1961.

Since December 1955 Rear Adm. William F. Raborn's Special Projects Office had led the Polaris program. Rickover had hoped for the job but could not get enough support to overcome Navy opposition. Because Rickover was notorious for expanding his role in any enterprise of which he was part, Adm. Arleigh A. Burke, chief of naval operations, Raborn, and others were determined to confine Rickover to the reactor propulsion system. Later Rickover had lost the fight to have the submarine powered by the two-reactor propulsion plant being developed by the Knolls Atomic Power Laboratory for the radar picket submarine *Triton*. He had argued that the Polaris submarine needed the two reactors and two propellers to operate safely under ice. Rickover's job in the Polaris program remained organizing for the production of the single reactor plant for the forty-one missile submarines and for training the officers and men responsible for operating the propulsion plant. Because each of the submarines would have two crews, the increased burden was substantial.[2]

Now Rickover was trying again for a greater part of the program. That same morning of the hearing, Sen. Henry M. Jackson, a close friend of Rickover and a member of the Senate Committee on Armed Services and the Joint Committee on Atomic Energy, issued a statement. Much had to be done to speed up Polaris: the missile had to be produced in numbers, it had to be "married" to submarines, and the ships had to be placed in operation. As matters stood, Raborn was in charge of the entire program. Simply keeping the development of the missile on track was a full-time job, and although Raborn should remain responsible for it, someone else should develop the submarine. It was not hard to guess the man Jackson had in mind.

Rickover had another ally. For some days before the hearing, Edwin L. Weisl, the subcommittee's chief special counsel, had visited Naval Reactors to see how Rickover ran the nuclear propulsion program and to hear his philosophy on managing a major technical effort. With this background, Weisl began by asking Rickover how he had "brought in the first nuclear submarine ahead of schedule against tremendous obstacles and odds."

Using no notes, Rickover, occasionally discursive, replied that understanding the proper roles played by government and industry was the answer. Government could not rely on industry to carry out a large-scale research and development project. Doing so led to progress slower than it ought to be, costs higher than they need be, and a final product not as good as it should be. To get what it wanted, the government had to make the technical decisions. The government, therefore, had to have its own people—people strong in technology as well as administrative ability. He described the history of the nuclear propulsion program and how "over the years we have achieved a very complete coordination between the Government and industry . . . and this coordination exists today." The man in charge mattered more than organization; he had to be willing to risk his career and fight bureaucracy and inertia in government and industry.

Apparently shocked to learn that Rickover had no more to do with the Polaris program than providing reactors, Weisl asked, with an air of incredulity, "You mean to say you are not involved in developing the nuclear submarine that would launch the Polaris?" He drew from Rickover the admission that he had never been consulted on the matter, although his organization was capable of large-scale development work.

In later sessions Weisl asked other Navy witnesses about the limited part that Rickover had in the program. Burke, Rear Adm. Rawson Bennett, director of naval research, and Rear Adm. John T. Hayward, assistant chief of naval operations for research and development, believed Rickover had been consulted, but each in his own way expressed the thought that Rickover's projects were too important for him to be drawn away from them.

If Rickover had tried to enlarge his part in the Polaris program, he had failed: Burke and others were determined to keep him out. If Johnson had thought to get a ringing endorsement from an outstanding leader of technology on congressional efforts to shape the missile organization, he had failed: Rickover thought the subcommittee was overemphasizing that aspect. A strong leader, not organization, was the key to success.[3]

A few weeks later Rickover and I. Harry Mandil, accompanied by their wives, were in England to consult with the British on ways to assist their nuclear submarine program—part of the post-*Sputnik* effort to increase cooperation between the allies.

The origin of their trip came from a meeting in Washington on 24 October 1957 between a delegation from the United Kingdom under Prime Minister Harold Macmillan and their American counterparts. Discussion ranged over several ways in which the two powers could cooperate more closely on the military applications of nuclear energy. Submarine propulsion was one possibility; perhaps the British could procure from the Americans a propulsion reactor and its fuel, or perhaps even a nuclear-powered submarine. That course would require amending the Atomic Energy Act and thus come under the scrutiny of the Joint Committee on Atomic Energy.

The White House sent several amendments to the act to the joint committee on 27 January 1958. They would be considered by the subcommittee that, under Sen. John O. Pastore, dealt with international cooperation in atomic energy. Its members would lean heavily on Rickover's advice when they considered submarine propulsion. He was thoroughly familiar with the subject. Since May 1957 he had been helping the British to develop a reactor plant, but under the law the assistance was sharply limited and frustrating to both parties.

Between 27 January and 1 February 1958 Rickover and Mandil assessed the British program. In their visits to government and contractor facilities in London and elsewhere, they found the British candid: they wanted an operational nuclear submarine as soon as possible. The two Americans had been to Britain before, and although they saw some progress since their last visit, it was not much. Shortly before returning to the United States, they were to meet with Lord Louis Mountbatten and a number of officers and officials involved in the British program. The only thing to do, Rickover decided, was to talk frankly to Mountbatten before the meeting.

Rickover knew Mountbatten from earlier trips. A highly decorated officer who was a member of the royal family, he had proved himself in combat and in high command. Mountbatten was the first sea lord, a position roughly equivalent to the American chief of naval operations. Poles apart in background and social position, the two men had nevertheless taken to each other at once. It amused Rickover to learn that they were born the same year and that, while he was growing up in Makow in czarist Poland, Mountbatten and his family were occasional guests of Nicholas II at St. Petersburg.

Bluntly Rickover told Mountbatten that the only way for the British to get a submarine in the near future was to have a British concern—Rolls Royce, the obvious choice because it was already taking part in the effort—contract with Westinghouse. Having witnessed the *Nautilus* operations during recent NATO exercises, Mountbatten did not hesitate.

On their return to the conference, Mountbatten announced that the British would procure an American reactor. The statement was greeted in dead silence, in an atmosphere of disappointment that was almost tangible. Yet during the remainder of their stay, Rickover and Mandil observed with admiration that they were treated with great courtesy and consideration by men who believed that years of their work had been pushed aside by the Americans.

Rickover testified before the Pastore subcommittee on 27 February and 28 May 1958. His first appearance began on a strained note. Lewis L. Strauss, commission chairman, and other members of the staff were waiting and ready to resume their testimony from the previous session. Pastore announced that he was changing the schedule: Rickover would testify first and "then if he desires we can excuse him." Rickover never knew why Pastore gave him precedence over the chairman, but he could see that Strauss was upset from the way the back of his neck reddened—a sign that veterans of such hearings used as a barometer of the chairman's feelings.

Rickover observed that proposals to help the British often used the term "exchange." Thus, under the amendments, the British and Americans would exchange information. The legislators should make no mistake: in submarine propulsion the British had nothing of value for the Americans. But another perspective should not be overlooked. Because of their common background and heritage, the Americans, by helping the British, were also helping themselves. He drew the line at assisting any other nation; there was too great a risk that the information would go straight to Moscow.

In his 28 May testimony, Rickover described the arrangements he had worked out. Rolls Royce and Associates would purchase the reactor from Westinghouse as a commercial transaction so that the respective governments would not be directly involved. As Rickover put it, Westinghouse, not Bettis, would be the British contact. The British would get an S5W, the same reactor that was to propel the fast attack and the Polaris submarines. Congress passed the legislation in August, and the president signed it that same month.

The Royal Navy commissioned the *Dreadnought,* its first nuclear submarine, in 1963. Inevitably the British had encountered difficulties. Some with the steam plant were caused by assuming that the technology and design in this area were already well established and did not need detailed scrutiny. Rickover had encountered the same problem in the American program. The British went on to develop their own reactor for their later submarines. Here they found their difficulties were not with reactor theory but with reactor engineering. That, too, had been Rickover's experience.

Rickover's contact with Mountbatten diminished in the 1960s as Rickover found in Sir Solly Zuckerman, chief scientific advisor to the ministry of defense, a skillful and perceptive individual through whom he made his contacts with the British. Rickover and Mountbatten had a disastrous meeting late in the lives of both men. The latter had come to Washington on some mission. After a small luncheon at the British embassy, the two men went to another room. Eleonore B. Rickover, the admiral's second wife, was waiting in a sitting room. When the two men reappeared she saw her husband's face pale with anger. Abruptly he said to her that they were leaving. On the way home he told her what had happened: Mountbatten had inadvertently implied to Rickover that he might receive a knighthood in return for his support. "Can you believe he didn't know me any better than this—that I would fall for a knighthood?" A few moments later he remarked, "You missed becoming a Lady." She replied that she was very proud of him and that she was already a lady.

Events had made Rickover the "stepfather" of the British nuclear Navy. Its officers and officials found him hard to deal with, hard to predict, and often abrasive, but without him they would never have gotten their first nuclear submarine to sea.[4]

In the aftermath of the *Sputnik*s, Capt. Evan P. Aurand, Eisenhower's naval aide, thought of a way to remind the world of American superiority in one realm of military technology. A voyage of the *Nautilus* crossing the Arctic Ocean and passing beneath the North Pole was sure to catch widespread attention. Under Commander Anderson, she had already operated beneath ice in August and September 1957 and come within 180 miles of the Pole. Only damage to periscopes and a crowded schedule had kept her from making the final dash. Enthusiastic from the first about the plan, Eisenhower made one stipulation: he would announce the success of the voyage. In the ship's first venture under the ice someone had scooped him; he did not want that to happen again.

The *Nautilus* would make her first real attempt for the Pole in June 1958. Passing through the narrow Bering Strait, which divided Siberia and Alaska, she would steam submerged across the Arctic Ocean, pass directly under the Pole, and continue onward, coming out of the ice in the broad and deeper waters between Greenland and Iceland.

On the eve of her departure, Rickover went to Seattle to inspect the ship and to give Anderson some special instructions for the propulsion plant in case of an emergency. Rickover opposed the voyage. The submarine had not operated long enough to be so far from support. If anything happened to her beneath the ice there would be little anyone could do.

In the Chukchi Sea, north of the Bering Strait, the *Nautilus* had to turn back; there was scant space between the shallow sea bottom and the float- ing ice above. Going farther could trap the ship, crushing her as if she were in a vise. Turning around, she headed for Pearl Harbor.

On 23 July she left for her second try, reaching the Pole on 3 August. A celebratory cake, a reenlistment, and the appearance of Santa Claus marked the historic event. Such activities seemed trivial; in the history to reach the Pole so many lives had been lost slogging through ice, fighting bitter winds, and suffering from the piercing cold. But as the submarine's first attempt showed, even in the nuclear age dangers remained. The *Nautilus* surfaced on 7 August off Iceland at the very position Anderson had plotted before the voyage began. A helicopter from Reykjavik picked him up and delivered him to the airport. Anderson flew to Washington while the *Nautilus* went to Portland, England, before returning to the United States.[5]

On 8 August Eisenhower greeted Commander and Mrs. Anderson in the conference room at the White House. The room was crowded with distinguished guests, among them Thomas S. Gates, secretary of the Navy, Adm. James S. Russell, acting chief of naval operations (Burke was out of town), and several other high ranking officers. Lewis L. Strauss, former chairman, and John A. McCone, his successor, represented the Atomic Energy Commission. They saw the president present the Legion of Merit to Anderson and heard Aurand read the citation.

The moment they arrived Anderson and his wife realized Rickover was not there. Once clear of the ceremony, they sped to Rickover's office. They found him about to leave for Shippingport, a trip hurriedly invented to give the impression that he had been too busy to attend the reception. The Navy's slight had hurt him deeply; the Andersons' gracious tribute meant much to him.

The next morning James C. Hagerty, the White House press secretary, met with reporters. The questions soon turned to Rickover's absence. Hagerty explained: the space was small and many people who participat- ed in the historic event were not invited because "we simply couldn't get them into the room."

Years later Russell recalled the incident. The White House wanted the Navy to hold down the attendance. Knowing Rickover had violently opposed the voyage—which was an operational matter—Russell decided it wasn't necessary to invite him. Probably Russell wasn't very sympathet- ic to Rickover: as a young officer he had a bruising encounter with him. "I went away saying if I ever meet that guy in a black [sic] alley I'm really going to let him have it." After the White House ceremony, however, "all hell broke loose."

Gleefully the newspapers picked up the story. The gifted cartoonist Herblock depicted the *Nautilus* approaching the dock and being greeted by a rotund supercilious figure labeled "administration" standing alongside a heavyset, dull-looking, and high-ranking naval officer. The official, holding a medal in his hand, was remarking, "This Splendid Achievement Made Possible By a Man Whose Name I Forget."[6]

The Navy's blunder gave the members and staff of the joint committee an opening they were waiting for. Rickover had been a rear admiral since 1953. He could remain in that rank for seven years and then would have to retire. But, if promoted to vice admiral, he could remain until he was sixty-two.[7]

John T. Conway of the committee staff drafted a speech chastising the Navy for its neglect of Rickover. Drawing heavily upon that draft, Sen. Clinton P. Anderson addressed the Senate on 11 August in a speech titled "The Little Man Who Wasn't There," the name coming from a popular novelty song. The White House in its news release, Anderson began, pointed out that the 116 men in the *Nautilus* were more than had ever been assembled at the North Pole at one time. In reality, he continued, there were 117 men, for the one man who had made the voyage possible was there in spirit. Anderson ridiculed the excuse that there was not enough room for Rickover at the ceremony; he doubted if Rickover weighed 125 pounds, and he certainly did not take up much room. Rickover's absence was not caused by the lack of room, Anderson declared, but by the lack of space "within the Navy for a man who is, and has been, outspoken in his criticisms of old, outmoded Navy concepts." Unless Rickover was promoted to vice admiral, the nation would lose his services. And, Anderson announced, he was introducing a resolution calling for Congress to bestow a Gold Medal on Rickover.[8]

On 18 August both houses of Congress voted unanimously to award Rickover the medal. Eisenhower approved the legislation ten days later and designated Rickover to be vice admiral on 23 October, with his date of rank to be 24 October 1958.[9]

Neither the Navy's position nor its reputation was helped by newspaper stories on the launching of the *Triton* on 19 August. Although, reporters observed, nothing had been settled officially, it was clearly understood in Navy circles and by Rickover and Ruth that she would christen the submarine. Instead, Mrs. John M. Will, wife of Vice Admiral Will, was accorded the honor. Neither of the Rickovers ever forgot the snub, and Ruth always refused later invitations.[10]

In one of her rare interviews, which the *New York Post* reported on 14 August, Ruth said that she didn't care to christen the ship, but her husband wanted her to have the honor: "But it would have been nice if once— just once—they'd have let George enjoy the fruits of his successes," she said. "But you don't know the Navy. . . . The stupid windbags who run it, they are really out to hurt my husband. . . . Doesn't it frighten you that such dumb people have our fate in their hands?"[11]

Eisenhower appointed Rickover to be his personal representative to greet the *Nautilus* when she arrived in New York. The city planned a parade up Broadway to City Hall. The Navy wanted to look its best: in August that meant whites would be the uniform of the day. Rickover claimed he didn't have any whites and wanted khaki. Somehow Jean Scroggins, a young lady in his office whose tact and efficiency were an important factor in running Naval Reactors, assembled the proper uniform. Even then he protested, probably more out of deviltry than anything else.

He flew up to New York with Chet Holifield of the joint committee and Conway. They boarded a Navy tug and met the submarine at the Ambrose lightship on Monday, 24 August. The weather was gray with lowering clouds and rain squalls. A couple of captains offered to assist Rickover to make the dangerous crossing from the tug to the submarine; he pushed them aside, telling them to keep their "God damn hands" off him, that he had been boarding Navy ships for years. Once he and the other guests were on board, the *Nautilus,* her crew lining the deck, entered the harbor. Helicopters hovered overhead, ships whistled, and tugs and fireboats, shooting huge plumes of water into the air, accompanied her.

The weather on Wednesday was perfect for the parade: a mild temperature, bright sun, clear sky. Rickover wanted the captain and the crew to go first—they were the heroes—but the parade officials wanted Rickover to go first because he was the president's representative. After a compromise had been worked out, the procession began at the Bowling Green about noon. Anderson and Rickover rode in a cream-colored convertible; behind them came twenty jeeps filled with the rest of the ship's company.

Clouds of tickertape drifted down on the motorcade and the tumultuous welcoming crowd, lined six deep along the route. Over the uproar shouts of "Well done, skipper!" and "Attaboy Ricky!" could be heard. The parade ended with a reception at City Hall and a luncheon at the Waldorf-Astoria.[12]

If in 1958 Rickover had gained additional prominence in the national scene and promotion to vice admiral, the next year saw him winning greater recognition in education and taking part in international affairs.

Rickover's first book, *Education and Freedom*, came out in March 1959. Made up of a number of his speeches that drew upon his own experiences and the studies he and Ruth were making of education, its diversity of focus did not blur its essential unity. Briefly put, our children, he wrote in the first chapter, titled "Education Is Our First Line of Defense—Make It Strong," needed an education better than the country had ever had or ever needed. "Only massive upgrading of the scholastic standards of our schools will guarantee the future prosperity and freedom of the Republic," he declared. He had found that developing nuclear power demanded better-trained engineers than the average engineer, and that all who were involved in the effort had to raise their thinking to a higher level. The purpose of schools was to challenge students to develop their intellectual promise. Individuals trained to respect intellectual honesty and scientific fact were an elite upon which the future of the nation depended.

Rickover's prominence guaranteed that his views would attract attention. The *Book Review Digest 1959* presented a mixed reception. F. P. Kilcoyne in the *Catholic World* noted, "To say that [Admiral Rickover's] view is narrow is not to minimize the seriousness of the problems to which he points." Irwin Goodwin in the *Chicago Sunday Tribune* thought Rickover's antagonists, which "number many professional school officials, will gag at his proposal for an intellectual elite—even tho the same officials often boast about athletic elites." Myron Lieberman in the *Nation* considered the book "more blinding than illuminating" and a "marked disservice to American education. Its valid points are submerged in sensational and quite irresponsible ranting about our educational situation."

Rickover would enter the arena of educational reform many times in the future, in speeches, in congressional testimony, and in his books: *Swiss Schools and Ours: Why Theirs Are Better* and *American Education, A National Failure: The Problem of Our Schools and What We Can Learn from England*, the first published in 1962 and second a year later.[13]

He had gotten into the field of education, Rickover remarked in private conversations, because he wanted something to keep him in the public eye—something that was no business of the Navy. That explanation, how-ever, did not account for the effort he and Ruth spent in research and writing or for their moral indignation over the failure of schools and society to sow the desire for learning in that short season when the minds of children were most fertile. He referred to education in other countries—Great Britain, Holland, Switzerland, Russia—showing how much more they required of their children than did the United States. Admittedly, such an analysis was difficult because the others had national standards while the Americans did not.

Rickover believed standards were necessary. He thought they should be voluntary, not imposed on schools, but available as a yardstick by which parents could measure the performance of the schools to which they sent their children. One thing he emphasized: standards should be drawn up by scholars, not by members of the educational establishment.

He saw education as a part of the competition between the United States and the Soviet Union. In this context the Americans were impeded by the theories of progressive educators teaching life adjustment. Later his views shifted, and to the earlier obstacles to education he added one more: television. He remembered how the schools of his youth had taught him all the fascination of learning.

In 1959 he visited the Soviet Union, but it was not education that led him there, it was the unlikely combination of diplomacy, Shippingport, and Vice President Richard Nixon's ambitions for the presidency.

Eisenhower and the Soviet premier Nikita S. Khrushchev were moving guardedly toward lessening the tensions between their two countries. As one part of the effort the Russians were to open a trade fair in New York and the Americans to open a trade fair in Moscow. Frol Kozlov, the first deputy premier and heir apparent of Khrushchev, arrived for the ceremony in New York and a tour of the United States. He would visit a number of atomic energy facilities, among them Shippingport.

On 11 July 1959, Kozlov, escorted by a contingent from the State Department and a number of reporters, arrived at the power station where Rickover and key management waited. While going through the station the two men began joshing each other. Rickover began one explanation by remarking, "Even a politician ought to be able to understand this." Kozlov claimed that the plant wasn't working; he couldn't hear any noise. Once Rickover patted the portly Kozlov on the stomach, remarking that the communist official was fat while the capitalist admiral was thin because he worked so hard. For a moment Rickover thought he had gone too far, but Kozlov grinned and the banter continued. At the Pittsburgh airport they spoke of peace. Rickover declared, in words catching the attention of the reporters, "It's all right to talk about peace. Now you go home and do something."[14]

Nixon, after opening the fair in Moscow, was to see Soviet atomic energy projects. Knowing nothing about atomic energy, he wanted someone in his entourage who did. He turned to John A. McCone, chairman of the Atomic Energy Commission, a fellow Republican and Californian. McCone suggested three candidates, Rickover among them. Promptly Nixon chose Rickover. McCone was particularly pleased with the choice. The Soviet nuclear-powered icebreaker *Lenin*, under construction at Leningrad, was on the vice president's itinerary. If Rickover could see its propulsion plant, the Americans would get a glimpse of the status of Soviet reactor technology.

Although never having met Rickover, Nixon knew his reputation and admired him. Furthermore, the Nixon party would return to the United States through Poland, and the presence of Rickover, born in czarist Makow, would prove the promise of America. The Navy felt differently about Rickover and tried to persuade McCone that better-qualified officers were available. Later Rickover recalled that the Navy told McCone that it had better-looking officers to accompany the vice president.

Rickover was eager to go. He hoped to use his contact with Kozlov to find some way of easing the relationships between the two states. (If the hope ever had a chance, it was thwarted when Kozlov died of a heart attack.) Rickover wanted to take with him Mandil and Theodore Rockwell, two of his senior engineers, but higher powers decided that their inclusion made the purpose of the trip technical rather than diplomatic. Rickover talked to Nixon and won his consent to offer the Soviets a wide-ranging agreement to exchange information on all power reactors, all reactors producing fissionable materials for weapons, and all nonnaval propulsion reactors. Precisely what authority Nixon had to make the offer is not clear; Eisenhower at his press conference just before Nixon's departure stated that the vice president was not part of American diplomatic machinery.[15]

The Nixon party left Baltimore's Friendship International Airport at 9:30 P.M. on 22 July. The flight was long and the plane was crowded. The vice president and the admiral had a chance to exchange only a few words. At 2:50 P.M. on 23 July the plane landed at Vnukova Airport, where Kozlov

greeted it. The reception was cool, in part because the Senate had recently passed and Eisenhower had signed the Captive Nations Resolution,
which called for setting aside the third week in July of each year to
commemorate those nations that had lost their freedom and independence. Obviously aimed at the Soviet Union, the resolution irritated many
of its officials.

On Friday, 24 July, Nixon and Ambassador Llewellyn Thompson made
a courtesy call on Khrushchev and others at the Kremlin. That afternoon
Nixon, Mrs. Nixon, Thompson, and Rickover, seated in the first car of a
motorcade, passed through streets lined with spectators to Sokolniki Park
to preview the American trade exhibition. Its ten acres included a pond
with boats, a children's playground, rows of cars, and a place where visitors could obtain free Pepsi-Cola. A model home was located almost at
the back of the area.

Khrushchev and Soviet officials were already at the fair. The Russian
leader declared on meeting Rickover, "You must be the Admiral who has
been making warlike speeches against the Soviet Union." To which Rickover replied, "No. Are you the Khrushchev who has been making speeches against the United States?" The conversation ended with an exchange
of platitudes on the need for peace. Rickover's notes do not refer to the
"kitchen debate" between Nixon and Khrushchev, which was so important to the vice president's future.[16]

On 25 July Rickover went with Nixon to the Kremlin, where the vice
president visited several high officials, among them Khrushchev and Kozlov. In talking with Kozlov, Nixon said that Rickover, representing the
president and the vice president, wanted to explore areas of atomic energy information that could be added to those in which exchanges were
already taking place. Rickover stated that he was authorized to arrange for
the exchange of information on all reactors. The proposition was interesting, Kozlov replied, and it would be considered, but the Soviet Union
could not act quickly. For one thing, the Captive Nations Resolution had
caused relations between the two countries to deteriorate.[17]

At a luncheon Khrushchev held, Rickover engaged in a spirited conversation with a functionary named Zukhov on exchanging information on
Navy yards and reactors:

Rickover: Although the United States is a democracy it can act fast.
    Can the Soviet Government also act fast?
Zukhov: A committee has been set up to take care of these matters.

Rickover: I have authority from my government to make arrangements
as to exchanges of reactor information. Who, in Russia, should I deal
with? Do you have the authority?

Zukhov: I have the authority.

Rickover: Let us exchange information on Navy Yards. We will be glad
to have you visit our Navy Yards if we are granted permission to visit
yours.

Zukhov: We will take the matter up with the committee which is
working with the State Department.

Rickover: Let us do it fast—this afternoon. Whom will you designate
to sit down with me and work out a list of Navy Yards.

Zukhov: How many yards?

Rickover: As many as you wish—1, 2, 3, or all.

Zukhov: We will have to refer it to a committee.

Rickover: I have authority from the Navy to make these arrangements.
Can't Russia act as fast as the United States?

Rickover turned to reactors. Zukhov reiterated that a committee would
take up the subject, and, furthermore, the U.S. Constitution did not permit
Rickover to make such offers without congressional authority. As Zukhov
continued to repeat that argument, Rickover saw no use proceeding.

Zukhov's appraisal of Rickover's offer was shrewd. Both countries were
carrying on negotiations to allow some degree of cooperation in atomic
energy, and Rickover's proposals were not part of that effort. Moreover,
the Soviet official must have known of Eisenhower's statement that the
vice president was not on a diplomatic mission; therefore, Rickover had
no authority to negotiate.

That evening at a dinner at the American embassy, Rickover talked to
Khrushchev for about fifteen minutes. One exchange revealed an interesting glimpse of Soviet education. Under a new ruling, Soviet students who
had completed secondary school had to work for one or two years before
entering the university. Rickover said to Khrushchev that he

considered this a mistake on his part, as many students might lose interest if
their education was interrupted by one or two years. He replied that many students were going on to universities because of influence—their parents could
afford to keep them in school—and because they wanted to keep on going from
one school to another. He, himself had not had too much schooling, but had
made out well. I replied that I agreed with him, that in general there were many

"educated fools" in all countries, and there were professors who goofed also; however, Mr. Khrushchev and the Russian leaders were exceptional people and he must not judge all people by himself. He said there were cases of women particularly who spent years at a university and then got married and did nothing more professionally. We both agreed that it was not necessary for a girl to go to college to learn to have children. He ended by saying he was determined that those going on to a university should do some work between secondary school and the university.

On 27 July the Nixon party flew to Leningrad, where it would see the *Lenin*. The icebreaker had been launched in December 1957. The Americans were given a brief tour during which they were led out onto a catwalk, where they looked down into the reactor compartment; then they were ushered out and shown a short film that did not include shots of the propulsion plant. That was it.

Nixon and Rickover were incensed. The vice president had a schedule to keep but gave Rickover permission to remain. Raymond L. Garthoff, a young CIA estimates officer fluent in Russian, stayed with Rickover. Storming and shouting, Rickover demanded to see the compartment. He was told it was locked. A number of burly Russians, listening to the dispute, stood silently along the bulkhead. Rickover asked who they were. Workmen, came the reply. He asked to see their hands. American workmen, he snorted, had calluses—these men had none. Garthoff suspected they were secret police and probably knew English. Rickover, having the same thought, made his remarks even more inflammatory and insulting. Occasionally in an aside to Garthoff he would murmur, "How'm I doing?" After his hosts checked with Moscow, he was finally permitted to make a brief inspection of the compartment. He stayed for three hours, asking questions and taking notes.

That evening he rejoined Nixon and the others. Members of the official escort reported that Rickover had not been diplomatic, a criticism Nixon swept aside by declaring the admiral had gotten to see the plant—that was his purpose. In his book *Six Crises* Nixon wrote that Rickover "had turned in a particularly outstanding job." The American press agreed. McCone sent a message to Rickover: "Well done. All press reports your efforts and final inspection of Lenin well received." On 27 July the *Washington Daily News* headlined "Rickover Gets Good Look at Atom Ship after 'Run-Around,'" and the *Chicago Daily News* of 28 July proclaimed, "Rickover Sees Atom Ship."[18] Another, more personal, high point came one evening when the Americans saw the ballet *Spartacus*. Rickover was in the group seated in the czar's box.

On its way back to the United States, the Nixon party stopped briefly in Poland. The reception in Warsaw on 2 August was overwhelming. Although little or no publicity had been given to the visit, cheering crowds packed the route and threw flowers into the cars. On two occasions while in Poland, Rickover gave advice to Nixon. Once the vice president received an apparently impromptu invitation to speak in an auditorium. Rickover, noticing that the backdrop featured a large hammer and sickle, recommended that Nixon decline, advice the vice president accepted. Another time Nixon's car brushed against a man on a bicycle, knocking him down. The immediate impulse was to continue, but Rickover quickly advised Nixon against it. Jumping from the car, the vice president helped pick the man up. Fortunately, the man had suffered no injuries, and the gesture won great applause.

Nixon introduced Rickover to the milling crowds, explaining that he had been born in a small town near Warsaw, had migrated to the United States, and had become an American hero for building the world's first atomic submarine. To himself Nixon observed that Rickover, outwardly unemotional, was greatly moved by his reception.[19]

Nixon and his group landed at 4:07 P.M. on 5 August at Washington National Airport. The vice president had enhanced his political future, and Rickover had learned a great deal from the *Lenin*.

The icebreaker had three pressurized water reactors. Inspecting them as painstakingly as he could, Rickover concluded that the Soviets had much to learn. The reactor compartment was poorly laid out and there was not sufficient attention paid to safety. Physicists, he suspected, were responsible for the shortcomings, and he repeated his longstanding conviction that reactor development was more a matter of engineering than physics. The *Lenin* looked ready to go to sea, even if the Russians said they had not yet tested the reactor. Rickover was inclined to disbelieve the statement: if the reactor had not been tested, he would have seen numerous instrumentation devices and cables. (Later sources stated that the icebreaker was commissioned in 1959.) He thought the Russians probably did not yet have atomic submarines.[20]

The *Lenin* held one major lesson for Rickover: the layout of the plant, components, and auxiliaries were important intelligence targets. He determined that Americans must not allow uncleared individuals or foreign nationals to see their naval nuclear propulsion plants.[21]

Rickover talked to Ruth and their son Robert about the Soviet Union. Living conditions looked better than they were; apartment buildings appeared fine from the outside but were terribly overcrowded inside. He went to Chicago, alone as always, to see his parents. They marveled that he, the son of a Jew who had once been a conscript in the czar's army, had sat in the czar's box in Leningrad to watch a ballet.

A little over a year later, on 8 November 1960, Abraham Rickover died of heart failure. He was eighty-five, the father of three, the grandfather of five, and the great grandfather of five. Retiring at seventy-six but unable to remain idle, he had resumed his trade as a tailor and worked a few more years. Rickover, again without Ruth or Robert, flew to Chicago for the services. "Hold Rites for Dad of Rickover" the *Chicago Daily News* headed its brief obituary.

Abraham Rickover had won some success, for he had realized his dream of becoming the owner of a small apartment building. Rickover would speak with admiration of how hard his father worked, his pride, and his determination to refuse charity. The reminiscences, however, did not contain warm anecdotes, possibly because his father was absent from home so much of the day or because Rickover, an intensely private person, chose not to relate them.

The Kozlov-Nixon visits were to be followed by an Eisenhower-Khrushchev exchange. The Russian premier came to the United States in September 1959, and plans called for the American president to visit the Soviet Union in 1960. First, however, the two leaders would meet that spring with Prime Minister Macmillan of Great Britain and President de Gaulle of France in Geneva, Switzerland. Captain Aurand, the president's naval aide, thought a submerged voyage around the world by the *Triton*, timed to end just before the conference, would add to American prestige.

The submarine was still new. She had begun her sea trials at the end of September 1959. Under Capt. Edward L. Beach she had made a few short coastal voyages and, as 1960 opened, was preparing for her shakedown cruise. Suddenly summoned to Washington, Beach was asked if his ship could circumnavigate the world submerged. He was not informed of the purpose of the voyage but was told it had to be completed on 10 May. Rickover visited the submarine and discussed some power settings that would give Beach more flexibility in operating the two-reactor plant.

Beach set sail on 16 February and, following a course roughly paralleling that of Magellan, surfaced on 10 May off Rehoboth Beach, Delaware.

A helicopter whisked him to the White House, where he rejoined his wife and received the congratulations of Eisenhower and several others. Unlike the ceremony for the polar voyage of the *Nautilus*, Rickover was present.[22]

By her submerged voyage around the world, the *Triton* had given an extraordinary demonstration of the capabilities of nuclear propulsion. Its effect on the summit, however, was overshadowed by the loss of a U-2 high-flying reconnaissance aircraft shot down by the Soviet Union. That event ended whatever hopes existed of Eisenhower visiting the Soviet Union.

Rickover had become a national figure. A play, *The Captain and the Kings*, starring Dana Andrews playing a role based on Rickover, had an exceedingly brief run in New York. More important, Rickover was sought after as a speaker at various occasions and was a frequent witness before congressional committees. These activities gave him no respite from his real responsibilities—developing reactors and training people.

Rachel Rickover and her children Fannie and Chaim in Poland, c. 1903–4. Abraham Rickover was already in New York. *Eleonore B. Rickover*

Rachel, Fannie, and Chaim arrived in New York on 26 March 1906 on board the *Finland*. *U.S. Naval Institute*

Hyman, Augusta, and Fannie
Rickover in New York, c. 1908.
Eleonore B. Rickover

At the 1916 Republican
presidential conven-
tion, Western Union
messenger boy Rick-
over stationed himself
to see everything and
collect most of the
tips. *Eleonore B. Rickover*

Rickover in front of Bancroft Hall. At night he rigged a blanket to hide the light and studied in the shower stall. *Eleonore B. Rickover*

Rickover thought the practice cruises were the best part of academy life, for they had none of the pettiness of Bancroft Hall. Days began at 5:30 with two hours of swabbing decks and polishing bright work. *Eleonore B. Rickover*

As an upperclassman, Rickover was no longer worried by the uncertainties of his plebe year, when he had wondered if he could "survive" at the academy. His grades were respectable. *Eleonore B. Rickover*

The destroyer *La Vallette* was Rickover's first ship. Her commanding officer found him hardworking, efficient, and studious. *Eleonore B. Rickover*

Ensign H. G. Rickover on watch in the *La Vallette* during a high-speed run. *Eleonore B. Rickover*

Captain C. S. Kempff, commanding the *Nevada*, commented on Lieutenant (jg) Rickover in March 1927: "Has done excellent work. . . . Thoroughly honest and painstaking in all his work." *U.S. Naval Institute*

Rickover and Ruth Masters, probably just before their marriage in October 1931. He wrote of her death in 1972: "She was at once the most human and intelligent person I ever knew, the greatest influence on my life and career." *Eleonore B. Rickover*

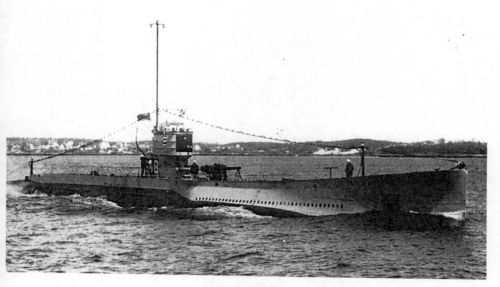

In December 1932, after two and a half years as engineer and executive officer in the *S-48*, Rickover wrote: "I hope that never again in my naval service will I ever be subject to conditions such as these." *U.S. Navy*

Rickover (in front, walking the plank) crossing the Equator in *S-48*.
Eleonore B. Rickover

Captain Frank Jack Fletcher of the *New Mexico* in February 1937 wrote that Lieutenant Rickover was "more than any one man responsible for the NEW MEXICO winning the engineering competition two years in succession." *U.S. Naval Institute*

The minesweeper *Finch* of the Asiatic Fleet was Rickover's only command at sea. He was severely criticized by his superiors for giving higher priority to making up for years of neglected maintenance rather than keeping up her appearance.
U.S. Naval Institute

Rickover atop a water buffalo in the Philippines. While stationed at the Cavite Navy Yard near Manila, he and Ruth traveled at every opportunity. *Eleonore B. Rickover*

Commander Rickover, head of the electrical section in the Bureau of Ships, visiting a defense plant (probably General Electric) during World War II. *Eleonore B. Rickover*

Captain Rickover (*second from left*), with other Bureau of Ships officers, inspecting a submarine main generator at the Westinghouse East Pittsburgh plant in October 1944. Rear Admiral Earle W. Mills (*far right*) would play a key role in starting Rickover's career in nuclear propulsion. *Eleonore B. Rickover*

Rickover found mud the ever-present enemy on Okinawa. *Eleonore B. Rickover*

Undated photography, probably taken by Rickover, of Ruth and their son Robert. *Robert M. Rickover*

Rachel and Abraham Rickover in 1949. Both were in their mid-seventies. Because they disapproved of his marrying out of the Jewish faith, he never visited them with Ruth or Robert. *Eleonore B. Rickover*

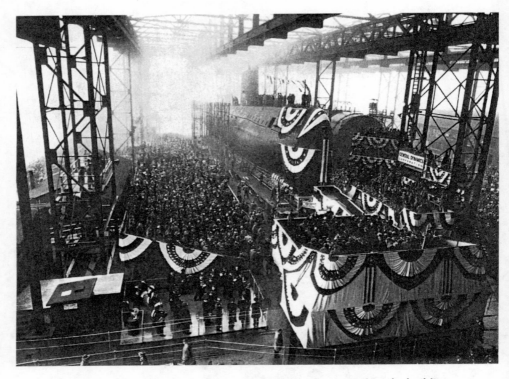

The first nuclear-powered ship, the submarine *Nautilus*, poised on the building ways at Electric Boat on 21 January 1954. Just before launching, a breeze suddenly swept away the fog, and flags and bunting began to ripple. *General Dynamics Electric Boat*

Nautilus getting under way from Electric Boat for initial sea trials, 17 January 1955. Once clear of the pier, Wilkinson ordered the engines all back full. Then it happened: the scream of metal on metal filled the engine room. *U.S. Navy*

Rickover boarding the *Nautilus* in New York on 24 August 1958 on her return from the first voyage beneath the North Pole. *Associated Press*

Meeting with President Kennedy, 11 February 1963. The president wanted his views on the multilateral force. It was to be made up of Polaris submarines manned by an international crew. Rickover had strong ideas but did not know how Kennedy would receive them. *White House*

In the ceremony held at the Oval Office on 3 December 1973 promoting Rickover to four-star admiral, President Nixon remarked: ". . . this man, who is controversial . . . did not become submerged by the bureaucracy." *White House*

The surprise Bednowicz-Rickover wedding, 19 January 1974. Rickover later declared: "When you meet a very charming, gracious, witty, intelligent, and beautiful woman," a marriage doesn't have to be explained.
Eleonore B. Rickover

Rickover on board the aircraft carrier *Nimitz* on initial sea trials, March 1975. She was the first of the two-reactor carriers, a propulsion system forced on Rickover because Secretary of Defense Robert S. McNamara would not accept the four-reactor propulsion plant for political reasons. *U.S. Navy*

Nuclear surface ships steaming in formation in the eastern Mediterranean, 1976. *From the foreground back:* the cruisers *California, South Carolina,* and the carrier *Nimitz. U.S. Navy*

Initial sea trials of the *Los Angeles* (SSN 688), the first of a class of high-speed attack submarines, on 27 June 1976. Rickover fought for them, convinced they were essential to meet the growing Soviet threat. *Newport News Shipbuilding and Drydock Company*

A month after President Carter's inauguration, Rickover was pleased to find that the president welcomed his views and wanted to keep receiving them. The admiral presented Carter with the workbook he kept as a member of the nuclear propulsion program. *White House*

Rickover at the White House with Secretary of Energy James R. Schlesinger as the Light Water Breeder Reactor at Shippingport, Pennsylvania, achieved full power on 2 December 1977, the 35th anniversary of the world's first man-made, self-sustaining nuclear chain reaction. *White House*

At the Rickover residence, 31 May 1979. Eleonore had not told her husband that she had invited the president of the United States and his wife and daughter to dinner. *White House*

Rickover played a major part in developing the Trident missile submarine. This picture shows the *Ohio*, the first of the class, under construction at Electric Boat in 1978. *General Dynamics Electric Boat*

Rickover in his office at Naval Reactors, Arlington, Virginia, late 1970s. *Eleonore B. Rickover*

Rickover had a stormy meeting with President Reagan, 8 January 1982, with John F. Lehman, secretary of the navy, present. The admiral had nourished the hope that he could remain on his job. He could not. *White House*

On 29 January 1982, the Senate took the first step in awarding Rickover a second Congressional gold medal. Admiral Thomas B. Hayward, chief of naval operations, Sen. John W. Warner, Eleonore Rickover, Admiral Rickover, and Sen. Henry M. Jackson gathered to celebrate in the vice president's office off the Senate chamber. *Eleonore B. Rickover*

Rickover at Electric Boat on 27 August 1983, the day of the launching of the *Hyman G. Rickover* (SSN 709). Admiral James D. Watkins, chief of naval operations at Rickover's left, Adm. Kinnaird R. McKee, Rickover's successor as director of naval reactors, at his right. *General Dynamics Electric Boat*

Rickover's eighty-sixth birthday at his home in Arlington, Virginia. Members of Naval Reactors staff behind Rickover. *From left to right:* Gene Rogers, David Scott, Carl Schmitt, Tim Foster, and Souren Hanessian. The cake's proportions and color were those of the "pinks." *Eleonore B. Rickover*

Rickover Hall, the engineering building at the Naval Academy, and the bronze bust of Rickover in its lobby. The nose on the bust has become shiny from midshipmen rubbing it for good luck during examinations. *J. Martin and USNA Archives*

The Program at the End of 1960

On 15 April 1959, at the end of the ceremony at which Rickover received the Gold Medal that Congress had voted him, he declared, "We shall let nothing deter us from building a nuclear Navy in the shortest possible time."[1] Rickover had the facilities in place to meet his goal, and he certainly had the determination to fight for it.

The achievements of nuclear-powered ships, listed in the annual report the Atomic Energy Commission published at the end of 1960, showed the potential of nuclear propulsion.[2] In that year three Polaris submarines were operating. In addition, two attack submarines had ventured into the Polar regions. The *Sargo* had made the first midwinter cruise beneath the Arctic ice and had surfaced at the North Pole on 9 February. In August the *Seadragon* had made the dangerous voyage across the top of North America and, en route, had surfaced at the Pole. The *Triton* had ended her submerged voyage around the world on 10 May.

Fourteen submarines were in operation, twenty-one were under construction, and Congress had authorized construction of an additional eleven. Two surface ships, the guided-missile cruiser *Long Beach* and the aircraft carrier *Enterprise,* had been launched, while the guided-missile destroyer leader (or frigate) *Bainbridge* was on the building ways.

The Navy was using seven yards to build the nuclear fleet. Five were privately owned: the Electric Boat Division of the General Dynamics Corporation at Groton, Connecticut; the Newport News Shipbuilding and Dry Dock Company at Newport News, Virginia; the Bethlehem Steel Company at Quincy, Massachusetts; the Ingalls Shipbuilding Corporation at Pascagoula, Mississippi; and the New York Shipbuilding Corporation at Camden, New Jersey. Two were Navy yards: one at Portsmouth, New Hampshire, the other at Mare Island, California.

In the Bettis and Knolls laboratories Rickover had created the technical excellence on which the program depended. They had developed all the reactor plants but one. The exception was a small propulsion system for a hunter-killer submarine developed by Combustion Engineering at Windsor, Connecticut. It was the company's first and last project. The ship turned out to be not only more expensive but also slower and larger than had been planned.

Describing, even briefly, the various reactor plants had become easier since the adoption of a system of designating them. The nomenclature consisted of three characters: an initial letter, a number, and a final letter. The first letter indicated the shipboard propulsion purpose for which the reactor was developed: *S* for submarine, *D* for destroyer, *C* for cruiser, and *A* for aircraft carrier. The number designated the model of that type developed by the designer. The final letter indicated the designer of the plant: *W* for Westinghouse, *G* for General Electric, and *C* for Combustion Engineering. Because the Mark I at Idaho was the first reactor plant developed for submarine propulsion by Westinghouse, it became the S1W, while the *Nautilus* reactor plant became the S2W.

The S3W/S4W and the S5W did not have land prototypes. The S3W/S4W powered the *Sargo* and *Seadragon* as well as two other fleet-type submarines and a submarine that carried the guided missile Regulus. Because of their low speed, the Navy would not build any more of the fleet-type or Regulus-missile submarines. In contrast, the more powerful S5W plant would drive many submarines. As of 1960, Congress had authorized thirty-seven of them, of which twenty-three were fast attack and fourteen were Polaris.

Rickover had five land prototypes in operation. Three were for submarines. He was using the S1W, built at the National Reactor Testing Station in Idaho for the *Nautilus* as a flexible test facility for improved submarine reactor systems, components, and cores. The S3G advanced reactor, located at West Milton, New York, served as the prototype for the S4G plant of the *Triton* and was being used in development work. West Milton had been the site of the sodium-cooled S1G, the prototype for the S2G reactor plant in the *Seawolf.* Because the pressurized-water reactor plants were proving superior for naval operations, Rickover dropped the sodium-cooled approach. In 1958 Electric Boat began installing a pressurized-water propulsion system for the *Seawolf.* The S1C at Windsor, Connecticut, was the land prototype for the hunter-killer submarine *Tullibee,* which had just been placed in commission.

Two land prototypes were for surface ships. The A1W in Idaho was the only prototype with two reactors. They drove one propeller shaft. Eight A_1Ws would power the four shafts of the *Enterprise* and two A_1Ws would make up the C_1W two-reactor plant for the *Long Beach*. The D_1G at West Milton was providing data for the D_2G two-reactor plant of the *Bainbridge*.

Although land prototypes were crucial in the development of reactor propulsion plants, Rickover also used them for another important purpose: every officer and every sailor who would operate the shipboard plants received his training on the prototypes.

The S_5G natural circulation reactor was developing one of the most promising concepts. It made use of the convection current that flowed in a liquid held at two different temperatures in the same system. Cooler, denser water forced warmer and lighter water to rise. Robert Panoff, Rickover's submarine project officer, believed that the approach might make possible eliminating or slowing down many components that had rotary or reciprocating elements. Through their vibration, they transmitted noise through the hull to the sea. Chief among these were pumps. Rickover saw natural circulation primarily as a means of simplifying the reactor propulsion system and, by doing so, returning to engineering practices that aimed at ruggedness, reliability, and easy maintenance, virtues he believed had been too often neglected or lost in the Navy's post–World War II efforts to adopt high-speed, lightweight machinery.

The S_5G prototype developed by Knolls would be built at the National Reactor Testing Station. Whether the reactor plant would operate reliably in a submarine, subject to the motion of the sea and the rapid maneuvers demanded of a combatant ship, was a question that had to be answered. Bettis and Knolls ran test loops on platforms that rocked and rolled to mimic the pitching and rolling of a ship. Although providing valuable data, such tests could not furnish all of the needed information. For that purpose, a land prototype able to simulate a ship at sea was essential. May 1961 saw its construction begin in Idaho. Under the conceptual design developed by Willis C. Barnes, an engineer officer who was later to leave the program and rise to flag rank, the prototype, floating in a basin, would be rocked by gyro stabilizers to achieve a roll angle of fifteen degrees to either side. Wave dampeners would prevent water from breaking over the sides of the basin.[3]

Much of the research and development work at the laboratories went into the improvement of reactor components to reach higher levels of reliability. Most of the effort, therefore, was highly classified, but in a few areas the results could be announced. In February 1957 the *Nautilus* was refueled at Electric Boat. On her first reactor core she had traveled sixty-two thousand miles, and on her second she would steam ninety thousand miles. Rickover's ultimate goal was a core that would last the life of a ship, which, for submarines, might reach thirty years.[4]

In September 1955 Adm. Arleigh A. Burke, chief of naval operations, had decided that all of the Navy's future submarines would be nuclear-powered. Even with all her imperfections, the *Nautilus* was deadly, her speed enabling her to outrun torpedoes and outmaneuver the surface enemy. Even before she was at sea the Navy had begun planning to build classes of nuclear submarines.[5]

Rickover had earlier begun reorganizing Bettis and Knolls to relieve them of the burden of multiple procurement. In 1956 he established the Plant Apparatus Department (PAD) outside Pittsburgh and, three years later, the Machinery Apparatus Operation (MAO) near Schenectady. The purpose of both organizations was to procure all components for reactor plants that were not prototypes or the first propulsion plant of its type. Neither PAD nor MAO ever procured reactor cores.

Procurement of conventional components, such as steam generators, pumps, and valves, proved difficult because the vendors had to be taught and often forced to meet the unprecedented standards that Rickover insisted that nuclear technology demanded; they had to understand that specifications were not goals but targets that had to be met.[6]

The table in the commission's 1960 annual report showed one important fact. Congress had authorized eleven submarines in addition to those in operation or under construction; in contrast, no more nuclear surface ships had been authorized since the *Bainbridge* in the 1959 building program.

One reason was expense. In January 1960 Burke sent an ad hoc committee under Rear Adm. Miles H. Hubbard to the yards where the three surface ships were under construction to investigate the causes of the escalating costs. On 25 February the committee issued its report. In every area building costs were going up. The costs of the *Enterprise* and *Bainbridge* had increased 1.5 times over their original estimates, and, because of exceptional circumstances, the costs for the *Long Beach* had grown 3.7 times. The increase for the nuclear propulsion plants of all three ships was 1.5 times, not out of line with the general trend.

The report came down hard on nuclear propulsion, declaring that no more nuclear surface ships should be built until those under construction had been tested at sea. It saw little chance that the pressurized water reactors would ever become competitive with oil-fueled propulsion plants. The technology cost too much, and pressurized water propulsion systems were too heavy for the horsepower they produced. It was far better to spend funds on improving the antiaircraft and antisubmarine capabilities of surface ships.[7] Whatever influence it had, the report reflected an attitude, if not necessarily the reasoning, that was widespread among senior officers of the surface Navy.

With nuclear propulsion for surface ships a contentious issue, Burke thought a treatise covering the subject from all angles, good and bad, would provide a common source for Navy statements, speeches, articles, and testimony. Milton Shaw, Rickover's surface ship project officer, worked closely with the office of the chief of naval operations on the paper.

"A Treatise on Nuclear Propulsion for Surface Ships" was completed in early 1961. In summary, the treatise acknowledged that nuclear propulsion would not have the same impact on surface ship operations as it did on those of submarines. Rough estimates, based on the best data available, indicated that nuclear surface ships could cost about one and a half times more than their oil-fired counterparts. Consequently, the Navy could buy three conventionally fueled frigates for the cost of two nuclear frigates. But nuclear propulsion could give surface ships virtually unlimited endurance at high average speed; they did not have to depend on tankers, themselves valuable and vulnerable targets, for fuel.[8]

Coming years would see the arguments become more elaborate and sophisticated, but the basic question was always the same: Were the military advantages that nuclear propulsion gave to surface ships worth their cost? The newly elected administration of John F. Kennedy would have to deal with the matter.

Breakthrough on Nuclear Carriers

LIKE ALL LEADERS of major enterprises, particularly those associated with national defense, Rickover was deeply interested in politics. That was especially true of the presidential election of 1960. Ever since their trip to the Soviet Union in 1959, Rickover had admired Vice President Richard Nixon, the Republican candidate, but they had not kept in close contact. While testifying before Sen. Lyndon B. Johnson's Subcommittee on Preparedness, Rickover had met John F. Kennedy, the Democratic candidate. The young senator from Massachusetts had made no particular impression; he was simply an attractive man who asked intelligent questions.[1] In a vigorous campaign pledging a rapid buildup of the nation's defense, Kennedy won a narrow victory in the popular vote.

Without doubt the naval nuclear propulsion program would feel the impact of the new administration. From that perspective, Rickover was interested in three presidential appointments: Robert S. McNamara, secretary of defense; John B. Connally, secretary of the Navy; and Glenn T. Seaborg, chairman of the Atomic Energy Commission. McNamara, who had served a few weeks as president of the Ford Motor Company before coming to Washington, had won a reputation as a strong, effective, and scientific manager. Connally was an astute and ambitious politician from Texas, and Seaborg was a brilliant chemist who had played an important role in the Manhattan Project and won a Nobel Prize for his work on transuranium elements.

Rickover did not know McNamara or Connally but had met Seaborg occasionally in the early uncertain days of the propulsion program. Seaborg remembered vividly one meeting with Rickover, back in 1947, when the Naval Group from Oak Ridge had stopped at the radiation laboratory at the University of California, one of the places on their itinerary to ascertain the status of reactor development. Seaborg never forgot the intense conviction with which Rickover spoke of naval nuclear propulsion. Now chairman of the AEC, Seaborg was convinced that naval ship propulsion was "obviously one of the best uses, if not the best, for nuclear power."[2]

Rickover could gather some idea of what the new administration thought about nuclear-powered ships from the Navy's fiscal year 1962 budget, presented to Congress early in the calendar year 1961. As drawn up by the departing Eisenhower administration, it called for three Polaris submarines, three attack submarines of the *Thresher* class, and seven oil-fired guided-missile frigates. It did not request an attack aircraft carrier, not surprising considering that the oil-fired *America* had been authorized in the preceding year. The only major change the Kennedy administration asked for was in the Polaris program: it called for ten of the submarines and would get them.[3] The number of nuclear-powered surface ships authorized remained unchanged; it consisted of the aircraft carrier *Enterprise*, the guided-missile cruiser *Long Beach*, and the guided-missile frigate *Bainbridge*, all under construction.

The seven frigates caught the attention of Rickover and his friends on Capitol Hill. In drawing up its proposed budget, the Navy had asked for two nuclear frigates, a request the Eisenhower administration had denied. The Kennedy administration, however, in its strong effort to build up the nation's defense, might accept an initiative from Congress to insert them in the building program. William H. Bates (R-Mass.), a Navy veteran and a member of the House Committee on Armed Services and the Joint Committee on Atomic Energy, set the stage in the Armed Services Committee while Rickover lined up the Navy.

On 19 March 1961 Rickover telephoned Adm. Arleigh A. Burke, chief of naval operations, to find out if he still wanted the two nuclear ships. Burke did. On 18 April Rickover briefed Connally on the nuclear program. Mentioning that he (Rickover) would be asked to testify before the House Armed Services Committee, he asked if he could state that the secretary approved substituting two nuclear for three of the conventional ships. Connally agreed enthusiastically.

On 24 April Rickover came before the House committee. It was his first appearance. The committee chairman, Carl Vinson, a Democrat from Georgia, had been elected to Congress in 1914 and had made naval affairs his interest. The changes Bates was proposing to the Navy building program, Vinson explained to the members, were why Rickover, an unscheduled witness, had been invited to testify. Rickover began by straightening out the impression left by an officer in earlier testimony. He had stated that Rickover was developing a single-reactor plant for a surface ship. Consequently, it was better to wait for it than to build the two-reactor ships under consideration. A great deal of work had to be done, Rickover declared, before the single-reactor plant was ready. Building the two nuclear frigates under consideration was the best way to reduce costs. Both would be powered by the D2G reactor plant, which was being installed in the frigate *Bainbridge* already on the building ways. In his view, a steady construction program was the best way to lower costs. The question of the smallest combatant surface ship suitable for nuclear propulsion arose. In Rickover's view eight thousand tons was the minimum because a nuclear propulsion plant took up too much room and weighed too much for a smaller ship.

The results of his appearance were less than Rickover had hoped. Whereas the House Armed Services Committee proposed two nuclear and four conventional frigates, the Senate committee wanted the seven conventional ships. A conference committee fashioned a compromise authorizing seven frigates, one of which would be nuclear. It would be named the *Truxtun*. Still, next year would bring another chance. In one other way the hearing had been important. L. Mendel Rivers of South Carolina, whose district included the Charleston Navy Yard, enthusiastically welcomed Rickover's appearance. In a few years the relationship between the two would lead to their alliance against McNamara.

One thing Rickover probably did not know: although the secretary of defense had not opposed the congressional action, neither had he given his wholehearted approval. He was just beginning a study on the application of nuclear power to the surface fleet.[4]

The Navy's first nuclear-powered surface ship, the *Long Beach*, got under way for her initial sea trials at 6:30 A.M. on 5 July 1961 from Bethlehem's yard at Quincy, Massachusetts. Five and a half years earlier her commanding officer, Capt. Eugene P. Wilkinson, and Rickover had taken the *Nautilus*, the first nuclear-powered submarine, on her initial trials; now they were together again. For more than two days the cruiser steamed about 820 miles, sometimes in heavy fog. The two-reactor plant operated beautifully. Because her weapon systems had not been completely installed, she was hardly a combatant ship. That job would require extended time in a yard.[5]

One incident during construction of the ship revealed the gulf between the care given to the propulsion plant components and that accorded the weapon systems. The spare main coolant pump received meticulous attention as the shipyard work force moved it slowly and precisely from the pier to its place below decks. Sometime earlier, however, the ship had received its first Talos, a surface-to-air missile, and the workers had not given it the same attention: while lifting the missile on board, they had damaged it.[6]

Rickover was driving himself very hard. In the morning of 25 July 1961, while walking down the corridor to his office in N Building (a World War II temporary structure located just behind Main Navy) and talking with Cdr. John W. Crawford Jr., a senior engineer officer in Naval Reactors, Rickover remarked that his hands felt cold. Crawford immediately said he should go to his office and lie down. Rickover replied that he didn't need to do that. Crawford insisted and called a doctor from Main Navy. After an examination, the doctor had Rickover (with a sheet over his head to prevent identification) put on a stretcher and taken to the medical rooms in Main Navy. A more thorough examination at the Bethesda Naval Hospital showed he had suffered a heart attack. He was placed in Tower 16, the VIP area.

That day nurse Lt. Eleonore A. Bednowicz was assigned to that area. In appearance she was a small, slender woman, but in manner she was efficient, brisk, and hardworking—and she stood for no nonsense. She did not meet Rickover until seven o'clock the next morning. Her first sight of him she was always to remember: he looked so little in bed. He quickly proved to be a good patient, interested in his treatment and in the life around him. Bednowicz made arrangements so that when Ruth Rickover visited her husband, the two of them could have lunch together. Later she met their son Robert when he came down from Yale.

Rickover quickly resumed much of his normal activity, beginning to read the "pinks" on his first day at Bethesda. Soon he was leaving the hospital for several hours. Treating his hospital room as his office, he frequently left papers scattered about. Once, while he was testifying before a congressional committee, Eleonore straightened them, although she had been warned by the chief nurse that he objected strenuously to anyone touching them. On his return he angrily asked who had disturbed his papers.

"Admiral," she declared firmly, "this is my ship."

He looked thoughtfully at her. "She was tough," he later remarked. He admired her quick intelligence, professionalism, and sense of humor. Moreover, he was attracted by her way of life, based on her deep Catholic faith. He would call her to his room every day before she left, giving her some things to read and flowers he had received. One of his first gifts to her was a copy of Milton's sonnet "On His Blindness," which he had memorized while in high school and which contained the line "They also serve who only stand and wait."

In late September he was back in his office with only a few restrictions on his activities. As a concession to his medical advisors he had a bed moved into his office, placed next to his desk so he could "rest" and yet reach the telephone.[7] His doctors told him he had to get more exercise. He had always liked walking, but now he strode vigorously four miles every day, outside if the weather was good, inside if it was not. When circumstances prevented him from going the full distance, he made up the shortage as soon as he could.

His interest in Lieutenant Bednowicz continued. He wrote to her, sent her flowers when she was in the Great Lakes Naval Hospital for major surgery, and visited her when she was stationed on Guam and his business took him there.

On Sunday morning, 29 October 1961, at 9:14, sixteen minutes ahead of schedule, the *Enterprise*, under the command of Capt. Vincent de Poix, got under way to leave the Newport News yard for her sea trials. She was huge, displacing eighty-five thousand tons and drawing 37 feet of water. Her flight deck measured 1,100 feet in length and 252 feet in width. Rickover had warned the pilot that her propulsion plant would respond promptly to orders for power. Disregarding the advice, for in his experience steam plants did not answer so quickly, the pilot called for power before the last line to the dock had been cast off. The *Enterprise* immediately began to move, snapping one big hawser. It was the start of an outstanding sea trial.

In the early stages of planning the propulsion plant, Rickover, Milton Shaw, his surface ship project officer, and others in Naval Reactors, talked over the number of reactors the carrier needed. The choice was between eight and four; in either case the total power output had to be the same. The eight-reactor plant would not be as great a leap forward in technology, and working out the means for controlling the operation of the shipboard plant would be more complicated. Furthermore, the eight-reactor plant would require doubling the number of associated equipment, which was expensive. On the other hand, the four-reactor plant was pushing the technology into new areas, for increasing the power output was far from a matter of simple extrapolation. The decision came down to eight reactors, two per propeller shaft.

In looking back on the construction of the *Enterprise*, the fight that came most sharply to Rickover's mind dealt with the catapult system. Carrier aircraft built after World War II were so heavy that they needed catapults to launch them. After testing several types, the Navy had settled on the steam catapult developed by the British. Steam drawn from the propulsion plant was stored in an accumulator and fed through launching valves into catapult cylinders located beneath the flight deck. In the length of a few hundred feet, pistons in the cylinders towed an aircraft from rest to that speed at which it could take to the air.

The steam catapult, however, delivered a heavy shock to the aircraft. For that reason the Bureau of Aeronautics, responsible for catapult development, began investigating other possibilities in 1952. The internal combustion approach, in which ignition of gas and air would provide the force, looked promising. The bureau was also working on a compressed air concept, but its development was not as far along. Either would be better for the aircraft and neither would require steam from the propulsion plant. The latter point was important, the bureau argued, because Rickover's nuclear propulsion plant might not be able to provide enough steam to enable the carrier to maneuver at high speed and operate the catapults at the frequency needed in combat.

The argument infuriated Rickover and Shaw. The propulsion plant could be designed to meet the requirements of ship and catapults. Furthermore, Rickover thought the plan of the bureaus was too risky because it placed the success of the carrier on two developmental projects. If the ship was fitted with catapults that could not handle the latest and heaviest aircraft, the Navy would have to admit its newest and most expensive carrier was a failure. Put more bluntly, the Navy would be getting an inferior carrier because of the catapults. In the search for the blame, Rickover had no doubt who would be the scapegoat.

On 13 December 1955 the Bureau of Aeronautics assured the Bureau of Ships that the internal combustion catapult would be ready for the *Enterprise* on 1 September 1961. There was, therefore, no need to compromise the ship's characteristics by providing steam catapults. A few days after the assurance was received, an experimental internal combustion catapult device exploded in a test at Lakehurst, New Jersey. On 21 February 1956 Rickover obtained agreement from the chief of naval operations and the two bureaus that he would design the steam system so that the ship could use steam catapults if either of the other two types could not be developed. Had he not done so, the ship would have been a failure.

Work on the internal combustion approach continued, but despite encouraging reports, success remained elusive. On 24 September 1960, Newport News launched the carrier. Two days later the Bureaus of Ships and Weapons (the latter a new entity formed by merging the Bureaus of Aeronautics and Ordnance) agreed to use steam catapults. On 10 November, Shaw at the A1W demonstrated to several high-ranking officers and civilians that the *Enterprise* plant could handle catapult and ship requirements. Installing the steam catapults on the ship continued almost to the last minute, before she moved down the James River into Chesapeake Bay.

Sea trials began on 29 October 1961, once the carrier was well beyond Cape Henry and the Chesapeake lightship. Much of the early effort went toward establishing a base against which to measure later performance data. Then came steaming and steering at various speeds, reversing and going ahead, and running at full power for four hours. There were no aircraft on board to launch, but the catapults were tested again and again by having them accelerate equivalent aircraft weights at the frequency that would be demanded during combat. The tests answered once and for all the question of nuclear propulsion and steam catapults. Late in the morning of 3 November the *Enterprise* reentered Chesapeake Bay with a huge broom, the traditional symbol of a clean sweep over an enemy, lashed to her highest antenna. That afternoon she was back in the yard, having passed the trials with flying colors.[8]

The *Enterprise*, however, might be the only nuclear carrier the Navy would get. The budget McNamara sent to Congress early in 1962 for the fiscal year 1963 contained an attack carrier, but it would have an oil-fired propulsion plant. Although the Navy wanted another nuclear carrier, and although Rickover had testified that Bettis was developing a four-reactor plant that would be an advance over the eight-reactor plant of the *Enterprise*, Congress authorized and appropriated funds for the conventional ship.[9] As yet unnamed, it bore the Navy designation CVA 67, which meant it was the sixty-seventh attack carrier in a line stretching back to 1919.

The decision on the CVA 67 was a blow to Rickover. It would be the second conventionally powered carrier that Congress had authorized since the *Enterprise*. If no more nuclear carriers were to be built, there would be no need for more nuclear escorts, and the nuclear surface Navy would consist only of the four ships already authorized.

The key to reversing the decision on the CVA 67 was McNamara. In taking him on, Rickover was fighting a secretary of defense who had become the leading figure in the Kennedy administration. McNamara was centralizing power in his office, primarily by imposing budgetary discipline over the three armed services. The Defense Reorganization Act of 1958 gave him the authority to do so, and although his predecessors had gone slowly in bringing it into effect, McNamara had moved swiftly. He won high praise from the public for making analytical (and therefore presumably rational) decisions on defense issues. He soon began getting intense criticism from military officers, who felt that their years of experience were being denigrated, and from members of Congress who felt that their influence was being curtailed.

Rickover began marshalling his forces. For two days, beginning on 31 March 1962, the Joint Committee on Atomic Energy met in the *Enterprise* off Guantánamo, Cuba, and heard firsthand from her officers the tactical military advantages that came from nuclear propulsion. The technology for surface ships, Rickover declared, was at the same point that it was for submarines when the joint committee first went to sea in the *Nautilus* in 1955. "You are the ones who forced the nuclear submarine Navy," he said. "I think without your forcing we will not have a nuclear surface Navy."[10] Some months later the nuclear carrier showed her superiority to conventional carriers in a deployment to the Mediterranean and during the Cuban crisis. Many senior officers, impressed by her performance, regretted they were going to be saddled with the CVA 67.

Rickover turned to the Atomic Energy Commission. Meeting in the *Enterprise* on 18 December 1962 with Seaborg and two new commissioners, James T. Ramey, formerly executive director of the joint committee staff, and John G. Palfrey, former law professor at Columbia, he described the four-reactor plant Bettis was developing. It now had a higher power rating than the version rejected a year earlier. The four reactors would cost less to fabricate and operate than the eight reactors of the *Enterprise*. The three commissioners heard Rickover declare that it would incorporate advanced power reactor technology as well as improve national defense. Both objectives, he observed, were commission goals.[11]

On 7 January 1963 Seaborg wrote McNamara that the nuclear-powered surface ships were meeting the Navy's design objectives, but no more of them had been authorized, although the commission had made important advances in reactor technology. The cost of the initial fuel loading for the eight-reactor plant was $64 million; that for the four-reactor plant was estimated at $32 million—and it would last twice as long. He asked McNamara to reconsider his decision on the CVA 67.

Rickover turned to Fred Korth, who had replaced Connally as secretary of the Navy in January 1962. Korth had taken office as an admirer of McNamara's management system but was soon disillusioned. Very quickly Korth discovered that Rickover could be unduly aggressive, but there was no denying his achievements. The facts that Seaborg had put in his letter Korth repeated in his memorandum to McNamara on 23 January 1963, which Rickover had helped prepare. Perhaps McNamara would find it helpful to establish a special task force to consider the CVA 67 issue; should that be the case, Korth would nominate Rickover and Vice Adm. William A. Schoech, deputy chief of naval operations (air), as Navy members. Because of congressional interest in nuclear propulsion for surface ships, Korth continued, the matter was urgent.

So began a lengthy exchange of correspondence. McNamara answered Seaborg on 2 February that the decision on the CVA 67 was under review; he replied to Korth on 22 February that members of his (McNamara's) staff had met with Rickover and Schoech, but the subject of nuclear propulsion had not been examined sufficiently for a rational decision. A "comprehensive, quantitative study of this matter . . . in the broadest possible context" was what was needed. It was easy to surmise from the terms of reference for the study that the answers would be complicated and challenges of interpretation inevitable. In the meantime, construction of the CVA 67 would have begun.

Korth replied on 4 April that it was difficult to put an exact dollar value on the benefits of nuclear propulsion because so many of them could be achieved in no other way. The Navy's most recent review, however, recommended nuclear power for all future attack carriers, including the CVA 67, and for all frigates. In addition, the review advocated developing a new nuclear-powered guided-missile destroyer and continuing to support the commission's nuclear propulsion program. On 20 April McNamara replied: the recommendations did not answer his questions, and for that purpose he was providing a table for the data he wanted. It took time for Korth to respond, and when he did so on 26 September, he cited a study, still under review, showing five task groups with nuclear CVA 67s had a combat effectiveness equal to six task groups with oil-fired CVA 67s.

McNamara saw no reason to prolong the issue. Congress had authorized an oil-fired CVA 67, and he did not think Congress would reverse itself. On 9 October he asked Korth to proceed with building the carrier as soon as possible. This was not making a final policy decision against nuclear propulsion, the secretary of defense explained, because that question would be reopened when the Navy completed its study.[12]

Rickover was certain no study would ever convince McNamara to build more nuclear surface ships. Of course costs were important, but too many military advantages could not be expressed in dollars and cents. Nothing more could be done, however; the decision was final.

Or was it?

David T. Leighton, associate director for surface ships, thought it was worth one more try and had no trouble persuading Rickover to join in the effort. They saw Sen. John O. Pastore, chairman of the Joint Committee on Atomic Energy, probably on 9 October. That same day the senator wrote to McNamara and, pointing out the committee's well-known stand in favor of nuclear-powered surface ships, told him it would soon hold hearings on the subject. The next day Rickover and Leighton saw Korth. A very relaxed secretary of the Navy, his feet on his desk, agreed to write one more letter to the secretary of defense. It expressed surprise over McNamara's decision of 9 October. Shortly after Rickover and Leighton left Korth's office, they learned the cause of the secretary's calmness. Caught up in the controversy over the TFX, a plane McNamara thought could meet the requirements of the Navy and the Air Force, Korth had announced his resignation.

Pastore called the meeting to order on 30 October at 10:00 A.M. The attendance showed its importance. Eleven of eighteen members and most of the staff were present. So were Korth, Seaborg, Adm. David L. McDonald, chief of naval operations, Rickover, four other admirals, several captains, officers who had commanded nuclear surface ships, and many high-ranking civilians. McNamara was absent: other obligations had kept him away.

Much of the testimony on this and the following day could have been predicted. Navy and commission witnesses argued for a nuclear CVA 67 and for building a nuclear surface fleet. Harold Brown, director of Defense Research and Engineering, spoke for McNamara. For three basic reasons the secretary of defense could not make such a wide-ranging decision: the cost of an all-nuclear carrier task force, including its escorts, was not known; analysis of nuclear and nonnuclear task forces showed the superiority of the nuclear force in some situations, but some of these were unrealistic; and the effect that an all-nuclear surface fleet would have on reducing logistic support had not been adequately studied.

In the general discussion during the meeting, Rickover made two main points. He had the reactors of the four-reactor plant designed and was building one. Not only would the power output of the four-reactor plant equal that of the eight-reactor plant of the *Enterprise*, but it would have nearly double the core life. He could have the plant ready for installation to meet the ship's construction schedule. The decision on the CVA 67 had broader ramifications than the ship itself. The loss of momentum in research and development, some of which applied to submarines, would be hard to recover.

His second point dealt with the rapid improvements of weapon systems—leaps forward that occurred every ten, even five, years. But a ship had to last twenty or even thirty years and therefore needed a good propulsion system. "In my opinion," he said, "it is foolhardy to put in a propulsion plant which you have today when you know something else is better."[13]

Although held behind closed doors, the hearing attracted some press attention. At a news conference that fell on the second day of the hearings, Kennedy was asked about the CVA 67. The Navy would get an oil-fired carrier, he replied, because that was what the Navy needed. Whether future major ships should be nuclear-powered was a decision that would be made later.[14]

McNamara was the sole witness during the committee hearing on 13 November. In his introductory remarks Pastore said that everyone understood that the CVA 67 had been authorized as a conventional ship, but the committee wanted to know why McNamara did not try to change that authorization and, more important, what the future held for nuclear propulsion for surface ships.

In two and a half hours of questions and answers—some exchanges were sharp—one point was clear. McNamara would not go back to Congress. It had considered nuclear propulsion and made its decision. Nothing since had happened for him to reopen the issue. Of course a nuclear-powered carrier was better than a conventional carrier, but that was not the point. "We don't buy the best there is in terms of technology in any one of our weapon systems," the secretary said. "We would be fools. . . . We would be foolish if we bought the best in technology in terms of the most advanced, in terms of speed, and range of firepower, when we don't need it."

The recent Cuban missile crisis had shown that it was patrol aircraft, escort vessels, and transport aircraft that were desperately needed. The fact that the *Enterprise* was nuclear-propelled was not important. Nor, he claimed, was cost a factor in his decision, an argument the committee members had difficulty understanding given his earlier declaration. The initial investment for the nuclear version, including the nuclear fuel, and the procurement of an additional aircraft squadron, was $440.4 million, compared to $277.2 million for the conventional ship, which did not include the fuel oil she would consume over her lifetime. A comparison of lifetime investment and operating costs of nuclear and conventional carriers showed that the nuclear version cost $480.5 million more than the conventional carrier over its lifetime. Included in that figure was $380.8 million to procure and operate the extra squadron of aircraft. For its part, the joint committee could see no reason for charging the procurement and operating costs of the extra squadron against nuclear propulsion.

Bickering over costs of nuclear propulsion and interpretation of analytical studies only showed the great gap separating the views of the joint committee and McNamara. The committee cited naval officers on the military advantages of nuclear-powered ships. In the final analysis, most of the benefits came down to their ability to steam at virtually unlimited distances at high sustained speed and the fact that they were not dependent for their fuel on tankers or storage facilities ashore. Compared to conventionally powered ships, that freedom gave them greater tactical and strategic flexibility, and increased ability to respond to emergencies and to remain on station.

McNamara declared that his decision on the CVA 67 applied only to that ship and should not be construed as a policy decision against nuclear propulsion. The Navy urgently needed smaller and cheaper reactor plants for escorts. A few years might see a ship construction program that would give the Navy the number of ships it needed. More carriers would be built, and he hoped that they would be nuclear (an astonishing remark, considering his testimony that nuclear propulsion for the CVA 67 did not significantly add to the nation's defense). The real potential for nuclear propulsion was with the "literally tens of major ships that we will be building other than . . . aircraft carriers." But that day would come only when the size, weight, and cost of the nuclear propulsion plants came down. He thought one thing was certain: "You don't have to build power plants in order to reduce the size and weight of them."[15]

Rickover had lost a battle but not necessarily the war. The CVA 67 would doubtless be conventional, but what of future carriers? Pastore, in transmitting the committee report to President Lyndon B. Johnson, then only a few weeks in office, pointed to overwhelming testimony from all witnesses—except McNamara—on the superiority of nuclear to conventional surface ships. Although such unanimity from that source was to be expected, the views of these men, most of whom were influential figures, could not be disregarded. Congressional mood was increasingly hostile to McNamara. The feeling in the Navy, where McNamara was considered a liar, was even stronger.[16]

The issue of the CVA 67 was not completely dead. Sen. Henry M. Jackson wrote on 3 April 1964 to Paul H. Nitze, who had succeeded Korth as secretary of the Navy, that Bettis had incorporated more advances in the four-reactor plant. Time, he went on, had not run out for making the CVA 67 nuclear-powered. On 24 April, Rickover and McNamara, along with Seaborg, Ramey, and Gerald F. Tape, a new AEC commissioner, flew to Pittsburgh to visit Bettis. During the tour of the laboratory McNamara refused to even consider the new four-reactor plant. A remark during a briefing on the development of the D1W reactor caught his attention. Originally intended for a destroyer, its power rating had been greatly increased. Two would be able to propel a carrier, but the ship would be smaller than the *Forrestal*, the first attack carrier built after World War II. The two-reactor plant opened a way out for McNamara. He could not accept a four-reactor propulsion system after the recent hearings. The two-reactor plant could be presented as something different.

McNamara asked if a two-reactor plant could be developed. Rickover replied that building a four-reactor plant was the best way to provide the technology for a two-reactor plant. McNamara began to stride off; he wasn't going to build a four-reactor ship to get a two-reactor ship. "You can forget both of them," he declared. Rickover and Leighton glanced at each other. The night before they had considered broaching the idea of the two-reactor carrier if McNamara rejected the four-reactor ship. But it was the two-reactor ship or none. Rickover told McNamara that developing the two-reactor propulsion plant for a carrier would be difficult but feasible. McNamara urged further development.

Intense activity filled the weeks that followed the return from Bettis. By the summer of 1964 enough of the design and development problems had been defined for McNamara to make the official request to the Atomic Energy Commission to develop the two-reactor plant. Harold Brown, director of defense research and engineering, drew the job of informing the joint committee. On 6 August he met with Pastore and Melvin Price and with Rickover and Leighton. Referring to the CVA 67, Brown said, "Let's face it, Bob made a mistake, and we have to get him off the hook."

In a memorandum to McNamara on 26 August, the assistant secretary of defense (comptroller) summarized the arguments for and against nuclear propulsion for carriers. He asked if those planned for the 1967, 1969, and 1971 budgets should be nuclear-powered. McNamara replied, "Yes."[17]

The two-reactor decision, Rickover remarked in recalling the struggle, was a prime example of a technical decision made on political grounds. For several reasons the four-reactor plant was the better choice. Simple arithmetic offered one. If the ship lost power from one of four reactors she could depend on the remaining three; if she lost power on one of two reactors, she could fall back on only one—and that one had to be able to produce power for the carrier and its planes under combat conditions. The technical problems were formidable. The reactor would have the highest power rating that Rickover, Naval Reactors, the laboratories, and the contractors had ever developed for a ship. No one knew what the size and weight of a two-reactor plant would be; no one knew the specifications of such major components as main coolant pumps, or what the difficulties of fabricating them would be. Still, Rickover and the organization he had created were not novices in reactor development and were already moving in the direction of more powerful reactors.

The Newport News Shipbuilding and Dry Dock Company launched the CVA 67 on 27 May 1967. On the floor of the House, Holifield stated that the ship "was obsolete when it was launched." Named the *John F. Kennedy*, the Navy commissioned her on 7 September 1968. She would be the last of the Navy's conventionally propelled attack carriers. Still, Rickover and the forces he had mustered had won the fight for nuclear propulsion of the next attack carriers. The Navy would commission the *Nimitz* on 3 May 1975. She would be the first of the Navy's carriers to be driven by the A4W/A1G two-reactor plant developed by Bettis and Knolls.

It is sometimes profitable to consider a victory from another perspective, to ask what would have happened if the struggle had been lost. Such speculation can provide no complete answers, but it is possible that had it not been for Rickover and the forces he had mobilized, the Navy's nuclear surface fleet would have numbered only one attack carrier, one cruiser, and two frigates.

Meeting with Kennedy

LATE IN THE MORNING of Monday, 11 February 1963, Rickover was driven the few blocks separating Main Navy from the White House. President Kennedy wanted his views on the multilateral force, frequently referred to as the MLF. Rickover had strong ideas on the subject but was not sure how the president would receive them.[1]

The multilateral force was a very complicated answer to a very complicated problem concerning the North Atlantic Treaty Organization. Established in 1949, NATO was formed to defend its members against a Soviet attack. A large part of the strength of the alliance rested upon the predominance of the United States in nuclear weapon and their delivery systems. Because of this superiority, Americans argued that other members did not need to develop their own nuclear weapons programs. Such efforts were a costly burden on fragile national economic systems, led to the proliferation of nuclear weapons, and risked reviving national rivalries that were such an unhappy part of European history. The British were an exception to this general policy. Because they had helped develop the atomic bomb during World War II, they had the technical knowledge to undertake their own programs. Moreover, Great Britain was the closest ally of the United States in a troubled postwar world.

In the 1950s two forces threatened the alliance that had become the cornerstone of American foreign policy. France, under the leadership of Charles de Gaulle, had embarked upon its own nuclear program, partly to gain prestige and partly to pursue its own European goals. Furthermore, other members of the alliance were uneasy over the dominant role of the United States in NATO nuclear policy. One way to increase NATO unity was to enlarge the role of the allies in their nuclear defense. Toward the end of the Eisenhower administration, devising the means to achieve this goal was assigned to Robert R. Bowie, an authority on international affairs and a former head of the policy planning council of the Department of State.

The MLF was the heart of Bowie's solution. It would consist of a number of ships, either submarines or surface, armed with Polaris missiles. The crews would be drawn from the participating nations and assigned to the ships in such a manner that a contingent from one nation could not seize control and become an instant nuclear power. Eisenhower was enthusiastic about the plan, Kennedy less so. Nonetheless, at Ottawa, Canada, in May 1961, he declared that the United States was willing to commit to NATO five or more Polaris submarines, providing certain agreements were reached. He left to Europe the initiative for undertaking the negotiations. But nothing happened.

The military assistance of the United States to Great Britain took many forms. One was a joint effort to develop a long-range missile that could be launched from an aircraft. But because the technical problems proved too severe, the Americans abandoned the project. The Americans had other long-range missile-delivery systems, but the British did not. To maintain their status as a great power, they wanted to build a Polaris submarine force. The Americans were reluctant to give them that assistance, mainly because they had earlier refused to help the French develop nuclear weapons. Aiding the British would only further alienate de Gaulle. Still, it might be possible to help the British but keep the unity of the alliance if they and the Americans, with French participation, formed a multilateral force. Although de Gaulle refused to join, the Americans offered membership to other NATO states. On 24 January 1963 the White House announced that a delegation would soon leave for Europe to begin talks.

Because Polaris submarines would make up the multilateral force, the administration had to consider Rickover's views. He was, after all, responsible for the training of the officers and men who manned the reactor plant and for the plant's safe operation. In addition, he was a public figure and was certain to be consulted by the Joint Committee on Atomic Energy. That body would have to consider legislation to bring the MLF into being. Glenn T. Seaborg, chairman of the Atomic Energy Commission, believed that although McNamara had outlined the scheme in broad terms to Rickover, the administration was underestimating the admiral's importance.[2] Finding that a presidential press conference was scheduled for 7 February and that Kennedy might be asked if he had talked to Rickover, Seaborg called the White House.

A few days later Rickover received a telephone call: he was to see the president at noon, 11 February. On that morning, Rickover, dressed in a dark business suit, left his office, joking as he went out the door that he did not know whether he would have a job when he returned.

According to the president's appointment book, Rickover was ushered into the Oval Office at twenty-two minutes after twelve. (Rickover would not have known the exact time—he never carried a watch, not wanting to be bothered with it.) Except for a brief session with a photographer, he and the president were alone, Kennedy seated in his famous rocking chair, Rickover at one end of a couch. Kennedy wanted the admiral's views on a multilateral submarine force.

Rickover thought it was not a good idea to base the force on submarines. They were complex and could only be manned safely by highly intelligent and specially trained officers and men working closely together. Mixed manning was bound to cause difficulties because of language and training differences, and these could only lower the operational effectiveness and safety. But that was not all. Inevitably, classified information would fall into Soviet hands. That was a subject too often overlooked by many people who did not know the work and cost it took for the United States to develop nuclear propulsion. Other countries wanted the results but without the effort and expense. Rickover saw no reason for the United States to risk the technological advantages it had. There was, after all, no requirement to share all military secrets with allies.

Kennedy spoke of policy matters. It was important to have a multilateral force in NATO to keep the alliance from breaking up, he said. "If we had absolutely to make it work we could make it work," Rickover replied. The conversation was going well and Rickover felt at ease, so much so that he felt free to say that some officials, asserting that they knew Kennedy wanted the multilateral force, were making statements that might later embarrass him.

The discussion turned to education. To Rickover's surprise, the president had read one of his books. Rickover took advantage of the opportunity to present his idea of a national education standard. Intrigued by the approach, Kennedy said he would look into it. The president knew many children were not getting an adequate education. Especially concerned about underprivileged youth, he speculated about their ability to acquire a good education. Rickover thought that question depended a great deal on motivation, home, background, and the influence of religion. These topics brought up the part played by parents. In answer to a question from Rickover, Kennedy said his parents had been quite strict with him, making him study and work during his boyhood. Their wealth had made no difference. Alluding to his own background, Rickover said that he had worked hard. Working hard and having goals early in life, both men felt, spurred the growth of character and mind.[3]

Rickover had spoken with the president about forty-five minutes. He did not know what Kennedy would decide on the multilateral force. The point that apparently most impressed the president was the chance of compromising classified information. Rickover thought a decision would come soon. It did. That afternoon he got a call from Edward R. Murrow, a well-known former correspondent for CBS but now head of the United States Information Agency and an old friend. At a session of the National Security Council, Murrow related, Kennedy had said that Rickover had convinced him that the multilateral force should be on surface ships only.

It seems fair to credit Rickover with a major influence in stopping a submarine-based multilateral force, but he was not the sole factor in Kennedy's decision. At the council meeting the president also spoke of the difficulty of getting congressional approval. Negotiations went forward on a surface-ship multilateral force, but without result.

Kennedy had raised Rickover's expectations in one area he could not fulfill: a national education standard. The president saw that Rickover got reports from the commissioner of education, but those reports stopped after the assassination. Had Kennedy lived, Rickover thought, the national standard might have gained a powerful advocate.

Thresher

ON 9 APRIL 1963 the attack submarine *Thresher*, under the command of Lt. Cdr. John W. Harvey, left the Portsmouth Naval Shipyard for sea trials after an eight-month overhaul. She rendezvoused with submarine rescue vessel *Skylark* and, after several tests, proceeded to deep water about two hundred miles off Cape Cod. At 6:37 the next morning she began her deep dive. At 9:13 the *Skylark* received the first of a few garbled messages: "Experiencing minor difficulties. Have positive up angle. Attempting to blow." Several times the rescue vessel tried to regain contact but failed. That night Adm. George W. Anderson, chief of naval operations, announced that the submarine was overdue and presumed missing.[1] There was no possibility that any of the sixteen officers, ninety-six enlisted men, and seventeen civilian technicians had survived the plunge of the submarine to the bottom.

Rickover wrote longhand letters of sympathy to the families of the men who were lost, checking meticulously to make sure the names, relationships, and addresses were accurate. He was one of many high-ranking officers attending the memorial service on 15 April at the Dealey Center Theater at the New London, Connecticut, submarine base. Because the theater was packed, loudspeakers carried the messages of condolences to many who crowded just outside the doors or sat on the steps of nearby buildings. Vice Adm. Elton W. Grenfell, commander of the Atlantic submarine force, declared, "The wonderful safety record of our submarines in recent years has led many people to believe the loss of a submarine was unthinkable."[2] To Rickover the loss was not unthinkable: over and over again he had emphasized safety in training and had fought continuously to raise the standards of workmanship in the yards.

The Navy had already begun its formal investigation of the loss of the ship and its men. Late in the evening of 11 April a court of inquiry, under

Vice Adm. Bernard L. Austin, held its first meeting. The court had little direct evidence with which to work. The water where the *Thresher* began her last dive was more than eight thousand feet deep. (Not until June was some debris on the bottom identified as hers, and not until 28 August was her wreckage found.) Two individuals who were neither members of the court nor witnesses were present at every session: John T. Conway, executive staff director of the Joint Committee on Atomic Energy, and Edward J. Bauser, also of the staff. The committee chairman, Sen. John O. Pastore, had sent them to make sure that the committee was kept informed. Conway and Bauser, at first suspected of being a pipeline to Rickover, kept to themselves, having no contact with either members of the court or witnesses. Austin soon realized the value of their presence: from their observations they could explain the course of the inquiry to the committee.

Conway and Bauser were to play another important role. Out of respect to those who had lost their lives, and to those they had left behind, the two staff members thought as much information as possible about the disaster should be made public. Furthermore, they did not want the Navy to conceal or whitewash poor construction practices. Largely through their efforts the joint committee decided to release an unclassified version of its own hearings, an action opposed by the Navy. For years the joint committee hearing remained the best source of information on the loss of the ship.[3]

Rickover was reluctant to testify before the court of inquiry. His reasons fell into two main categories: those dealing with the submarine force and the Bureau of Naval Personnel and those concerning the Bureau of Ships and the design and construction of the *Thresher*. Nevertheless, he could not avoid appearing.

The sudden expansion of the submarine force, resulting from the high priority given to getting the Polaris fleet at sea as rapidly as possible, required an increasing number of nuclear-trained officers. Rickover could not provide them. He was already taking all the submarine officers who met his standards. The shortfall in the number of officers needed in the submarine force was being met by assigning those at sea one tour of sea duty after another. (The normal practice called for following time at sea with a tour of shore duty—a period of normal family life and staff assignments that would prepare them for positions of greater responsibility.) Many officers had complained of the strain to Vice Adm. William R. Smedberg, chief of naval personnel. He argued vehemently that some young and outstanding diesel submarine officers had been rejected because Rickover's standards were too high.

As for the submarine itself, Rickover had opposed the rapidity with which the *Thresher*, the first of her class, had been designed and built. She incorporated several technical innovations, among them the ability to reach greater depths and achieve quieter operation than her predecessors. But the shipbuilding programs called for several of her class to be under construction before she had gained any operational experience. If a serious problem developed, time-consuming and expensive changes might have to be made to the ships already being built. Furthermore, he did not think highly of the Portsmouth Navy Yard, which built her.

One further point remains to be made. Rickover's responsibilities for the *Thresher*'s propulsion plant were less than many casual observers of naval affairs might have expected. When a ship with a new reactor type put to sea, Rickover was responsible for the entire propulsion plant, including the reactor, its auxiliaries, and the steam plant. For later ships using the same reactor type, Rickover was not responsible for the steam plant but remained responsible for the reactor plant. An S5W reactor propelled the *Thresher;* that same reactor plant was already driving the *Skipjack*, the first of another class of submarines.

Rickover and his engineers had misgivings over the bureau's layout of the *Thresher*'s steam plant but found their advice unwelcome. They saw too much piping, carrying seawater essential for cooling the propulsion plant, brought into the submarine. That piping had to resist the same ocean pressure as the hull.

Portsmouth had laid the submarine's keel on 28 May 1958 and the Navy had commissioned her on 3 August 1961. She and those that soon followed compiled an outstanding record—until 10 April 1963.

Rickover appeared before the court of inquiry on 29 April. He was ill at ease. He and Austin agreed to begin with a statement that to date there was no evidence that the reactor plant had any direct relationship to the loss of the ship. Rickover soon got to the main cause of the disaster. "I believe," he said, "the loss of the *Thresher* should not be viewed solely as the result of a specific braze, weld, system or component, but rather should be considered a consequence of the philosophy of design, construction and inspection, that has been permitted in our naval shipbuilding programs. I think it is important that we re-evaluate our present practices where, in the desire to make advancement, we may have forsaken the fundamentals of good engineering."[4] He went on to detailed technical suggestions. At the end of his remarks he promised to help all he could. In his own mind, he was disturbed that the court had so few questions to ask him.

The brazes and welds to which he referred were two types of joints used in piping systems. The court's investigation brought out the difficulties that brazers and welders had in making sound joints. Silver-brazed joints were a serious problem because there was no good way to make sure the joints were sound. They were, however, less expensive than welding and, more important, were the only way to make certain joints. Considering the brazed joints dangerous, Rickover in September 1961 had banned them in all seawater systems that went through reactor compartments, but he lacked authority to ban them in the steam plant.

The court found that testing procedures and records at Portsmouth were poor. And Smedberg illustrated the officer personnel problem by pointing out that Harvey and his executive officer were new to the ship and, of the eleven officers, only three had been with her for any significant time.

Robert Panoff, Naval Reactors' project engineer for submarine propulsion plants, was puzzled by the message from the *Thresher:* "Attempting to blow." Sounds heard by the *Skylark* showed that the submarine had tried to surface by blowing water from her ballast tanks. Something had gone wrong, for the sounds had stopped abruptly. Panoff thought blowing the tanks of the *Tinosa,* a sister ship under construction at Portsmouth, might give a clue. It did. The blowing stopped after a few seconds.

Air passed into the tanks through valves that were fitted with strainers to keep out particulate matter. The strainers were not in the specifications but had been added by the contractor. At high pressure, droplets of moisture formed on the strainers and turned to ice, blocking the air from entering the tanks.

The court reconstructed the loss of the *Thresher* as best it could from sound data from the *Skylark* and other sources. It seemed likely that the ship was at the deepest point of its deep dive when a silver-brazed joint failed, releasing seawater into the ship under high pressure. Telephoning that she was experiencing minor difficulties, she tried to surface but could not. Probably water from the leak short-circuited the electrical equipment, causing the reactor to shut down. Without reactor power and unable to blow her tanks, the submarine plunged to her death.

Adjusting some data to make the reconstruction more consistent, the court had computer runs made. The best found that several minutes passed from the time the reactor plant stopped or slowed down until the submarine collapsed. Within that time the reactor operators had presumably tried to restart the reactor and failed. In going over the court's findings, some officers, including the director of submarine warfare in the office of the chief of naval operations, believed the failure stemmed from the strict adherence Rickover required in start-up procedures. The reactor operators might have driven the ship to the surface had they taken shortcuts to regain power.

Naval Reactors engineers, led by Panoff, took the data and compared them with the assumptions on which the computer runs were based. They found that the acoustical evidence was weak as it applied to slowing down or stopping the reactor plant. Moreover, the information provided by the court for the computer runs was subject to different interpretations. New computer runs showed that the *Thresher*, at the point where the court postulated the reactor shutdown, had sufficient power to surface. Nonetheless, the fact remained that no computer run or any other analysis could provide a sure account of the loss of the ship.

The court of inquiry held its last meeting on 5 June 1963 and began drawing up its finding of facts. In summary, it believed the *Thresher* was at test depth when a leak in the engine room occurred, possibly from a silver-brazed joint. The leak might have short-circuited the electrical system, causing the reactor to shut down. Attempts to blow the ballast tanks failed. The weight of the inrushing seawater pulled the ship down to collapse depth. As for Portsmouth, the yard was overconfident of the soundness of silver-brazed joints, and its testing procedures and documentation were inadequate. But no one individual or group of individuals was responsible for the loss of the submarine.

The Joint Committee on Atomic Energy held hearings on 26 and 27 June and 24 July 1963, and again on 1 July 1964. In them an angered Rickover attacked the charge that the rigid training of reactor operators kept them from departing from procedures to speed up the recovery of propulsion power. For all normal situations the rules were rigid, but not in dire emergencies. Nothing, he declared, could restrict the actions of a commanding officer to safeguard his ship in an emergency. "Common sense tells you this is not so."[5]

Although this was true, a commanding officer had to know the steps he could take in the event of a sudden shutdown when he had no time to improvise them. That was one area in which Naval Reactors had not given sufficient attention. After the loss of the *Thresher*, Rickover improved procedures and trained the operators for fast recovery of propulsion power.

The Navy tightened up its standards for submarines under construction and took measures to improve the safety of those in operation. Rickover took more officers into the program, drawing many of them from sources other than the submarine force. Strangely, it was the loss of the *Thresher* that eased the problem of the officer shortage. The Navy had to incorporate safety measures in the attack and Polaris submarines under construction and in operation, which gave time to narrow the gap between the number of officers trained and those needed.

Vice Adm. Lawson P. Ramage, who had become the deputy chief of naval operations (fleet operations and readiness), appeared before the joint committee and spoke of the number of valuable lessons the Navy had learned from the loss of the *Thresher*. Chet Holifield, the committee chairman, commented, "The Chair will just say it is indeed sad that we had to have the tragic loss of 129 lives in order to put in the safeguards which have been put in since that time."[6]

*** 15

Every Two Years

VICE ADM. Hyman G. Rickover, USN, would have to retire in January 1964. Title 10, United States Code, left no doubt about that. It stated that an officer had to retire when he became sixty-four. The secretary of the Navy, however, could call a retired officer back to active duty.[1] Rickover wanted to continue to lead the propulsion program; the Navy wanted him out.

Rickover told the members of the Joint Committee on Atomic Energy, meeting in the *Enterprise* in March 1962, "As long as I am able and both I and others feel I can do a useful job, I would like to stay on." The program was changing rapidly, he explained, and while developing reactors remained the major effort, refueling and maintaining the growing number of nuclear-powered ships in the fleet was demanding increasing attention. These activities involved large amounts of radiation and required utmost care in planning and training. The committee members agreed. "I do not think Congress is going to stand idly by and watch you put on the shelf," Melvin Price declared. "We will have to get into this thing."[2]

The Navy held a sharply contrasting view. On 7 February 1963, Capt. Tazewell Shepard, President Kennedy's naval aide, informed McGeorge Bundy of the National Security Council of the approaching Rickover deadline and that the Navy believed "there are a number of officers who can direct the Navy's reactor program now that the pioneering is over."[3]

Fred Korth, secretary of the Navy, was a Texan familiar with the Washington scene from having served in high administrative positions in the Department of the Army. The Rickover task before him was not easy. He had to accommodate the intense desire of the Navy to oust Rickover with the deep conviction of the Atomic Energy Commission that the technical excellence of the program depended upon Rickover's continued leadership. A lawyer with the reputation of being a skilled negotiator, he had his task cut out for him.

Talking with Rickover on 14 February, Korth found him willing to lead the program as a civilian employed by the commission. In all probability this move would satisfy the commission, but it offered nothing for the Navy. On 25 February Korth saw Glenn T. Seaborg, commission chairman. The secretary outlined three possibilities. He could annually reappoint Rickover; Congress could legislate Rickover's reappointment for a specific period, say, five years; or the commission could retain Rickover as a civilian. Korth thought Rickover would oppose the annual reappointment because it would not give enough continuity. The Navy, for its part, would not welcome legislation setting the length of Rickover's leadership, because that would be congressional intervention into the department's business. The best solution seemed to be Rickover as a commission official acting with the same authority he was now exercising.

Korth then turned to issues that bothered the Navy. Under commission mandate, Rickover selected officers for nuclear training. Selection and training were traditionally Navy functions, and Korth wanted Seaborg to consider returning them to the Navy, leaving final certification of competence to Rickover. In addition, Korth thought the program should have a deputy director, someone who could take over if anything should happen to Rickover. Korth knew that Rickover didn't want a deputy but thought highly of Capt. John W. Crawford Jr., a veteran of the program who had served in the commission, in shipyards, and in Rickover's headquarters. Maybe Rickover would accept him.[4]

Korth had laid his cards on the table. The commission would get Rickover's leadership of the program beyond January 1964; the Navy would get the selection and training of officers and a deputy director who was a naval officer.

On 25 February, after talking to Rickover, Seaborg telephoned Korth. Rickover would accept a civilian appointment—but he absolutely refused to give up selection and training, and he stalled on the matter of a deputy. Seaborg probably had expected the reaction.

Rickover saw selection and training as essential elements in meeting his commission obligation to ensure the safe operation of the Navy's propulsion reactors. He could not meet that charge unless he personally interviewed, selected, and trained every officer who would have any responsibility for the reactor plant. The Navy had another way of looking at the matter: only by Rickover's approval could an officer enter the nuclear program and eventually achieve command of a nuclear ship. Through his control of a major program he was creating the "Rickover Navy."

The question of a deputy was complicated and would arise several times over the years. Crawford had held the title since 1960. It gave him the legal authority to sign fitness reports for the junior officers, thus relieving Rickover of that task. But neither Crawford nor his predecessors in that position were deputies in the usual sense of the term. By definition, a deputy was an assistant having equal authority to that of his superior, and could exercise that authority when that superior was absent or incapacitated. That was the type of deputy that many observers, in this instance Korth as well as many members of the joint committee, thought Rickover should have.

Rickover could not have forgotten the bitter promotion struggle of 1953, a fight he won only because the Navy did not have a qualified officer to replace him. That defense would not hold up if Crawford became his deputy with authority such as Korth was proposing. It would not hold up if any engineering duty officer was brought into the program for any length of time. More than one individual noticed that Rickover had interviewed several such officers, some of outstanding caliber, and rejected them. There was another aspect to the matter: senior members of Naval Reactors did not want a deputy. They wanted direct access to Rickover. In talking with Seaborg on 27 February, Rickover suggested any of his four assistants—David T. Leighton, I. Harry Mandil, Robert Panoff, or Theodore Rockwell—for the position.[5] Significantly, all were civilians.

Korth had made his first moves to settle the questions of Rickover's continued leadership, his authority over selection and training, and his acceptance of a deputy. In none had he made much progress.

From their offices on Capitol Hill the joint committee members and staff watched the situation closely. Sen. John O. Pastore, committee chairman, strongly favored retaining Rickover as a civilian but wondered how the change would affect the program. Maybe it would take legislation to keep it as it was. He wanted to act before the issue became a matter of public controversy. He saw signs of this happening in a *Saturday Evening Post* editorial of 16 March 1963 titled "Let's Solve the 'Rickover Problem.'" It accused the Navy of jettisoning the man who had done so much for national defense—words that echoed the 1953 promotion struggle—and it proposed presidential appointment of Rickover as a civilian to lead the program as the solution. Pastore urged Korth and Seaborg to meet in his office with other committee members.[6]

Korth, Seaborg, and James T. Ramey, formerly the committee staff director but a commissioner since 31 August 1962, met with Sen. Clinton P. Anderson and Reps. Chet Holifield and Melvin Price on 21 March 1963. From the outset the committee members made clear to Korth that the issue was how—not whether—Rickover should be retained. Korth explained the courses he was exploring. Holifield and Anderson, not seeing how a civilian Rickover could exercise real control over selecting and training naval personnel, thought legislation might well be needed. By stating that he wanted time to work out a solution, Korth fended off that idea.

The secretary raised the matter of a deputy. He suggested Rear Adm. Vincent de Poix, the first commanding officer of the *Enterprise*. Seaborg pointed out Rickover's reluctance to designate a deputy. On that matter the group believed Rickover would not only have to yield but also accept an officer for the position.[7]

Seaborg kept the White House informed. In his biweekly report, he wrote that Rickover should be retained as a civilian and continue to select and train personnel, for these functions were an essential part of reactor safety. An accident involving a naval reactor would not only endanger the lives of the ship's company but also raise serious domestic and international questions about health and safety. These views, Seaborg noted, were shared by the joint committee. If Korth could not solve the problem fairly soon, Pastore, Anderson, and Holifield would introduce legislation to take care of the matter. Seaborg did not say anything about a deputy, a matter probably too minor for White House attention.[8]

Weeks went by. On 8 April Korth surprised Rickover, the commission, and the joint committee, by announcing that the Navy would continue to avail itself of Rickover's services beyond his retirement. How this would be done had not been decided, but it would be announced within the next few months.[9] Ramey, who was following the matter for the commission, believed the Navy was stalling. He saw Kenneth O'Donnell, a longtime close associate of Kennedy and now a special assistant at the White House. Some weeks later Ramey learned from O'Donnell that the president thought Rickover should stay.

More weeks went by. On 11 June Rickover had a stormy meeting with Korth. The secretary insisted on a deputy and suggested Rear Adm.

Eugene P. Wilkinson, the first commanding officer of the *Nautilus* and the *Long Beach*. Rickover absolutely refused, declaring that his key engineers—Leighton, Mandil, Panoff, Rockwell, and Crawford—would quit in protest. Rickover then saw Seaborg, who remarked that there was a feeling that Rickover should choose one of the five. On 21 June, Korth again saw Rickover. The secretary stated that the admiral could stay on as a civilian if he had a deputy. Again Rickover refused. Korth offered another choice: Rickover could be recalled to active duty but on indefinite tenure, which meant he was subject to annual reappointment by the secretary. Rickover also rejected that scheme.[10]

On 21 June Korth announced he would recall Rickover to active duty immediately on his retirement in February. In nice, bureaucratic language he stated, "While I recognize that Vice Admiral Rickover has earned a peaceful retirement, I feel that the Navy and the country needs his continued service so long as he is willing and able to contribute."[11]

The announcement stunned the commission. Korth had acted without informing it—or the joint committee. Rickover would not be a civilian but be reappointed annually by the secretary of the Navy, whoever that might be. Seaborg urged Korth to hold to the earlier understanding, declaring that it was hard to see how the Navy and the commission could meet the program commitments until there was certainty of Rickover's leadership.[12]

Leighton, Mandil, Panoff, and Rockwell turned to the joint committee. As they saw it, the real issue was not whether Rickover be retained as an officer or a civilian, but *that* he be retained. Understanding that Rickover was willing to serve as a civilian, they asked for a meeting with the committee to convince it that the change would not affect the program. Because they were well known to the members and the staff, it was not difficult to arrange an invitation to testify. On 15 August 1963 at 2:00 P.M. they appeared in the committee room.

Mandil, chief of the reactor engineering branch, had been in the program since 1949; Rockwell, the technical director, also since 1949; Panoff, assistant manager for submarine projects, since 1950; and Leighton, surface ship project officer, since 1953. All were members of the inner circle upon whom Rickover often relied, not only for technical advice but also for their views on political issues, roughly defined as including relationships with the Navy, the AEC, contractors, and Congress.

The number of committee members attending the meeting indicated the importance they gave the subject. Senators Pastore and Anderson, and eight congressmen, among them Holifield, Price, Craig Hosmer, and William H. Bates, listened closely. Although all four engineers took part in the discussion, perhaps Panoff summarized it best. "One thing ought to be made clear," he said. "There is nothing that Admiral Rickover does in his present job that requires a vice admiral or any other naval officer to do it. It has been Rickover the individual, the brains between his ears and his stubbornness. He has never used the stripes on his arm to get anything done in that job."

The legislators listened and questioned but were not convinced that a Mr. Rickover could exert the same authority as an Admiral Rickover; they did not seem to understand that Rickover's authority for interviewing, for sea trials, and for so much of what he did depended upon his acting as an agent of the commission. During the discussion of the hazards of annual reappointment, Anderson remarked that the joint committee had saved Rickover before. "We haven't failed you yet," he added. On that note, the meeting broke up at 3:40 P.M.[13]

Did Rickover really want to become a civilian? Those men closest to him weren't sure, but they suspected that he would rather be an admiral than a civilian. If so, it was not surprising, considering his struggle to reach flag rank.

Korth resigned his office on 1 November 1963.[14] During much of the year he had been embroiled in a controversy over the TFX, a project of Secretary of Defense Robert S. McNamara for the joint Air Force–Navy development of a high-performance aircraft. His successor, Paul H. Nitze, took his oath of office on 29 November 1963. A Harvard cum laude graduate who had done well in Wall Street, he had come to Washington during World War II and had served in several posts. At Kennedy's request, he had become assistant secretary of defense for international affairs. Able, intelligent, and exceedingly ambitious, he had hoped to become deputy secretary of defense.

On 13 December, Anderson, Pastore, Holifield, and Price went to the White House. Twenty-three days earlier they would have talked with Kennedy; now it was Lyndon B. Johnson who sat in the Oval Office. The committee members proposed that Johnson direct the AEC and the Navy to arrange for Rickover to be the civilian head of the program.[15]

The next morning Seaborg received a telephone call from Nitze. He had seen Johnson, who told him to see Pastore and Anderson right away. Nitze did so, telling them that "he had sent forward papers, which would come before the Senate next week, requesting that on January 2nd, [sic] when Rickover reached age 64, mandatory retirement age, he be retired as a Vice Admiral (rather than as Rear Admiral). Then, Rickover would be recalled to active duty, as a Vice Admiral, for a two-year period; and, during that time, efforts would be made to work out his future and the future of the position which he holds."

The joint committee thought the scheme made sense. Nitze found Johnson willing to accept it. In talking with Seaborg, Nitze said that the two-year period was not a definite limit because Rickover could be reappointed. Nitze believed Rickover wouldn't like the arrangement but would prefer to stay on as a civilian. In that case, Nitze felt, the Navy would demand greater control over selecting personnel.[16]

Rickover did not like the arrangement: he did not like having to be reappointed every two years, a stipulation that did not relieve the uncertainty of his continuing leadership. He told Nitze he would serve him loyally and do the best he could, but people would leave the program. At some time, Rickover continued, he would have to tell Nitze that he could no longer do the job. Seaborg thought that at the end of two years perhaps the civilian issue could be reopened. Rickover believed the Navy would never accept that decision. Anderson said that he, Pastore, Holifield, and Price were satisfied, and added that if Rickover's men thought the situation would be catastrophic, they didn't have much faith in the commission or the joint committee.[17]

On 27 December 1963, Nitze sent Rickover a memorandum stating the terms of the two-year extension—that it involved no diminution in Rickover's authority, and that he was not barred from another extension.[18]

The question of a deputy remained. Crawford's name was still the one most often mentioned. He had retired from the Navy in July 1963. He hated to leave but saw no other choice. He and other engineering officers had been assured that serving in nuclear propulsion would enhance their career prospects. The assurances, however, had proved hollow, a fact that was made evident when eligible engineering officers in the program were not, despite their outstanding records, promoted as rapidly as nonnuclear engineering duty officers. Crawford went to work for former Commissioner Thomas E. Murray as manager of production, Murray Manufacturing Company.

In February 1964 Crawford received a telephone call from Cdr. Michael Ricinak, who had served in Naval Reactors from 1956 to 1958 but was now an aide to Paul Fay, undersecretary of the Navy. Fay, who had been personally close to Kennedy, had been asked by Nitze to arrange for a naval officer to be Rickover's deputy. Fay had talked to Rickover, who said that Dunford, Crawford, and others would be acceptable but all had retired from the Navy and would not return. Ricinak remarked that Crawford would come back; the purpose of the call to Crawford was to explore that possibility.

Crawford hesitated, having no illusions about the difficulty of being Rickover's deputy. But if Rickover had to have a deputy and if Rickover had said that he was acceptable, Crawford was willing to serve. By doing so he would be a successor imbued with Rickover principles and management philosophy, someone acceptable to both the Navy and the commission. He came to Washington in mid-February, saw Fay, and had a brief session with Nitze.

Crawford explained that Rickover would never have a deputy in the usual meaning of the title. He was, however, willing to return and do the same type of work he had done earlier as deputy. He would succeed Rickover when Rickover left. Crawford would be advanced to the rank of rear admiral when the first member of his Naval Academy class was so advanced.

Crawford studied the memorandum on the way back to New York. The paper was unsigned and filled with ambiguities. A few days later Crawford got a telephone call from Fay. With some embarrassment the undersecretary said that the arrangement, after a conversation with Rickover, had fallen through. Crawford felt some relief. The position of "heir apparent" would never have been an easy one. For some time the relationship between Rickover and Crawford was strained, but in later years it once again became friendly.[19]

In August 1964 Rickover confronted another crisis: Mandil, Panoff, and Rockwell left the program. Mandil's health was deteriorating, Rockwell no longer felt the work challenging and thought that Rickover was subjecting him to niggling and ever-increasing supervision, and Panoff, brilliant and ambitious, saw himself clashing ever more frequently with Rickover. In 1961 Rickover had lost Milton Shaw, another fine engineer, who went on to become technical assistant to the assistant secretary of the Navy for research and development. Rickover replaced Shaw as surface ship project officer with Leighton, but losing Mandil, Panoff, and Rockwell at one time was another matter.[20] Years later, in recalling their departure, Rickover admitted that it was a severe blow.

He missed Mandil most. He admired Mandil's engineering skill, his professional attitude, and his philosophy. Looking back from later years, he thought Mandil was the best engineer he ever had. There were personal associations, too. He and Ruth had gone to Europe with Harry and Beverly Mandil, and it was to Beverly Mandil that Ruth Rickover asked the question, "Why did they do this to George?"

In viewing the loss so personally, Rickover overlooked the stability of the program as well as the caliber of the engineers he had so carefully trained and from whom he demanded such excellence. His relationship with Leighton continued to be close. He also turned to William Wegner, an academy graduate of the class of 1948 who entered the program in 1955. In addition to serving in Washington headquarters, Wegner had been Rickover's representative at the Ingalls Shipbuilding Corporation at Pascagoula, Mississippi, and later the nuclear power superintendent at the Puget Sound Naval Shipyard. He became deputy to Rickover, taking on roughly the same responsibilities as his predecessors in that capacity. Those duties were limited, with virtually none dealing with technical matters. Wegner, who resigned from the Navy in 1964, would remain with the program until August 1979.

It was possible to look upon 1963 and 1964 as marking a new phase in Rickover's career. Every two years the Joint Committee on Atomic Energy wrote to the chairman of the Atomic Energy Commission and to the secretary of the Navy or to the secretary of defense, announcing that it was time to extend Rickover's leadership for another two years. None could have foreseen that this procedure would allow Rickover to remain in government service until January 1982, far longer than a civilian could have done. In fact, he would come to depend upon a new generation of personnel who would serve in the program.

New Classes of Surface Ships and Submarines

AT THE BEGINNING of 1965, Rickover could see his future marked by reappointment every two years. The first two-year period had already begun, for it started with the date of his mandatory retirement, 27 January 1964. He had mixed feeling about the reappointment process, resenting the necessity of restarting the procedure periodically but appreciating it as a reminder to friends and foes alike of the backing he had in Congress.

That support he continued to need as struggles over surface ships and submarines entered a new phase. The fight for surface ships would lead to new classes of attack aircraft carriers and escorts; the conflict over attack submarines would lead to the *Los Angeles* (SSN 688) class.

After his trip to the Bettis laboratory in April 1964, Secretary of Defense Robert S. McNamara agreed to ask Congress for a nuclear carrier in fiscal years 1967, 1969, and 1971. These, added to the *Enterprise*, already in commission, would represent a big stride toward creating a nuclear surface fleet. Nothing concerning administration budget requests and congressional action was certain, however. Attack carriers were exceedingly expensive to build, and the Navy's budgets were stretched tight with competing claims.

Rickover worried over the prospects for nuclear escorts. Two were in commission: the *Long Beach* (originally designed to carry only missiles, among them the Polaris) and the *Bainbridge*. A third, the *Truxtun*, was under construction. In fiscal year 1963 the administration had asked for and Congress had funded a fourth escort, but because the weapon system being developed for the ship was not ready, McNamara canceled its construction. Since then he had not included any nuclear escorts in his construction programs. The one he sent to Congress early in 1966 for fiscal year 1967 included the nuclear carrier *Nimitz* and two escorts, both of which were planned to have conventional oil-fired propulsion plants.[1]

Rickover and his congressional friends decided to change the two escorts to nuclear propulsion. They had hopes for success: in 1961 they had substituted nuclear for conventional propulsion for the *Truxtun*. Rickover and L. Mendel Rivers, an ally then and now chairman of the House Armed Services Committee, worked closely together.

Born in 1905 in the poverty-stricken rural town of Gumville, South Carolina, Rivers had worked his way through law school and had practiced his profession in Charleston before his election to Congress in 1940. Ambitious, tough, and irascible, he fought hard. Newspaper reporters portrayed him as a hard-drinking redneck, but others knew him to be very bright, extremely hardworking, demanding on his staff, and contemptuous of mistakes and incompetence.

In recalling his association with Rivers, Rickover saw certain common elements in their backgrounds and philosophies. Coming from humble origins, both had fought to reach positions of power, agreed that the defense establishment under McNamara was poorly managed, and shared the conviction that the executive branch of the government was usurping the prerogatives of the legislative branch. They were not, however, friends. Rickover never had the personal ties with Rivers that he did with Henry M. Jackson, Clinton P. Anderson, and John O. Pastore in the Senate, or with Chet Holifield, Melvin Price, William H. Bates, Charles Bennett, and Melvin Laird in the House.

Rivers quickly put his own stamp on the hearings. He sat behind a podium on which he had fixed a plaque bearing words from Article 1, Section 8 of the Constitution:

> The Congress shall have the power
> To raise and support armies
> To provide and maintain a navy
> To make rules for the government and regulation of the land
>   and naval forces

He would point imperiously to the plaque when officials and officers from the armed services or the defense establishment were testifying.

Rickover, at times accompanied by David T. Leighton, his project officer for surface ships, occasionally breakfasted with Rivers on Capitol Hill to plan hearing strategy. Rivers ran a tight committee. Rickover watched, almost in awe, as the chairman marked up bills and slashed out items without consulting other members.

The *Nimitz* passed through the congressional gauntlet unscathed, but the guided-missile destroyers did not. Prospects for changing them to nuclear propulsion brightened momentarily on 10 March 1966 when McNamara unexpectedly told the House Armed Services Committee that he saw no sense for having a nuclear-powered carrier if it could not achieve its full potential because it lacked nuclear-powered escorts. He thought the Navy already had such a balanced unit, probably referring to the *Enterprise* and the escorts *Long Beach* and *Bainbridge*. He agreed that each nuclear carrier should be part of a balanced force. The lead time to build *Nimitz*, however, was greater than it was to build two nuclear-powered guided-missile destroyers. It was not necessary, therefore, for the two escorts now under consideration to have nuclear propulsion.[2]

The Senate committee acted first. It authorized a nuclear escort (for which long-lead-time items had been funded the preceding year) and deleted the two guided-missile destroyers.[3] The House committee was to hear Rickover on Monday, 2 May, in his first appearance before that body since 1961.

He was at home on Sunday when his telephone rang at 11:00 P.M. It was Paul H. Nitze, secretary of the Navy, reminding him that the administration's program called for the two destroyers. Rickover replied that the committee had asked him to compare the nuclear- and conventionally powered ships. Certain that the nuclear ships were superior, he would state that conviction to the committee. If a choice had to be made on which to cut, the nonnuclear ships should be the ones to drop.

The exchange of remarks, already pointed, apparently grew even sharper. Rickover's notes record Nitze stating that "*he* was Secretary of the Navy and was responsible for the welfare of the Navy and I should not take it upon myself to mastermind what the Navy or the Secretary of Defense should do." Rickover replied that the committee had asked for his opinions, not those of the Navy or the Department of Defense.[4]

Calling the committee to order at 10:19, Monday morning, Rivers excluded everyone from the room except committee members, their staff, and Rickover and Leighton. Congress, Rickover began, was important not only for the part it played in providing for national defense but also for its role in the nation's life. Recently Congress had allowed its constitutional responsibilities to be usurped by the executive branch, with its appointed officials who believed representatives and senators, chosen by the electorate, lacked the competence to judge important issues.

Rickover compared the two guided-missile destroyers and the two nuclear escorts. The nuclear ships would cost $278.3 million, which included $24 million for their cores, but would give at least ten years of operation without refueling. The initial cost of the two oil-fired ships was $145.1 million, not including the fuel. The two types were not identical in other respects: the nuclear ships were larger and each would have twice the number of missile launchers, as well as twice the number of torpedo tubes as the proposed destroyer. The nuclear frigates would also have helicopter landing facilities and accommodation for a screen commander.[5]

Reporting on 16 May, the committee proposed authorizing two nuclear frigates. The first was the *California*, for which long-lead-time items had already been approved, and the second was the *South Carolina*. Almost as an aside, the committee also recommended constructing the two guided-missile destroyers—they could escort the oil-fired carriers *John F. Kennedy* and *America*.

Tired of the McNamara tactics of delay, Rivers wrote mandatory language into the House report: "Notwithstanding the provisions of any other law, the Secretary of Defense and the Secretary of the Navy shall proceed with the design, engineering, and construction of the two nuclear-powered guided missile frigates as soon as practicable." He declared, "If this language constitutes a test as to whether Congress has the power to so mandate, let the test be made and let this important weapons system be the field of trial."[6]

The following day Rivers issued a press release, The shift to nuclear propulsion had its opposition, but if to get nuclear ships Congress had to take the helm, "we'll do it."[7]

On 14 June his colleagues in the House gave Rivers a standing ovation as he opened the debate on the bill. Some observers believed the applause expressed sympathy for Rivers, who had been the subject of a critical article by the columnist Drew Pearson, alleging that the congressman, absent from the House for some days, had been in the Bethesda Naval Hospital for heavy drinking instead of bursitis. Whatever the case, the House passed the bill by the lopsided vote of 356 to 2.

John W. Finney in the *New York Times* on 15 June emphasized the constitutional question: whether Congress or the president as commander in chief had the power to determine how congressional authorizations were to be carried out. At least one member of the press saw the event as a victory of Rickover over McNamara.[8] Whether that interpretation was correct, the vote of the House showed a restiveness, a feeling against the secretary of defense and perhaps the administration.

A conference committee took up the task of reconciling the Senate authorization of the *California* and long-lead-time items for the *South Car-olina* and the House authorization of the two nuclear frigates and two con-ventional destroyers. Rickover saw a dangerous flaw in the House version. Leighton drew up a memorandum at the request of Senator Jackson. The conference committee might compromise by proposing one nuclear and two conventional destroyers. If that happened, "the Secretary of Defense will be in the beautiful position of saying he only needs two ships and therefore the nuclear frigate shouldn't be built. Further he will be able to say that building two ships of one type is much cheaper than building one nuclear frigate and one conventional destroyer. Therefore including the one nuclear frigate and two conventional destroyers makes it virtually impossible to get the nuclear frigate actually built." But if the conference committee decided in favor of the two nuclear frigates, Congress would be giving the administration the number it wanted. Completing the mem-orandum, Leighton went on leave.

Retitling the memorandum "Notes for Senate-House Conference on FY 67 Military Authorization Bill" and dating it 20 June 1966, Rickover sent it to several members of the committee.[9]

In the end Congress authorized and appropriated funds for the *Califor-nia* and the long-lead-time items for the *South Carolina* and dropped the conventional ships. The Senate conferees defused the constitutional issue of the "mandatory language" by stipulating that the contracts should be entered into as soon as practicable "unless the President fully advises the Congress that its construction is not in the national interest."[10]

Rickover was in trouble. Paragraph 1149 of chapter 11 of *Navy Regula-tions* stated that no one in the Navy could, in an official capacity, apply to Congress, to either house, or to any committee, for legislation or for appropriations "except with the consent and knowledge of the Secretary of the Navy," nor was any person to answer a congressional request for information except through the secretary or as he authorized or as pro-vided by law. By retitling the memorandum intended only for Jackson and by readdressing it to the conference committee, Rickover had broken reg-ulations.

What he had done could not be concealed. On 9 July Nitze asked Rick-over for copies of any communications he had sent to the conference committee. Three days later Rickover replied there were no such com-munications, but he had answered informal and personal requests for his views coming from individuals who were senior members of committees having jurisdiction over issues. Anything he had sent was consistent with his testimony of 2 May. Still, if Nitze believed it would not be a breach of confidence with those who had received the notes, he would be pleased to furnish them. Nitze replied on 17 July that he wanted them. Rickover complied three days later.[11]

His friends on the joint committee swung into action. On 20 July Holifield and Price telephoned Nitze to tell him that they, as well as Jackson, had individually asked Rickover to prepare the document. Moreover, it was risky for Nitze to make an issue out of the matter because it could have political repercussions, particularly in view of the criticisms that the Republicans were making about the conduct of the war in Vietnam.[12]

Rickover went to Jackson's office on 26 July. The senator said that the previous day he had met with Nitze. The secretary was carrying out the orders from McNamara, he said, because Republicans were using Rickover's testimony and his note to the conference committee to embarrass the administration. To his knowledge, Rickover replied, no one, Democrat or Republican, had made public use of the material. Jackson thought a meeting between Rickover and the Democratic joint committee members would be helpful. Rickover accepted the proposal but maintained he could not be placed in the position where he would never contact members of Congress unless he had notified and obtained permission from someone in the Department of Defense. Jackson said he would take care of the situation and that Rickover should not worry.[13]

John T. Conway, executive director of the committee staff, wanted to keep the matter out of the public eye. Only a few weeks earlier thousands of people had marched through Washington protesting the war in Vietnam, and Chicago as well as New York had also seen demonstrations. Having Rickover, a prominent figure and master of the colorful phrase, defend himself by exposing his differences with McNamara and Nitze, two important members of the Johnson administration, was the last thing the Democratic members of the committee wanted.

Conway planned the meeting, now enlarged to include Nitze. On 3 August the secretary was to come to the joint committee room, but Conway thought something more secluded would be better. Senators had small rooms near the Senate chamber where they could take a break without having to return to their offices in another building. A staff member met Nitze and promptly took him to Pastore's "hideaway." It was crowded; there was not even room to sit down. Jackson, Anderson, Pastore, Holifield, and Thomas G. Morris were present. So was Rickover.

Almost immediately Rickover burst out, accusing Nitze of being the worst secretary of the Navy in the history of the United States. For a moment, it seemed, the careful plans for a quiet meeting and a calm discussion had been ruined, but Jackson got things back on track by asking Nitze to explain the problem. The secretary replied that Rickover had sent a document dealing with authorization matters for members of Congress. The document recommended an action that was contrary to the policy of the Department of Defense. Nitze said he had no objections to statements Rickover made in hearings, but this instance violated Navy regulations. Jackson replied that he, among others, had asked Rickover for the information. Rickover, therefore, had not volunteered the information and hence had not broken regulations.

Rickover declared that any rule by an executive agency preventing free expression of opinion by a member of the armed forces to individual members of Congress on any subject was illegal, but he was not taking his stand on the legal aspects of the situation. Furthermore, he had not sent opinions that Nitze did not know about because they were consistent with his earlier testimony. But, if in the past he had acted only in accordance with official policy of the Navy, there would be no nuclear Navy now.

Holifield bore down on the political issue, warning that, as a member of the Democratic Party, he was willing to go to the president to prevent any rash action that would hurt the administration. Nitze conceded that no disciplinary action would be taken. The meeting ended with a vague agreement, probably all that could be obtained considering the circumstances. Nitze understood that Rickover would not send letters on budget matters to Congress except through the secretary. Rickover's interpretation was different: if he received a written request for information from a congressman, he should give the secretary a copy of that request. "Whether this was to be done before hand or afterwards was not clear," Rickover stated.[14]

The incident, however, was not closed. At Nitze's request Rickover came to his office in the afternoon of 9 August. Nitze handed Rickover a multipage document containing the judge advocate general's opinion. It found that it was illegal for a member of the armed services to deal with a congressman without first going through official channels. Rickover glanced quickly through the document and said he did not agree. Nitze said that Rickover had not read it. An extended discussion followed, in which Nitze pointed out that McNamara was angry because Rickover had written to members of Congress. Nitze then gave Rickover a single-page memorandum. Noticing that there was a place for his signature at the bottom, Rickover asked what was in it. Nitze explained that it was a statement of what Rickover would do in his future relations with Congress. Rickover refused to sign. Nitze said he didn't have to sign it—just read it. Rickover also refused to do that. "I told the Secretary that he had the option of firing me if he wished," Rickover recalled. Nitze replied that Rickover should stay because of the value of the work he was doing.[15]

As 1966 ended, Rickover could have looked back with some satisfaction as far as the nuclear surface fleet was concerned. Congress had authorized the *Nimitz*, the first of her class of carriers, and the *California*, the first of her class of escorts. Nonetheless, heavy weather lay ahead for the nuclear surface fleet: each additional ship had to be fought for, in battles made more difficult by the growing ravages of inflation.

Authorization of the *Nimitz* and the *California* was taking place just as the fight for developing a new attack submarine was moving toward a climax. The *Permit/Sturgeon* class, employing the S5W plant, although highly successful, was inevitably becoming obsolete. When it would reach that stage was hard to tell: the Soviet Union was building a large submarine force, and from information reaching him, Rickover was convinced that Soviet submarines could achieve higher speeds than they were given credit for. He saw no time to lose in developing a new high-speed attack submarine.

The decision was not Rickover's alone to make. Determining ship characteristics was a major undertaking involving technical aspects and operational features. Furthermore, designing, developing, and building a submarine was an expensive business that was bound to have a serious impact on the Navy's budget. The views of two civilian officials, above the Navy in the bureaucracy of the defense establishment, had to be considered. They were John S. Foster, director of Defense Research and Engineering and, above him, McNamara. Finally, it was Congress that authorized and appropriated funds.

Rickover exerted great influence on submarine design. On the technical level, reactor propulsion systems took years to design and develop. Certain key decisions, such as the reactor and shaft horsepower, plant arrangements, dimensions, and center of gravity, had to be made early and, once made, could not be easily changed.[16] On the policy level, members of Congress looked to Rickover for advice.

He believed high speed was one of the most important qualities for a submarine to possess. In late 1963 he had begun work on the propulsion plant for a high-speed submarine that could escort surface ships. On

18 August 1966, Adm. David L. McDonald, chief of naval operations, issued development objectives for a high-speed submarine, a document calling for pre-design tradeoff studies of different concepts. Rickover's approach, known in naval circles as "Rickover's submarine," faced mounting opposition. Because of its propulsion plant, the ship would be big and heavy—characteristics that adversely affected the speed that could be achieved. According to procedures, the submarine should have come under the scrutiny of Rear Adm. Elmo R. Zumwalt Jr., who had reported in August 1966 as the first head of the recently formed systems analysis division in the office of the chief of naval operations. With the quiet collaboration of others, Rickover sidestepped Zumwalt, avoiding the delay inherent in tradeoff studies.[17]

To overcome opposition, Rickover mobilized his support. On 8 February 1967, Rear Adm. Philip A. Beshany, director of the submarine warfare division in the office of the chief of naval operations, telephoned Rickover that he would recommend developing a high-speed submarine. Although not a nuclear-trained officer, he had commanded a squadron of Polaris submarines. In March he became coordinator of the nuclear submarine project. He was familiar with the issues: the need to explain over and over again the value of speed in tactical engagements and to confront the argument that the Rickover submarine was too big, too expensive, and not needed. The new submarine had to have more, however, than just speed; improvements in other areas had to be factored in.[18]

On 4 March 1967 Rickover briefed the commanders of the Atlantic and Pacific submarine forces, asking for their support in developing a high-speed submarine and for their help in outlining its characteristics. He pointed to the lack of submarine design capability in the Navy and in industry, and to the increasing burden imposed by the bureaucracy in the Navy and the Department of Defense. The submarine operators should look to him as their most effective spokesman. They should support him in working for one-of-a-kind submarines to try out new concepts, or for a prototype to gain operating experience before committing a whole class to a design.[19]

He appeared before the joint committee on 16 March and described all the difficulties in getting a new project approved. At every step there were "nay sayers": words he often used to describe officials who preferred the safety of holding up actions rather than approving them. "The rules for starting a new project have now been changed," he remarked. "Before you can get permission you have to write a book and guarantee exactly what the new item will do. But when you are engaged in development you do not have time to write a book. Further, how can you honestly promise, before you start a development, exactly what it will do when it is finished. I have fought the redtape jungle for many years, but it is becoming very difficult to get any new project through the Navy and the Defense Department. You must justify everything eight ways to Sunday."[20]

Opposition to Rickover's ship gathered around another concept called the "conform submarine," being designed under the leadership of Capt. Donald H. Kern, chief of the submarine desk, which had cognizance of submarine design. The name came from "concept formulation," a technique in which several studies analyzed possible designs and, after various tradeoffs, selected the one deemed best. Kern had been design superintendent at Portsmouth and played a major role in developing the single-propeller diesel-electric *Barbel* class. The conform submarine proposed to make use of a natural circulation reactor (S5G), counter-rotating propellers to give high propulsion efficiency, and the smallest possible hull.[21] In the bureaucratic struggle over a new high-speed submarine, the conform submarine seemed the best way to block Rickover.

Rickover's submarine would be powered by the S6G reactor plant. Tom A. Hendrickson, chief of submarine fluid systems, was Rickover's technical chief and project officer for the new plant. His job was to "submarinize" the D1G/D2G reactor plant, which the Knolls Atomic Power Laboratory had developed for the frigate *Bainbridge*. Because procurement of long-lead-time components would determine the delivery date of the ship, Rickover wanted the Navy to seek their authorization in the fiscal year 1968 and the entire ship the following year.

According to one source, Kern and Rickover signed an agreement on 20 September 1967. Under its terms, Kern would back Rickover's ship until it was authorized, and then Rickover would back Kern's conform.[22] None of the Naval Reactors engineers ever saw the agreement and it is hard to see what Rickover, or Kern, would have gained by it. Rickover was not noted for helping a competitor and, once his ship was authorized, it was unlikely he would support Kern. Prototypes were expensive; building two would place a heavy strain on the budget and cause delay in beginning a new class of submarines because each prototype would be matched against the other. Kern's support of Rickover would have given the sanction of the submarine desk to Rickover's prototype.

On 8 December 1967 Rickover and Hendrickson took a forty-page paper giving the Navy's position for going ahead with the Rickover high-speed submarine to James K. Nunan, assistant director for sea warfare in the office of Defense Research and Engineering. They were shown huge stacks of documents that systems analysis required before making major decisions, and the forty-page paper was rejected as inadequate.

Systems analysis was a technique devised to provide quantitative comparisons of several approaches to a complex problem. Reaching an optimum solution was not an easy matter, for shifts in one variable affected other variables. That was the reason for the number of studies shown to Rickover and Hendrickson. Rickover believed, and some others agreed, that McNamara used systems analysis to substantiate decisions he had made or proposed to make. Numbers provided a veneer of certainty that looked impressive and was time-consuming to challenge. The results of the studies were sometimes startling. Some dealing with strength of the submarine force calculated that twenty-five Soviet submarines would be lost for every American submarine in a war. With that superiority there was no need to build a new high-speed submarine quickly or to continue the construction of attack submarines beyond the number authorized.

At the end of 1967, Rickover was blocked in his fight for his high-speed submarine. In a memorandum of 5 December 1967 Alain C. Enthoven, assistant secretary of defense (systems analysis), declared that no decision should be reached on building either the conform or high-speed submarine until studies were completed. Nunan recommended to Foster on 18 December that the high-speed submarine should not be funded: "It was the wrong boat, at the wrong time, for the wrong reasons." Two days later McNamara met with Paul R. Ignatius, secretary of the Navy. Although agreeing that the Navy needed high-speed submarines, McNamara questioned the Navy's approach and would allow no money for research and development or for procurement of long-lead-time items.[23]

An unexpected event, one of those that radically change positions on bitterly debated issues, occurred in January 1968. Worried about the quality of intelligence on the Soviet submarine program, Rickover had exerted pressure so that his deputy, William Wegner, could get access to information collected and analyzed by the office of Naval Intelligence and the Central Intelligence Agency. He found their findings flimsy at best and discovered that neither shared information with the other. He and Capt. James F. Bradley, director of undersea warfare in the office of Naval Intelligence, searched for ways to determine how fast Russian submarines could travel.

On 3 January 1968 the *Enterprise* left Alameda, California, for her third deployment to Vietnam. Far to the north, her presence known to American intelligence through a number of listening devices on the ocean floor, a Soviet submarine of the *November* class was operating. Off the coast of California, a Russian spy ship, which monitored American military communications, met the carrier. The Russian sent off a brief transmission: the submarine turned south.

It was a superb opportunity. If the submarine shadowed the carrier, and if the carrier built up speed, and if the submarine continued to follow, it might be possible to find out how fast the submarine could go. Rickover called Adm. Thomas H. Moorer, chief of naval operations, urging that the Navy seize the opportunity.

On 5 January 1968 the evidence was in. The *November* submarine was able to keep up with the *Enterprise* at thirty knots. It was a stunning discovery. The Russians had placed fifteen *November*s in operation between 1958 and 1964. The speed the *November* demonstrated was far greater than the twenty-five to twenty-seven knots the American intelligence community credited the class, and it was far greater than the *Permit*s and *Sturgeon*s could make. Moreover, the Soviet Union had a large submarine construction program, far exceeding that of the United States.[24]

Rickover and Hendrickson took a revision of their 8 December 1967 paper to Foster's office on 6 February 1968. Superficially, the revision bore little resemblance to the earlier document, but Hendrickson had taken it, divided it into chapters, double-spaced the typing, inserted a table of contents, added headings, printed sections on heavy paper, separated them by dividers, and put the entire contents between thick cardboard covers. It was a handsome and imposing piece of work that received many compliments, but it was word for word the same as the original forty-page paper of 8 December. It remained the basic document for the Navy's position.[25]

Moorer set up an ad hoc panel on 8 March 1968 to determine the characteristics of the high-speed submarine. Officers with operational experience with nuclear submarines made up the membership—no technical people, although technical information was made available. That same day in a telephone call to Seaborg, Foster said he did not find the intelligence on the Soviet program conclusive; he was not convinced that selecting Rickover's high-speed submarine was the course to take. A few more knots were not important because, although the ship gained speed, she would give off more noise. Finally, to increase the speed, the weight of the hull had to be reduced, which meant that the new submarine would not be able to operate as deeply as the *Sturgeons*. Foster warned the panel he would not approve a high-speed submarine if it had no more capability than the *Sturgeons*.[26]

The panel reported on 30 April 1968: "The information derived from the study to date supports the decision of the SECNAV and the CNO to build the high-speed submarine in the FY 1970 program. Some further refinements of the operational configuration selected by the Panel can be expected. These refinements will optimize the design, but can only be minor in nature, and will not affect the basic decision to proceed."[27]

In June 1968 Rickover and Foster testified before the Senate and House Armed Services Committees and the Joint Committee on Atomic Energy. Rickover wanted an immediate decision to go ahead with the high-speed submarine; Foster was willing to accept the reactor but wanted to consider other parts of the propulsion plant and wanted to wait until 1 July to make his decision. Rickover declared that for years he had been fighting for a high-speed submarine, for years he had been warning of the growing Soviet submarine fleet, for years the office of the secretary of defense and the director of Defense Research and Engineering had demanded studies. There was no time for more delay. Foster argued that he wanted to consider nonnuclear parts of the propulsion plant, presumably those elements that were part of the conform approach. Rickover replied that only meant more studies, for most of the components under consideration had not received much research and development work. Foster, on the defensive, received rough treatment from the congressional committees.[28]

During the turmoil in Washington Rickover suffered a personal loss. His mother Rachel, in her early nineties, died on 10 March. He hurried to Chicago, alone as usual, for the services.

He was proud of his mother, of her courage as she, with her two children, waited on Ellis Island for her husband to appear. He remembered how, in their first years in New York and Chicago, when they were struggling to get by, she would hold back her own servings at meals so that her husband and her children could have more. He was proud that at the age of sixty-five, she took courses in citizenship, reading and writing, and English. She went to school for two hours a day for five days a week for two years.

Three days after her death he was back in Washington, testifying before the preparedness investigating subcommittee of the Senate Armed Services Committee.

Foster had promised a decision on the high-speed submarine on 1 July 1968. A physicist who had been director of the Lawrence Radiation Laboratory at Livermore, California, where he had specialized in the design of nuclear weapons, Foster wanted to see firsthand the advantages of speed. An exercise was quickly set up: a submarine of the *Permit/Sturgeon* class would try to intercept a faster submarine of the *Skipjack* class. For the intercepting submarine, Foster asked for the *Dace*. Under Cdr. Kinnaird R. McKee, she had compiled an outstanding record, including highly classified missions to gather data on Soviet submarines. McKee knew the boundaries of the area in which the operation was to be undertaken and the rules under which he had to operate, but nothing else. With Foster on board, McKee, by skillful maneuvering and with the high state of training of his officers and men, was able to find and "sink" the faster *Shark* with a simulated torpedo, but it was a close call. The exercise impressed Foster with how difficult it was to overcome the advantage of speed.[29]

On 1 July Clark M. Clifford, secretary of defense after McNamara resigned in February, announced that the ship would be built. The *Los Angeles* was the lead ship of the 688 class. She, the *Baton Rouge*, and the *Philadelphia*, also 688s, were authorized in the fiscal year 1970. The class would number sixty-two, have an estimated speed greater than that of the *Sturgeon*s, but would not be able to operate as deeply.

Whether the conform submarine was a lost opportunity has been debated. Because it was never built, the answer can never be known. Certainly its characteristics on paper were impressive and superior in many respects to those of the *Los Angeles*, but whether its objectives could have been realized was another matter. It was not a risk the congressional committees wanted to take.

For most of the 1960s McNamara was secretary of defense. He and Rickover loathed each other. In the case of the new *Nimitz* class of carriers and the new *Los Angeles* attack submarines, Rickover had prevailed with the indispensable help of Congress. Some time during this period (the date cannot be fixed) McNamara went to Capitol Hill to see L. Mendel Rivers. The secretary of defense said he intended to take disciplinary action against Rickover. The chairman of the House Committee on Armed Services asked the reason. Because Rickover comes to members of Congress, McNamara replied:

> Mr. Rivers asked Mr. McNamara what disciplinary action he intended to take. Did he intend to give Admiral Rickover a court-martial? He told Mr. McNamara that if he wanted to give Admiral Rickover a court-martial that was fine, but then he would run into Mr. Rivers, Mr. Bates, Mr. Philbin, Mr. Hosmer, Senator Anderson, Mr. Holifield, the Speaker of the House, the entire House of Representatives, the entire Senate, the Jews, the Catholics, the Protestants, and any one else you wanted to name. He told Mr. McNamara if he wanted to do it, to go ahead and do it, but he couldn't imagine why he wanted to do it.
>
> At that point Mr. McNamara said "thank you" and departed.[30]

Rivers did not have a great deal of patience with what he deemed stupidity. In a voice that could be heard outside his office he shouted, "Do you know what those God-damned fools want to do? They want to court-martial Rickover."

Troubles, Sorrow, and Happiness

RICKOVER MUST HAVE watched the presidential election of 1968 with particular interest. Certainly he had met Hubert H. Humphrey, the Democratic candidate, but it was Richard M. Nixon whom he knew best. When Rickover had his heart attack in 1961, Nixon, then in private practice in New York, urged him to slow down a little, although admitting that the advice would "be more likely to fall on deaf ears in your case than perhaps any other person I know." In thanking him, Rickover referred to their official visit to the Soviet Union in 1959: "I will always remember the courteous way in which you treated me and how you helped me during the Russian trip."[1] There is no evidence, however, that they had kept in close contact.

Nixon selected Melvin R. Laird, an eight-term congressman from Wisconsin for secretary of defense. Fourteen years on the Subcommittee on Defense of the Appropriations Committee had given Laird a thorough knowledge of military affairs. Many officers in the Pentagon welcomed his appointment with a sense of relief; in his confirmation hearings he had declared he would cut back systems analysis and give more respect to the views of the service secretaries. Rickover knew Laird well and respected him. Often they had planned strategy while walking from the congressman's office to hearings. Laird was his own man, but like all veteran legislators, knew he had to ask the right questions to get the facts he needed. If Rickover knew John H. Chafee, former governor of Rhode Island who became secretary of the Navy, their contacts had been slight. Glenn T. Seaborg, a stalwart advocate of naval nuclear propulsion, began his ninth year as chairman of the Atomic Energy Commission, and Adm. Thomas H. Moorer continued as chief of naval operations.

On nearly every front the new administration faced acute problems—inflation, racial conflict, and social unrest—and in one way or another all were linked to the war in Vietnam. They affected the Navy, which, in a time of tight budgets, was trying to maintain old and worn-out ships, build new ones, and start new programs. The Trident missile submarine effort ranked high in the latter category.

On Monday, 12 May 1969, Rickover left his office in Main Navy to meet with Rear Adm. Levering Smith and Rear Adm. Jamie Adair. Smith was the director of the Strategic Systems Project Office, formerly the Special Projects Office, which had developed the Polaris missile system; Adair was the commander of Naval Ship Systems. Together they represented the basic elements of a sea-based missile system: the weapon, the ship, and the propulsion plant. Their meeting marked the entrance of Rickover into what was to be called the Trident Program. An unknown chronicler in Naval Reactors recorded, "From this time on NR was heavily involved."[2]

Rickover had no part in originating Trident. Robert S. McNamara, secretary of defense, had taken that step on 1 November 1966 by asking for a wide-ranging study of ballistic missile concepts and missile characteristics to counter a future Soviet threat. Called STRAT-X, the study drew upon the three services, major defense contractors, and other sources. Completed in August 1967, it found that ULMS, the acronym for undersea long-range missile system, promised the greatest survivability and cost effectiveness. Because characteristics of ship and missiles had yet to be determined, it would be years before the new system would go to sea.

By that time the Polaris submarines would be nearing obsolescence. Operating about 240 days a year, the ships were receiving hard service. Moreover, advances in several technologies, among them the means to achieve more quiet operation, could not be backfitted into the Polaris fleet. Finally, missile development was increasing ranges. The A1, carried by the first Polaris submarines, could reach one thousand nautical miles; those envisaged for ULMS would have a range from forty-five hundred to six thousand miles. All these factors, including the dimensions of new missiles, dictated building submarines that would be larger than the Polaris ships.

Greater ranges would enlarge the areas in which the new missile submarine could operate and reach its targets, and they also opened the possibility of making fundamental design changes. One scheme called for a huge submarine that, with its missiles, would be towed to sea and placed on the ocean floor. It would not need a propulsion plant because a small reactor could provide the electric power required to operate the missile systems and to meet the needs of the crew. The reactor for the *NR-1*, a deep-submergence research vehicle that Electric Boat would launch in January 1969, might be able to do the job.

Naval Reactors knew nothing of STRAT-X or ULMS. One submarine officer, aware of the effort and worried over the direction it was taking, contacted William Wegner, who informed Rickover. Finding the scheme ridiculous, Rickover wanted nothing to do with ULMS.

Opinion within ULMS began shifting to the S5W reactor plant, which was propelling most of the attack and all the Polaris submarines. It was easy to see the motives of those shaping ULMS; they hoped to follow the example set by the Polaris program in which Rickover's role was limited to providing the S5W reactor plant and training the officers and men charged with its operation. That prospect dimmed rapidly when Rickover realized that ULMS was going to be big; he intended to play a major part in it.

He had a nuclear propulsion plant in mind. Bettis was working on the D1W reactor plant. Originally the project was planned as a single-reactor plant for a destroyer, but for several reasons its original purpose had been discarded and its power rating increased. When the encounter in January 1968 between the *Enterprise* and the *November* submarine revealed the unexpected speed of the Soviet ship, Rickover wanted to use a submarinized version of the D1W propulsion plant for a submarine that could operate at greater speed and depth than the *Los Angeles* 688 class. Unable to get support for the ship, he saw in ULMS another chance for the reactor plant.[3]

ULMS was gaining momentum. On 28 May 1969, John S. Foster, director of Defense Research and Engineering, agreed that the Navy should look at various combinations of missile sizes; the number of missiles, ranging from sixteen to thirty, per ship; and the operating characteristics of the submarine.[4]

While thinking about the power plant for a very large missile submarine, Rickover was preparing to take the smallest nuclear submarine on sea trials. On 16 August he left Electric Boat in the *NR-1*, the world's first nuclear-powered deep-submergence research vehicle. She had a speed of about four knots, a length of 150 feet, a diameter of 12 feet, and a submerged displacement of four hundred tons. She also had retractable bottom wheels, viewing ports, television and still cameras, a claw to recover objects, and a manipulator to grasp and cut.

Since 1964 Rickover had been thinking of such a submarine to explore large areas of the continental shelf. Although the intelligence applications were obvious, he had little use for the Central Intelligence Agency and resisted their efforts to influence design and equipment. It was research that interested him. Electric Boat began erecting the hull in June 1967. He closely monitored construction progress, some observers believing he took more personal interest in the *NR-1* than in other work in the yard. One afternoon in his office, he suddenly realized the vehicle did not have a name. Because Naval Reactors was commonly known as NR, he chose *NR* to honor the organization and *1* in the hope that the future would see another in operation, able to dive to even greater depths.[5]

NR-1 did well in the trials. At one point Rickover, prone before a viewing port, watched in fascination life-forms on the bottom. They moved so slowly, perhaps because of the need to conserve energy.

The *NR-1* went on to an impressive career, helping to recover a Navy F-14 fighter and its Phoenix missile lost from an aircraft carrier, searching for parts of the space shuttle *Challenger*, which exploded on 28 January 1986, and undertaking oceanographic studies. Years later, when Rickover was gone, it took part in underwater archaeology, a field he would have found fascinating.

From the sea trials of the *NR-1*, Rickover returned to the technical work, to following the ULMS program, and to watching closely the fight in Congress over the building programs for nuclear attack carriers.

In August 1965 McNamara had approved a plan calling for the authorization of a *Nimitz*-class attack carrier in fiscal years 1967, 1969, and 1971. Congress fully funded the *Nimitz* in 1967, and the Newport News Shipbuilding and Dry Dock Company laid her keel in June 1968. The other two carriers began falling behind schedule. As it turned out, the *Dwight D. Eisenhower* was authorized in 1970 instead of 1969, and the *Carl Vinson* in 1974 instead of 1971. Inflation and its impact on the economy were the culprits. The effect could be seen in the rise of the cost estimates for the *Nimitz*. The original estimate was $427.5 million; by April 1970 that figure had risen to $536 million.[6]

To relieve the pressure on the budget, the appropriations for each of the two carriers were stretched out to cover more years. Under this fiscal maneuver, advanced procurement of long-lead-time items continued. These were the nuclear propulsion components that had to be ready at certain stages of the ship's construction. Some other construction costs were deferred to the next year or years. Thus work on the ship went on,

but at a slower rate and at less cost during a given year. No one liked defer-
rals. By forcing readjustments to production and building schedules, they
raised the total cost of the ship.

Fights in both Houses over authorization and appropriations for the
carriers revealed strong opposition—not just to the *Eisenhower* and *Vinson*
but also to the number of attack carriers in the fleet. The Navy stated that
it needed fifteen. Walter F. Mondale, Democrat, and Clifford P. Case,
Republican, challenged that number in the Senate on 12 August 1969.
Moreover, they called for a wide-ranging study on carrier strength and the
duplication of carrier- and land-based aircraft missions. Until that report
was completed, they proposed withholding funds for the *Eisenhower*.
Mondale and Case shifted their ground, modifying their amendment on
9 September and again on 12 September. Because funding of advance procurement for the last two years showed that Congress intended to build
the ship, the two senators would not try to withhold its funds. They did,
however, offer an amendment deferring advance procurement for the *Vinson* until the Senate and House Armed Services Committees completed a
joint study by 30 April 1970.

Rickover did all he could to make the case for the ship, providing information that the Navy could use to answer public inquiries and, at the
request of his old friend Sen. John C. Stennis, writing a lengthy letter for
the *Congressional Record*.[7]

In early 1970 the Nixon administration ambushed Congress. Although
asking for advance procurement funds for the *Vinson* in the fiscal 1971 budget, it stipulated that they would not be obligated until "completion of
studies in process to assess future requirements for attack carriers." The
"studies" turned out to be a study that would be made by the National
Security Council (NSC) and completed sometime in September, or perhaps later.[8] The administration had neatly trapped Congress. No matter
what the Armed Services Subcommittee concluded, the administration
would take no action until it completed its own study, whenever that
might be.

A badly puzzled Stennis called the Joint Armed Services Subcommittee
to order on 7 April 1970 in room S-146 in the Capitol. He did not see how
it could make recommendations on the *Vinson* and the required number of
attack aircraft carriers to Congress without knowing the findings of the
National Security Council study. Although he was alone in that view, it
would have great influence in the Senate.

For six days the Joint Armed Services Subcommittee received a wealth of material on the need for fifteen attack aircraft carriers, on comparing the strengths and weaknesses of air power from land bases and from carriers, and on the actual costs of attack carriers in operation. Oil-fired carriers received little attention, although at one point Rear Adm. James L. Holloway, who made most of the Navy's presentation at the hearings, remarked that nuclear-powered carriers cost about one-third more to build than their conventionally powered counterparts. In his appearance on 8 April, Mondale declared that eliminating aircraft carriers was not his purpose—he had never advocated that—but he could see little justification for requiring fifteen for the foreseeable future.

Rickover had prepared a long and elaborate statement, which he gave on 15 April 1970. It was largely for the record because for this audience, many of whom had often heard him, he needed only to summarize and expand on some points. Statement and summary showed the difficulties he faced. He said nothing about the number of attack carriers the Navy needed—that was not his job—but if the Navy was to have them, they should be the best. It was even more important that they be the best if there were to be fewer of them.

He pointed out that long-lead-time propulsion components had to be ordered seven years before the ship was to be delivered. Because the components had to be installed during the early stages of the ship's construction, any delay in their delivery held up its completion. Splitting advance procurement for budgetary reasons into two successive years, as was done for the *Eisenhower,* had its downside. The deferral not only added to the ultimate cost of the ship but also cast doubt on the Navy's commitment to its carrier program and opened gaps in production lines that had been so carefully established at great cost and effort. Furthermore, vendors and fabricators of nuclear components were finding the market for civilian nuclear power plants increasingly attractive. As of 1 January 1968, the cumulative rating and dollar value of reactors ordered by electric utilities since 1961 showed an astonishing upward curve. Components for nuclear power stations took about as long to fabricate as those for the Navy. Production capability once lost to the Navy would be hard to recover.

He saw no reason for holding up the subcommittee's report to Congress until the NSC finished its study. Going ahead might convince the council of the importance of the carrier; waiting might have the opposite effect.[9]

The Joint Armed Services Subcommittee issued a brief report on 22 April 1970 recommending approval of the president's request for long-lead-time construction items for the *Vinson.* The Senate Armed Services

Committee, however, refused to authorize the funds. In the House committee, L. Mendel Rivers tried to force the administration's hand by urging that none of the appropriations for shipbuilding should be obligated
until the NSC had advised the president of its recommendation for the
ship. He lost in the conference committee. He and other House members
were "grieved," but "it was virtually impossible to change the mind of the
adamantine Senate conferees when faced with the absence of the will to
make decisions on the part of the administration."[10]

The NSC never made a study, at least dealing with the *Vinson*. An astute
president had seen in the Mondale-Case amendment a chance to delay the
ship even further. Congress was to authorize her in fiscal year 1974, Newport News was to lay her keel on 11 October 1975, and Rickover was to take
her on trials on 24 January 1982. It was the last ship in which he would do
so.

Some individuals with whom Rickover had worked for years were leaving
the stage and others were taking their place. After heart surgery, too often
postponed, Rivers died in the University Hospital in Birmingham, Ala-
bama, on 28 December 1970. F. Edward Hébert became chairman of the
House Armed Services Committee. Rickover's relationship with him was
good, if not as close as it had been with Rivers. In November 1971 Seaborg
resigned from the AEC after serving as chairman for more than ten years,
far longer than any of his predecessors or those who were to follow. In the
introduction to volume 1 of his journal, Seaborg wrote, "The commissioners and I had good rapport with Rickover, but we couldn't claim that we
gave much direction to his program. Brilliant, articulate, and irascible,
Rickover was his own man."[11] James R. Schlesinger became the new chairman. Brusque, impatient, and often sarcastic, he thoroughly knew the
atomic energy program from earlier government service and was to go on
to hold Cabinet positions.

One change Rickover did not welcome. On 1 July 1970 Adm. Elmo R.
Zumwalt Jr. became chief of naval operations, replacing Moorer, who
became chairman of the joint chiefs of staff. "You could talk to him," Rickover said of Moorer, an accolade he bestowed on few.

At fifty, Zumwalt was the youngest officer to become chief of naval operations. Rickover considered Zumwalt a protégé of Paul H. Nitze, whom he
disliked, and an advocate of systems analysis, a discipline he despised.
Years earlier Rickover had interviewed Zumwalt for prospective com-

manding officer of a nuclear frigate or prospective executive officer of the nuclear cruiser *Long Beach*. Preliminary sessions with three longtime members of Naval Reactors explored technical background and aptitude with questions that were formal and professional. Meetings with Rickover, however, were often stormy ordeals in which the candidates were subjected to questions to test their quickness of mind and their ability to think and recognize basic principles. Because the questions often delved into personal matters, many individuals found them demeaning. Several high-ranking officers tried to get Rickover to change his interview technique but without success. The transcript of the Zumwalt interview in Polmar and Allen's *Rickover* gives a fair picture. Rickover accepted Zumwalt, who, however, declined so he could take command of the Navy's first guided-missile frigate.[12]

Zumwalt had no doubt that, as chief of naval operations, he would have trouble with Rickover. When Nitze was secretary of the Navy, Zumwalt was his executive aide and followed closely the twists and turns of the struggle over the recall of Rickover to active duty after his retirement. Zumwalt and Rickover had clashed over a study to determine how many major fleet escorts (cruisers) the Navy needed and how many of these should be nuclear-powered. Based on data from systems analysis, Zumwalt found the arguments for nuclear propulsion weak. Rickover declared that systems analysis was too narrow in its conclusions and did not take into account the ability of nuclear-powered ships to meet unforeseen tactical and strategic situations.

The new chief of naval operations faced three main problems: the carrier and submarine forces for too long had taken priority over other parts of the fleet, the Navy was dangerously short of the ability to confront an increasingly strong Soviet navy, and the Navy's personnel policies and practices had to be overhauled drastically to bring an end to racial injustice.

The material condition of much of the surface Navy was poor. Funds were not available to maintain the older ships, which were wearing out, or to build new ones having much improved characteristics. Too much money, Zumwalt believed, was going into nuclear-powered ships—the carriers, escorts, attack and missile submarines—and not enough into smaller and less costly ships such as patrol frigates. These could be used for escorts or for missions not needing expensive and large ships. Zumwalt tried to reach an agreement with Rickover, increasing the rate of submarine procurement for three years in exchange for support of the design and testing of new surface vessels. Rickover opposed Zumwalt's surface ship programs, particularly in Congress. On the other hand, they worked closely together to get congressional approval of the *Carl Vinson* and the Trident submarines.[13] Rickover did not, however, challenge Zumwalt's personnel policies.

Having taken part in STRAT-X while director of the Navy's division of systems analysis, Zumwalt was familiar with ULMS, as Trident was still named. Now, as chief of naval operations, he had to decide on the general characteristics of the ship. Zumwalt and Levering Smith, head of the Strategic Systems Project Office, strongly opposed Rickover's proposed propulsion plant, arguing that it meant building a large and expensive submarine that was not needed. Nonetheless, Zumwalt on 28 October 1970 recommended to Laird a submarine powered by the large reactor and carrying twenty-four missiles. David Packard, deputy secretary of defense, as well as some advisory groups, questioned the need for the additional speed and recommended more studies.[14]

Rickover insisted upon a panel of experienced submarine officers to consider the propulsion plant. To get the perspective of submariners, Zumwalt set up a panel composed of officers who had commanded nuclear attack and Polaris submarines. It concluded that a large, slow submarine was vulnerable and would have difficulty breaking sonar contact. Finally, it was important that the ship have the ability to undertake distant patrols. For these reasons speed and power were essential. Zumwalt found safety the most persuasive argument. Because of her size and weight, a large submarine could gain momentum that would bring her quickly to crush depths unless she had sufficient power to recover.[15]

Because of frequent clashes with Smith, Rickover pressed for a reorganization that would lessen the influence of the Strategic Systems Project Office. In a stormy meeting on 19 January 1971, with Zumwalt, Smith, several senior officers, and John W. Warner, undersecretary of the Navy, Rickover won agreement that an officer, not part of Naval Reactors, the Strategic Systems Project Office, or the Naval Ship Systems Command, should become project officer. Rear Adm. Harvey E. Lyon, former executive officer in the *Patrick Henry* and commander of the *Alexander Hamilton* and *Pollack*, was selected. (The first two were Polaris ships, the third an attack submarine.)

On 26 February 1972, the Navy agreed on the general characteristics of the ship. It would not have the large propulsion plant Rickover advocated; it and the huge submarine it required cost too much. Instead, the ship would have the S8G reactor (the eighth submarine reactor developed by General Electric). If less powerful than Rickover wanted, it was nonetheless more powerful than the S5W plant used in Polaris. The new missile submarine would have a forty-two-foot-diameter hull, a dimension that was determined by the size of the missile, and twenty missile tubes. On the grounds of cost effectiveness, Melvin R. Laird, secretary of defense, increased the number of tubes to twenty-four. Rickover thought twenty-four too many for one ship. He saw Laird, who warned him that the change would require presidential approval. Bringing up the issue would reopen controversies and possibly jeopardize the entire effort. Reluctantly, Rickover let the matter drop.[16]

On 16 May 1972 Laird changed the name of the program from ULMS to Trident, the three-pronged spear carried by Neptune, the Roman god of the sea. That same year Congress authorized the construction of the S8G prototype. General Electric would begin its construction at West Milton, New York, in January 1973.

On 25 May 1972, Rickover came home to 4801 Connecticut Avenue to find Ruth dead from a heart attack. Determined as always to maintain their privacy, only he, his son Robert, then living in New York, and Wegner and Leighton and their wives were present as her ashes were interred the next day at the Arlington National Cemetery.

Rickover was proud of Ruth and her writings. The one he mentioned most often was *International Law in National Courts*, her doctoral thesis published in 1932 by Columbia University. She also wrote "International Organization of European Rail Transport," a major article in the May 1937 issue of *International Conciliation*, published by the Carnegie Endowment for International Peace, as well as some handbooks for the endowment. All were scholarly, highly technical, and meticulously researched.[17]

At the time of her death they had been working on biographical essays of the men after whom the Polaris submarines were named. Seeing the lack of unity and the decline of the Protestant work ethic as the chief dangers to American society, they wanted to show the importance of leaders who could set a moral tone. Determined to complete the book, he worked on the essays whenever he had the chance. On at least one occasion he sat in an airport waiting room, scanning books drawn from his briefcase and making notes. Naval Reactors engineers who were with him saw to it that he had vacant seats on either side and that he was not interrupted. *Eminent Americans: Namesakes of the Polaris Submarine Fleet* appeared in 1972. Rickover dedicated it to Ruth: "She was at once the most human and intelligent person I ever knew, the greatest influence on my life and work."[18]

He found in her papers a manuscript recounting their travels in the Far East. While he worked over the pages to get rid of anachronisms, Chief Barbara J. Whitlark of his office ferreted out the English spellings of local place names, checked maps, and prepared the manuscript for printing. The Naval Institute Press published *Pepper, Rice, and Elephants: A Southeast Asian Journey from Celebes to Siam* in 1975. Although well written, it sold relatively few copies. Not wanting to be under any obligation, Rickover offered to make up any losses the press had incurred.

He did not look well. His eyes were tired, his cheeks had fallen, and his walk, if no less firm and determined, did not have the vigor it once possessed. He was not taking care of himself. Because his nights were sleepless, he thought of becoming a night watchman at a local drugstore and reading until it was morning and he could go to his office.

His work required his time while the fights in Congress over Trident demanded his attention. The years of 1972 and 1973 saw the main battles taking place on the Senate floor over the Strategic Arms Limitation Talks, known as SALT I. In Moscow on 26 May 1972, Nixon and Leonid I. Brezhnev, general secretary of the Central Committee of the Communist Party of the Soviet Union, signed a treaty limiting antiballistic missile systems and a five-year interim agreement limiting strategic offensive weapons. From the standpoint of many critics the Soviet Union gained more than the United States. Consequently, it was exceedingly important to accelerate the pace of Trident before a treaty at the end of the interim agreement might impose further restrictions.

Debate in the Senate revealed deep differences of opinion. The Armed Services Committee report of 14 July 1972 spoke of ten submarines at a cost of $13.5 billion, the first becoming operational in 1979. With some reason, the report observed that Trident "promises to be one of the most expensive weapon systems ever developed by the United States." Lloyd M. Bentsen led one group in arguing that the interim agreement removed the urgency behind Trident and that longer development and construction time could prevent costly mistakes. He proposed delaying the program for a year but continuing missile research and development. Strom Thurmond and others among those taking the opposite side declared that the Trident schedule should be accelerated and, among their authorities, cited

Moorer, Zumwalt, Levering Smith, and Rickover. Bentsen's amendment lost on 27 July by a vote of forty-seven to thirty-nine. A shift of only five votes would have changed the result.

The struggle grew even more bitter in 1973. The question was not whether the program should continue, but whether it should continue at the quickened pace. Debate in the Senate, beginning on 20 September, centered over the next few days around the amendment proposed by Thomas J. McIntyre of New Hampshire. Along with several other senators as cosponsors, he proposed cutting in half the $1.7 billion requested by the administration for Trident. He pointed out almost half the members of the Armed Services Committee were against acceleration and preferred a more orderly development that would spread costs and avoid the waste and errors that would result from having ten Trident submarines under construction before one was at sea. He wanted, therefore, to reduce the authorization for development and procurement by $885 million. The Senate took the unusual step on 25 September of debating behind closed doors from 1:24 until 4:00 in the afternoon. Two days later the Senate rejected the amendment by the narrow vote of forty-nine to forty-seven. In the final outcome, the amount authorized was about $2 million less than what the Navy wanted.[19]

The press followed the debates and the activities of those who made frequent visits to senatorial offices. Rickover and Zumwalt found themselves described as the Navy's "shoe leather brigade."

Quotations and references in the debates are hardly a precise measure of what has to be, by its very nature, an inexact subject—the influence of one individual on the fortunes of an important and complicated piece of legislation. Yet when all is said and done, powerful legislators in addressing their colleagues do not quote and cite authorities by name unless those individuals have reputation and standing.

In the early morning of 16 November 1972, Rickover returned to Washington National Airport from a business trip. He decided to walk to his office, a distance of about a mile. Shortly after his arrival he collapsed. He was rushed to the Bethesda Naval Hospital, where doctors declared him exhausted, a diagnosis soon changed to a heart attack.

Wegner was on the West Coast when he received word that Rickover had died. Later news soon corrected that information. As deputy director, Wegner was urgently needed in Washington. While he was flying in, David T. Leighton, associate director for surface ships, was at Newport

News, speaking in place of Rickover at the keel laying for the submarine *Baton Rouge*. Warner, secretary of the Navy since 4 May 1972, was also at the ceremony.

Wegner was at his office when a telephone call alerted him that an officer representing Adm. Isaac C. Kidd Jr. was on his way over. Kidd, an unrestricted line officer, headed the Naval Material Command. The Naval Ship Systems Command, of which Naval Reactors was a part, came under Kidd. Obviously ill at ease and clearly without qualifications, the officer said he had been sent to Naval Reactors to take charge. He was, however, on his way to New York.

Wegner pointed to the stack of documents on his desk that called for decisions; he declared that the staff had to be informed of the change, as did the laboratories and major contractors. Saying that Wegner should carry on, the officer left. Wegner called Leighton at Newport News. He talked to Warner, who asked what Rickover would want. Leighton replied Rickover would not want a change. Warner called Kidd and got the matter straightened out.

The episode showed two things: the eagerness of the Navy to take charge of the program and the need for Rickover to have a deputy in case he was incapacitated. Wegner's position was soon clarified but not publicized: he was designated Rickover's successor until the chief of naval operations and the secretary of the Navy appointed a successor. It did not, however, cover what would happen if Rickover should not be reappointed.[20] Rickover soon returned to work and Wegner continued to handle personnel matters and much of Rickover's contacts with the Navy.

Rickover was receiving honors. In April 1973 Warner announced that the new engineering complex under construction at the Naval Academy would be named Rickover Hall. The idea was Warner's, not Rickover's. To be completed in 1974, it would house more than three hundred thousand square feet of classroom and faculty office space and contain all the latest features for teaching modern naval engineering and design, including a tow tank for hydrodynamic demonstrations and ship design experiments, as well as a variety of aircraft engines, maintenance equipment, and scale models of deep-draft ship power plants. It was a nice sentiment, but it smacked somewhat of an honor awarded to a man at the end of an illustrious career.

So, for that matter, was the bill introduced in April 1973 by the House Armed Services Committee authorizing the president to promote Rickover from vice admiral to full admiral—from three to four stars. It was an honor giving him no additional authority. Yet only one other engineer officer had achieved that status: Samuel S. Robinson, chief of the Bureau of Ships when Rickover reported to the Electrical Section in 1939. Robinson got his fourth star in January 1945 and retired a year later. Rickover, however, intended to continue leading the propulsion program.

At ten minutes past noon on 3 December 1973 a small number of individuals gathered in the Oval Office at the White House, among them Secretary of the Navy Warner, Moorer, Zumwalt, Senators Jackson, George Aiken, and Strom Thurmond, and Rep. Chet Holifield. President Nixon began with a brief reference to the trip he and Rickover had made to the Soviet Union and Poland and then spoke of the technological breakthroughs the admiral would leave "as a monument." Nixon continued, in words probably summing up in his mind the outstanding quality of Rickover: "This man, who is controversial, this man, who comes up with unorthodox ideas, did not become submerged by the bureaucracy." After Warner read the commission appointing Rickover to the rank of four-star admiral, Nixon signed the document.

Rickover, reading from index cards, spoke of how much he owed to others and concluded, "Today we are faced with grave issues, foreign and domestic. We do not need excited change. All of virtue and justice are not embodied in one party and none in the other. We must all accept responsibility and work for the restoration to the country of quiet and harmony without which these issues cannot be resolved." More than one reporter believed Rickover was expressing sympathy to the president beleaguered by Watergate. That was correct. Rickover had worked over the phrasing several times, trying to catch the tone he wanted to convey to a man he liked.[21]

On 17 January 1974, Rickover was one of several senior officers appearing before the House Seapower Subcommittee of the Armed Services Committee meeting at Norfolk, Virginia, to learn about the Navy's need for new construction. In his testimony, he agreed that the Navy needed more ships and that nuclear propulsion was too expensive for many of them. He turned to an idea proposed by Bob Wilson, a Republican committee member from San Diego. The congressman had in mind legislation along the lines of the Vinson-Trammell Act. Passed in 1934, it authorized the Navy to construct ships up to the limits set by the Washington naval treaties of 1921 and 1922, and the London conference of 1930. Because the

United States had fallen so far below these restrictions, the Vinson-Trammell Act in effect authorized a shipbuilding program that would be carried out over several years, thus making it possible for long-range planning. The nuclear propulsion program needed something like that.[22]

Rickover asked Leighton to assist George Norris, counsel for the Seapower Subcommittee, who would draft the legislation. He had been counsel to the Joint Committee on Atomic Energy, where he had played a major role in drafting the Atomic Energy Act of 1954. Later he went into private practice, although still in the field of atomic energy, before returning in 1966 to join the staff of the Seapower Subcommittee. A strong feeling of respect had grown up between Norris and Rickover, Leighton, Wegner, and other members of Naval Reactors.

Wilson, Craig Hosmer, Holifield, Melvin Price, and Samuel Stratton spoke in favor of the bill in the House, as did Jackson and Thurmond in the Senate. The House passed the bill on 22 May, the Senate on 11 June. After further shaping in the conference committee, the bill went to the White House, where it was signed on 5 August 1974 as Title VIII of the Department of Defense Appropriation Authorization Act of 1975.

Title VIII declared that it was the policy of the United States to modernize the Navy's strike forces by constructing nuclear-powered major combatant ships, defined as submarines for strategic and tactical missions, aircraft carriers, their escorts, and such ships as were required to carry out independent operations for which high-speed endurance was essential. Each year the president sent his budget to Congress, the secretary of defense was to submit at the same time a written report on the application of nuclear propulsion to the strike force, including contract data. Furthermore, all major combatant ships requested from Congress were to be nuclear-powered unless the president fully advised that their construction was not in the national interest.[23]

Nixon signed the legislation on 5 August, pointing out several inflationary features of the act—one of which was Title VIII. "I shall recommend nuclear propulsion for ships only when the added cost of such propulsion is fully justified in the national interest," he declared.[24] Nixon was not the president who would have to deal with Title VIII. Unable to withstand the onslaught of Watergate, he resigned on 9 August.

Rickover had mixed feelings about Nixon. He still admired the man but disliked many of his actions. Rickover had grave doubts about the constitutionality of the president impounding funds that Congress had authorized and appropriated. As for Watergate, it was, Rickover remarked on

30 June 1973, "a hell of a situation." To a few of his close associates, Rickover said he ought to see Nixon, to see if there was not some way out. There is no evidence that Rickover did so.[25]

Rickover had known Gerald R. Ford, the new president of the United States, for many years. Elected to Congress in 1948, Ford soon became a well-liked and respected member of the House Subcommittee on Department of Defense Appropriations and often heard Rickover testify. Trying to check the ravages of inflation, Ford did not find construction of nuclear-powered surface ships in the national interest. More important, Title VIII lost support in Congress, which in 1978 declared that the United States would modernize its naval forces by building advanced, versatile, survivable, and effective combatant ships. Nuclear propulsion was no longer an essential element in the legislation.

The Vinson-Trammel Act came at a time when the national economy was in a depression and a naval construction program offered employment. Title VIII was passed when the economy was suffering from inflation. Moreover, whether several hundred legislators could impose a long-term program against the wishes of a president was questionable.

Rickover was meeting each day with a new buoyancy. On 21 January 1974, the *Chicago Sun Times* disclosed "the best kept secret since the Manhattan Project": Adm. Hyman G. Rickover had married Cdr. Eleonore Ann Bednowicz at 11:00 A.M. on 19 January at St. Celestine Church in Elmwood Park, Illinois.

They had first met in 1961, when he entered the Bethesda Naval Hospital after his first heart attack. For some time they had kept in contact, but after Ruth's death, she had not heard from him, although she did call on him in 1972 when he was in the hospital with his second heart attack. Later, while stationed at the Great Lakes Naval Hospital as education coordinator, she was assigned to an educational planning board that was to meet at the Bethesda Naval Hospital. While driving through a constant rain from Chicago to Washington over the Pennsylvania Turnpike, she suddenly found she was inches away from a huge truck. Her car spun around and went down the embankment backward. She was uninjured and her car was undamaged. Her immediate thought was that God had saved her for some purpose, though what it was she did not know. Two truck drivers stopped and got her back on the road. They had seen her Great Lakes sticker on her car and had been at Great Lakes for their naval training. An intense Catholic, she promised to pray for them.

At the planning board she found that, except for her, all the members were doctors. During the assignment she was staying at a friend's house, Nancy Furmanchik, a Navy nurse who also knew him. One evening she suggested inviting the admiral to dinner. Although not having thought of seeing him, she did call him. He accepted immediately and from that time on saw her as often as possible and called her every day. While she was back in her apartment at Waukegan, Illinois, he telephoned her from a factory floor: would she marry him? She had not expected the question, even though they had been good friends for a long time. She wanted a week to think it over. She prayed for guidance. He was thirty years older than she, five years older than her father. Her father was stunned and her mother was in tears. But they had much in common. Both had a lively sense of humor and the same outlook on life, both were strong-willed, and both were dedicated to their professions.

Keeping their marriage plans a secret was no mean task. They had to get a license and a ring. Rickover, a public figure, was recognized at one time or another by a taxi driver, a train conductor, and an employee of Peacock, the famous Chicago jeweler from whom they purchased their wedding rings. His denials that he was Admiral Rickover were probably not convincing, yet somehow the press was kept at bay. But it was a close call; the night before the wedding reporters began calling every Bednowicz in the telephone book. Because her picture had been flashed on television, her family left their home and stayed in seclusion at her brother's home; she stayed with her sister in River Grove.

They kept the wedding party small. She had her mother and father, her three brothers and her sister; he had his son, his sister Augusta, and a few nieces and their husbands. That was the first time Robert met his Chicago relatives.

After the wedding the couple left on their honeymoon to Greece and Turkey. Before the flight left, she watched with amused pride as he excused himself, and asked if she minded if he took his daily walk. She remained in the VIP waiting room, sipping champagne with a perfect stranger. There was one unexpected interruption. He had forgotten his wallet at her sister's home and her brother brought it to the airport. Not until later did she learn that her husband never carried a wallet—all he would have in his pocket was change to make telephone calls.

They had an idyllic honeymoon. They saw the treasures of the Sultans of Turkey in Istanbul, cruised among the Greek Islands, and wondered at the ancient Minoan cities on Crete.

They came back to Washington on 2 February 1974. They had to find a new place to live; 4801 Connecticut held too many memories and Eleonore did not want to live there. He found an apartment at Buchanan House, a new building just around the corner from National Center 2, where Naval Reactors was located after the demolition of Main Navy. A window from the study overlooked the entrance of National Center 2. In the morning, when he got out of his car to enter the building, he looked up and waved to her.

Eleonore changed his life. They were active socially, entertaining and being entertained at small dinner parties, and attending larger gatherings such as receptions and concerts. Rickover had to take some teasing from his friends in Congress on marriage. "Don't tell me you had to," joshed Chet Holifield during a Joint Committee meeting on 25 February 1974. But as Rickover told the committee, "When you meet a very charming, gracious, witty, intelligent and beautiful woman," a marriage does not have to be explained.[26] Once again he had someone to share his life and whose life he could share.

The Bitter Battle: Shipbuilding Claims

FIGHTS FILLED Rickover's career. None, however, was as bitter as his struggle in the late 1960s and 1970s with shipbuilders over the money they claimed the government owed them. Inflation fueled by the war in Vietnam inflamed the differences. By 1965, shipbuilders were facing an unprecedented upward swing in labor and material costs. By early 1969 ship construction costs had increased about 15 to 25 percent over those a mere two years earlier.[1] The antagonism Rickover aroused in his long campaign over the next decade to prevent payment of unsubstantiated and possibly fraudulent claims became a major element in forcing him out of the naval nuclear propulsion program.

March 1969 marked the beginning of the struggle, for that was when the Navy and the Todd Shipbuilding Corporation (which did not build nuclear ships) settled a claim. Todd had stated that the government owed it $114 million; the Navy had paid $96.5 million, about 84 cents on the dollar.

The Todd claim, called an "omnibus" or "total cost" claim, was something new. Rather than substantiating the basis for the amount claimed, the company simply cited alleged government deficiencies and then claimed a lump sum based on how much would cover all their projected costs and return the desired profit. Other builders, encouraged by rapidly growing claims, quickly followed suit. Because the omnibus claim bore no relation to cause and effect and was based instead on what the contractor wanted, Rickover recognized it as undermining the sanctity of the contract that bound shipbuilder and Navy. He insisted that the claims should be, as in the past, evaluated on their contractual merits.

As always, Rickover worked closely with Congress. In the Subcommittee on Priorities and Economy in Government of the Joint Economic Committee, he had an exceptional platform. He and its chairman, Sen.

William Proxmire of Wisconsin, shared a common determination to safe-guard the government against contract abuses by private industry. Prox-mire had a flair for publicity; with much fanfare he annually awarded the "Golden Fleece" to that government agency that had been most profligate with the taxpayers' money. In his appearances before the Proxmire com-mittee, Rickover caught the attention of the press: it sought colorful sto-ries, and he, wanting to publicize the sums at stake and the principles involved, was willing to oblige. In the course of these hearings, Proxmire published important correspondence and documents that otherwise would have been buried forever in files.[2]

Claims grew out of the fixed-price type contracts that were commonly used in Navy shipbuilding. Such arrangements involved an agreed-upon target price and generally a higher ceiling price, which represented the government's maximum liability. Within the ceiling price, the contrac-tor's profit would depend on his incurred costs. The lower the costs, the greater the profit. If the contractor's costs rose to the point that his entire target profit had been consumed, he had then to bear all subsequent costs. Rickover favored fixed-price contracts, even with high ceiling prices, because they gave the builders incentive they would not otherwise have to control their costs.

Constructing a warship was a complicated and expensive business tak-ing years. The builder provided materials, labor, and facilities, while the Navy or the government (the two terms were frequently interchangeable) furnished certain components, equipment, and information. If these were defective and caused delays, the contractor would be entitled to an equita-ble adjustment in the contract price. Similarly, shipbuilders were entitled to contract price adjustments for Navy changes in a ship already under construction to compensate for additional work, schedule delays, or high-er costs. Under approved procedures, the Navy had traditionally eval-uated such claims on their merits, audited the alleged cost, and then nego-tiated settlements. By providing the Navy with nothing to evaluate except a list of allegations and with no connection between the amounts claimed and the allegations, the Todd claim frustrated the process and threatened to make contract pricing meaningless.

The danger proved real as other builders seized upon the new approach. In May 1971 eleven claims totaled $579 million. Of these, $98.1 million were for Newport News and $22.7 million for Electric Boat. Only one claim, filed by Newport News, was for nuclear work. The eleven claims and those expected by the end of the year came to an impressive

$790 million. That same year the General Accounting Office, established by Congress in 1921 to scrutinize the receipt and disbursement of public funds, stated, "The practices presently being followed in settling claims could lead to an erosion of the contractor's incentive to control costs with a corresponding decline in the effectiveness of firm-fixed price contracting."[3] Behind that balanced prose was the warning that contractors might simply bid low to get the work, then seek to recover whatever it really cost and their corresponding profit through large unsubstantiated claims.

Once Rickover could have listed seven yards—five owned by industry and two by the Navy—building nuclear-powered ships; by 1974 only Newport News and Electric Boat remained. Both were building the *Los Angeles*–class (SSN 688) attack submarines, but only the New England yard would build the Trident missile submarines and only the Virginia yard could build aircraft carriers and cruisers. Conglomerates owned the yards. Electric Boat had been a division of General Dynamics since 1952, and Newport News had been bought by Tenneco in 1968.

Rickover had a low opinion of businessmen. "I believe that businessmen are, as a rule, the most stupid group, from a large viewpoint. Money apparently warps people's judgement and causes them to have an unreal attitude," he wrote to Ruth Rickover on 14 July 1935.[4] The passage of almost forty years had not changed his impression. He saw in conglomerates, with their focus on profits rather than quality of work, absentee management at its worst.

The tide of claims continued to rise, reaching $893.2 million at the beginning of 1974.[5] Of this amount, Newport News and Electric Boat accounted for $100.2 million, not all of it, however, for nuclear work. Congress closely followed the issue. The members of the Seapower Subcommittee of the House Committee on Armed Services were particularly knowledgeable. In the summer and fall of 1974, its chairman, Charles E. Bennett of Florida, a veteran legislator and old friend of Rickover, held several hearings on claims.[6] Because of their importance to defense, Electric Boat and Newport News held special interest.

Joseph D. Pierce, president and general manager of Electric Boat, testified on 1 August. A tough, hard-bitten engineer, Pierce had known Rickover for years. Although thoroughly familiar with the technical complexities of submarine construction, he was uneasy and unskillful in the fine art of balancing corporate politics and the demands of Rickover. His yard was having manpower problems. To prepare for the SSN 688 class and the Trident missile submarine programs, Electric Boat had added six thousand people to its work force between September 1972 and July 1974. Because skilled workmen had to be taken off their jobs to train those just coming in, productivity had fallen. But he was optimistic; a training program should bring results, and the hiring effort had not exhausted the local labor market.

He turned to the new contract signed with the Navy on 25 July 1974 for the first Trident submarine with an option for the next three. He admitted the risks: the ship was a new design and would be built in a new facility. Among the uncertainties, he spoke of the "unpredictability of today's economy," an oblique reference to inflation. Still, Electric Boat and the Navy had considered the risks and agreed upon a fixed-price incentive fee contract calling for the delivery of the first Trident as early as possible. The parties agreed on a target price and an unusually high ceiling price in view of the potential risks. Moreover, the Trident contract provided for escalation and for compensation for such problems as those coming from late deliveries of material.[7]

John P. Diesel, president of the Newport News yard, sharply criticized the Navy in his appearance on 6 August. He charged that the Navy, failing to get adequate funds from Congress, was trying to make up the shortfall by pushing many of its responsibilities and construction costs onto the contractors. Escalation clauses in the contract did not give adequate protection against double digit inflation. Admitting that Newport News was feeling the effects of its campaign to increase its manpower, Diesel charged that the demanding and intrusive presence of the Navy, of which the office of Rickover's representative was one element, prevented management from using its workforce effectively and thereby added to the labor costs the yard had to meet. Yard and Navy faced each other in a spirit of hostility and animosity.

Newport News had thirteen nuclear ships under construction—two aircraft carriers, four cruisers, and seven submarines—yet from seven years of work the company expected almost no profit. Unless guaranteed a 7 percent profit of its total program cost, he warned, Newport News might not accept new Navy construction.

He proposed building new ships under a cost-plus-fixed-fee contract, at least until inflation was brought under control and the volume of claims reduced. In that approach the builder and the Navy would estimate the ship's cost but recognize that plans and requirements change. The builder, however, would be paid a fixed fee regardless of the final cost. Asked what incentive the yard would have to keep the cost down, Diesel replied that it was the professional pride of the builder, an answer that did not convince the committee.

In his appearance on 23 September, Rickover rejected the arguments of the builders, particularly those given by Diesel. Some of the companies, perhaps experiencing losses or less profit than anticipated, laid the blame on several causes, among them inflation, flawed procurement policies, and poor contract administration. All had one common theme: the Navy was to blame. Newport News was having financial difficulties with its new construction contracts, but that, Rickover declared, was the result of the yard's decline in productivity, which, in turn, was caused by the rapid manpower buildup. In that process Newport News had not reached the level of skilled labor needed to make its contract schedules. That was not the fault of the government.

He, along with David T. Leighton, assistant director for surface ships, and Thomas L. Foster, director for fiscal matters, took up the question of escalation. The builders received escalation payments based on two indexes. The one for materials reflected the cost of special commodities used in ship construction, and that for labor was on a special index derived from data supplied by various shipbuilding companies. Together the indexes followed pretty accurately the impact of inflation on the shipbuilding industry. As long as shipbuilders performed to contract cost and schedule, the escalation clause would fully protect them no matter how high the inflation. Very few defense contractors, Rickover pointed out, had such favorable terms.

The shipbuilders had signed contracts that they had negotiated with the Navy; they knew what they were doing. It was not the responsibility of the government to rescue them from their failures, and it was not the taxpayer who should foot the bill. "As I see it," Rickover said, "when you make a contract you should fulfill it." He had been asked why he was fighting so hard over claims. It was not to make the country honest, he declared. "Even the Lord Jesus Christ could not do that." His goal was to use the money Congress appropriated to get ships, not to bail out shipbuilders.[8]

To casual observers, the hearings suggest a compromise: the builders claimed they were losing money, and the government needed the ships; both sides, therefore, should make a deal. Nonetheless, Rickover strongly objected to such horse-trade settlements. More to the point, he realized that maintaining the integrity of government contracts was key to sound business and good products. Failure to enforce contract provisions for short-term expediency only encouraged companies to submit low-ball bids to win contracts and then submit claims to make them profitable. Rickover became a thorn in the side of those who simply wanted somehow to wipe the slate clean.

Hiring more workers spawned more troubles at Electric Boat. Rickover knew about the chaotic condition of the yard, but not the full extent of its financial situation. The contract overruns were far greater than the company was representing. Corporate executives at Electric Boat and General Dynamics were concealing the full extent of their overruns, in the hope that the government would eventually rescue them through a liberal claims settlement.

The quality of the work force was not the problem at Newport News: it had stopped the manpower buildup before it could cause as much damage to the technical excellence of the yard as it had at Electric Boat. Newport News, however, was experiencing overruns that would deal their profit projections a heavy blow. In an attempt to ameliorate part of the problem, the company argued that the Navy's option for the *Arkansas* (CGN 41) construction could not be enforced because the Navy had made so many design changes and because of the rise in inflation. In sharp contrast, Rickover and the Navy argued that the option was still valid. In August Newport News stopped work on the ship. Under court order the company resumed work pending resolution of the dispute, but the Navy had to pay its costs and a profit.

Relations between the yard and Rickover continued to deteriorate. In February 1976 Diesel wrote to Adm. James L. Holloway III, chief of naval operations, tightening the pressure on the Navy. As president of the company, Diesel saw his job as determining whether Newport News should undertake any new construction for the Navy until there was solid evidence that the future relations would be very different. He admitted the implications of withdrawing were far-reaching, an understatement considering it was the only yard capable of building nuclear surface ships.[9]

By 1 April 1976 claims had reached $1.719 billion and involved seventy ships. Contracts for nuclear ships accounted for 69 percent of the claims: those submitted by Electric Boat came to $300 million for eighteen submarines; those by Newport News to $894.3 million for one aircraft carrier, two cruisers, and thirteen submarines.[10]

To William P. Clements, a blunt, outspoken business leader and former governor of Texas who became deputy secretary of defense in 1973, the situation could not go on. The Navy needed the ships, the yards were vital national assets, and the reputation of the Navy was suffering. He proposed using Public Law 85-804 to get rid of most of the claims. Passed by Congress in 1958, it enabled the president to authorize any department or agency to amend or modify contracts notwithstanding any other law or regulation. The secretary of defense could exercise this authority by making a formal determination that such action was necessary to facilitate the national defense and by notifying Congress in advance. Whether the status of the Navy's shipbuilding program warranted such extracontractual relief was open to question, but at least the law offered a way out.

Clements proposed to modify the contracts of four builders: those with Electric Boat and Newport News dealt with nuclear ships, those with the Ingalls Shipbuilding Division of Litton Systems and the National Steel and Shipbuilding Company with conventional ships. He announced that he would change the existing contracts so that their escalation provisions would approximate those in the Trident contract. He would pay the contractors what they would have received had those provisions been in effect. In exchange, the four builders would drop their claims, thus avoiding the need for audits. In the first days of April 1976 he opened negotiations with the builders.

Rickover argued against the scheme in a meeting with Clements on 7 April. Acknowledging that Public Law 85-804 gave Clements the authority to settle the claims of the four builders, he said that doing so would only create new difficulties. What would Clements do about other defense contractors? How would he get congressional support for paying a conglomerate if it was already reporting high profits? More important, a one-time settlement was not a final solution. In fact, the builders might draw the opposite conclusion: claims instead of contract performance were the keys to profits.

Rickover then proposed a provocative and controversial alternative. The Department of Defense was apparently concluding that it was unable to enforce its shipbuilding contracts because the shipbuilders could hold vital ships in hostage. The additional sums to be paid to bail out at least some of the shipbuilders would exceed the asset value of the shipyard. Rather than just give away the money and risk a repetition of the problem, the Navy could buy the shipyards and hire industry to operate them under long-term contracts. For over thirty years the Atomic Energy Commission and its successor agencies had followed that practice in operating their facilities, an arrangement often labeled GOCO, for government-owned–contractor-operated.

Rickover's GOCO proposal was conditional. If forced by hostage taking to pay such large amounts, and if the government had to cover contractor costs regardless of responsibility, why not, for roughly the same amount, buy the facilities to ensure their continuing availability and hire contractors to operate them on a cost reimbursement basis? Put another way, if the government could not enforce its contracts for vital materials, it should take advantage of the large sums it proposed to pay to set up an alternative arrangement. Government and contractors could devote their entire energies to building ships rather than fighting each other over contract issues.[11] There was little support for the idea. Many quickly derided the proposal as "nationalization of the shipbuilding industry." But it highlighted the problem the Navy was facing.

In early June Clements reported he could not reach agreement with the four shipbuilders. Proxmire called for new hearings. Rickover was scheduled to testify on 7 June, and Clements was scheduled on 25 June.

Rickover's testimony focused mainly on Newport News, stating that it refused to certify that its claims were current, accurate, and complete. In an apparent effort to swamp and frustrate Navy analysis, the yard submitted sixty-four two-inch-thick volumes of claims, which turned out largely to be a collection of imaginative entitlement theories together with rough estimates of what amounts should be paid if the theories were correct. The volumes contained little, if any, cause-and-effect substantiation. The conglomerates had made the claims so large and confusing that outsiders did not want to get bogged down in who was right and who was wrong. "Just settle" was the attitude. The claims experience simply reinforced Rickover's cynicism about conglomerate management. "The conglomerates wouldn't care if they were building ships or manufacturing horse turds," he remarked. "Their goal is to make money, no matter how."

As Rickover intended, the press leapt on his statement. Angered by the slur, Clements asked to see Rickover and Holloway. Because Rickover would be on the *Los Angeles* during her sea trials, the meeting had to be postponed until 29 June.

On 11 June Proxmire, citing Rickover's testimony and numerous examples of apparent fraud in the claims documents, asked J. William Middendorf III, secretary of the Navy, and E. Grey Lewis, the Navy's general counsel, for a formal investigation of the Newport News claims under federal false claims and fraud statutes.

On 14 June Diesel officially informed Clements that Newport News wanted the carrier *Vinson* and five 688-class submarines removed from the yard unless the company received prompt and full compensation for its work. He ended his letter with a nice touch: Newport News would help the Navy move the carrier to the Puget Sound Navy Yard and the submarines to the Navy yard at Mare Island.[12]

Rickover felt increasing pressure from his superiors in the Defense Department. That same day in the confines of his office, he said that Newport News was blaming the impasse on him and a few of his people, mainly Leighton and Foster. He would not quit. As he was speaking, Leighton came in, reporting that the pressure against Rickover appeared to be orchestrated, but nobody knew who was behind it. Rickover thought he "was taking on everyone now." Later, on 24 June, Rickover heard that Clements wanted to get rid of him, but that Donald H. Rumsfeld, secretary of defense, had said, "No. Not now."[13]

On 25 June Clements told the Proxmire committee that Electric Boat and National Steel had accepted his offer in principle but Newport News and Ingalls had not. The proposals drawn up under Public Law 85-804, however, had to apply to all four yards or none. He vehemently denied that he was trying to bail out the shipbuilders or settle the claims at face value, but he was trying to remove them as a cause of the rancorous disputes. Had he been successful, the country would be getting the ships it needed without the long delay and great expense in conducting audits. Something had to be done to repair the ties between the shipbuilders and the government: Rickover's declaration about horse turds was evidence of that. His efforts collapsed, Clements asked, "What do we do now?"[14]

Soon after his return from the trials of the *Los Angeles*, Rickover and Holloway had their delayed meeting with Clements. At least the three had no trouble finding common ground: resolving the claims problem was the Navy's highest priority. Rickover volunteered the idea that establishing a three-man ad hoc board was the quickest way to this goal. Only the board would analyze the claims and determine their value. For the board to succeed, the contractors could not be allowed to circumvent it through Navy or Defense Department officials. Moreover, neither he nor any member of his organization, Rickover continued, should be a member of the board or have anything to do with it, save for providing technical information. Holloway agreed with the plan, adding that it was similar to one that Adm. Frederick H. Michaelis, chief of naval material, was considering. The board would be placed in his organization.

Michaelis issued the charter of the Navy claims settlement board on 13 July. It would be headed by Rear Adm. Francis F. Manganaro, an engineering duty officer, with a captain in the Supply Corps and a civilian lawyer as the other members. For help, the board would draw on other parts of the Navy. In July 1976 it began its first assignment: it was the Newport News claim of $151 million (part of total claims of $892 million) on the cruisers *California* (CGN 36) and *South Carolina* (CGN 37). Both were already in commission.[15]

While this settlement was in progress, the fight over the *Arkansas* continued. Rickover felt intense pressure to keep him out of the claims issue. He considered asking for a court of inquiry as that would bring the matter before the public. It would mean the end of his career, but that might be coming to an end anyway.[16]

The Manganaro board, which had begun its work in the last year of the Ford administration, resolved the Newport News claim of $151 million for the two cruisers in February 1977, the first year of the Carter administration. The board awarded $44.4 million, at first glance about 30 percent. Because of the cost sharing provision in the contract, however, Newport News got 60 percent of the maximum amount possible. Nonetheless, the settlement confirmed Rickover's conviction that the value of the claims was vastly exaggerated. Diesel professed encouragement over the way the board had dealt with the claim, but pointed out others remained.[17] In March the Manganaro board began analyzing two claims filed by Electric Boat totaling $544 million, not for work on the Trident ships but for the *Los Angeles*–class submarines.

Management was a major part of the problem at Electric Boat. David Lewis, an outstanding figure in the aerospace industry, had become chairman of the board and chief executive officer of General Dynamics in 1971. Awed by seeing Rickover's ability to allocate contracts for the 688-class and Trident missile submarines, and by the prospect of huge profits, Lewis saw Rickover as a customer who had to be satisfied. For that reason Lewis had replaced Pierce in 1976 because of Rickover's complaints. In his place Lewis named Gordon MacDonald, a senior General Dynamics executive with a financial background but no shipyard experience. He found thousands of new workers had yet to be trained, materials control was near collapse, and productivity was falling fast. Electric Boat could not absorb the workload it had contracted for.[18]

Although well aware that the financial condition at Electric Boat was not good, Rickover had no way of knowing how bad it really was. As time passed and rumors spread, Rickover thought that the amount of claims would increase, but he did not suspect that the overrun had grown to nearly $1 billion.

Unlike the voluminous Newport News claims, those of Electric Boat consisted of only a few volumes that, in essence, asserted that all delays and cost increases were totally the financial responsibility of the government. Since General Dynamics officials obviously knew that this was not the case and tried to attribute all company problems to the Navy, Rickover highlighted and forwarded them to his superiors, recommending investigation for fraud.[19]

General Dynamics, as was the practice of the shipbuilders, was carrying the claim on its books as an asset, assuming for financial reporting purposes that the Navy would ultimately reimburse all incurred costs, thus avoiding any losses. Investor doubt of the value at which it was listed could wreak havoc with the corporation's stock. Lewis wanted a provisional payment on the claim of $120 million, which he badly needed to meet cash-flow problems at the yard. In its nearly completed evaluation of the claim, the Manganaro board did not find the claim of $544 million worth the desired provisional payment. In October Lewis went to Capitol Hill, warning those senators and representatives having influence on military affairs that Electric Boat would have to stop work on the 688 attack submarines unless the Navy resolved the claims in the company's favor. He did not reveal that the $544 million claim was not the total overrun. His foray was exactly the reason Rickover had insisted that the settlement board should make its findings free from outside pressure.

That same month Lewis replaced MacDonald with P. Takis Veliotis. The new general manager of Electric Boat had come from the General Dynamics yard at Quincy, Massachusetts, which built commercial ships. Greek-born, he had grown up in a family-owned shipping business. Seeing no future in Greece, he moved to Canada and found a place in a Quebec shipbuilding company. Highly intelligent, ambitious, exceedingly tough, and a fine engineer, he learned the business thoroughly. As general manager at Quincy, he had taken a troubled yard and made it prosper. At Electric Boat Veliotis ruthlessly replaced management and slashed the work force. Rickover heartily approved.[20]

Both men were in the *Omaha* (SSN 692) on Saturday 20 November when she began her initial sea trials. At a depth of about one hundred feet one of the periscopes began leaking water at the rate of about a gallon a minute. A way was rigged up to dump the water to the bottom of the ship, and when the ship surfaced water was found in the other periscope. In addition, a bypass pump failed. Rickover thought quality control at Electric Boat was near collapse.[21]

The *New London (Conn.) Day* ran a series of articles on Electric Boat. It found idleness in the work force, absenteeism, shoddy work, and welding errors. The 24 October story reported that the highly respected accounting company of Arthur Andersen stated that the financial position of General Dynamics depended upon gains in productivity on the 688 submarines as well as recovering a substantial portion of its claims.

The claims dealt only with the 688s; presumably progress on the Tridents was not affected. Electric Boat had laid the keel of three of them: the *Ohio* (SSBN 726), *Michigan* (SSBN 727), and *Florida* (SSBN 728). But on 29 November at a news conference in Washington, Rear Adm. Albert L. Kelln, the Trident program coordinator, stated, "We're having difficulty with people, plans, production, material, scheduling." The first Trident would be deployed in 1981 instead of 1980, and its initial cost had soared from $723 million to nearly $1.2 billion. However, because of the liberal contract terms, the Navy would pick up the bill, and even with a year's delay in delivery, Electric Boat should make a profit on the contract. To anyone reading the newspaper account, however, the information was hardly reassuring.[22]

If that was not enough, the Manganaro board, nearing the end of its analysis of the $544 million claims, was finding they were not worth much. If the board's report was released before the end of the year, it would undercut the plans of General Dynamics to continue publishing annual reports to stockholders predicated on full recovery under Navy shipbuilding claims.

At this point Edward Hidalgo, assistant secretary of the Navy for manpower, reserve affairs, and logistics, moved in. Knowing from Lewis the seriousness of the situation facing General Dynamics (although not the full extent of the overrun), and keenly aware of the political ramifications of ceasing work on the 688s, Hidalgo on 1 December seized the files and documents from the board, stopping it dead in its tracks before any public release of its findings. The tactics were rough but effective.

Rickover was furious at Hidalgo's preemptive strike on the company's behalf. Proxmire called a hearing. Rickover and Manganaro testified on the morning of 29 December, Hidalgo that afternoon. At one stroke, Rickover declared, Hidalgo had done away with thousands of hours of painstaking work done by the board. As bad as that was, it might have been acceptable if a "giveaway"—if that was what Hidalgo intended—would really solve the problem. But it would not. Instead, it would encourage contractors to submit claims, confident that they could receive good terms. Hidalgo did not see what the fuss was about; in talks with company officials he had become aware that resolving claims could not reach the fundamental causes of the clash between the Navy and the shipbuilders. He had, therefore, created a new steering group, with subgroups to handle Electric Boat and other claims. All he had done was to straighten out organizational matters to get at the fundamental differences.

The next day Proxmire fired off a letter to W. Graham Claytor, secretary of the Navy. The words, if not provided by Rickover, carried his views. Hidalgo was evasive, nonresponsive, poorly informed, and unprepared. Furthermore, his explanation for removing the claims was unsatisfactory and showed his insensitivity to the possibility that some were fraudulent.[23]

On 6 January 1978 Rickover had lunch with Claytor and Charles W. Duncan Jr., deputy secretary of defense. During the heated discussion Claytor, red-faced and angry, declared Rickover was virtually accusing him of having knowledge of fraudulent claims. Rickover replied he had not said that—the fraudulence was alleged. Claytor said he was taking it personally. Maybe he had gotten his point across, Rickover shot back. Claytor and Duncan said that Newport News was angry and, because of Rickover, was threatening to stop work. The thing to do, Rickover declared, was to return the claims to the Manganaro board. Seizing them was going to be very hard to explain.

A few days later Rickover learned that the claims had been returned to the board. Puzzled, he wondered if his talks with Duncan and Claytor were the reason. If so, he remarked, it was the first time in his knowledge that a secretary of the Navy and an assistant secretary of the Navy had been overruled at the instigation of a naval officer. He was not then aware that Hidalgo by his maneuver had slipped General Dynamics past the date of disclosure.[24] He also did not know at that time that the White House had encouraged the Navy to return the claims to the board in the light of adverse appearances.

On Friday, 27 January 1978, President Carter met with the American Press Institute Editors in the Cabinet Room of the White House and took time to answer questions. One was whether he had gotten involved in the claims issue. Had he talked with Rickover about the General Dynamics claim that was causing so much trouble? Carter replied that they had talked about the General Dynamics claim as well as others. He wanted to be fair to the companies involved and keep them solvent, but not pay them for work they had not done. As the editors all knew, Rickover was very knowledgeable on claims and "very strict in protecting the public's interest." Carter's schedule called for him to have a meeting with his chief defense officials, probably the following week.[25]

The meeting soon took place. Hidalgo, Claytor, Duncan, and Vice Adm. Clarence R. Bryan, commander, Naval Sea Systems Command, briefed Carter. Because Rickover was urging a GOCO, if the Navy was unwilling or unable to enforce its shipbuilding contracts, much of their remarks dealt with problems that action would bring forth. Out of the discussion that followed, a settlement based on Public Law 85-804 seemed best. Carter wanted a solution by 30 June, and, he remarked to Hidalgo, it would be nice if it was acceptable to Rickover.[26]

In the following months the Manganaro board found that General Dynamics' claim of $544 million was worth about $125 million at best. Nonetheless, Hidalgo was willing to ask Congress for $431 million. The actual overrun, however, was $982 million. Although the figures varied somewhat during the negotiations, the difference between what Hidalgo could offer and the total overrun was about $500 million. Declaring a loss of about half a billion dollars would ruin the reputation of General Dynamics and its management, unless the Navy could be forced to pay more. Holding the 688s under construction as hostage was the best, perhaps the only, weapon the company had.[27]

On 13 March Veliotis officially informed Bryan that Electric Boat would stop work on the 688s on 12 April at 11:59 P.M. because of the Navy's breaches of contracts. In several pages the division's general manager set forth the Navy's faults: failing to make timely and adequate payments under the contract terms, and providing late, incomplete, and defective drawings, specifications, and other data, all of which blocked the company's ability to perform effectively and economically. Replying the next day, Bryan denied the Navy had breached the contracts; they remained valid and binding.[28]

Veliotis in his letter complained that Electric Boat had to make more than thirty-four thousand changes to the detailed drawings the Navy provided for the 688-class submarines. To those who knew nothing of shipbuilding, the number was a damning indictment of the Navy.

Several officers explained to several congressional committees that the changes were not contract changes, as the uninitiated might expect. The design process, performed by Electric Boat itself, proceeded in parallel with ship construction. The first issue of a drawing might provide only enough detail to support material buys requiring long-lead-time purchases. As more information became available, perhaps individual component drawings, or arrangements, or specific requirements, that information would be added by a plan revision. If the shipbuilder installed equipment in a wrong but acceptable location, that act would trigger a plan change. Bryan declared that Electric Boat had well understood this and was deliberately inaccurate and misleading in its presentation. The average number of revisions per plan was about the same as that for the *Sturgeon* (SSN 637) class, which preceded the 688 class. Most changes were minor, but that did not mean that making and recording them was not exceedingly important. They were a complete record of the ship as it was actually built and were essential in making repairs or alterations.

Rickover told members of the Subcommittee on Defense of the House Appropriations Committee on 16 March that it took about six thousand detailed drawings to build one nuclear attack submarine, and an average drawing went through about six or seven revisions over the full period of design and construction. The shipbuilder requested some revisions to record mistakes made in fabrication or the different procedures he intended to use. Still other changes were made to take advantage of less expensive construction techniques. Most revisions were very minor and many were simply clerical or administrative. From its long history of building nuclear submarines, Electric Boat knew all about revisions, and knew that they furnished little basis for claims.

Rickover went further: Electric Boat and Newport News were both building 688s. When the program began Electric Boat bid lower than Newport News, but a recent comparison of the first five submarines built by each yard was revealing: those by Electric Boat cost $50 million more per submarine than those of Newport News. In his opinion the situation at Electric Boat was so bad that he would not give any new construction to the yard for at least two or three years—not even a barge. To Veliotis, Rickover's remarks were a deadly insult.[29]

After tense negotiations, the Navy and General Dynamics agreed to delay the work stoppage at Electric Boat until 11 June. Six days before that date the yard increased the pressure on the government by issuing eight thousand layoff notices—a move designed to bring political pressure on the Navy. Claytor and Hidalgo continued negotiating with Lewis, finally reaching a complicated agreement.

The total overrun was $892 million. Earlier, however, the Navy had found an additional $50 million, bringing the overrun down to $842 million. As noted earlier, the Manganaro board had found the $544 million claim worth $125 million. Deducting the $125 million from the overrun brought that figure down to $717 million. The Navy and General Dynamics split that amount, each paying $359 million. Although this required General Dynamics to write off a $359 million loss, through a number of complicated steps the company was able to erase the overrun and even come out ahead. Its stock promptly climbed.[30]

Before submitting the proposed settlement to the Authorization and Appropriations Committees for their concurrence, James T. McIntyre Jr., director of management and budget, summarized the situation for the president on 23 June. After describing the arrangement that Hidalgo had made with General Dynamics, McIntyre noted the procedural steps that came next. He observed that the Navy's troubles with claims remained: those of Newport News had yet to be settled, and Electric Boat was failing to meet schedules and exceeding cost estimates on the Trident program. Carter approved plans for funding the claims, probably on 8 or 9 July, 1978.[31]

Rickover continued to warn Hidalgo, who became secretary of the Navy on 24 October, that Electric Boat was laying the groundwork for new claims. Relations between the two remained bitter.

Patrick Tyler, in his *Running Critical: The Silent War, Rickover, and General Dynamics,* painted a vivid picture of Rickover and his fight over claims. Its sharp focus did not, nor was it intended to, capture Rickover's outlook and philosophy. According to Tyler, Rickover was ambitious, egocentric, ruthless, and vindictive, but those qualities did not sum up the reason for his struggle.

Occasionally, after some stormy meeting with naval officers in the Pentagon, he would raise the rhetorical question, "Do the officers exist for the Navy, or does the Navy exist for the officers?" He could have rephrased the question for Electric Boat and Newport News: "Do the shipbuilders exist for the Navy or does the Navy exist for the shipbuilders?"

As he saw it, the Navy was the customer who paid the shipbuilder to build a ship; their relationship was spelled out by their contract which made provision for adjusting to changing circumstances. Rickover never denied that the builder should be reimbursed for defects and delays caused by the Navy, but the Navy had certain rights, such as making sure that the ship met specifications and standards, and also had certain obligations, among them a fiduciary responsibility to the taxpayer. Neither rights nor obligations could be exercised without access to facts. Submitting total cost claims, parts of which had been in gestation for years, without substantiating data, meant an inversion of the traditional responsibility. In such circumstances some officials seemed to believe that the Navy existed to provide profit for the builder—through inflated or fraudulent claims, if necessary—to maintain goodwill and essential capability.

Most concerned officials in the Navy and the Department of Defense came from the business world and would return to it in a few years. They sympathized with the executives of the shipbuilding industry. "We are all in this thing together" and "Let's get on with the job" were slogans, Rickover once remarked, that "meant that the government was going to pay." He was outraged by the chicanery and slipperiness employed by the lawyers representing the shipbuilders. He thought the essence of business, particularly public business, is that "a deal is a deal" and that both contractual and technical discipline could quickly dissipate if the customer starts feeling obliged to protect suppliers from the consequences of their own mismanagement or poor judgment. If you are not going to enforce contracts, why bother negotiating them? The struggle over inflated shipbuilding claims involved moral and ethical issues as well. Despite the personal risk, he felt he had to make this case.

The Admiral and the President

LATE IN 1970 Rickover received an invitation to the inauguration of the governor of Georgia. Puzzled, he asked who Jimmy Carter was.

If Rickover did not remember Carter, Carter remembered him. Graduating from the Naval Academy in 1946, he had served in surface ships and submarines. Attracted to the possibilities of nuclear propulsion, he applied for an interview with Rickover. That event made an indelible impression. Allowing the young officer to choose any topic, Rickover then questioned him. Carter soon realized that in one subject after another his own knowledge was superficial. Finally Rickover asked Carter for his standing at the academy. Proudly Carter stated that he was 59th in a class of 820. Asked if he had done his best, Carter hesitated a moment and then replied that he had not. "Why not?" asked Rickover. That question, Carter wrote, "I have never been able to forget—or to answer." In *Why Not the Best?* his presidential campaign biography, he wrote that it was a question every American ought to ask.[1]

Rickover selected him in July 1952 and sent him to Schenectady as one of the prospective engineering officers for the *Seawolf* (SSN 575). There Carter had few direct contacts with Rickover but nonetheless felt his imprint: the stress on dedication, hard work, responsibility, and performance. Because of the death of his father and his desire to lead a civilian life, one which would give him greater opportunity for more varied public service, Carter left the Navy in October 1953. It was rare for Rickover to allow an officer who had committed himself to the program to leave. Some people in Naval Reactors suspected the influence of Richard B. Russell of Georgia, a powerful figure in the Senate. Rickover did not attend Carter's inauguration as governor, but he and the governor began a casual relationship over the telephone, usually discussing education.

On 23 October 1974 Carter wrote a brief note to Rickover from the governor's office in Atlanta: "I wanted you to know that I have decided to run for President. . . . I do not intend to lose." Observing that Rickover and Sen. Henry M. Jackson, also contending for the Democratic nomination, were close friends, Carter did not ask for Rickover's support. He would, however, like Rickover's advice on developing a better understanding of the nation's defense establishment. "You have had," he concluded, "a great and beneficial effect on my life—more than you could know. That is why I want you to know my plans well before any public announcement is made." Rickover responded by sending some congressional testimony on energy and a speech on "The Role of Engineering in the Navy." He also urged cutting bureaucracy to reduce costs and increase efficiency.[2]

Immediately after winning his party's nomination in July 1976, Carter began his campaign. On 11 August he interrupted his quest for votes to address a handwritten note to Rickover. If elected, and if it was "within the bounds of military/political propriety," he would like Rickover's advice on several matters, among them the structure of the Defense Department, the method of letting contracts, and the emphasis to place on nuclear power.[3] Such matters were close to Rickover's heart, but it was hard for him to know how seriously to take Carter. Rickover could not but wonder if he was being used in the campaign.

Carter won a narrow victory over President Gerald R. Ford and assumed office on 20 January 1977 as a bitterly cold winter was shutting down factories and closing schools. He took emergency measures to lift restrictions on the availability and the transportation of fuel. On 2 February, from the library of the White House, he declared by radio and television the urgent need for a national energy policy.[4] In all that he was doing, there was one event he was particularly looking forward to: a luncheon that he and Rosalyn Carter would have with Rickover and Eleonore Rickover at the White House on 5 February.

Rickover wanted to discuss energy policy but wasn't sure he would be able to speak freely on the subject. Possibly James R. Schlesinger would be present. Former chairman of the Atomic Energy Commission, former director of central intelligence, former secretary of defense, he was now Carter's advisor on energy policy and would be the first secretary of energy, a department the new president was eager to establish. Rickover would not feel free to discuss energy policy if Schlesinger was present.

Rickover need not have worried. He and Eleonore were the only guests at an informal and gracious lunch. Newspaper photographs the next day showed Eleonore, Rosalyn, and Rickover, in his usual dark business suit, seated on a couch, while a smiling president, wearing slacks and a sport shirt, sat close by in an easy chair. The two wives liked each other immediately. While they visited the residential quarters of the White House, their husbands talked about shipbuilding claims, simplifying defense, and cutting down the bureaucracy. Carter asked to be told when Rickover thought he made mistakes.

The meeting had gone exceedingly well. Carter sent to the Rickover residence the photograph of the four of them, inscribed to Hyman and Eleonore and with the words that he hoped to be a president worthy of them. Having access to the president was an honor, but to be of help Rickover knew he had to accept certain restraints. He volunteered them: never try to influence budget matters and never be a spokesman for the Navy, an understanding that did not preclude his fighting in Congress for nuclear propulsion. Rickover was exhilarated. He might "do the country some good" by getting his ideas to the president; he might even be at the crest of his career.[5]

Rickover sent a copy of his speech "Thoughts on Man's Purpose in Life" to the Oval Office. Its philosophy appealed to Carter. Material possessions and high living standards led to empty lives; the void could only be filled by having a purpose in life, by making commitments, and by assuming responsibilities. Rickover related a Japanese custom that honored their outstanding artists—not by bestowing peerages or knighthoods but with the title "National Human Treasure." Carter replied, "You would certainly be a nominee for National Human Treasure."[6]

On 16 February Rickover sent his views on labor to the White House. Two days later he met with Burt Lance, a longtime Carter friend and associate and now director of the powerful Office of Management and Budget. He left a list of topics with Lance: abolish the Naval Material Command to rid the Navy of a layer of bureaucracy, strengthen the renegotiation board, which tried to recover excessive profits from private industry on government contracts, and require shipbuilders to certify the accuracy of their claims.[7]

Rickover was back at the White House on 25 February, pleased to find that Carter welcomed his views and wanted to keep getting them. As a light touch, he presented Carter with the workbook that he had kept while at the Knolls laboratory. Having reviewed the notebook and other evidence, Rickover designated the president a "fully qualified Naval Nuclear Power Engineer." Should he leave his present employment, he would be welcomed in the naval nuclear propulsion program, "subject, of course, to an additional interview." Carter replied, "After voluntary or involuntary retirement from my present assignment, I may get up the courage for another interview with you. I hope that my present performance will qualify me for the promotion."[8]

To many individuals who had tried to get rid of Rickover for years, his close ties to the commander in chief came as a shock. Reporters who followed defense matters found it incredible that the relationship between Rickover and Carter could last. Rudy Abramson, staff writer for the *Los Angeles Times*, in his article of 27 February pointed out the apparently irreconcilable: Rickover had a well-deserved reputation for fighting hard for nuclear propulsion, but Carter was presenting a budget for fiscal year 1978 to Congress that did not provide any new nuclear surface ships. It did not contain a nuclear aircraft carrier, already designated CVN 71 (later named the *Theodore Roosevelt*), and it proposed canceling CSGN 42, a nuclear cruiser fitted with the Aegis air defense systems. If there was a clash between president and admiral, concluded Abramson, "Heavy Seas May Await Rickover."

Time bore out only part of the prediction. Carter, Harold Brown, secretary of defense, and W. Graham Claytor Jr., secretary of the Navy, continued the Nixon and Ford policy of downplaying the importance of the Navy. Assuming a short war with Central Europe as its center, the Army and Air Force would carry the major burden, leaving the Navy with little to do.[9] But the relationship between Rickover and Carter remained close.

Rickover went to the White House on 8 April with a number of subjects. One was human rights. He thought Carter's strong stand was good: it appealed to the deeply ingrained sense of morality of the American people. He could not have been back in his office long when he received a note from Carter asking for some "energy principles" to use in an address to the nation. The request caught Rickover the day before he was to leave for Newport News and the sea trials of the attack submarine *Baton Rouge* (SSN 689). Energy, however, was hardly a new subject for him; he had been considering it for years.

He drew up a pessimistic response, doubting whether a democracy could face the energy problem with the urgency it demanded. Never before had humanity confronted such a bleak and dire future. Once people had lived on lands suitable for all their needs, but times had changed. Now they were living in areas that earlier would not have been settled, an expansion made possible by industry and the use of irreplaceable raw materials. That could not long continue. He listed several approaches to the problem, warning that many would be extremely unpopular and would not easily get the support of Congress or the public.[10]

Rickover swept into his office Tuesday morning after the sea trials. Quickly he withdrew a few typed pages from his briefcase. They contained sentences, marked with deletions and insertions, that Carter might use to introduce his speech. Rickover had a member of his staff go over the pages to ready them for retyping so they could be rushed to the White House.[11]

Then he went back to his usual work, checking progress in several technical areas, perhaps directed toward a major goal, such as developing long-lived fuel elements so that ships would need to refuel only once and, beyond that, fuel elements that would last the life of the ship. He was watching closely one technical project that was reaching an important stage of development. It was a radically different reactor core for use in civilian power reactors. It might be ready to demonstrate the feasibility of its approach at the Shippingport Atomic Power Station by the end of the year.

From the Oval Office on Tuesday evening, 18 April, the president declared that preparing to meet the energy crisis was the greatest challenge Americans faced. Because the country was running out of gas and oil, it had to take steps to conserve energy, to renew the use of coal, and to develop permanent renewable sources such as solar power. All the measures he was advocating would be difficult: the effort would be the "'moral equivalent of war,' except that we will be uniting our efforts to build and not to destroy."[12]

The quotation was in the material Rickover had sent to the White House. The words were those of William James (1842–1910), the American philosopher and psychologist. They had not only caught the eye of the president, they also captured the attention of the press. The future would see the first letters of the phrase form the acronym MEOW and become a scoffing identification of the speech.

Certainly Carter would take a short outing in a nuclear submarine—the only question was when. On 9 March Rickover suggested a one-day cruise out of Cape Canaveral in the *Los Angeles* (SSN 688), the lead ship of the class. The best date turned out to be 27 May.

As Rickover planned the event, the president and his wife would be standing in the cockpit atop the sail as the ship got under way. The space was small, but there they could be seen and photographed by the press. He would be on the ladder leading below, probably only his head would show. Certainly Carter would like to man the throttle, maybe when the submarine went from one-third to two-thirds speed ahead would be best.

On 20 May Rickover telephoned Cdr. John E. Christensen Jr., captain of the *Los Angeles*. No special touches. No special menu. Probably the president would eat with the crew. One more thing: no "fat slobs of officers" in sight. He sent R. Mark Forssell, his director for submarine systems, William M. Hewitt, his director for secondary components (those associated with the steam plant), and Capt. Austin Scott, a nuclear-trained line officer temporarily attached to Naval Reactors, to make sure the ship was in perfect condition. In addition they were to oversee the rehearsal of the maneuvers that the president would witness, and go over briefings to be sure they were free of Navy jargon and acronyms.

At 8:42 Friday morning, 27 May, the Carters arrived at the pier. Before boarding the *Los Angeles,* Carter held a brief good-humored press conference. At 9:13 two tugs pulled the submarine into the channel of the Banana River. The president and his wife, waving to the crowd lining the banks, and Christensen were the only ones on the sail. At 11:55, some thirty-five miles to the east of the cape and in choppy seas and under threatening clouds, the submarine dived. Briefly Carter and Rickover manned the controls.

Rickover changed part of the agenda. Carter would be at the throttle as the ship went to flank speed—the ship's fastest sustained speed. Forssell stationed himself behind the president. At one point Carter was watching one set of dials, not realizing he also had to keep track of another set. Under certain conditions the reactor would shut down. Forssell could see the headlines: "Carter Scrams Reactor While His Former Boss in Command." "Mr President," he warned, "you had better watch the steam flow."

Later during the submerged run Rickover pointed to the engineer officer of the watch and said, "You're dead." Although not part of the agenda, it was a test Rickover often used on initial sea trials to make sure the men were so well trained that one could take over immediately in an emergency. While the officer feigned death, the rest of the watch performed faultlessly.

The ship received one message: someone had leaked the "fat slob" story to the press. Rickover thought it best to tell Carter about the story instead of trying to conceal it. The president just laughed.

In the wardroom Carter sat in the captain's chair and relaxed. They talked about many things, the Protestant work ethic and the possibility of eliminating nuclear weapons. In that connection Rickover speculated that, given human nature, it might have been better if nuclear fission had never been discovered. Rickover wanted to talk to Carter of several matters but found the opportunity slipping away as the president eagerly inspected the rest of the ship.

On going ashore Carter met a crowd of reporters. "I'm very proud of what I have seen," he said. "It was a very exhilarating and gratifying experience for me." One question directed at Rickover asked if he was proud of seeing how far one of his former junior officers had come. "Well, it shows that any sailor or officer in the Navy can become President. . . . I am afraid we have introduced competitors to President Carter at the next election."

Carter had the background to judge what he had seen. On his return to Washington he penned a note to Rickover: "Your nuclear submarines are, I believe, the finest exhibition of superb engineering ever created by man."[13]

Except for topics from which he had barred himself, Rickover had no hesitation in advising Carter on any subject. In late July he took to the White House an article in the Outlook section of the *Washington Post* that dealt with communities and crime. Carter was interested in his views on ghettoes and how leaders of the community took care of their own. At a press conference earlier in the month a reporter had asked whether it was fair to deny federal funds to a poor woman to have an abortion while a wealthy woman could obtain one without difficulty. Carter had replied that life was unfair. It was not a religious issue with him, he remarked to Rickover. Then, came the reply, Carter was not logical, for he would deny abortion to the women who needed it most. And, Rickover added, we already have too many people in the world.[14]

In October Carter sent a note thanking Rickover for the many kindnesses he had shown to the Carter family—gifts such as personalized jackets, dolphin candlestick holders, and, especially for Rosalyn Carter, an inscribed copy of Ruth Rickover's *Pepper, Rice, and Elephants.*[15]

In one respect Rickover's official position changed. The Department of Energy, becoming an active entity on 1 October 1977, absorbed many of the functions of the Atomic Energy Commission. Rickover had watched the legislative maneuvers carefully. In all the reshifting and consolidation he wanted to be certain that some legislative legerdemain or mishap did not put the nuclear propulsion program completely into the hands of the Department of Defense, where it would no longer have the protection of a civilian agency. The act did keep the joint program. He was director of the Office of Naval Reactors in the new department and deputy commander for nuclear propulsion, Naval Sea Systems Command in the Navy. His responsibilities did not change.

Reflecting the new energy organization, the Joint Committee on Atomic Energy was abolished and its responsibilities split among other congressional committees. Rickover was to miss the joint committee. He had known many of its members and staff for years. They knew their subject, worked hard, and were a powerful source of support. Some had already left the committee; Chet Holifield, for instance, a great influence and friend, had retired from Congress in 1974.

While in the *Los Angeles,* Carter had accepted Rickover's invitation to take part in a ceremony marking the start-up of the Shippingport Atomic Power Station with its new reactor. Most civilian power reactors used uranium enriched in the uranium 235 isotope and water to remove the heat from the reactor core. Uranium 235 was scarce, and even before the end of World War II, nuclear scientists and engineers had begun exploring the possibility of breeding, a process in which the reactor could produce more fuel than it consumed. The adamantine laws of nuclear physics made it impossible for water-cooled reactors with enriched uranium fuel to breed, although that type was generating most of the electricity produced by nuclear energy. Breeder reactors under consideration and development were examining other fuels and coolants. Although the technical difficulties were great, once conquered, they could free atomic power from the restrictions of the uranium supply. Water reactors might be able to breed, however, if they used thorium instead of natural uranium as the source of nuclear fuel. This was the approach Rickover was pursuing at Shippingport in a "Light Water Breeder Reactor" program.

Not only were the engineering obstacles immense, but the effort faced heavy opposition from the nuclear engineers and scientists of the reactor development community. The breeding gain would not be as great as with the other concepts and would siphon off fiscal support needed by the other approaches. The project survived mainly by the support of the Joint Committee on Atomic Energy, most especially from Chet Holifield. But if successful, the approach would permit the conversion of existing light water power plants from fuel based on uranium to that based on the more plentiful thorium.

In August 1977 Shippingport with its breeder core reached criticality. Although the plant could not go to full power until several tests and measurements were completed, Rickover, for once, was in no hurry. The second of December 1942 at Chicago had seen the world's first nuclear chain reaction, and 2 December 1957 at Shippingport had seen the world's first full-scale civilian power station reach criticality. Rickover wanted 2 December 1977 to see the president of the United States bring the first light water breeder to full power.

Rickover was driven to the White House on the morning of 2 December with William Wegner, his deputy director, and David T. Leighton, associate director for surface ships and the light water breeder reactor. An electronic blackboard had been placed in the Oval Office for all the dignitaries, newspapermen, and photographers to see. Words written on the blackboard would also appear on a similar blackboard in the Shippingport control room. The ceremony began at 10:46. After an exchange of introductory remarks, Carter stepped to the board and wrote, "Increase light water breeder reactor power to 100%, Jimmy Carter."

While they waited for Shippingport to reach full power, Rickover explained the engineering represented by the core. It had a diameter of eight feet, a height of eight feet, and a weight of about ninety tons. It was built to the accuracy of one one-thousandth of an inch—the "accuracy of a Swiss watch." Soon the words flashed back from the Shippingport control room that the plant had achieved its goal. Whether the plant would actually breed, however, depended upon the results of years of operation and the analysis of the spent fuel.

In the congratulations that followed, Rickover introduced Leighton, who was a class ahead of Carter at the academy and might have hazed him, and Wegner, whom he might have hazed. "So I think that makes it quits," he concluded.[16]

The relationship between Carter and Rickover was continuing into the next year. Perhaps nothing more clearly illustrated its strength than Rickover's comments to Carter about his press conference of 15 December 1977 and his television appearances.

Some questions at the press conference dealt with his energy program. Carter remarked that there had been progress—not as much as he had hoped—but progress nonetheless. The crude oil equalization tax and natural gas policy act were the two most intractable problems, but "Congress had made substantial progress even on energy, which has been the only major failure this year."

The next morning Rickover scanned the transcript of the conference, probably in the *New York Times*. The lead paragraph in an accompanying story by James T. Wooten quoted Carter's remarks that his energy policy had been a "major failure." That effort, Wooten observed, had been hailed as the "moral equivalent of war" and, to the president's evident disappointment, was now deadlocked in Congress.[17]

Rickover hurriedly made some notes and called the White House. Unable to reach the president, he spoke to his secretary, Susan Clough. Carter was not a failure, Rickover declared, and could only have won if he had given in to the oil interests:

> There is no question that the public will ultimately understand, and he will be regarded as a far-seeing man who has attempted to protect the people of the U.S.
>
> It took about 400 years for the Lord Jesus Christ to have his message accepted. Up to that time he could be considered a "failure."
>
> As long as a man is trying as hard as he can to do what he thinks to be right, he is a success, regardless of the outcome.[18]

Rickover telephoned Carter on the evening of 1 February 1978. The next day the president was to address the nation on the controversial treaties dealing with the Panama Canal. Rickover offered advice: Carter should face the camera, not the prompter. He should be himself, a "warm, decent, loving human being." He should not be concerned if he made a mistake in speaking. "The people can tell if he is honest with them and will forgive the error," he advised. Rickover added that he didn't want to be presumptuous, but, "as he knew, I was deeply concerned that he do the very best possible." Carter replied that he understood.[19]

As spring passed into summer in 1978, the second year of the Carter administration, all signs pointed to a fight between the administration on the one hand and the Navy and the congressional Armed Services and Appropriations Committees on the other. Secretary of Defense Harold Brown on 10 April 1978 before the House Armed Services Committee listed the missions of the Navy and, in summary, declared that "our commitments require that we maintain a two-ocean Navy." A few days earlier Adm. James L. Holloway III, chief of naval operations, had testified to the house committee, "I do not think that the size of the Navy today, the 459 ships, realistically represents a two-ocean Navy." Within the Navy feeling ran strong against the administration's policy. Brown remarked in a press interview that serious problems confronted the Navy—shipbuilding overruns was one, aircraft procurement another—and he didn't like officers opposing the administration's policy making their own approaches to members of Congress or the congressional staff.[20]

Much of the struggle centered around authorizing and appropriating funds for the next aircraft carrier. Two types were under consideration. The administration favored an oil-fired or "conventionally propelled carrier" designated the CVV. The congressional leaders and Rickover argued for a fourth *Nimitz*-class carrier, the *Theodore Roosevelt* (CVN 71). The cost of the conventional carrier was reported at $1.4 billion, that of the nuclear ship $2.4 billion. Getting nuclear carriers authorized and funded was a familiar and never-ending battle, but Rickover was well aware that the stakes were the same: authorization of a conventional carrier could mean no more nuclear surface ships for the Navy.

On March 1 he compared the two ships before the House Armed Services Committee. To illustrate the difference between the CVN and the CVV, he had prepared a table for committee members. Consisting mainly of a bar chart, it showed the nuclear ship displacing about ninety-five thousand tons handling an air wing of eighty-nine to ninety-four aircraft. The conventional carrier would displace sixty-three thousand tons and handle fifty to sixty aircraft. The CVN had four catapults compared with two for the CVV. In category after category, such as capacity for aircraft fuel and aircraft ammunition, the nuclear ship was clearly superior. Propulsion endurance on one fueling was thirteen years for the CVN compared with a few days for the conventional carrier.

A recent Navy study assumed a thirty-year life cycle for the CVNs and CVVs. On that basis the Navy could buy and operate two and a half CVVs for about the same cost as two CVNs. The study analyzed a number of hypothetical engagements between Soviet forces and American carrier forces under various circumstances and in different parts of the world. In each case two American forces were considered: one built around a nuclear carrier and the other around the conventional ship, both costing the same, with the conventional force including more ships to make up the difference. In all but one—the projection of air power supporting a five-day land battle in the Pacific—the nuclear force was superior. Furthermore, the study assumed replenishment ships were available whenever and wherever needed, and that these ships were not attacked. "That," Rickover remarked drily, "is quite an unusual situation in a war area."

As in the past, he reminded the committee that Congress had establish-ed the nuclear submarine program and that Congress had forced the con-struction of the nuclear surface fleet. Only Congress could exert pressure for more nuclear surface ships.[21]

On a ship-to-ship comparison no one could have doubted which of the two carriers was better, but that was not the issue—that question had been settled years ago. Brown (a veteran of the 1963 and 1964 fight over the *John F. Kennedy*) agreed that a nuclear carrier was the more effective of the two ships but cost more to procure. Furthermore, the Navy had twelve large carriers. Three nuclear carriers were in commission and a fourth was under construction. That should be sufficient.[22]

The fate of the Carter administration's defense program was uncertain in the early months of 1978. Although the White House had not asked for a nuclear aircraft carrier, Congress might insist on one. Rickover was exert-ing all his influence on behalf of the ship, as were many other officers.

On 6 May Melvin Price, chairman of the House Armed Services Com-mittee, submitted his report to the House. It proposed authorizing a nuclear carrier at $2.129 billion. John Stennis, chairman of the Senate Committee on Armed Services, issued his report on May 15. It, too, rec-ommended authorization of a *Nimitz*-class carrier. The actions were a sharp challenge to a Democratic president from a Democratic Congress. Seeking a compromise, Claytor, speaking before the naval academy alum-ni association on 17 May, announced that the administration would accept a conventionally powered carrier but not the nuclear ship.[23]

If intending to blunt the congressional drive, he had failed. The House passed its authorization bill by a vote of 319 to 67 on 24 May, and the Sen-ate passed its bill by a vote of 87 to 2 on 11 July. To iron out Senate and House differences in the long and complicated bills, representatives from each house met in conference. Its report, printed on 31 July, authorized the nuclear carrier.[24] Although Congress had yet to appropriate funds for the defense budget, it looked as if it would do so.

Washington speculated that Carter might veto the authorization bill. Still, the action would be dangerous. If Congress overrode him, he would suffer a serious defeat at a time when his polls were already low.

At 4:00 P.M. on 17 August 1978 Carter held his thirty-sixth press confer-ence. To the reporters crowded into Room 450 in the Old Executive Office

Building, he announced that he had one statement to make and then would answer questions. He was brief: he was vetoing the defense authorization bill.

He turned at once to the carrier. It would be, he said, "the most expensive ship ever built." The aircraft it would carry and the ships it would need for escort would cost billions in years to come. Other items in the budget, cut to provide for the carrier, were more important to defense.

The questions that followed dealt with breakdown of Israeli-Egyptian negotiations, the state of the dollar and inflation, Congress and the energy bill, and relations with China. Fairly late in the conference, one reporter asked if Carter had discussed his decision on the carrier with Rickover. He had not.

When Rickover first visited him after the election, Carter recalled,

> he pointed out then that his inclination was not to try to influence my decision on individual items in the Defense budget, that he knew I had special problems as President and a special perspective that he could not have himself. And because of our close relationship in the past—which still exists, by the way—he was going to refrain from that particular aspect of my responsibilities.
>
> He does meet with me quite frequently, and we have very frank discussions, but, I think, more in general terms. And he's not had any inclination to try to influence me on this particular matter.[25]

Congress was scheduled to vote on overriding the veto on 7 September. The outcome was hard to predict. Debates in Congress showed that support among the legislators for such ships was no longer as strong as it had been in earlier years. Furthermore, to get funds for the carrier, Congress had taken amounts from the president's budget for items that included strengthening American ground forces in Europe, increasing airlift, adding electronic warfare equipment and electronically guided ordnance, and improving the readiness of the military forces. These, Carter had declared, were needed immediately while it would take years before the carrier could contribute to defense. The White House began putting immense pressure on Congress and seeking support from business and civic leaders.

What did Rickover think? Three highly regarded reporters seized their chance on Sunday morning, 3 September, when Rickover appeared on *Face the Nation*, a CBS television and radio program, to talk about education. George Herman and Ike Pappas of CBS News and Haynes Johnson of the *Washington Post* were eager to begin. Herman was first. Education was important, but what about the nuclear carrier? A lot of congressmen wanted to know whether it was needed. "The carrier issue is now up before Congress and is therefore not a subject in which I should become involved," Rickover answered. "Whenever I testify to Congress . . . I will tell Congress exactly what I think."

Herman moved to the claims struggle and Rickover's position that the government should take over the shipbuilding yards: had he had any reaction from Congress, the Pentagon, or the White House? Rickover replied, "I regret, this is also a subject under consideration right now by the Navy Department, and will be considered by Congress when it returns. I regret, therefore, I cannot, nor will I, comment on that." Herman accused Rickover of taking over the interview. "That is correct," Rickover said, "and I will stop doing it when we talk about education. . . . If you wish to terminate this discussion, that's perfectly all—"

The three reporters watched with incredulity as Rickover prepared to leave. They turned immediately to the subject of education. At one point Johnson asked Rickover how he felt Carter was doing. "I think that, under the circumstances, he's doing a darn good job, but people expect him to do everything," Rickover said. "He cannot. He doesn't have the power. He's only one single human being." Rickover had made one thing absolutely clear: *Face the Nation* was, as its announcer stated, "a spontaneous and unrehearsed news interview."[26]

On 7 September the House voted 206 to 191, 35 not voting, to sustain Carter's veto. Since it took both houses to override the veto, the House had settled the matter, at least for the year. Nevertheless, the relationship between Rickover and Carter remained unchanged.

Rickover saw almost the same pattern emerging in 1979 as Carter called for a medium-sized conventional carrier. If stage and players were the same, the background was different. Iran, long an American bulwark in the Mideast, was descending swiftly into the maelstrom of revolution. Oil production was dropping and oil prices from the petroleum exporting countries were rising swiftly. Once again Americans faced a future of inflation and the prospect of long lines at gas stations.

Before subcommittees of the House Armed Services Committee on 1 March 1979, Rickover pointed again to the Soviet naval strength, to the growing oil shortage, and to authorizing ships that would be operating into the next century. Suppose someone in the future were to return and ask, "You had all that information and you still authorized oil-fired ships that had to fight great distances from the United States, and you still did that? How would any of us answer that question? They will think we are nuts."[27]

Rickover was, in the minds of the legislators and the public, the expert on reactor safety. Never was this role more evident than in the analysis of the events which began in the early morning on Wednesday, 28 March, at Unit 2 at the Three Mile Island nuclear power plant, located on the Susquehanna River about ten miles south of Harrisburg, the capital of Pennsylvania. Because of a series of errors, the reactor core overheated and threatened massive releases of radioactivity over a wide area containing several communities. An alarmed world watched and waited.[28]

The day after the accident, Donald R. Connors, chairman of the Bettis advisory safety committee and responsible for emergency planning at the laboratory, received a telephone call from a representative of the regional office of the Nuclear Regulatory Commission at King of Prussia, a town near Philadelphia. He asked if Bettis facilities were available to measure highly radioactive samples of reactor coolant from Three Mile Island. Connors checked with Naval Reactors in Washington; Rickover said Connors could commit the entire resources of the laboratory if necessary.

In the following days Bettis was one of many organizations giving assistance. Being closer to the site of the accident than Knolls, Bettis had the greater share of the Naval Reactors effort. It analyzed samples from the coolant, the air in the containment building, and a waste tank outside the containment building. The laboratory also sent lead bricks, used to make temporary radiation shielding, by air and by flatbed trucks to the stricken plant.

After the immediate danger faded, attention turned to the underlying causes of the accident. With 152 reactors operating and a superb safety record, Rickover was prominent among those whose views were sought. On 24 May he testified in a crowded hearing room before the subcommittee on energy research and development of the House Committee on Science and Technology; on 23 July he and his senior engineers met in the Naval Reactors conference room with a commission Carter had established under John G. Kemeny, a mathematician and physicist; and on 8 August he spent six uninterrupted hours—no time off for lunch—in a nearby hotel meeting room with executives of several major utilities.

He believed useful lessons could be learned by comparing operating procedures and methods of naval reactors with those of commercial power reactors. No direct application of the Navy program procedures and methods, however, was possible because the technical requirements of reactors operating in combatant ships and the training of officers and men who operated them necessarily differed from those in a civilian power station. But principles drawn from the Navy program could be valuable for civilian power.

Nuclear technology levied its demands on all the organizations and people who came in contact with it. For nuclear civilian power plants, that included operators in the control room, supervisors, and individuals in the executive offices. Utility executives did not have to know how to operate the power plant, but they had to have enough knowledge to realize the need for excellence and the consequence of its lack. Companies that designed and built nuclear power plants and those which fabricated their components had to understand the necessity for conservative design practices. The discipline required by nuclear technology had to bind all who were a part of it into a tightly woven web.[29]

One theme ran throughout Rickover's remarks, whether to members of Congress, to the Kemeny commission, or to the utility executives. It was the need for strong, central control. He had established it in the Navy program, but many doubted if it could be done outside the military environment. "I do not agree," Rickover said. "I believe that adequate discipline can be obtained in commercial nuclear power."[30]

Carter had asked Rickover for his personal views on the accident. On 1 December 1979, he sent them in a lengthy letter to the White House.[31] Analysis revealed a pattern of events often found in catastrophic accidents involving manmade devices. Relatively minor equipment malfunctions were followed by operator errors, each happening under slightly different circumstances. A succession of such events produced conditions under which a human or mechanical failure could trigger catastrophe. Had these earlier events been corrected promptly, the accident would not have occurred.

For years he had urged the utilities to establish a central technical organization that would have a clear mandate for safety and the power to apply sanctions to enforce its standards. Many of its proposed functions he had laid out before the executives in his August meeting but, he observed, he had seen little evidence that they understood their problem or how to attack it. The Electric Power Research Institute was an example of what he had in mind. It performed research and development for organizations generating power by various means. He understood that another organization, the Institute of Nuclear Power Operations, had recently been formed, but these institutes were only steps in the right direction. Carter included key phrases from Rickover's letter in the remarks he made on the Kemeny commission report on 7 December 1979.[32]

Rickover was unduly pessimistic in his allusion to the Institute of Nuclear Power Operations. Established by nuclear utility executives in the wake of Three Mile Island, the organization had self-improvement and self-regulation as its mission. Imbued with the spirit of Rickover principles adapted to the civilian environment, the institute brought discipline and coherence to the American civilian nuclear power industry, attributes that, had they been adopted earlier, might well have changed the disappointing history of commercial nuclear power in the United States.[33]

Carter's request to Rickover that he summarize his personal views on Three Mile Island had come on the evening of 31 May 1979. Rickover and Eleonore and Carter and Rosalyn had been at Electric Boat on 7 April as part of the ceremonies for two Trident submarines, the *Ohio* and the *Georgia*. Annie M. Glenn, wife of Sen. John Glenn of Ohio, christened their ship, and Rosalyn Carter laid the keel of her submarine, a ritual in which she chalked her initials on a keel plate—letters a welder would burn into the plate.

On the flight back to Washington, Eleonore spoke to Rosalyn, inviting her and her husband to dinner. She wanted the dinner to be a surprise. Rosalyn was delighted and enthusiastic. "Jimmy would like that," she said, but she had to check his calendar to find a good date. It turned out that 31 May was the best. Security checks and precautionary measures to ensure the safety of the president filled the preceding days. Somehow she was able to keep all the preparations from her husband. She had, however, told him that an Air Force officer and his wife and daughter would be coming to dinner. When the knock came at the door, Rickover opened it and learned for the first time who the guests were.

Eleonore said to the president, "He doesn't look surprised."

"He is," Carter replied.

The Carters were glad to get away from the White House. After dinner the two wives talked, and Amy went into one of the bedrooms to do her homework, while the men talked for three hours on a number of subjects, including politics, race, society, and defense. Rickover brought up the subject of the carrier:

I told the President that I had never spoken out against any administration stand on the Navy or any other matter. He agreed with this. However, in connection with the aircraft carrier, I said I considered him to be in error in advocating a 53,000-ton carrier which could only carry a small number of planes. I said if there was to be an additional carrier, it should be nuclear powered for reasons he well knew—particularly with the oil crisis becoming more severe. I could see no purpose in spending money to build a 53,000-ton carrier or even a Kennedy Class carrier if his objective was to save money. I recommended that he cancel his request for any carrier other than a nuclear one. I said I knew it was not my decision to make—whether we should have an additional carrier or how many carriers were to be in operation—but if there were to be another carrier, it should be nuclear powered.[34]

If Carter made a comment, Rickover did not record it. After their guests had left, Rickover confessed to Eleonore that he had been worried whether there was enough food for two families.

A change in regulations made retirement attractive for some individuals in civil service. In the summer of 1979 a number of Rickover's senior engineers left Naval Reactors. William Wegner, deputy director; R. William Bass, project officer for operating submarines; Robert S. Brodsky, director, Reactor Safety and Computation Division, and Murray E. Miles, director, Nuclear Technology Division, formed a consulting firm named Basic Energy Technology Associates, or BETA. Philip R. Clark, who had been chief of reactor engineering, became president and chief executive officer of General Public Utilities Nuclear Corporation. As a group, they averaged twenty-four years with Rickover. Leighton remained for several months in order to complete a project.

To most people in Naval Reactors the departures caused no great impact, certainly not as much as those of Mandil, Panoff, and Rockwell fifteen years earlier. James W. Vaughan Jr., a graduate of Duke University who had joined the program in 1957, became deputy director. The others who moved into the vacancies were also veterans of years of service and familiar with Naval Reactors organization, operations, and Rickover.

By fall it was increasingly clear that Congress would authorize the CVN 71. The press reported in October that Carter, while still opposing the ship, would not veto the defense legislation of which it was a part. The House passed the authorization legislation on 26 October 1979, clearing the way for it to go to Carter.[35] Appropriation legislation soon followed. Newport

News would lay the keel of the *Theodore Roosevelt* on 31 October 1981 and launch her on Navy Day 1984, and the Navy would commission her on 25 October 1986.

Grim and foreboding events marked the end of 1979 and continued into the next year. In November Iranians overran the American embassy in Tehran, and on 27 December Soviet troops invaded Afghanistan. For the first time since Czechoslovakia in 1948, the Soviet Union had used its own forces to increase its sphere of influence. In his State of the Union address on 23 January 1980, Carter declared that any outside force trying to gain control over the Persian Gulf would "be repelled by any means necessary, including military force." In Chicago on 3 March, Cyrus R. Vance, secretary of state, in a speech to the Council on Foreign Relations, said that American policy had to be balanced between firmness and avoidance of confrontation. Rickover telephoned Vance on 11 March, recommending that the United States send a small body of troops, possibly a battalion, into Afghanistan to show the Russians that they could not do "anything they wished and with no consequences." Vance thought an armed conflict might result. Rickover did not think so; that, he said, would inevitably lead to war, and he did not believe the Russians would go that far. In his plan, the Americans would not confront the Russians but would leave Afghanistan when the Russians did. Vance replied he would give the matter further consideration.[36]

Rickover's available papers do not show any contacts with Carter during the election campaign of 1980. On 1 September, Rickover sent Carter a sea trial letter from the nuclear cruiser *Arkansas* (CGN-41). Across the bottom of Carter's copy Rickover wrote, "I believe you have passed the hurdle, and that your election is a foregone conclusion." Possibly he was referring to Carter's successful renomination for a second term on 13 August. As it turned out, Carter suffered an overwhelming defeat. Rickover then wrote to him that anyone who had done his best was a success. Carter answered, "As I leave office, my realization of your great contributions are matched only by my thanks for your personal kindness and consideration. I've never gone wrong by following your advice."[37]

The relationship between the admiral and the president was puzzling. Their social contacts were infrequent: the Rickovers were never invited to state dinners at the White House. Certainly mutual admiration bridged the differences between them. On 9 June 1980, Carter presented Rickover and twelve others with the Medal of Freedom, the highest award given to those who made outstanding contributions to the nation in the fields of religion, fine arts, science, and politics. All the recipients standing before him, Carter remarked, were united by their passionate commitment to the enhancement of the quality of American life. The words suited Rickover. At the luncheon and reception that followed, he spoke briefly. "Every human being should try to do the best he can," he said. "If he does that, then in his own mind and in God's he's great." That was the philosophy that each saw in the other.[38]

In 1979 Carter had renewed Rickover's tour of duty for another two years, an extension that would bring him to January 1982 and the administration of President Ronald Reagan.

End of a Career

RICKOVER WAS eighty-one when the Reagan administration took office in January 1981, but he did not look it. His color was good, and although his hair was white, the years had taken little of it. He remained slender, and his posture, except for a slight rounding of the shoulders, was straight. As those who argued with him could attest, his voice was as strong as ever. He admitted he could no longer work the same grueling hours as he had when the nuclear propulsion program was young and every dawn marked a new day of battle, but even so he arrived at his office around eight in the morning and left around seven in the evening.

He faced the new year uneasily. In the past he had occasionally confessed to weariness and a desire to lay down his burdens, but neither he nor those to whom he spoke took his words seriously. The program, after all, was an integral part of his life. His current two-year term of duty carried him through the end of January 1982, but he wanted to continue until 1984. He realized that the forces that had stood behind him for so many years were weakening. The Joint Committee on Atomic Energy no longer existed, and many of his congressional stalwarts had left. The functions of the Atomic Energy Commission had been merged into the Department of Energy, and atomic energy itself had lost its glamour and appeal. Continuing to lead the nuclear propulsion program depended on mustering enough support to persuade Caspar Weinberger, secretary of defense, and John F. Lehman Jr., secretary of the Navy, to retain him.

Rickover's relationships with Electric Boat remained bitter. While its general manager, P. Takis Veliotis, had succeeded in improving the quality of the waterfront work, the financial position of Electric Boat depended upon another round of shipbuilding claims against the government. As Rickover had warned his superiors, the settlement negotiated by Edward

Hidalgo, assistant secretary of the Navy in the Carter administration, had not ended the matter.

On 26 January 1981, Rickover, along with representatives of contractors and the submarine force, were conducting the initial sea trials of the *Jacksonville* (SSN 699), a 688-class submarine that Electric Boat had laid down almost five years earlier. During the trials the submarine maneuvered at various speeds and depths as officers, crew, and contractors conducted steering tests, cycled valves, checked equipment, scanned instruments, and examined test results. Rickover took the opportunity to look into the training of officers and crew. He was very proud that so many of the crew, perhaps 60 percent, had never been to sea before and yet handled themselves like veterans.

Tests of the propulsion plant culminated in a submerged four-hour full-power run that ended in an emergency stop, or "crashback." Most of those hours Rickover spent in his room working or talking over the progress of the trials. Sometimes he found the chance to read a biography or a history. Toward the end of the run he went aft to the maneuvering room, the compartment from which the propulsion plant was operated. At the last minute of the last hour of the run he gave the order to go to reverse at high power.

A crashback, by suddenly putting in reverse a submarine, displacing almost seven thousand tons, and traveling in excess of twenty-five knots, placed a tremendous strain on the propulsion plant, far greater than it was ever likely to undergo in service. The crucial moment came when the ship had lost all headway but not yet gathered sternway—then the ship was "dead in the water." SSN 688 class submarines were not designed to go astern while submerged. They could get into serious danger. It was Rickover who gave the order for the ship to go ahead. Although there was no question that he was in charge of the trials, the commanding officer was responsible for the safety of his ship.

The crashback of the *Jacksonville* threatened a clash between the two responsibilities. When the navigator reported that the ship's speed was zero, Rickover delayed giving the command to go ahead by one minute. In that time the ship gained sternway and, according to an Electric Boat official, reached a speed of nine knots and an upward angle by the stern. Dissatisfied with the performance of the planesman, Rickover had the evolution repeated four more times. On each occasion, he allowed the ship to gather sternway, although not as much as the first time.[1]

At the time of the *Jacksonville* trials, the Reagan administration did not yet have a secretary of the Navy. John F. Lehman Jr. filled that vacancy on 5 February 1981. Thirty-nine years old, an aviator in the Naval Reserve, ambitious, and ruthless, he determined to reverse the trends of the Carter administration. He would restore the importance of the Navy in national defense, fight for an aggressive naval strategy, and rebuild the fleet from about 450 ships to 600. To achieve that goal he had to "straighten out the contracting mess and settle the Rickover problem."[2]

He also had to straighten out the mess at Electric Boat. Before the Seapower Subcommittee of the House Armed Services Committee on 12 March, Vice Adm. Earl B. Fowler Jr., commander, Naval Sea Systems Command, laid out the causes of the delays in building Trident and 688 submarines at the yard. They included accepting and using steel that did not meet specifications, incomplete and unsatisfactory structural welding, and missing and improper weld inspection records. The government, by furnishing some equipment that had to be repaired and by revising designs, had added delays, but they were a minor part of the whole. Fowler stressed that all problems that could compromise the safety of the submarines had been, or would be, corrected before their first sea trials.

Correcting quality control failures was expensive because the ramifications extended to the yard, the ships under construction, and the ships completed. Although Electric Boat did not know what the cost would be, it was proposing an imaginative solution: for its own poor work it would ask its customer, the Navy, to pay compensation.

Since 1942 the Navy had acted as self-insurer of builder's risk in the construction of new ships. The Navy paid for the loss or damage from unexpected or accidental events. Fowler gave examples: fires, explosions, and accidental breakage. But, he emphasized, the Navy would not pay a contractor for the rework the contractor had to do because of the contractor's own poor performance.[3]

Five days later Lehman announced he was no longer asking Electric Boat and Newport News to bid on building four 688 submarines. Instead, he was awarding three of the ships to Newport News and holding up his decision on the fourth. Lehman made public his letter to David S. Lewis, chairman of the board of General Dynamics. It stated that the Navy could not count on the Electric Boat Division of General Dynamics to make its commitments. Furthermore, by this time, the average return cost of the first five 688s from Electric Boat was 50 percent higher than the first five 688s from Newport News. Electric Boat and the Navy, by working together, could agree upon the steps needed to correct the problems at t h e y a r d . In the spring he would assess the situation at Electric Boat before deciding on the fourth 688.[4]

To defend Electric Boat, Veliotis appeared before the Seapower Subcommittee on 25 March. He declared the problems were not as serious as Fowler claimed, that Electric Boat, not the Navy, had discovered some of the difficulties and corrected them, that Electric Boat had gone through some tough times but they were gone. The first Trident submarine, the *Ohio* (SSBN 726), he expected to deliver in October. The way to preserve the nation's industrial base for submarine construction was not to award three of the four 688s to Newport News, he said, but to divide them equally between the two builders. He also stated that General Dynamics intended to file an insurance claim of $100 million against the government because of the poor work done by Electric Boat. He had a hard time selling that argument.[5]

Electric Boat received another blow on 1 April when the Navy announced it would not exercise its option to construct the ninth Trident submarine. The Navy would begin negotiations before 30 September 1981 for the ship under revised terms and conditions.[6]

Rickover appreciated the vigor of Lehman's actions against Electric Boat but could not understand why Lehman had not yet asked to see him. The two had met casually at a cocktail party given in March by Adm. Thomas B. Hayward, chief of naval operations, and Rickover had given the secretary a tie clip shaped like a submarine. Since then Rickover had heard nothing. Puzzled and uneasy, he remarked, "You'd think he'd want to meet the guy who was responsible for one of his major programs."[7]

Rickover got some reassurance about his future on 26 March in a meeting with Hayward. The chief of naval operations had one basic question: Who should take over if Rickover should be incapacitated or die? His deputy, James W. Vaughan Jr., Rickover replied. Hayward raised the possibility of Vice Adm. Kinnaird R. McKee, a brilliant submarine officer, as Rickover's successor. Rickover replied that a nuclear trained officer had neither the technical background nor the experience to deal with contractors and Congress. Furthermore, Rickover saw no need to make a decision; he exercised daily and was in good health. If he felt unable to carry out his duty he would advise Hayward immediately. He wanted to stay on until he was eighty-four. Rickover got the impression that Hayward would not object but would oppose any further extension.[8]

At last Lehman asked Rickover to come to his office. In the late afternoon of 1 May they began a wide-ranging discussion by talking about nuclear war and what the United States should do if attacked. Rickover agreed with a statement of British Prime Minister Harold Macmillan: "What is the merit of posthumous revenge?" Rickover "saw no point in wiping out the human race just because this great calamity had befallen us. At that time there would be nothing we could do to redress the situation." Lehman disagreed: "He would retaliate." They went on to talk about the Naval Academy, the number of ballistic missile submarines and how many were required, the service life of submarines and the number needed, the delivery date of the first Trident submarine, the role of Rickover's representatives at the shipyards, and several other subjects. Lehman was surprised at the end of the forty-minute meeting when Rickover, after giving him a paper titled "Notes on the Naval Nuclear Propulsion Program," remarked that he would also give copies to the officers to whom he reported. It was customary and proper, Rickover explained, that they should know what matters he took up with his superiors.[9]

The meeting had passed without incident. Rickover probably did not know that Lehman, even before becoming secretary, had Weinberger's consent to force Rickover out of the program. Rickover did know that General Dynamics and other contractors were fighting against his reappointment, but that was nothing new. He also knew his congressional support was ebbing.[10]

As in past years, letters supporting Rickover's reappointment began arriving at the destinations where the decisions were made. James B. Edwards, secretary of energy, wrote to Weinberger on 6 May that his department considered Rickover the most qualified person to carry out the duties of deputy assistant secretary for naval reactors. Edwards raised the importance of Rickover's civilian role: a number of measures Rickover enforced in the naval program were being adopted by the civilian industry. Sen. Strom Thurmond from South Carolina, a member of the Senate Armed Services Committee, wrote to President Reagan that the country could not afford to lose "a man of Admiral Rickover's vision, integrity, and skill."[11]

His future still clouded, Rickover watched over the preparations for the initial sea trials of the *Ohio* (SSBN 726), the first of the controversial Trident submarines. Many people, among them congressmen and senators, had asked to go along, but he had turned them down. He remembered when the *Nautilus* (SSN 571) first got under way on nuclear power that the starboard reduction gear gave off a loud noise. Rickover had not wanted to return to the pier: too many people, among them newspapermen, were on shore watching every move. Investigation showed a loose screw—easily fixed—had caused the problem. Rickover thought the same kind of conditions governed the *Ohio;* trials were no place for spectators.

On 17 June under a dark blue sky as yet untouched by dawn, the huge submarine backed out of the yard into the Thames River. Lights from the pier, the shore, and a host of small boats streaked the black water with shimmering reflections. Soon the breaking day revealed the boats more clearly. Nuclear protestors manned some of them. The largest, a two-masted schooner, displayed large signs, one of which read "Freeze the Nuclear Arms Race." Rickover was pleased with the way the *Ohio* handled, how quietly she moved. The pilot left the ship when she was in midstream and was headed toward the sea.

"A beautiful ship," he told Rickover.

"How do you know?" Rickover replied. "You're just saying that because you think you should. Thanks, though."

A Coast Guard cutter and a Groton police boat as well as four Electric Boat tugs accompanied the ship. Veliotis, a huge man, stood on top of the pilot house of the *Hackensack*, one of the four tugs. He and Rickover glared at each other and turned away. A few miles beyond the harbor entrance the submarine began some surface tests, steering various courses and moving with small bursts of speed before going out to sea.

The trials went well, although some problems with the nonnuclear portion of the plant caused temporary delays and readjustment of the trial agenda. Noise in the reduction gear was one; determining its source took an expert brought by tug to the ship. When he could steal the time, Rickover read a book on Japan before the Meiji restoration. The four-hour full-power run and the crashback went well.

On 20 June the *Ohio* completed her initial sea trials. As was his usual practice when the propulsion plant trials were over, Rickover addressed the ship's company. After complimenting officers and men on the exemplary manner in which they had conducted the trials, he recalled his own service in submarines more than half a century earlier. It was a tough life, he said, particularly in the tropics:

There was no air-conditioning. We were constantly hot and perspiring—We developed rashes. When we turned in and tried to sleep, we were so tired that we didn't even bother fighting off bed-bugs and, in the upper bunk, the drip-ping of water that had condensed on the over-head interfered with sleep—and dreams. When we surfaced after sunset, we carried a bucket of fresh water topside and had a sponge bath. Sometimes we jumped over-side to cool off, but the salt water made the skin sticky.

So, you young noblemen on the Ohio do not know how fortunate you are. . . .

I wish you the best of luck. I hope you make full use of the opportunity the Navy has given you to lead a worth-while and industrious—therefore a happy life.[12]

Off the mouth of the Thames River, Rickover and some test personnel, mainly those dealing with the propulsion plant, transferred to a Navy tug before the submarine headed back to sea for other tests.

The crashback of the 688-class attack submarine *La Jolla* (SSN 701) did not go well. She left Electric Boat for her initial sea trials on 26 July. At the end of her full power run, about 6:45 in the morning of the next day, she began the maneuver. Instead of resuming ahead operation when she was dead in the water, she began to make sternway and to go down by the stern. Someone other than Rickover gave the order for the ship to go ahead. He had the crashback repeated. Again the submarine backed down, again began making sternway and again going down by the stern. When Rickover gave the order for the ship to go ahead, she began to move toward the surface. To keep her from surfacing, she began a dive that took her down at a steep angle to a depth that was greater than that before she had started the crashback. On her return to the proper submerged depth, she resumed the test agenda.

Some Electric Boat representatives, not involved in conducting the trials, had gone to the navigation center where they could observe the ship's speed and angle during the crashbacks. On July 31 Veliotis wrote to Hayward about the trials. Other submarines had developed sternway and suffered temporary loss of control during crashbacks, but on the *La Jolla*, he wrote, these conditions had created a situation where even a slight untoward event could have had disastrous consequences. He urged the Navy to investigate and take steps to prevent a recurrence of the risk.

An enclosure gave details. During the first crashback the ship reached a maximum astern speed of 5 knots and went 16 feet below the depth at which the maneuver had begun. During the second crashback she reached an astern speed of 11.6 knots with her bow taking an upward angle. In that crashback, when the propulsion plant answered orders to go ahead, the ship began moving toward the surface. To prevent her from surfacing she began a dive, reaching a downward angle of at least forty degrees and a depth of 240 feet below that at which she had begun the maneuver.

Hayward answered on 13 August that he did not regard crashbacks as hazardous; they had been successfully completed by every submarine delivered to the Navy. Nonetheless, the Navy was taking steps to improve communication during the trials between the officer of the deck in the control room and the engineer on watch in the maneuvering room.

Electric Boat released its letter to the press on 19 August. Newspaper headlines showed that the company had gotten the publicity it wanted: "Sub Takes Plunge during Sea Trials Mishap," "EB Says Rickover Lost Control of Sub during Test, Caused Alarm," "Navy News-Leak Taints Rickover," "Sub Builder: It's Time to Put Adm. Rickover on the Beach."[13]

As was his custom, Rickover had written a letter to Eleonore when the trials were over and the *La Jolla* was on her way back to Electric Boat. He gave a different account of the event:

> Once more, we have completed the trials ahead of time, and successfully. This has become a recurring event recently; I am concerned that my good fortune may end one of these days.
>
> And, of course, if the slightest thing goes wrong in a nuclear submarine, it immediately gets into the news. Further, there are always representatives of Electric Boat on board, and they have been instructed to note all that I do and report it at once—so an issue can be made of it.
>
> However, I pay no attention to these people and completely ignore them. I keep operating the way I always have, and it works.
>
> These representatives are never present where the action is; they stay in the wardroom, drinking coffee and complaining.
>
> On the other hand, there have been numerous occasions when, had it not been for the decisions I made to proceed with the trials, the ship would have returned to port, and the trials would have had to be run once more—causing delays in the delivery of the ships.
>
> Mr. Veliotis, I expect, will soon be leaving. I hope a straightforward and realistic man will replace him.
>
> All this is part of the occupational hazard of dealing with Electric Boat and Newport News. The managers, at both yards [are absent] more than half the time, and for over two years neither has gone out on a trial.
>
> This is the manner in which the commercial shipyards operate—absentee management. No wonder the cost is always exceeded, and is fantastic. But the civilian officials in the Defense Department and in the Navy generally support them. The present Secretary of the Navy, for a change, does not. So now, Mr.

Hidalgo, the ex-Secretary, has become an Electric Boat agent and is lobbying members of Congress, telling them we should give more business to E.B. and complaining about me.

Because we completed the trials several hours before the anticipated time, we will be back in New London this evening—in time to get a flight from Hartford to Washington, arriving about 10 P.M. This is good news, because I will then be able to see you today, rather than tomorrow evening. . . .

I will end by telling you once more that you are a rare and beautiful woman, from whom emanates a loving and beautiful nature, a lively intelligence, nobility of heart, and a courage and good nature that never fails.[14]

It could be argued that Rickover should not have let the incident occur. He knew from Charles A. Hansen, his own representative at the yard, that Veliotis and Electric Boat had criticized the way in which he had run the *Jacksonville* trials. Rickover knew that Veliotis, at a meeting on 19 February with Navy officers stationed at Electric Boat, had declared that Rickover was the root of all the problems in the Navy. He knew that Veliotis had said he would "use his influence and energies to make sure ADM Rickover was not reappointed."[15] He knew he was right when he wrote to Eleonore that the representatives of Electric Boat "have been instructed to note all that I do and report it at once—so an issue can be made of it."

In his mind he had not endangered the ship and her company. Capt. James R. Lang, commanding the *La Jolla*, stated in his letter of 25 August to the *New London Day* that "safety was not threatened, hazarded, or compromised, instead a well-built ship completed a very successful trial." One could argue that Rickover, Lang, and the Electric Boat representatives were unlikely to agree on the matter of safety. It is, however, important to note that the Navy revised its procedures for crashbacks after the *La Jolla* trials. A time limit was placed on their duration.

Certainly it would have been better for Rickover if the event had never occurred. Whether the *La Jolla* trials were a major factor in forcing Rickover out of the propulsion program is debatable. Aside from the flurry of newspaper articles that followed the release of the Electric Boat letter to Hayward, there seems to have been no additional hue and cry for Rickover to leave. Other forces were already working to that end.

As Rickover noted, Lehman was a welcome change from his predecessors. Rickover approved the spirit of the secretary's speech before the National Press Club on 19 August, blasting the arrogance and negligence of the management of General Dynamics' Electric Boat Division. The next day

Rickover telephoned Lehman. That morning, Rickover said, Veliotis had briefed his senior staff and distributed a handout on how unfairly Lehman and Fowler were treating Electric Boat, stressing that Lehman was black-mailing the yard by refusing to award it contracts. Veliotis wanted the employees to write their congressmen and form action groups to put pressure on the Navy. Rickover thought Electric Boat was learning that it could no longer get along with such tactics as it had in the past. Lehman laughed and said what Electric Boat did would make no difference in any action he took.[16]

The chances of Rickover's reappointment looked somewhat brighter. So often two adversaries of one opponent find common ground.

Lehman and David S. Lewis, chairman of the board of General Dynamics, were searching for a way to settle their disagreements. On 25 August they framed the general terms. One called for the Navy to end Rickover's duty at the end of January 1982 and for General Dynamics to replace Veliotis in November. Lehman was almost certain he could deliver Rickover: the congressional support that had protected Rickover was gone.[17]

Rickover's name came up in an ABC 20/20 television interview with Lehman on 22 September. In discussing the submarine program and Electric Boat, Lehman distanced himself from Rickover. Although he expressed "intense admiration" for the admiral, Rickover was about four layers below the layer that normally dealt with the secretary. Lehman had personally met Rickover only once and talked to him three times on the telephone. Of course Rickover was controversial and held strong views on nuclear power, submarines, and the way of doing business with contractors. "Eventually," Lehman said, "whether it be this year or sometime in the future Admiral Rickover has to be replaced sooner or later, as we all do."[18]

On 22 October Lehman, accompanied by Lewis and Sen. John H. Chafee of Rhode Island, former secretary of the Navy, held a news conference at the Pentagon. Usually, Lehman remarked, he did not have good news to announce, but this morning he did. General Dynamics and the Navy had made enough progress in solving the problems at Electric Boat to make it possible to award it a contract for the 688 submarine that had been withheld earlier. Furthermore, the Navy was requesting Electric Boat to submit options for up to three more 688s. He looked forward with confidence to the long-term Navy–Electric Boat relationship and the solid base on which to meet the submarine building needs of the Reagan administration. Someone asked if there were changes in Rickover's participation in sea trials. Lehman replied that he saw no reason to change Rickover's role. He nevertheless avoided a direct answer to the last question: "Have you made a decision about Admiral Rickover yet?"[19]

By November Lehman was ready to act. He and Weinberger had already worked out the steps to take and Reagan had given his approval. Rickover would be asked to remain on active duty two months after the end of January 1982 in order to help his successor. Furthermore, he would be offered the position of nuclear science advisor to the president.

Hayward had already asked Adm. James D. Watkins, commander in chief, Pacific Fleet, to return to Washington to help work out the transition from Rickover to a successor. Watkins, an extremely perceptive officer, had won Rickover's respect as chief of naval personnel. In November he and William Wegner, Rickover's former deputy, began planning the necessary steps. They saw their main mission as protecting the organization Rickover had created and the philosophy under which he ran it. Baldly put, this meant keeping the naval nuclear propulsion program from becoming submerged in the Navy's bureaucracy.[20]

Lehman had planned with Weinberger to see Rickover on Friday, 13 November, to tell him he would not be reappointed. On Monday, 9 November, however, a leak from White House sources, who obviously knew what they were talking about, said Rickover would not be reappointed. Eleonore Rickover heard the news on the radio at 4:00 in the afternoon. Her husband would be back home about 10:00 that night from sea trials of the *Boston* (SSN 703). She hoped that someone had informed him—that she would not be the one to tell him. No one had.

"Well, that's it," he told her.

But at his press conference of 10 November, Reagan gave the planners a minor jolt and Rickover some encouragement. A reporter asked the president if Rickover was too old to stay in his job. Reagan, seventy years old, quipped that Gladstone, prime minister of Great Britain in the latter part of Queen Victoria's reign, reached the height of his power when he was eighty-three. The Associated Press reported the remark as possibly indicating that Rickover's career was not yet finished but also observed there was not much support for the eighty-one-year-old admiral in Congress.[21]

That same day Lehman saw Rickover; the secretary would not recommend his reappointment to Weinberger or the president. Rickover took the news calmly.

Those who were making plans for the transition had also to consider Naval Reactors itself, not as an organization but as a closely knit group of individuals whom Rickover had trained and formed into a highly skilled team, people who were proud of themselves, of their work, and of Rickover. Past efforts to remove Rickover from the program had to face the question: If he left would his senior engineers also leave? If they did, could the excellence of the program survive? The matter had never been brought to the test, but now it could not be avoided.

On or about 11 November Hayward asked Vaughan to his office. The deputy director was thoroughly familiar with the program. Joining Naval Reactors in 1957, he had handled a number of tough assignments, among them radiological control, fuel materials development and testing, reactor plant mechanical components, and manufacture of the light water breeder reactor. The chief of naval operations said he knew that the strength of Naval Reactors was in its longtime civilians. For that reason he asked Vaughan to remain as deputy for at least a year to smooth the transition from Rickover to his successor by providing continuity of management. Sometime during this hectic period W. Kenneth Davis, deputy secretary of energy, reinforced Hayward's arguments. Vaughan agreed. He worked closely with Capt. Frank Kelso (later to become chief of naval operations), a nuclear-trained officer in the Bureau of Naval Personnel. Their task was to keep the relationship between Naval Reactors and the Navy that Rickover had created.

If "politics makes strange bedfellows" so do official ceremonies. The day after Lehman told Rickover he would not be reappointed, he, Rickover, and Veliotis were among those taking part in the commissioning of the *Ohio* at Electric Boat. By then the news had spread widely that Rickover would not be reappointed. More than eight thousand spectators heard Vice President Bush give a conventional speech. Vice Adm. Steven A. White, commander submarine force United States Atlantic Fleet, spoke next to introduce Rickover.

White, after the usual opening remarks, spoke of the pleasure of having Rickover present, declaring, "We are doubly pleased to see your charming wife Eleonore with you." Even in summary his next remarks were impolitic before the vice president and the secretary of the Navy. White declared it was Rickover who more than thirty years ago envisioned the war-fighting potential of the nuclear submarine. It was he who made the concept of a nuclear powered strategic missile submarine a possibility. It was because of him that the United States had an attack submarine force of awesome capability. It was his high standards, his search for truth, and

his call for perfection that were the basis of the excellence of the submarines and the men who sailed in them. "Please stand and join with
me," he said, "in giving a real submarine force welcome to Admiral
Rickover."[22]

"Not even my wife speaks to me that way," responded Rickover before
turning to his own speech. Neither it, nor the ones that followed by Lehman, Veliotis, and the others were exceptional.

Back in his office the next day, Rickover had Thomas L. Foster, who
handled fiscal, procurement, and legislative matters and knew well congressional machinery, sound out sentiment on Capitol Hill. Those to
whom he talked said Lehman had told the legislators that there was no
intent to dismantle Rickover's organization, but Rickover had to have a
deputy that was a naval officer. Foster found that the congressional feeling
favored Rickover staying on two more years but agreed he should have a
naval officer as deputy. As he had in years past, Rickover refused to consider a deputy; he felt everyone would be looking to the deputy as "heir
apparent," not to him, for decisions. The meeting in the office broke up
with plans for Rickover to talk to Sen. Henry M. Jackson and others over
lunch the next day.[23]

Early the next day, Friday, 13 November, Rickover and Carl H. Schmitt,
who handled security, public, and foreign matters, went to the Pentagon.
Rickover entered Weinberger's office. Lehman was already there. Weinberger said President Reagan wanted Rickover to stay on full-time as his
scientific advisor on nuclear matters after his term ended in January and
after he had provided for an orderly transition. Rickover would not
accept. Weinberger kept making the offer. Rickover refused seven times.
He told Weinberger and Lehman, who, apparently ill at ease, was avoiding
looking at him, that he had been doing a good job and that no one had told
him that he was not doing a good job. The question of a deputy came up.
Rickover replied that Vaughan was his deputy, and everyone in Naval
Reactors knew that Vaughan was his deputy.

Rickover and Schmitt hurried from the Pentagon to Jackson's office on
Capitol Hill. At the end of the brief meeting Jackson was to call Lehman
and ask that a hold be placed on any announcement. Jackson planned to
talk with his congressional allies. Rickover would join them at 11:00 or
11:30.

Rickover was back in his own office shortly before 9:00. Soon Schmitt
and Foster joined him. Vaughan entered with the news that a press release
had been written in Lehman's office. It said that the president had decid-

ed that Rickover would be relieved at the end of January, although he might stay on for some months to provide for an orderly transition. In addition Rickover was being asked to act full-time as the president's scientific advisor on nuclear matters.

Around 11:30 Rickover met with Jackson, Thurmond, and John W. Warner, former secretary of the Navy, and with representatives Samuel Stratton, Frank Horton, and Melvin Price. Calmly, Rickover said that he wanted to remain on duty. In the midst of the meeting word came of an announcement over the radio that the president would not reappoint Rickover.

So that was that.

Lehman held a press conference at 4:30 in the afternoon. He and Secretary Weinberger had every hope that Rickover would play an active role in selecting a successor and in overseeing the transition of the program to his successor. Although Admiral Rickover had made no decision about serving as an advisor, Lehman could not conceive of Rickover "not being called on frequently and daily for his continued advice on the naval reactors and military applications as well."[24]

Feeling angry and cheapened by the offer, Rickover remarked to Eleonore, "They must take me for a fool if they didn't think I could see through their plan. No one asked me for my advice while I was on active duty, and now to save face, they would relegate me to a room and I would wait for the telephone to ring." Since he was still on duty until the end of January, he continued to go to the office, even though, as he told Eleonore, he "felt as if he were kicked in the teeth" and did not want to go near "that damn place." He did his best, with some success, to bring to conclusion some contract negotiations. Because Shippingport no longer had congressional support, he took the necessary steps to shut down the plant, moves he made reluctantly because he had wanted to operate the station to get the most data possible. Hayward, disturbed by plans to abolish the Department of Energy, asked Rickover for a paper to use for protecting the interest of the Navy in the joint program.[25]

Sometime, probably on 7 December, Rickover was called to Lehman's office. Again he was offered the position of advisor to the president and again he refused. The conversation turned to the need to establish stability of the program through the orderly transfer of leadership to another officer. Rickover, Lehman remarked, could help by encouraging his engineers and managers to cooperate. Some casual phrasing led Rickover to believe he was being asked to be an advisor to Lehman and Hayward.

Only later, sometime after 15 December, did he learn there was no offer.[26] He was to see President Reagan on January 8, 1982. At times Rickover accepted the idea that his Navy career was over; at other times he thought how often he had faced defeat and survived. Members of his senior staff who were close to him warned him that he had no chance of staying in charge of the program. They predicted he would receive congratulations on a long and brilliant career filled with achievements and suggested he act the part of an elder statesman. Sometimes he accepted their view; other times he did not. If he could just once talk to the president in person . . .

He was waiting in a reception room down a corridor from the Oval Office when Lehman entered. Rickover realized he would not see the president alone. Already angry, Rickover was ushered into the president's office along with Lehman and two White House photographers. He saw Weinberger, James A. Baker, the president's chief of staff, and William P. Clark, national security advisor. Generally following a briefing paper that Lehman had prepared in which the president "would thank the admiral effusively for his historic contribution," Reagan spoke of his personal admiration for the admiral and the debt the nation owed him.

Realizing the meeting was ceremonial rather than substantive, Rickover broke in to ask that if all these things were true, why was he being fired? Bitterly he accused Weinberger and Lehman of lying to the president and giving in to the contractor demands. He went on to describe the callousness with which he was being treated, how he had to learn from his wife that he must leave. That he was too old, Rickover declared, was a dangerous argument, for it could be used against the president. At Rickover's request, Reagan saw him alone. Again Rickover warned Reagan of the risk in retiring him because of his age.

The meeting with Reagan accomplished nothing. The tirade was not only evidence of Rickover's deep disappointment at recognizing the end of his professional career but also the fury of a goaded man who felt manipulated, patronized, and humiliated.

Rickover continued to work for his remaining time. He took the *Carl Vinson* (CVN 70) on sea trials. They were the last trials he would conduct, and they went with textbook perfection. On 27 January she passed her four-hour full-power run at greater than design full power.

The next day he testified before the Joint Economic Committee with Sen. William Proxmire presiding. The committee had little to do directly with naval nuclear propulsion but it had been an excellent platform for Rickover to take on shipbuilders, lawyers, and contracting issues. His testimony, the last he would deliver before a congressional committee, did not have much content or focus. It ranged from the pernicious influence of large defense contractors to the statement that aircraft carriers would last no more than two days in war. He spoke of radioactivity, of how its intensity early in the earth's existence had made life impossible, how its gradual decrease allowed life to begin, but now mankind was restoring radiation that nature had taken so long to eliminate. He thought mankind would probably destroy itself, but, he asked, "What difference will it make? Some new species will arise eventually."[27]

Friday, the following day, he spoke to the people of Naval Reactors in the large conference room on the ground floor of National Center 2, the building in Arlington, Virginia, which held the program offices. He was brief. He spoke to them of how their efficiency, smartness, and spirit had shown what an expert technical group could and should do, of the difficulty they would have to live up to their reputation, of the need to be worthy of the public trust:

> I now say good-bye to you. This to me is a sad day, because it brings to an end my service in the Navy and the Energy Department. But I remain a servant of the United States, and so long as I can I will help that great Service to which I belong body and soul.
>
> What the future holds I cannot say; I will not prophesy. I thank you, and please remember that, although I have gone, I still remain a comrade and a friend. Good-bye.[28]

On Saturday, January 30, Rickover came into his office just as he had done for so many Saturdays. That morning Adm. Kinnaird R. McKee called on him. He and Steven A. White, both nuclear trained and then vice admirals, had each been considered to replace Rickover. Of the pair, McKee was increasingly favored. His exploits in gathering intelligence on the Soviet submarine force had won him a distinguished reputation among the very few highly placed and influential officers and officials who knew about them. He had served exceedingly well in positions of increasing responsibility, including superintendent of the Naval Academy and director of naval warfare in the office of the chief of naval operations. His relationship with Rickover was cordial and professional until it was clear that he would take over the program. Then, for a while, Rickover favored White.

McKee had much to think about. Rickover had trained a superb group of professionals in engineering and in other fields whose skills had given Naval Reactors a deservedly high reputation. Most of them, having spent their entire professional careers with Rickover, felt a deep loyalty to him. Their departure could cripple the program. Furthermore, after Rickover left, what would his attitude be? After some maneuvering, arrangements had been made for McKee to call on Rickover in his office. It was a short and quiet meeting. There would be no overlap. Rickover would leave at the end of the day and not come back; McKee would come in on Monday morning and, he was told, "all of this will be yours." Rickover said he would not keep track of what McKee was doing, would not give him advice unless asked for it, and would stay out of his way. After the change, McKee did call on Rickover and kept him informed, a practice Rickover appreciated.[29]

Although the meeting had gone smoothly, Rickover resented being forced out of the program he had led for so long. He groused, unfairly, that McKee had been given four stars while he had had to struggle to get his two stars.[30]

That same Saturday afternoon his office was dismantled. It was a small corner room with windows along two walls, almost always with blinds pulled, because they looked across a short distance to other drab buildings holding other Navy offices. Bookcases that lined the wall, his desk, his scarred rocking chair, his conference table with its chairs—everything was carried out. Finally, only a small metal table and chair remained. At the end of the day he got up and walked out. He could not hide his emotion. "I guess I'll never see this place again," he said.

He returned home at 5:45, saying to Eleonore, "I finished all my work."

Had he stayed in charge of the program too long? The question is not easy to answer. His short-term memory was failing, but his long-term memory remained clear. He knew the technical direction he wanted to go and so did his engineers and the laboratories. Some of his engineers thought that he had become too conservative and that it was time for a fresh look at old decisions and practices. Such comments did not by any means imply a lessening of his technical standards or a compromise on safety.

There is another aspect to his length of service. He had brought into the Navy a technical program that demanded a level of engineering far superior to that which had been previously required. He could never relax the vigilance with which he protected that engineering. Watkins, Wegner, and others who planned the strategy by which the effort would be transmitted from Rickover to a successor recognized the need to preserve the organization he had created.

The executive order Reagan signed on 1 February 1982, drawn up by Watkins and Wegner, codified the program structure Rickover had created. Naval nuclear propulsion would continue as a joint program under the Department of Energy and the Department of the Navy with the responsibilities divided between them as they had been in Rickover's tenure. There were two major changes. One established procedures for changing leadership. They stipulated that a four-star admiral or civilian equivalent should lead the program for eight years. Furthermore, the director should report directly to the chief of naval operations and have direct access to the secretaries of energy and the Navy and other senior officials in the departments concerning nuclear propulsion matters.[31] The essential elements of the executive order were put into law two years later and have remained in effect.

That same date, which was the Monday after the meeting with Rickover, McKee issued a memorandum to Naval Reactors personnel. He referred to key principles that Rickover had established and that had contributed to the unblemished safety record of the program, and how it took complete commitment to maintain them. "I want to convey to each of you in the strongest manner possible that these principles continue to govern," he wrote. "You need not question this or ask for further clarification. Every requirement, report, procedure and practice remains in effect. Regular reports which you have been making to Admiral Rickover should continue to be made to me."

Over the years many people had felt that senior members of Naval Reactors would leave when Rickover left. That fear proved groundless, for he had instilled in them the same sense of responsibility that he possessed.

Death

THE NAVY gave Rickover an office in a drab building located in the Washington Navy Yard. It was customary for the Navy to grant high-ranking officers an office and a secretary for a few months after their retirement to help them get their papers together, but Rickover's case was different. It was Congress that declared he should have adequate office space, administrative assistance, and transportation so that he could provide help and advice on nuclear matters to the Navy Department, the Department of Energy, and other government organizations. And it was Congress that stipulated he should have this support indefinitely.[1]

His office consisted of a small number of rooms. The one in which Rickover sat held a metal desk, the wooden rocking chair he had brought from his Naval Reactors office, a couple of metal bookcases, and one or two metal chairs for visitors. A Navy chief and a small staff of enlisted men had their desks in another room. A larger room, called the "library," contained metal racks holding several books and boxes of papers. A kitchenette provided coffee and the storage for the few ingredients of Rickover's spartan lunches. Windows in Rickover's office looked out on a street carrying traffic to a bridge over the Anacostia River. Both view and office were depressing.

The relationship between Rickover and his staff was tense. The Navy had assigned him good men, but they knew him only by his formidable reputation. Unlike his office secretariat in Naval Reactors, they had not been with him for years and did not know his ways and idiosyncrasies. Furthermore, they were governed by Navy regulations.

Invitations to speak flowed in, and so did requests from groups seeking to enlist him in a cause. He accepted some speaking engagements, provided the honoraria went to charity, but refused to join any organization.

Honors came his way. A ship would carry his name and Congress would award him a second Gold Medal. Senator William Proxmire of the Joint Economic Committee proposed a fifth star for Rickover. Had it been awarded, he would have been the only living five-star officer in any of the armed services and only the fifth naval officer to have five stars.[2]

Rep. Charles E. Bennett, chairman of the Seapower Subcommittee of the House Armed Services Committee and a close friend of Rickover, introduced a bill on 16 November 1981 with sixty-eight cosponsors to name the next *Nimitz*-class carrier *Hyman G. Rickover*. On 1 March 1982, the bill, with several additional cosponsors, was placed on the House calendar. Rickover wanted a nuclear carrier named after him, but opposition within the Navy was too intense.

Rear Adm. John D. H. Kane, a retired officer who was director of naval history, pointed to the tradition that the secretary of the Navy, not Congress, named naval ships. Furthermore, naval ships were not named after living persons, although he acknowledged the tradition had been breached in the case of the carrier *Carl Vinson* (CVN 70). The engineering building at the Naval Academy, which, Kane observed, would last longer than any carrier, was already named in Rickover's honor. Nevertheless, the Navy would not object to naming a submarine after Rickover.[3]

The proposal for Congress to award him a Gold Medal aroused little controversy. On 29 January 1982, the Senate passed a bill authorizing the presentation. In a small room off the Senate chamber, Adm. Thomas B. Hayward, chief of naval operations, Sen. John W. Warner, Sen. Henry M. Jackson, and others congratulated the admiral and Eleonore on the Senate action. Both houses easily passed the legislation, which President Reagan signed on 23 June 1982. It would be Rickover's second Congressional Gold Medal; his first was awarded in 1959 after the Polar voyage of the *Nautilus* (SSN 571). Only President Taylor had received more than one.[4]

Months would pass before the launching of the submarine *Hyman G. Rickover* and the Gold Medal ceremony. Such recognitions, high honors though they were, could not engage his mind and keep him occupied.

He continued the fight against shipbuilders by urging the Department of Justice to investigate the possibility of fraud in their claims against the government. He found it a frustrating task. No longer did he have at his call members of his staff who were thoroughly familiar with the issues, had worked for him for years, and could be in his office within seconds. Finally, the shipbuilders and the government were reducing the differences between them. Rickover was struggling to carry on a battle with almost no resources and few allies.

Rickover had to have something to do. The Navy, he said, had no use for him. It did not ask for his advice—and neither did the Department of Energy nor the Nuclear Regulatory Commission. For the first time since grade school in Chicago, more than seventy years ago, he had no purpose to engage his mind, no goal for which to strive. In earlier days he occasionally quoted Browning—"Ah, but a man's reach should exceed his grasp / Or what's a heaven for?"—and inevitably, his thoughts turned to education as his "reach." No longer satisfied with speeches on the failures of American education, he sought a direct way to help younger people of high school age.

At a social gathering late in 1981 he and Eleonore Rickover met Joann P. DiGennaro, a young attorney in the office of the general counsel of the International Trade Commission. Intelligent, energetic, and ambitious, she was willing to abandon her career in government to devote herself to directing a nonprofit organization. It became the Admiral H. G. Rickover Foundation. Rickover had three aims in mind: to sponsor seminars relating to energy issues, to consider international trade as it affects the flow of technology, and to exchange scholarly ideas on educational issues.

Rickover focused his attention on the Rickover Summer Science Institute. It would be directed toward students who had not yet graduated from high school but showed great promise in science and mathematics. Each year a group would spend some weeks in the summer in the Washington area. Most, perhaps fifty, would come from the United States, but a considerable number would come from abroad, mainly from the Near East and Far East.[5]

In the summer of 1982 Rickover, Eleonore, and DiGennaro visited Israel and Egypt, and in December of that year and into January of the next, he, Eleonore, DiGennaro, and her husband visited China and Japan. In both instances the senior officials of the host countries wanted Rickover's views on their atomic energy programs. Moreover, they welcomed him as a famous American.

The foundation depended upon Rickover. He thought arranging for the students to work in government laboratories with leading scientists could be its great contribution. Only he, however, could gain access to department and office leaders. Only he could attract the financial support it needed. The "Salute to Admiral Rickover" dinner on 23 February 1983 at the Sheraton Washington Hotel demonstrated how influential he was: former presidents Nixon, Ford, and Carter were present, as were Rosalyn Carter, leading members of Congress, and prominent figures of past administrations. No major officials in the Reagan administration attended.

All the speakers paid tribute to Rickover in pleasant and gracious sentences that revealed sincere admiration. A remark by Rickover, when recalling his long service in the Navy, drew the greatest laughter: "I obeyed all orders—that I agreed with." The guests fell into rapt silence as he went on to recall his youth and his struggle to get an education. He spoke of his desire to make possible for young people the advantages he did not have. That was the reason for the foundation: it would stress excellence through learning.

Congressman Bennett, the last to speak, announced that a 688-class submarine, under construction at Electric Boat and scheduled for launching in August, would be christened the *Hyman G. Rickover*.[6]

Not everyone favored the Rickover Foundation. Eleonore Rickover did not. She worried over the strain its activities would place on her husband's health. Moreover, she and DiGennaro disliked each other.[7] Some of his closest associates who had served with him decades earlier did not want to see him involved in an enterprise in which he would become the most important fund raiser. He was the only financial asset the foundation possessed, they believed, and therefore destined to be under tremendous pressure. Others who knew him well also had reservations but observed that, at least, Rickover now had something to do.

As Bennett had announced at the tribute dinner, the *Hyman G. Rickover* would be launched in August. The date turned out to be the twenty-seventh of that month. The Rickovers flew up in a small Navy plane. Although well accustomed to such ceremonies, he was strangely ill at ease. At Trumbull airport naval officers and senior Electric Boat officials greeted them. In weather that was hot, hazy, and still, they were driven first to a large hall in the yard and then to the waterfront and into a huge cavernous structure, already crowded with guests, that sheltered the ship on her building ways. Admiral Rickover, Eleonore Rickover, Adm. James D. Watkins, chief of naval operations, and Adm. Kinnaird R. McKee took their places on the podium.

After the usual speeches and a kiss from her husband, which, he announced, "wasn't part of the program," Eleonore Rickover mounted the steps to a small platform. At the proper instant she broke a bottle of champagne against the hull and declared, "In the name of the United States I christen thee Hyman G. Rickover. May God bless her and all who sail in her and may God bless their families and loved ones, for they also serve who only stand and wait." She had added the phrase referring to the families and loved ones to the traditional wording, not telling anyone ahead of time lest someone raise an objection.

The *Hyman G. Rickover* (SSN 709), with Capt. Fredrik Spruitenburg, prospective commanding officer, his officers, and his men on deck, slid smoothly down the ways and into the Thames River.

A luncheon and reception in honor of Eleonore Rickover, sponsor of the ship bearing her husband's name, followed at the nearby Branford House on the campus of the South Eastern Branch of the University of Connecticut. At the end of the luncheon, served on the outside terrace, came the speeches. In her remarks Eleonore Rickover revealed that her husband was nervous because he wanted to know what she was going to say and she would not tell him. Many members of her audience, she said, had heard him speak and not known what he was going to say. Now he was in their position. A hushed audience heard her speak informally and graciously of her pride in her husband and of the honor of christening a ship bearing his name. "I want to take this opportunity and extend the honor that is accorded to me and salute the Navy wife," she said. "As I do this I think about how important she is, because she allows her husband to have the best of both worlds, and maybe they don't think about that too often. And in this salute I want to include the first Mrs. Rickover, who deserves this honor far more than I do."

Rickover took the occasion to remember the close relationship that had existed between the Navy and Electric Boat at the beginning of the nuclear program, and how that tie continued until General Dynamics took over Electric Boat and the local manager had "attempted to impose his will on the United States Navy."[8] His audience knew the reference: it was to P. Takis Veliotis, who had fled the United States for Greece in the face of allegations of fraud.

In the midmorning of 1 November 1983, Strom Thurmond, president pro tempore of the Senate, and Tip O'Neill, Speaker of the House of Representatives, awarded Rickover the Gold Medal Congress had voted him in June 1982. In the National Hall of Statuary in the Capitol, more than 150 guests listened to congratulatory messages from Reagan, Nixon, Ford, and

Carter. The heart of Rickover's brief remarks were in one sentence: "It was the backing Congress gave me that made the nuclear ship program possible."[9]

Earlier Rickover had complained that no one asked for his advice on nuclear matters. That situation changed on 2 September 1983 when William G. Kuhns, chairman and chief executive officer of General Public Utilities, asked Rickover for assistance. The corporation managed the two-reactor nuclear power plant at Three Mile Island, south of Harrisburg, Pennsylvania. The accident that had caused so much alarm in March 1979 occurred at Unit 2. The undamaged Unit 1 had been shut down, but, despite changes in management and organization, including the recruitment of Philip R. Clark, a longtime senior engineer at Naval Reactors who became president and chief executive officer of General Public Utilities Nuclear Corporation, the corporation could not get the approval of the Nuclear Regulatory Commission to restart it. Kuhns believed that Rickover's evaluation of the soundness of the organization and its senior management could do more than anything else to prove that Unit 1 was ready to operate. No one, after all, had a higher reputation for integrity in technological matters than Rickover.

Rickover recruited James M. Dunford, Jack C. Grigg, and Robert V. Laney, retired veterans of Naval Reactors, to assist him. They carried out detailed inspections of the plant and training facilities, scrutinized documents on management structure and performance, and interviewed representative samples of managers and employees. On 19 November Rickover stated in his report that General Public Utilities Nuclear Corporation had the management and integrity to operate Unit 1 safely.

Nonetheless, the Nuclear Regulatory Commission did not act.

Rickover had made five recommendations in his November report. He did not consider them essential to starting up the unit, but he believed they would enhance its operation. He, Dunford, Grigg, and Laney returned to Three Mile Island on 16–17 April 1984 to see if the management had incorporated their recommendations. They found it had taken the appropriate steps. In his report of 19 April, Rickover reaffirmed his earlier findings. He criticized the Nuclear Regulatory Commission for its failure to act. "Havering by a responsible government agency can cause delay and results in discouragement of those who are technically and financially responsible for the operation of our nuclear facilities," he stated. "I strongly recommend that GPU Nuclear Corporation be author-ized to operate TMI-1 without further delay."[10]

TMI-1 resumed operation in October 1985. How much Rickover's reports weighed in the decision of the Nuclear Regulatory Commission could not be determined but certainly they played their part. Looked at from another point of view, had he recommended unfavorably, TMI-1 could not have started up again.

Rickover's world was collapsing. He had demanded a high fee for serving as a consultant to General Public Utilities because he needed the money for the foundation. He traveled frequently to appeal for funds, a task he disliked. Often the high point of these trips came when someone in an air-port, suddenly recognizing him, thanked him for all that he had done for the country.[11]

The Navy men in his office resented working on foundation matters. They knew that such activity, along with using Navy office machinery and supplies for the foundation, was against regulations. One or more of them complained to their superiors in the Navy and to members of Congress. In April Admiral Watkins sent an officer to call on Rickover. Upset, Rickover declared that the Navy was not using him and he could not sit and do nothing. Nonetheless, he issued orders to the naval personnel in his office not to work on foundation matters.

On 18 July 1984 the *Washington Post* broke the story that Rickover had received gifts from General Dynamics. For some time the Department of Justice had been investigating allegations that the corporation had delib-erately bid low to "buy in" to the program of building 688-class sub-marines and had filed false claims. Department officials interviewed Veli-otis in Athens. Rickover stated to the press that Veliotis should be allowed to return to the United States and testify. While refusing to take that step, the former general manager at Electric Boat turned over documents to substantiate his charges. Those papers included references to gifts Gener-al Dynamics had given Rickover.[12]

On 21 November 1984, John F. Lehman, secretary of the Navy, estab-lished an ad hoc gratuities board to investigate the gifts to Rickover. It found that no one in General Dynamics and its Electric Boat division believed Rickover had been or could be influenced by the gratuities, which were mainly submarine-shaped tie clasps, coffee mugs, mint julep cups, and paperweights. Such items were often distributed when a ship was launched and on other similar occasions. In two instances Electric Boat had purchased, at Rickover's request, pieces of jewelry for his wife, but no one believed that these had affected his attitude toward Electric Boat. Having never found Rickover easy to get along with, its officials found it simpler to give him what he wanted. The fact remained, however, that giving and accepting gratuities was illegal. The board assessed their total value at $67,628.33.

Lehman, acting under the defense acquisition regulation, announced on 21 May 1985 that the Navy would cancel two contracts with General Dynamics and demand that the corporation pay $676,283.30 (ten times the value of the gratuities) to the Navy. He was also sending a letter of censure to Rickover. At his news conference Lehman stated, "If his behavior towards General Dynamics was an indicator of what General Dynamics was getting for its money they sure got a bad deal, because he was always rigorous in negotiating with General Dynamics, very tough."

In his lengthy response to Lehman on 7 June, Rickover declared, "I can emphatically say that no gratuity or favor ever affected any decision I made." Except for the jewelry given to Eleonore, all the gifts were sent individuals who had given essential support to the propulsion program: they included some people in Naval Reactors, members of Congress and congressional staffs, and presidents of the United States. Often they were given as part of the tradition of ship launchings.

His response was defiant. "Let me first say, as I have said repeatedly, my conscience is clear on this subject."[13] A proud man, he felt bad about taking the gifts and the damage it did to his reputation.

At seven o'clock Wednesday morning, 4 July, he suffered a slight stroke. His right side and leg were numb and he could not move them. He could talk with difficulty and was coherent. Eleonore called Capt. William Baker (MC), USN, a doctor and a longtime friend of the Rickovers. She asked if Rickover could be brought to the Bethesda Naval Hospital by car instead of by ambulance. After hearing that it was all right, she called the chief from his office and Robert S. Brodsky, who had worked in Naval Reactors and, with his wife Lois, had often entertained the Rickovers in their home. Together they got Rickover into a wheelchair and into the car. At the hospital a CAT scan showed no brain damage. At first Rickover did not want to live, but soon he began fighting back. In a few days he was out of intensive care, speaking over the telephone with a voice that was clear but weak.

Admiral Watkins, whose relationship with Rickover went back twenty-five years, wanted to remind the public of Rickover's tremendous contributions to the Navy and to the nation. These, he thought, might be overshadowed by the attention the news media had focused on the gifts. Watkins sent the statement he had made before the ad hoc board on gratuities to Sen. William Proxmire for publication in the *Congressional Record.* It appeared on 11 July 1985.

Watkins wrote from personal observation of the hours of the day and the days of the week that Rickover worked, of his fights against Electric Boat, Westinghouse, and General Electric, and, above all, of "his talent in designing and building the marvelously reliable nuclear propulsion plants upon which so much of our national security depends." Watkins had concluded, "In Admiral Rickover, the American people got a great bargain!"[14]

Rickover was back with Eleonore in their condominium on 19 July when Eleonore found she could not waken him. They were flown by helicopter back to the Bethesda hospital. The flight required the permission of President Ronald Reagan because he was at the hospital and no helicopters were permitted to land while he was there. Examination at Bethesda revealed that Rickover had suffered a new stroke; the trouble seemed to be a transient ischemic attack (TIA), a precursor to another stroke. Eleonore remained with him, seeing that he got the care he needed and making sure that the doctors knew about his individual characteristics: a short-term memory loss and that his temperature, for example, was slightly below that usually regarded as normal and had to be observed closely and treated if it rose because of his susceptibility to pneumonia.

They returned to their condominium in Arlington to which they had moved after leaving the Buchanan House near to the offices of Naval Reactors. Books lined a part of one wall of a spacious and gracious living room, pictures and awards another, while windows along other walls gave beautiful views looking over a part of Arlington, across the Potomac, and into Washington. Men from Naval Reactors and their wives came calling. For years Rickover had vehemently eschewed any social contact with the people who worked for him, convinced that all too often such relationships interfered with the professional discipline their jobs required. Now, always neatly dressed and groomed, he enjoyed the sessions and wide-ranging conversations while Eleonore saw that he husbanded his strength.

On Rickover's eighty-sixth birthday, Carl H. Schmitt, deputy director of Naval Reactors, had a special cake prepared for him. Its proportions and color were those of the "pinks," the carbon copies Rickover got from the sections each working day on which he scrawled comments ranging from technical matters to sentence structure. The letters *NB* iced in one corner of the cake stood for the Latin *nota bene,* or "note well," and emphasized a point he wanted to make.

In February, while Eleonore was helping him out of his chair into a wheelchair, they both fell. They went to the Bethesda hospital, where they found he had broken a rib. Not wanting to stay at the hospital, they returned home. But he was very ill. On 19 March he went back to Bethesda. Because he was suffering from an infection and a temperature of 103 degrees, doctors from the National Institutes of Health were called in. He stayed at Bethesda for twenty-nine days before going back home. He was treated with antibiotics and chest therapy for pneumonia. In April Eleonore severely strained her back. Much earlier she had arranged for him to have nurses around the clock. One of those in attendance, Joan Barnes, had a beautiful singing voice, which gave Rickover a great deal of comfort. She observed that he was always ill at ease when Eleonore was not nearby. Knowing he would not last much longer, he said he did not want to undergo the indignities of "heroic measures." Eleonore promised him he would not.

Husband and wife grew closer together. His thoughts often turned to religion and philosophy. For some time he had not wanted to talk about the foundation. In February he decided to sever his connection with it. In May it became the Center for Excellence in Education.

He would receive only a few visitors. One was Theodore Rockwell, who had joined the program in 1949 and had witnessed and taken part in some of the earlier struggles, when Rickover's future and that of the program were in doubt. He had left the program in 1964 but, after Rickover had been forced from the program, became closer to him. In one conversation they talked about his achievements, and which, if any, were long lasting. Rockwell thought it was Rickover's impact on the people he educated and trained: "The need for excellence, quality, professionalism, and integrity." Rickover accepted that judgment.[15]

The end came on 8 July 1986 at his home. His last word was "Eleonore."

Across the nation the press noted his death. There was one jarring note. On 9 July, Robert Rickover, living in Toronto with his wife Jane, gave an interview in which he asserted that his father was "ruthlessly exploited at a time when he was not mentally competent." He went on to state that

DiGennaro was among those who manipulated his father in order to get money for the foundation. In Robert and Jane's view, Rickover's record should show his leadership in the development of nuclear power and his growing realization that mankind would either destroy itself with nuclear weapons or by nuclear power plant accidents. When Rickover assessed the ability of General Public Utilities to start up Unit 1 at Three Mile Island, they thought he no longer had the ability to make such an evaluation. That charge was denied by Laney, a member of the Rickover group that went to the plant, by William G. Kuhns, chairman of the utility, and by DiGennaro.[16]

As many people had observed, Rickover did have short-term memory lapses in his later years, but they saw him as far from senile, even during those critical and desperate times when he was in the hospital. The strokes weakened his voice but did not affect his coherence. He did have serious reservations about nuclear power, but so did many people after the 1979 accident at Three Mile Island. His doubts rested upon the willingness of society to lift its standards of responsibilities so that the benefits of nuclear energy, in spite of its potential dangers, could be realized.

Most newspaper obituaries paid tribute to the technological revolution he led, the battles he fought, the excellence he demanded, the successes he achieved, and the contributions he made. As all who knew him agreed, these summations could not begin to capture the greatness of the man.

Engineering Legacy

RICKOVER WAS one of the great engineers of our time—perhaps of any time. Often asked to describe his engineering principles, he did so with great reluctance, believing that they would be taken as a recipe for achieving success rather than as a philosophy for stimulating thought. In the wake of the accident at the Three Mile Island nuclear power plant in March 1979, however, he could not avoid discussing these principles before various organizations. One was the House Subcommittee on Energy Research and Development of the Committee on Science and Technology. From the testimony given before that committee, he prepared a memorandum for all his section heads, project officers, and field representatives titled "Principles of the Naval Nuclear Propulsion Program," which was distributed widely throughout Naval Reactors on 20 August 1979. This chapter draws heavily upon that document; the extracts below closely paraphrase some of its sections.[1]

Rickover believed a successful technical program required strong technical control.

> It was impossible to achieve that control if responsibility and authority were divided and each assigned to a separate group. Design, manufacture, assembly, test, operation, maintenance and selection and training of personnel were so closely related that they had to have close technical coordination and direction. He had created a technically competent staff and established procedures where he was promptly and directly informed of problems.
>
> He personally interviewed each applicant to make sure of the candidate's technical competence, attitude, and motivation. Those he selected were trained in the details of reactor plant design, construction, and operation, and taught to manage the program by a thorough knowledge of the technical facts, logic, common sense, and hard work.

Although, strictly speaking, his relationship to his staff might not be considered a principle of engineering, it was an integral part of the engineering excellence he created. He held his people responsible for doing their work. That meant he made certain that their working conditions were conducive to doing their work; he refused, for example, to allow them to attend extraneous courses, conferences, and meetings. His people had access to him. He found, too, that they were stimulated and challenged by their work and the possibility of moving into positions of increased responsibility. Many of his engineers remained with him for a decade or more, giving the program a continuity and a corporate memory that would have been difficult to achieve otherwise.[2]

> All organizations and contractors involved in the program had to have technically trained and qualified people. That included design engineers, field representatives, technical auditors, and inspectors.
>
> All who made decisions in acquisition, design, operation, maintenance, and training, had to have a fundamental understanding of the technology and a commitment to the technical aspects of the job, as well as the determination to see that careful attention was paid to technical details.

He placed great emphasis on another skill that, if not an engineering principle, was critical to engineering success. In reports, letters, and meetings, he insisted upon precision. He detested vague expressions such as "aspect" or "basically"; he refused to accept promises "to work harder" or "to do better" as solutions to difficulties. Being informed that an answer to a problem required "more good people" told him nothing he needed to know—unless it was about the individual making the request.

He believed that conservatism in design was essential in a highly technical field. It was necessary, therefore, to

> recognize from the outset the uncertainty and inaccuracy in available technical knowledge. Otherwise at some stage it would be necessary to add design features or systems; these would increase plant complexity, make it more difficult to understand how the plant actually functioned and how to operate it. Finally, these additions reduced reliability and safety.
>
> Make sure that plant design, its equipment and its procedures were such that the plant operators could be expected to understand, operate, and maintain it properly.

He used full-scale mockups, made of cardboard and wood, as one method to match the layout of the reactor and machinery plant to the requirements of its operators. In that way he could see the proposed location of every valve, pipe, and large component, and he could determine whether their placement gave enough room for the crew to operate and maintain them. It took training to use a mockup properly. Strolling through it was not enough; it was necessary to pause, think, visualize, and analyze the various activities that would take place. The mockups had to be full-scale; anything less would give a false picture and cause trouble later.

> Use simple systems design so that reliance was placed primarily on direct control by trained operators rather than on automatic control.
>
> Design, build, operate, and maintain the plant so as to prevent accidents, rather than relying on systems and procedures to cope with accidents after they occur.
>
> Use formal documentation for all parts of the program—design decisions, manufacturing procedures, operating procedures, inspection requirements, inspection results, and for any waivers. Technical facts, recommendations and decisions had to be thoroughly reviewed by senior personnel in all the disciplines involved.

Charged by the commission with the responsibility for the safe operation of the Navy's propulsion reactors, Rickover developed engineering principles to carry out this obligation.

> Operating a nuclear power plant properly required knowledge and understanding of the characteristics of many systems and components, and of their interactions. Ultimately reliance had to be placed on the operator. However Naval Reactors provided, insofar as practicable, detailed procedures for those operations and casualties which could be foreseen. Preparing such procedures allowed deliberate, thorough consideration by a number of people of all the factors involved. Where procedures were provided, Naval Reactors required verbatim compliance. An operator could not revise a procedure on his initiative: he could recommend a change but not implement it until it was approved.
>
> In a true emergency, operators had to do what they judged necessary. Knowledge and understanding of approved procedures and operating situations allowed an operator to understand the plant and decide what to do when he had to act on his own.
>
> It was naive to allow routine operation of a plant with many deficiencies such as "alarms" or with abnormal conditions present, and then expect operators to respond properly to alarms which indicated casualties.
>
> Top management had to be technically knowledgeable and be fully involved

in seeing that training was done properly. It was insufficient and misleading for management to deal, as many did, solely with the total number of man months of training or the length of the program, or the cost, or the facilities, or to delegate training to a subcontractor, thereby leaving the vital "details" to someone else.

Rickover's engineering principles created an extraordinary center of engineering excellence in Naval Reactors. He could summon into his office engineers who, through years of experience, were experts in their fields and had learned to present their views to Rickover and to one another forcefully. An officer of a ship at sea, if a component was not operating correctly, could call Naval Reactors and talk to an engineer who knew that component thoroughly—not just its specifications, but its design—who could visualize its location in the ship, and who was aware of whether the problem had occurred on other ships. No other part of the Navy had such a center of technical competence. The continuity of personnel and documentation enabled Rickover to upgrade his plants, to "breed excellence," as one engineer put it. If one component showed signs of trouble, he was able to have his engineers check records, dates of manufacture, name of vendor, operating history, and see if components on other ships were showing similar signs. From such analyses he could decide the steps to take: whether, for example, specifications should be changed.

He never claimed that Naval Reactors was faultless and that he did not have to reemphasize his principles. In his August 1979 memorandum, he stated,

> You and your people are—and must feel—personally responsible for seeing that these principles are applied. This requires particularly that you enforce the principle of accountability with the prime contractors. When the prime contractors make a mistake, it should be brought to their management's attention. Vigilance and effort are required to do this—but it is essential. Routine work or "getting on with the job" must not be used as reasons to inhibit you from raising such issues. To succumb to this would result in sloppy work, mistakes, unnecessary expense and delay, and improper operation in the long run.
>
> You and your people, at all levels, must fully understand and apply this.

Referring to Rickover's principles, one senior engineer wrote,

> I believe much of Rickover's significance lies in his rare fusion of "Get the job done" with "Do it right." To accomplish either one is much easier than to

accomplish them both. He never allowed them to be separated, or allowed one to override the other. His engineers felt intense pressure directly from him to accomplish the two goals together, so we felt no conflict.

These two goals become mutually enforcing when both are achieved. The fact that he got the job done earned him the independence and freedom to do it right. The fact that it was seen to be done right got him the support to get it done. The fact that the goals were non-negotiable was exhilarating to the engineers and was the key to obtaining and retaining competent staff.[3]

The engineer works upon the frontier between technology with all its demands, and human nature with all its foibles. That means, as Rickover often declared, the engineer must not be, nor allow himself to be, shielded from the "real world." He must get out of his office and down to the shop floor to see, to inspect, to know what is going on.

Engineering principles are Rickover's legacy, as are the people he trained—the engineers, managers, and operators. Upon them rests the responsibility of seeing that his principles endure, and upon them rests the obligation to transmit them to the people they train.

In Memoriam

MORE THAN a thousand people entered the Washington National Cathedral on 14 July 1986. On that hot and humid Monday, a typical summer morning in Washington, they had come to attend the memorial service of Adm. Hyman G. Rickover, USN, Retired.

The admiral's wife, Eleonore B. Rickover, in a dress of dark navy blue—her husband's favorite color—was escorted to her place by Vice Adm. Bruce DeMars. There she joined a small group of relatives and friends she had invited to the ceremony. She had chosen Cdr. Bruce E. Kahn for the invocation and responsive reading. When the admiral was in intensive care at the Bethesda Naval Hospital, she had met Rabbi Kahn, who had shown her deep understanding and great sympathy. She had asked former President Jimmy Carter to read John Milton's sonnet "On His Blindness," which her husband had memorized when he was a schoolboy in Chicago. Its most quoted line—"They also serve who only stand and wait"—she had used when christening the *Hyman G. Rickover*. She had asked Adm. James D. Watkins, former chief of naval operations, to deliver the eulogy. Over the years he and Admiral Rickover had built strong ties between them based on trust and respect. Rear Adm. John R. McNamara of the chaplain corps, whom she knew well, would deliver the homily.

Vice Admiral DeMars had organized the ceremony for her, making the arrangements at the cathedral, contacting President Carter, arranging for Admiral Watkins to be flown back to Washington, and making sure that all the myriad details would go smoothly.

Secretary of State George P. Schultz represented the administration of President Ronald Reagan. To his right were former President Jimmy Carter and Mrs. Carter, and to his left Sen. Strom Thurmond, chairman of the Senate Committee on Armed Services, and Mrs. Thurmond. Behind them were Secretary of the Navy John F. Lehman, Adm. Kinnaird R.

McKee, director of the Naval Nuclear Propulsion Program, and Mrs. McKee.

As the Navy band ended its prelude of Bach chorales, the cathedral fell silent. The congregation rose to its feet as the Navy Ceremonial Guard, moving with precision, marched down the long, high-vaulted nave to present the colors. Everyone remained standing as the band played the National Anthem.

Rabbi Kahn chose Psalm 90:1–4 and 12–17 for the responsive reading. It began, "Lord, thou has been our dwelling place in all generations . . ."

Admiral Watkins caught the spirit of Admiral Rickover in the eulogy when he referred to a statement by Voltaire that the admiral often cited: "Not to be occupied, and not to exist, are one and the same thing." Watkins concluded, "And I can think of no man who better epitomized that tough standard, for Admiral Rickover was *occupied*. He was a unique individual who accomplished great deeds through hard work and struggle, and thereby gained respect of a nation and the world. He was an original thinker who dared to peer beyond boundaries set by others, and therefore accomplished that, about which, others only dreamed. This is the special American, naval professional, visionary, intellectual, scientist, iconoclast and most importantly, teacher."[1]

It was a superb eulogy. It could not mention all the contributions Admiral Rickover had made during his eighty-six years. It could not list the many students of international and military affairs who credited him with developing one of the major technologies that gave the West its victory during the cold war. It could not recount his struggles to establish standards to measure the adequacy of the education that American children were receiving. It could not cover the many efforts he made to defend the government against those business and industrial interests that thought the government belonged more to them than to the taxpayers.

In *How the Battleship Maine Was Destroyed*, he brought together qualified individuals to examine the technical evidence that surrounded a controversial event that shaped American history. Considering how emotions had swayed the technical analysis of the loss of the ship, he warned, "With the vastness of our government and the difficulty of controlling it, we must make sure that those in 'high places' do not, without most careful consideration of the consequences, exert our prestige and might. Such uses of our power may result in serious international actions at great cost in lives and money—injurious to the interests and standing of the United States."[2]

A eulogy extols the virtues and achievements of its subject. Not everyone who dealt with Admiral Rickover would agree with all the excellencies with which he was portrayed. "There is no motion without friction," he occasionally remarked. An individual always in motion, he generated much friction and created many enemies. Any student of his life will encounter evidence of this hostility from men, women, and organizations who found themselves abruptly wrenched from their accustomed routine by the demands of the program he led. They are part of the admiral's life and cannot be overlooked. Without doubt he will always remain controversial.

He was a great man to whom the nation and all who strive for excellence owe much.

NOTES

Abbreviations

ACE	Army Corps of Engineers
AEC	Atomic Energy Commission
BuNav	Bureau of Navigation
BuShips	Bureau of Ships
CA	Collection of Author
CNO	Chief of Naval Operations
DDE	Dwight D. Eisenhower Presidential Library
DOD	Department of Defense
E	Entry number (used in designation of documents from NARA)
HASC	House Armed Services Committee
HGR	Hyman G. Rickover
JCAE	Joint Committee on Atomic Energy
JCL	Jimmy Carter Presidential Library
JFK	John F. Kennedy Presidential Library
JWC	John W. Crawford Jr.
LBJ	Lyndon B. Johnson Presidential Library
NARA	National Archives and Records Administration
NAVSEA	Naval Sea Systems Command
NHC	Naval Historical Center
NRD	Division of Naval Reactors
NSD	Naval Supply Depot
NY Pearl	Navy Yard, Pearl Harbor
PWR	Pressurized-Water Reactor
RMR	Ruth M. Rickover
WHCF	White House Central Files
WMH	William M. Hewitt

Introduction

1. For an excellent summary of the program, see "A Description of the Naval Nuclear Propulsion Program," 31 January 1982, in Joint Economic Committee, *Economics of Defense Policy: Adm. H. G. Rickover*, 97th Cong., 2d sess., 28 January 1982 (Washington, D.C.: GPO, 1982), pt. 1, 68–103. Part 1 contains testimony; part 2, selected congressional testimony and speeches by Rickover; part 3, Navy contracts and government policies; part 4, shipbuilding claims; part 5, lawyers and legal ethics; part 6, cost accounting standards, independent research and development, and miscellaneous matters. (Hereafter cited as *Defense Policy*, followed by part number.)

2. "Thoughts on Man's Purpose in Life," *Defense Policy*, pt. 2, 721.

Chapter 1. Becoming an Officer

1. Naturalization Commissioner, *Supreme Court of the State of New York, First Judicial District, Declaration of Intention to Become a Citizen . . .* , 24 February 1898, Rickover Papers.

2. For data presented at Ellis Island, see List or Manifest of Alien Passengers for the U.S. Immigration Officer at Port of Arrival, INS, M682, Pass. & Crew List of Vessels Arriving at New York 1897–1942 from March 27 to March 29, 1906, vol. 1495, RG 85, NARA.

3. Ibid.

4. Citizenship documents are attached to Declaration of Intent to become a Citizen, 24 February 1898, Rickover Papers.

5. A summary of state labor laws, although difficult to use for individual states, is in U.S. Department of Labor, *Growth of Labor Law in the United States* (Washington, D.C.: GPO, 1967), 5–17, 24; Norman Polmar and Thomas B. Allen, *Rickover* (New York: Simon & Schuster, 1982), 34.

6. This and other quotations at Marshall are from *Review: John Marshall High School Commencement—Semi-Annual* 11, no. 4 (February 1918): 7, 19, 22–23, 25, 57.

7. *Chicago Evening American*, 7 June 1916; Kristie Twaddell, "Old Photo Admiral's Top Prize," *Chicago Evening American*, 20 September 1967.

8. Congress had set the number of nominations at five on 20 December 1917. See *Annual Report of the Secretary of the Navy for the Fiscal Year 1918* (Washington, D.C.: GPO, 1918), 74. For date of notification, see Acting Chief of BuNav to Rickover, 9 April 1918, Rickover Papers.

9. Official documents used "mental examinations" when referring to examinations in history, geography, and so on. I have used the "academic" to convey the meaning to a modern reader. For requirements, see "Regulations Governing of Candidates into the Naval Academy as Midshipmen," *Annual Register of the United States Naval Academy, Annapolis, MD. October 1, 1918, Seventy-fourth Academic Year, 1918–1919* (Washington, D.C.: GPO, n.d.), 229–43.

10. BuNav to Rickover, 13 June 1918, Rickover Papers.

11. Class standing is from *Annual Register of the United States Naval Academy, 1919–1920* (Washington, D.C.: GPO, 1920), 154–55.

12. "Reminiscences of Admiral Stuart S. (Sunshine) Murray, USN (Ret.)," 1:18–20, and "Reminiscences of Captain Henri Smith-Hutton, USN (Ret.)," 1:7, both in Interviews Conducted by the U.S. Naval Institute, NHC.

13. Rickover to Smith-Hutton, 20 June 1973, Rickover Papers.

14. *Annual Register of the United States Naval Academy, 1921–1922* (Washington, D.C.: GPO, 1922), 34.

15. Registrar, Naval Academy to Rickover, 8 January 1963, Rickover Papers.

Chapter 2. Sea Duty, Shore Duty, and Love

1. M964, Records Relating to United States Navy Fleet Problems I to XXII, 1923, Roll 1, NARA.

2. Rickover emphasized this point several times in conversations with me.

3. Standing of the ship is in Seymour to BuNav, 10 April 1924, Rickover Papers.

4. Fitness Report, 24 October 1923–31 March 1924, and Seymour to BuNav, 10 April 1924, Rickover Papers.

5. For assignment to the plotting room and recollection of Rickover's abilities, see "Reminiscences of Rear Admiral Charles J. Wheeler, USN (Ret.)," 138–41, Interviews Conducted by the U.S. Naval Institute, NHC. The ship had two submerged torpedo tubes; Rickover was also torpedo officer.

6. Fitness Report, 21 January–1 April 1925, Rickover Papers.

7. Annual Report of the Chief of Naval Operations, 1 July 1925, in *Annual Report of the Navy Department for the Fiscal Year (Including Operations to November 15, 1924) 1925* (Washington, D.C.: GPO, 1925), 72–73; Records Relating to United States Navy Fleet Problems I to XXII, Microfilm 964, Rolls 3–4, Fleet Problems IV and V, NARA.

8. Fitness Reports, 1 October 1925–31 March 31 1926, 1 April 1925–11 June 1926, Rickover Papers.

9. Quotation from Lt. Cdr. C. S. Kempff, "Shiphandling with Electric Propulsion," U.S. Naval Institute *Proceedings* 43 (August 1917): 1705–12.

10. Chief of the Bureau of Medicine and Surgery to Chief of BuNav, 2 July 1926, Rickover to Chief of BuNav, 13 November 1926, Seymour to Bureau of Engineering, 15 November 1926, Acting Chief of BuNav to Lt. (jg) Hyman G. Rickover, 22 January 1927, Rickover Papers.

11. Fitness Report, 1 October 1926–31 March 1927, Rickover Papers.

12. Charles Lucke, "Advanced Engineering Education," *Journal of the American Society of Naval Engineers* 26 (May 1914): 509, 516.

13. Biographical data from "Personal Information," unsigned paper, n.d., Rickover Papers. For her views on international law, see RMR to HGR, 29 August 1929, RMR, Rickover Papers.

14. BuNav to Rickover, 18 October 1928, Rickover to BuNav, 3 April 1929, and endorsements by Todd and Church, Rickover Papers.

15. BuNav to Rickover, 17 April, 4 May 1929, Rickover Papers.

16. HGR to RMR, 5 July 1929, Rickover to Chief of BuNav, 5 July 1929, Rickover Papers; Clay Blair Jr., *The Atomic Submarine* (London: Odhams, 1957), 31–32. In HGR to RMR, 22 July 1929, Rickover Papers, Rickover refers to receiving orders to New London.

17. Handwritten note by Arendt on margin of a company letter to him by an official whose signature is illegible, 22 August 1929, Rickover Papers.

18. RMR to HGR, 13 September 1929, RMR.

19. HGR to RMR, 8 September 1929, Rickover Papers.

Chapter 3. Submarines and Marriage

1. HGR to RMR, 12 October 1929, Rickover Papers.

2. For S-class submarines, see Gary E. Weir, *Building American Submarines, 1914–1940* (Washington, D.C.: Naval Historical Center, 1991) and Robert H. Barnes, *United States Submarines* (New Haven, Conn.: H. F. Morse Associates, 1944).

3. HGR to RMR, 16 March 1930, Rickover Papers.

4. HGR to RMR, 21, 22, 23 November 1929, Rickover Papers.

5. HGR to RMR, 9 December 1929, Rickover Papers.

6. *Base Newspaper* 11, no. 17 (14 June 1930), Submarine Base, New London, Connecticut.

7. HGR to RMR, 3, 5 February 1930, Rickover Papers.

8. RMR to HGR, 11 February 1930, RMR.

9. HGR to RMR, 8, 12 February 1930, Rickover Papers.

10. HGR to RMR, 6 March 1930, Rickover Papers; RMR to HGR, 9 March 1930, RMR. For an excellent account of the German influence on American submarine design during this period, see Weir, *Building American Submarines*, 28–35.

11. RMR to HGR, 18 March 1930, RMR; HGR to RMR in two letters, both dated 19 March 1930, Rickover Papers.

12. HGR to RMR, 26 March 1930, Rickover Papers.

13. HGR to RMR, 14 May 1930, Rickover Papers.

14. HGR to RMR, 10 March 1930, Rickover Papers.

15. Edward L. Beach, a wartime submarine commander, in his *Salt and Steel: Reflections of a Submariner* (Annapolis: Naval Institute Press, 1999), 179–80, has a different view of Rickover and the *S-48* than the one offered here.

16. HGR to RMR, 22 July 1930, Rickover Papers.

17. The age of the battery was the probable cause. The fire is described in the *S-48* Log and in Commanding Officer to CNO (Division of Fleet Training), 17 September 1930, E 993, Box 4975, Folder SS159/S62, RG 19, NARA; HGR to RMR, 18 September 1930, Rickover Papers; RMR to HGR, 20 September 1930, RMR.

18. "Reminiscences of Rear Admiral William D. Irvin, USN (Ret.)," 98–99, Interviews Conducted by the U.S. Naval Institute, NHC.

19. HGR to RMR, 29 July 1931, Rickover Papers.

20. Senior Medical Officer, U.S. Submarine Base, Coco Solo, Canal Zone, to Commanding Officer, USS *S-48*, 29 June 1931. Date of qualification for command comes from Fitness Report, 6 July–30 September 1931, Rickover Papers.

21. HGR to RMR, 1, 5, 16, 22 August 5, 6 September 1931, Rickover Papers.

22. RMR to HGR, 11 June 1931, Rickover Papers.

23. Commanding Officer to CNO (Division of Fleet Training), 10 December 1931, General Correspondence 1925–1940, SS 159-162/S31 to SS159-162/S8-(28), RG 19, NARA.

24. HGR to RMR, 22 February 1932, Rickover Papers.

25. This account of the expedition is based on conversations with Rickover and Clayton B. Garvey, a petty officer in the ship; *New York Times* Clippings, Rickover Scrapbooks, Rickover Papers; Cdr. Richard H. Knight, "Seismology and the Navy," U.S. Naval Institute *Proceedings* 60 (August 1934): 1110–20.

26. Rickover to BuNav, 5 April 1932, and endorsements of 5, 6, 7 April 1932; BuNav to Rickover, 28 May 1932, Rickover Papers.

27. Entry in Fitness Report, 1 October 1932–31 March 1933, Rickover Papers.

28. Rickover to Chief of BuNav, 5 January 1933, and endorsements of 5, 6, 8 January 1933, Rickover Papers.

29. BuNav to Rickover, 20 January 1933; HGR to RMR, 25 February, in which he enclosed a copy of his request, both Rickover Papers.

30. RMR to HGR, 9 March 1933, Rickover Papers.

31. "Reminiscences of Rear Admiral William D. Irvin," 94.

32. HGR to RMR, 30 March 1933, Rickover Papers.

33. HGR to RMR, 11 July, 9, 21 August 1933, Rickover Papers.

34. Quotation is from Weir, *Building American Submarines*, 113–14. See also John D. Alden, *The Fleet Submarine in the U. S. Navy: A Design and Construction History* (Annapolis: Naval Institute Press, 1979).

35. Weir, *Building American Submarines*, 108–10.

36. Alden, *Fleet Submarine*, 46.

37. HGR to RMR, 23, 25, 27, 28 September 1933, Rickover Papers.

38. Rickover's translation was issued by the Department of Intelligence, Naval War College, Newport, Rhode Island, July 1936, and bears the designation 3336-1351/7-1-36. A copy is in NAVSEA.

39. H. G. Rickover, "Quarterly Marks and Promotion of Enlisted Personnel," U.S. Naval Institute *Proceedings* 60 (March 1934): 403–5.

40. Rickover, "International Law and the Submarine," U.S. Naval Institute *Proceedings* 61 (September 1935): 1213–27.

41. In August 1934 Rickover applied for submarine duty on the Asiatic Station. See First Endorsement, Chief of Naval Material to BuNav, 20 August 1934, and his

fitness reports for 1 October 1933–31 March 1934, 1 April–30 September 1934, and 1 October–23 March 1936, Rickover Papers.

42. *New York Times*, 30 January 1933.

Chapter 4. Engineering Duty Only

1. "U.S.S. New Mexico Engineering Organization 1934," given by HGR to the author.

2. M964, Records Relating to United States Navy Fleet Problems I to XXII, Roll 18, NARA; reference to the atmosphere of the maneuvers are in the *New York Herald*, 30 December 1934 and 11 January 1935, in "Professional Notes," in the U.S. Naval Institute *Proceedings* 61 (March 1935): 420–21.

3. HGR to RMR, 10 June 1935, Rickover Papers.

4. Brockett to Rickover, 6 February 1980, Rickover Papers. Rear Admiral Batcheller allowed me access to a copy of his reminiscences dealing with training.

5. Office of the Chief of Naval Operations (Division of Fleet Training), *Report of Engineering Performance, 1934–1935, United States Navy F.T.P 153* (Washington, D.C.: GPO, 1935), 3, and "Analysis of Engineering," table 4, NHC.

6. "Reminiscences of Rear Admiral Charles E. Loughlin, USN (Ret.)," 1:24–28, Interviews Conducted by the Naval Institute, NHC.

7. Volume, month, and pages of U.S. Naval Institute *Proceedings* follow each article citation: Adm. F. B. Upham, "Promotion by Selection," Discussion, 61 (January 1935): 98; Lt. A. E. Becker Jr., "Selection and Promotion in the Navy," 61 (May 1935): 671–82; Lt. Cdr. Robert B. Carney, "Selection, Security and Morale," 61 (June 1935): 814–17; Lt. Winston Folk, "This Selection Business," 61 (November 1935): 1612–23; Lt. (jg) J. S. Holtwick, "Fitness Reports and Selection," 62 (July 1936): 964–68; Cdr. R. O. Davis, "Facing the Issue—Selection," 62 (May 1936): 646–48; Lt. Cdr. A. O. R. Bergsen, "Middle of The Road in Promotion," 62 (June 1936): 804–8; Cdr. Francis S. Craven, "Selection and Morale," 62 (August 1936): 1105–11. Quotation is from Davis.

8. HGR to RMR, 3, 11 August 1935, Rickover Papers. Quotation is from 11 August.

9. The above quotation and the one following are from HGR to RMR, 28 June, 14 July 1935, Rickover Papers.

10. HGR to RMR, 3 March 1936, Rickover Papers.

11. HGR to RMR, 25 March 1936, Rickover Papers.

12. HGR to RMR, 15 March 1936, Rickover Papers. His date of promotion was 1 July 1937.

13. HGR to RMR, 18 April 1936, Rickover Papers.

14. These paragraphs are based on Brockett to Rickover, 26 February 1980, Rickover Papers, and "Reminiscences of Rear Admiral Charles E. Loughlin," 1:37; *New Mexico* Log, NARA; and conversations with Rickover.

15. Office of the Chief of Naval Operations (Division of Training), *Report of*

Engineering Performance, 1935–36, United States Navy F.T.P. 160 (Washington, D.C.: GPO, 1936), 3, FRC 68-A-5149, NHC.

16. HGR to RMR, 8, 29, November 1936, Rickover Papers.

17. M964 Records Relating to United States Navy Fleet Problems I to XXII, Roll 22, NARA.

18. James L. Jordan, "A Little-Known Side of Admiral Rickover," *San Diego Union*, 18 November 1981, and "Reminiscences of Vice Admiral Wm. R. Smedberg, III, USN (Ret.)," 1:43, Interviews Conducted by the Naval Institute, NHC. The two accounts differ. Jordan, who was the fueling officer, remembers the incident occurring in 1936, when it could only have happened in 1937, and does not mention the *Concord*'s men boarding, whereas Smedberg, who was on the cruiser's bridge, recalls the executive officer in whites, which seems unlikely in the early months of the year off Dutch Harbor. I have derived the date of the incident from the *New Mexico*'s log. The ship fueled the *Concord* only once at Dutch Harbor. See also "Reminiscences of Vice Admiral Ruthven E. Libby, USN (Ret.)," 1:44–55, Interviews Conducted by the Naval Institute, NHC.

19. Commanding Officer to Chief of BuNav, 26 February 1937, Fitness Reports, 1 October 1936–24 April 1937, 25 April–2 June 1937, Rickover Papers.

20. Rickover to BuNav, 14 September 1936, HGR to RMR, 31 October 36, Rickover Papers.

21. Brockett to Rickover, 20 January 1982, Rickover Papers. Quoted with permission of Mrs. William A. Brockett.

22. Quotations from Bremerton, 16 March 1937, in "Notes 1937, Tsingtao-Chefoo," RMR, Rickover Papers.

23. RMR to Kay, 3 October 1937, "Notes 1937, Tsingtao-Chefoo," RMR. His commission was signed 29 July 1937 and his date of rank from 1 July 1937, Rickover Papers.

24. *Finch* Log; Lt. J. P. Rockwell and Lt. H. G. Rickover to CNO, 17 July 1937, General Correspondence AM5/S3-1(4) to AM9/SL9-4 to S3-1, RG 80, NARA.

25. Senior Member, Material Inspection Board, to Commander in Chief, Asiatic Fleet, 10 September 1936, Second Endorsement, Commander Train to Commander in Chief, Asiatic Fleet, 17 September 1936, Second Endorsement, Commander Train Asiatic Fleet, 24 February 1937, General Correspondence AM9/S3-1(1) (371231) to AM10/S3-1(2) (S310101), RG 80, NARA.

26. Commanding Officer USS *Finch* to Commander in Chief, Asiatic Fleet, 21 August 1937, Rickover Papers. Rickover kept a copy of the list.

27. Description of voyage and quotations are from HGR to RMR, 22 August 1937, Rickover Papers.

28. *Chicago Daily Tribune*, 4 October 1937, has a story, photograph of Rickover, and a sketch map showing where the refugees boarded the *Finch*.

29. Naval Message: *Finch* to BuNav, 4 September 1937; Chief of BuNav to Rickover, 7 September 1937; HGR to RMR, 2 October 1937, Rickover Papers.

30. Fitness Report, 21 August–5 October 1937, Rickover Papers.

31. HGR to RMR, 2 October 1937, Rickover Papers; RMR to Elmina, 15 November 1937, RMR, Rickover Papers.

32. Reference to orders is in Rickover to BuNav, 31 August 1938, Rickover Papers.

33. Notes, Cavite, 15 November 1937, RMR.

34. Theodore Rockwell, *The Rickover Effect: How One Man Made a Difference* (Annapolis: Naval Institute Press, 1992), 27–28.

35. "Reminiscences of Vice Admiral William Paden Mack, USN (Ret.)," 1:115, Interviews Conducted by the U.S. Naval Institute, NHC. The *John D. Ford* was awarded four battle stars and was decommissioned in 1945.

36. For an account of their travels, see Ruth Masters Rickover, *Pepper, Rice, and Elephants: A Southeast Asian Journey from Celebes to Siam* (Annapolis: Naval Institute Press, 1975).

37. Rickover to BuNav, 31 August 1938; L. M. Atkins, First Endorsement, date illegible, Rickover Papers; Notes, Cavite, 12 September 1938, RMR, Rickover Papers.

38. For accounts of the trips, see Mrs. Rickover, Korea, Manchuria, Peking; Home Trip—July 11–October 4, 1939, RMR; Peiping, China . . . S.S. CANTON . . . 7 June 1939–21 June 1939, fifty-two pages of notes beginning with Yunnanfu, 25 June 1939, and ending with landing in Calcutta, Rickover Papers. They used geographic place names that are no longer in use. I have changed them to the modern form.

39. Rickover's account is in Burma Road, Rickover Papers. Rickover to Director of Naval Intelligence, 28 August 1939; Office of Naval Intelligence to Rickover, 9 October 1939, Rickover Papers. Mrs. E. B. Rickover has the penciled notes from which the report was drawn.

40. Berners Hotel, 3 August 1939, Rickover Papers.

Chapter 5. The Electrical Section and the War

1. "Reminiscences of John C. Niedermair, Naval Architect," 268–69, Interviews Conducted by the U.S. Naval Institute, NHC.

2. *Electrical Section History*, NAVSHIPS 250-660-24 (Washington, D.C.: Bureau of Ships, 1946), 4–5.

3. Data on battleships derived from Appendix 1 of *Dictionary of American Fighting Ships* (Washington, D.C.: GPO, 1959), vol. 1, and on aircraft carriers from Appendix 1, vol. 2 of the same series, published in 1963.

4. Rockwell, *Rickover Effect*, 30.

5. "Reminiscences of Rear Admiral Schuyler N. Pyne, USN (Ret.)," 134–36, Interviews Conducted by the U.S. Naval Institute, NHC.

6. NY Pearl to BuShips, 19 March 1942, NHC.

7. *California* Log, NARA.

8. Chief of BuNav to Rickover, 18 March 1942, Rickover Papers; Chief of BuShips to Commandant, Navy Yard, Puget Sound, to Rickover, 27 March 1942, E 1266, RG 19, NARA.

9. "Lecture to Be Given at the Post Graduate School Naval Academy . . . by Commander H. G. Rickover . . . 7 January 1943," Rickover Papers.

10. Rickover, Memorandum of Conference Held in the Office of the Manager, NY Pearl, 11 April 1942. See also C. D. Swain, Production Officer, Memorandum for File, 11 April 1942, both from E 1266, RG 19, NARA; Wallin, *Pearl Harbor: Why, How, Fleet Salvage and Final Appraisal* (Washington, D.C.: Navy Department, Naval History Division, 1968), 230.

11. Wallin, Salvage Officer, to Commandant, NY Pearl, 15 April 1942, NHC. Progress can be traced in many reports bearing the general title "U.S.S. California (BB44) Reconditioning of Electrical Propulsion Equipment," located in E 1266, RG 19, NARA. The reports used here are dated 30 April and 15 May 1942. See also Commandant, Puget Sound Navy Yard to Chief of BuShips, 9 May 1942, from the same collection.

12. "Lectures to Be Given at the Post Graduate School Naval Academy . . . by Commander H. G. Rickover . . . 7 January 1943, Rickover Papers.

13. For shock, see "Applications and Development of Electrical Equipment in the United States Navy to be presented by Captain H. G. Rickover, U.S.N. Before the Pittsburgh Section of the American Institute of Electrical Engineers," Rickover Papers; W. P. Welch, *Mechanical Shock on Naval Vessels*, NAVSHIPS 250-660-26 (Washington, D.C.: GPO, 1946) acknowledges Rickover's role on vi. For the anvil, see G. W. Faurot to author, 11 November 1995. On switchboard, see John W. Simpson, *Nuclear Power from Underseas to Outer Space* (LaGrange Park, Ill.: American Nuclear Society, 1994), 4–5.

14. E 1266, Boxes 724, 736, 752, RG 19, NARA has many documents illustrating the activities of the sections.

15. Herman A. Liebhafsky, *Silicones Under the Monogram: A Story of Industrial Research* (New York: John Wiley, 1978), 224–26.

16. *Electrical Section History*, 44.

17. Remarks of Adm. H. G. Rickover, USN, at the 1981 Egleston Medal Award Dinner, Columbia School of Engineering and Applied Science, New York, 5 November 1981, Rickover Papers.

18. Richard G. Hewlett and Francis Duncan, *Nuclear Navy, 1946–1962* (Chicago: University of Chicago Press, 1974), 127.

19. Rickover was very proud of the report and kept a copy. "NSD Mechanicsburg—Handling of BuShips Maintenance Parts—Report on," Rickover Papers. Quote is from Fitness Report, 1 April 1944–24 March 1945, Rickover Papers.

20. He was promoted commander for temporary service on 2 January 1942 and commander on 21 April 1942 to rank from 2 January 1942. He was promoted captain for temporary service on 26 June 1943 and captain on 7 August 1947. See Rear Admiral Hyman G. Rickover, U.S. Navy, Transcript of Service Record, 18 October 1956, Rickover Papers.

21. Fitness Report, 1 April 1944–24 March 1945, Rickover Papers.

324   ★   Notes to Pages 84–92

22. For Okinawa I have relied heavily on Benis M. Frank, *Okinawa: The Great Island Battle* (New York: Elsevier-Dutton, 1978), letter dated 5 June 1980 to the author from James S. Bethea, Rickover's executive officer at Okinawa. A collection of various reports in the Rickover Papers was intended for a history of the base.

23. Naval Operating Base (Task Unit 99.3.4), Tentative Operation Plan No. 1-45, 15 April 1945, Ship Repair Department, Base History, Naval Operating Base, Administrative History, Appendix 38 (26) to 38 (30), Box 73, NHC. The plan did not mentioned Rickover by name, but he had already been selected to command the repair base. On the importance of the base, see Vice Adm. W. W. Smith, Commander Service Forces, U.S. Pacific Fleet to Vice Adm. W. S. Farber, Sub-Chief of Naval Operations, 11 June 1945, and "Synopsis 9-11-45" of draft history of Okinawa, both in Rickover Papers.

24. For activities after leaving San Francisco and views on the death of Roosevelt, see HGR to RMR, 1, 2, 5, 12, 18 April 1945, Rickover Papers; RMR to HGR, 14 April 1945, RMR.

25. Rickover to Capt. H. E. Eccles, Commander Service Force, U.S. Pacific Fleet, date illegible but probably 5 May 1945, Rickover Papers.

26. HGR to RMR, 4 May 1945, Rickover Papers.

27. Rickover to Capt. H. E. Eccles, probably 5 May 1945, Rickover Papers.

28. HGR to RMR, 31 May 1945, Rickover Papers.

29. Vice Adm. W. W. Smith to Vice Adm. William S. Farber, Sub-Chief of Naval Operations, and Smith to Adm. Royal E. Ingersoll, Commander, Western Sea Frontier, both 11 June 1945; HGR to RMR, 9 July 1945, Rickover Papers.

30. Draft synopsis dated 11 September 1945, Okinawa papers, Rickover Papers.

31. Ibid.

32. HGR to RMR, 26 July 1945, Rickover Papers.

33. Draft synopsis of the base history and a document titled "Running Report" in Rickover Papers.

34. O'Grady was an enlisted man; I do not know his rate.

35. HGR to RMR, 9 August 1945, Rickover Papers.

36. HGR to RMR, 12 August 1945, Rickover Papers.

37. HGR to RMR, 16, 29 September 1945, Rickover Papers.

38. HGR to RMR, 16, 24 October 1945, Rickover Papers.

39. Record of Proceedings of the Okinawa Post-War Advance Board Convened at the Naval Operating Base, Okinawa, Ryukyu Islands, 9 November 1945, from Folder, Okinawa, Ryukyu Islands (1945–48), in Field Liaison and Records Section, Base Maintenance Division (3OP-422 H 1930–1965), NHC.

40. HGR to RMR, 6 November 1945, Rickover Papers.

41. Ruth Masters Rickover refers to the leper colony in her *Pepper, Rice, and Elephants*, 189–90.

42. Fitness Report, 1 September–25 November 1945, Rickover Papers.

Chapter 6. Atomic Energy

1. For the Nineteenth Fleet, see Blair, *Atomic Submarine*, 58–62. Fitness Reports of 28 February, 8 May 1946, Rickover Papers.

2. HGR to RMR, 4 May 1946, Rickover Papers.

3. Hewlett and Duncan, *Nuclear Navy*, 15, 16–20, 27–32, 34–35; Notes from Chronology of Nuclear Energy for Propulsion of Ships, 14 June 1946–24 December 1949, CA.

4. Kenneth D. Nichols, *The Road to Trinity: A Personal Account of How America's Nuclear Policies Were Made* (New York: William Morrow, 1987), 232–33.

5. HGR to RMR, 13 July 1946, Rickover Papers.

6. Dunford, 4 January 1987, and Roddis, 6 January 1987, to the author. The quotation is from "1945–1947: Early Days of the Nuclear Navy," a paper Roddis presented on 7 July 1982 before the Charleston chapter of the Navy League of the United States.

7. Conference Notes provided by Roddis to the author.

8. Reports Written by Naval Group at Oak Ridge, Tennessee, NRD.

9. HGR to RMR, 4 October 1946, Rickover Papers.

10. Hewlett and Duncan, *Nuclear Navy*, 38; Rockwell, *Rickover Effect*, 42.

11. Hewlett and Duncan, *Nuclear Navy*, 75.

12. Seaborg to Oppenheimer, 4 August 1947, *Journal of Glenn T. Seaborg, 1946–1958* (Berkeley: Radiation Laboratory PUB-676, July 1980), 1:300; for Teller's opinion, see Blair, *Atomic Submarine*, 86–87.

13. Hewlett and Duncan, *Nuclear Navy*, 49–51.

14. Beach, *Salt and Steel*, 168–85.

15. Hewlett and Duncan, *Nuclear Navy*, 57–58, 60–61.

16. Gary E. Weir, *Forged in War: The Naval-Industrial Complex and American Submarine Construction, 1940–1961* (Washington, D.C.: Naval Historical Center, Department of the Navy, 1993), 158 n. 29. Quotation from Richard G. Hewlett and Francis Duncan, *Atomic Shield, 1947/1952*, vol. 2 of *A History of the United States Atomic Energy Commission* (University Park: Pennsylvania State University Press), 191.

17. Chief of Naval Personnel to Rickover, 15 February 1949, Rickover Papers.

18. On recruitment and T-3, see Rockwell, *Rickover Effect*, 65–66.

19. Theodore Rockwell, "Admiral H. G. Rickover's Impact on Nuclear Power," based on invited opening paper, Chairman's special Session at the Joint International Conference, 16 November 1992, of the American Nuclear Society and the European Nuclear Society commemorating the 50th Anniversary of the Birth of Nuclear Power.

20. Rickover, "The Decision to Use Zirconium in Nuclear Reactors," in *History of the Development of Zirconium Alloys for Use in Nuclear Reactors . . .* , NR:D:1975 (Wash-

ington, D.C.: United States Research and Development Administration, 1975), 3–13; Rockwell, *Rickover Effect*, 87–90.

21. For the impact of the Soviet detonation of 29 August 1949, see Hewlett and Duncan, *Atomic Shield*, 219–21.

22. A copy of the hearing is in NRD.

23. Deputy CNO (Operations) to Deputy CNO (Logistics), 27 February 1950; Hearing . . . Shipbuilding and Conversion Program 1952, Fiscal Year 1952, 28 March 1950; Chairman of the General Board to CNO, 11 April 1950, General Board Subject File, 1950–January 1951, Box 18, RG 19, NARA.

24. Statistics derived from Donald E. Fry, comp., Chronological Listing of NR Personnel from 1946 to Present in "1992 NR Sea Stories," unpublished document gathered for the 1992 Naval Reactors reunion.

Chapter 7. Promotion

1. Hewlett and Duncan, *Nuclear Navy*, 164–67.

2. Ralph Gerber, "The Engineering Duty Only Officer Today," and Rexford V. Wheeler and Sheldon H. Kinney, "The Promotion of Career Officers," U.S. Naval Institute *Proceedings* 78 (March 1952): 293–97; 80 (June 1954): 637–46; "Reminiscences of Admiral Stuart S. (Sunshine) Murray," 2:639–40; Polmar and Allen, *Rickover*, 186.

3. ALNAV 67, issued 11 July 1951, NHC.

4. "Reminiscences of Admiral Stuart S. (Sunshine), Murray," 2:641–42.

5. Polmar and Allen, *Rickover*, 183–88.

6. Quotations from a copy of *Statement of Representative Sidney R. Yates (Dem. Ill.) before the Senate Armed Services Committee on 5 March 1953 re Hearing on Captain Hyman George Rickover, USN*, Scrapbook 1, Rickover Papers.

7. Robinson to Rickover, telegram, 8 June 1952, in Scrapbook 1, Rickover Papers.

8. *New York Times* and *Washington Post*, 15 June 1952. A Portion of Dean's remarks are in his letter to Kimball, 8 July 1952, Rickover Papers. For Truman, see Harry S. Truman, *Public Papers of the Presidents of the United States: Harry S. Truman, 1952–53* (Washington, D.C.: GPO, 1966), 425–30.

9. ALNAV Two One, 3 June 1952, Scrapbook 1; Rickover to Chief of Naval Personnel, 22 July 1952, Rickover Papers.

10. Citation is in Rickover Papers; photograph in *New York Times*, 8 July 1952.

11. ALNAV 35, 19 July 1952, NHC.

12. Fitness Report, 1 September 1950–28 February 1951, which was made out by Hafstad. Hafstad to DuBose, 20 June, 26 August 1952, Rickover Papers.

13. Hafstad to DuBose, 26 September 1952, Rickover Papers.

14. *Time* 60 (4 August 1952).

15. Durham to Kimball, 16 December 1952, JCAE, Box 95, JCAE Outgoing Mail, December, January 1953, RG 128, NARA.

16. *Washington Evening Star*, 16 January 1952, Scrapbook 1, Rickover Papers.

17. Rockwell, *Rickover Effect*, 138. In two conversations Rickover told me that on hearing the news from Chalk River, he thought the pressurized-water approach was dead.

18. These paragraphs on the promotion struggle rely on several conversations with Rickover and members of his staff who were in Naval Reactors at the time. Rockwell's *Rickover Effect* is indispensable.

19. Scrapbook 1, Rickover Papers, has the story as it appeared on 4, 5, 6 February 1953 in the *Portsmouth (Ohio) Times*.

20. *Congressional Record*, 83d Cong., 1st sess., 22 January 1953, vol. 99, pt. 1, pp. 498–99.

21. Ibid., 12 February 1953, 1024–29.

22. Ibid., 1026.

23. All quotations are from Scrapbook 1, Rickover Papers.

24. *Washington Post*, 19 February 1953, Rickover Papers.

25. Senate Committee on Armed Services, *Report of Hearing . . . Held on Nominations as Covered by Reference Numbers 2AF, 1AF, 2A, N, 2N, 3N, 105, Executive Session*, 26 February 1953, Sars-T.13, RG 46, NARA. I cannot explain the difference between the thirty captains recommended for promotion in note 11 above and the thirty-nine captains mentioned here.

26. *Congressional Record*, 83d Cong,. 1st sess., 2 March 1953, vol. 99, pt. 2, pp. 1553–62. Quotation is on 1556.

27. Rickover, conversation with author.

28. A copy of the statement is in Scrapbook 1, Rickover Papers.

29. Rickover's memorandum is dated 3 March 1953, but the title and context indicate the conversation took place on 4 March, Rickover Papers.

30. Senate Committee on Armed Services, *Hearing Held . . . Nomination of Captain H. G. Rickover to Be a Rear Admiral*, Executive Session, 5 March 1953, RG 46, NARA.

31. Saltonstall released the letter on 9 March 1953. See Scrapbook 1, Rickover Papers.

32. Edwin E. Kintner, "Admiral Rickover's Gamble: The Landlocked Submarine," *Atlantic Monthly* 203 (January 1959): 31–35, and by the same author, "The First Days of the Mark I," *Journal of the American Society of Naval Engineers* 72 (February 1960): 9–13.

Chapter 8. *Nautilus*

1. For January date, see Hewlett and Duncan, *Nuclear Navy*, 158. For 1954, see Rockwell, *Rickover Effect*, 183.

2. Rockwell, *Rickover Effect*, 144–45.

3. Rickover to Wilkinson, 25 March 1953, Rickover Papers.

4. *Washington Times-Herald* and *Washington Star*, 20 August 1953.

5. Rickover to File, 5 January 1954, Rickover Papers; Cutter's account, which is less detailed, is in "Reminiscences of Captain Slade D. Cutter, USN (Ret.)," 2:374–82, Interviews Conducted by the U.S. Naval Institute, NHC.

6. Beach, *Salt and Steel*, 232–36.

7. *New London (Conn.) Evening Day*, 21 January 1954.

8. Strauss to Cole, 14 October 1954, Submarine-*Nautilus* Folder, Box 465, General Correspondence, JCAE Records, RG 128, NARA.

9. Diary of Maj. Gen. K. D. Nichols (hereafter cited as Nichols Diary), 5, 6 January 1955, ACE.

10. DOD Press Release No. 41-55, Rickover Papers.

11. These paragraphs are based on several conversations with Rickover and others. The best description of the trials is by Rockwell, who participated in them, in his *Rickover Effect*, 188–95. Wilkinson's account, as told to Hugh Morrow, "We Took the Atom Sub to Sea," which appeared in *Saturday Evening Post* 227 (9 April 1955): 17–19, 84, and (16 April 1955): 38–39, 148–51, is less satisfactory. See also "Reminiscences of Carleton Shugg," 23–24, Interviews Conducted by the U.S. Naval Institute, NHC; and the log of the *Nautilus*, Logs of U.S. Naval Ships and Stations 1955, Box 718, Records of the Bureau of Naval Personnel, RG 24, NARA.

12. Weir, *Forged in War*, 178–86, 195.

Chapter 9. Shippingport Atomic Power Station

1. Hewlett and Duncan, *Nuclear Navy*, 196–98.

2. Richard Pfau, *No Sacrifice Too Great: The Life of Lewis L. Strauss* (Charlottesville: University of Virginia Press, 1984), 139, 150, 186; Roger M. Anders, *Forging the Atomic Shield, Excerpts from the Office Diary of Gordon E. Dean* (Chapel Hill: University of North Carolina Press, 1987), 249.

3. Hewlett and Duncan, *Nuclear Navy*, 227–28.

4. Commission Meeting 885, 9 July 1953, AEC. Rickover gave me an unpublished paper titled "Thomas E. Murray and the PWR," which consists of chronologies and quotations. Excerpts from the Cole letter are on 17–18.

5. Murray, "Far More Important than War," 22 October 1953, Electric Companies Public Information Program, Rickover Papers. For Murray's account of the PWR, see his *Nuclear Policy for War and Peace* (New York: World Publishing, 1960), 157–61.

6. Dwight D. Eisenhower, "Radio and Television Remarks on the Occasion of the Ground-breaking Ceremonies for the Shippingport Atomic Power Plant, September 6, 1954," *Public Papers of the Presidents of the United States: Dwight D. Eisenhower, 1954* (Washington, D.C.: GPO, 1960), 840–41; Nichols, *Road to Trinity*, 328; Simpson, *Nuclear Power*, 107.

7. Nichols Diary, 22 November–22 December 1954, ACE; quotation is from Strauss, Memorandum to Murray, 28 February 1955; Murray, Memorandum for Chairman Strauss, 25 February 1955, Rickover Papers.

8. Francis Duncan, *Rickover and the Nuclear Navy: The Discipline of Technology* (Annapolis: Naval Institute Press, 1990), 197–203. See also Francis Duncan and Jack M. Holl, *Shippingport: The Nation's First Atomic Power Station* (Washington, D.C.: History Division, Department of Energy, 1983). Norman Friedman, *U.S. Submarines Since 1945: An Illustrated Design History* (Annapolis: Naval Institute Press, 1994), 7. Friedman was mistaken in writing that Shippingport was a failure.

Chapter 10. A National Figure

1. Dwight D. Eisenhower, "Radio and Television Address to the American People on Science and in National Security," *Public Papers of the Presidents of the United States: Dwight D. Eisenhower, 1957* (Washington, D.C.: GPO, 1958), 791.

2. Weir, *Forged in War*, 241, 244, 252–53; Richard W. Dyke and Francis X. Gannon, *Chet Holifield: Master Legislator and Nuclear Statesman* (Lanham, Md.: University Press of America, 1996), 176–77; Hewlett and Duncan, *Nuclear Navy*, 308–9; Friedman, *U.S. Submarines Since 1945*, 197.

3. Preparedness Investigating Subcommittee of the Senate Armed Services Committee, *Inquiry into Satellite and Missile Programs*, 85th Cong., 2d sess., 6 January 1958 (Washington, D.C.: GPO, 1958), 4–33; Jackson statement, 23–24; for Hayward, Bennett and Burke, see vol. 2, 1730–31, 1939.

4. For the American side of the negotiations I have used, see JCAE, *Amending the Atomic Energy Act of 1954*, 85th Cong., 2d sess. (Washington, D.C.: GPO, 1959). Rickover's testimony on 27 February 1958 is on 159–74, and his testimony on 28 May 1958 is on 465–509. He referred to his trips to the United Kingdom in January 1958 on 164 and 172. For the British side, I have relied on Philip Ziegler, *Mountbatten* (New York: Alfred A. Knopf, 1985), 558–59, and Solly Zuckerman, *Six Men Out of the Ordinary* (London: Peter Owen, 1992), 169–97. Vice Adm. Sir Ted Horlick's article, "Submarine Propulsion in the Royal Navy," *Proceedings of the Institution of Mechanical Engineers* 196 (1982), which deals with nuclear propulsion on 67–70, is very helpful. The stormy meeting between Rickover and Mountbatten is from conversations of Admiral and Mrs. Rickover with me.

5. William R. Anderson and Clay Blair Jr., *Nautilus 90 North* (New York: World Publishing, 1959) describe the voyage.

6. News Conference on 9 August 1958, James C. Hagerty's Press Conferences July through September 1958 (2) File Folder, Box 52, Papers of James Hagerty, DDE; "Reminiscences of Admiral James S. Russell, U.S. Navy (Ret.)," 1:75, 2:348–50, Interviews Conducted by the U.S. Naval Institute, NHC; Rockwell, *Rickover Effect*, 246–50; *Washington Post*, 15 August 1958.

7. "Re: Promotion of Rear Admiral Hyman G. Rickover, USN, to rank of Vice Admiral, by rider to the Defense Appropriation Bill for fiscal 1959," n.d., Rickover, Adm. H. G. Folder, Box 20, JCAE Records, RG 128, NARA.

8. The draft is in Submarines-*Nautilus* Folder, Box 465, General Correspond-

ence, JCAE Records, RG 128, NARA; *Congressional Record*, 85th Cong., 2d sess., 11 August 1958, vol. 104, pt. 13, pp. 16911–13. Quotation is on 16912.

9. *New York Times*, 19 August 1958; *Washington Post* and *Washington Times Herald*, 29 August 1958, from a folder of newspaper clippings in my possession. Dates of promotion are from Secretary of the Navy to Rickover, 7 November 1958, Rickover Papers. The Gold Medal ceremony took place on 15 April 1959 in the New Senate Office Building.

10. *Washington Evening Star*, 13 August 1958, *Washington Post*, 16 August 1958, Scrapbook 11, Rickover Papers.

11. *New York Post*, 14 August 1958.

12. *New York Times*, 26, 27, 28, August 1958.

13. *Education and Freedom* was published in 1959 by E. P. Dutton; *Swiss Schools* in 1962 by Little, Brown; and *American Education* in 1963 by E. P. Dutton. In his scholarly appraisal of Rickover and education, William J. Haran in his doctoral thesis presented at the Loyola University of Chicago, "Admiral Rickover, USN: A Decade of Educational Criticism, 1955–1964," concluded Rickover often misunderstood and oversimplified the philosophy of education but showed the need for reform.

14. Conversations with Rickover, *Pittsburgh Press, Washington Sunday Star, New York Times*, all 12 July 1959.

15. When I interviewed Mr. Nixon in April 1978 in connection with writing *Rickover and the Nuclear Navy*, I remarked that I had been unable to find any trace of Rickover in the State Department archives on the preparation of the trip. The former president said that was not surprising. Rickover came along as his guest and the department had nothing to do with it. Rockwell, *Rickover Effect*, 265, 269–70. For Eisenhower, see news conference of 22 July 1959, Dwight D. Eisenhower, *Public Papers of the Presidents of the United States: Dwight D. Eisenhower, 1959* (Washington, D.C.: GPO, 1960), 541.

16. Nixon gives his account of his trip to the Soviet Union in his *Six Crises* (New York: Pocket Books, 1962), 262–304. Rickover spoke to me about his selection when we were talking about the trip. The chronology of his memoranda is not easy to follow. I have used the daily reports of the *Washington Post* to put them in order. They are Memorandum of Discussion with Mr. Khrushchev on the Opening of the American Fair, Friday, 24 July 1959; Tour of Futuristic Kitchen at American Fair, Friday, 24 July 1959; Memorandum of Discussion Between VADM H. G. Rickover and Mr. Zukhov, at a Luncheon Given by Mr. Khrushchev at the Kremlin; Discussion with Mr. Khrushchev at Dinner Given by American Ambassador, at Which Were Present Mr. Nixon and the Leading Members of the American Delegation, as Well as Mr. Khrushchev and Leading Members of the Russian Government. "Tour of Futuristic Kitchen" has nothing on the "kitchen debate."

17. Vice President's Kremlin Conversation with Kozlov, 25 July 1959, Memorandum of Conversation, Department of State, *Foreign Relations of the United States,*

1958–1960, vol. 10, pt. 1, *Eastern European Region, Soviet Union, Cyprus* (Washington, D.C.: GPO, 1993), Doc. 97, 353–58.

18. *Washington Post*, 28 July 1959; Nixon, *Six Crises*, 310 n.; McCone to Rickover in care of Ambassador Thompson, 19 July 1959, Rickover Papers.

19. Nixon, *Six Crises*, 307–10.

20. On the *Lenin*, see Raymond V. B. Blackman, ed., *Jane's Fighting Ships, 1969–70* (New York: McGraw-Hill, 1969), 562.

21. Duncan, *Rickover and the Nuclear Navy*, 176–77.

22. Edward L. Beach, *Around the World Submerged* (New York: Dell, 1962).

Chapter 11. The Program at the End of 1960

1. JCAE, *Review of Naval Reactor Program and Admiral Rickover Award*, 11, 15 April 1959 (Washington, D.C.: GPO, 1959), 46.

2. This chapter is based heavily on AEC, *Major Activities in the Atomic Energy Programs, January–December 1960* (Washington, D.C.: GPO, 1961). For the Navy program, see 140–46, and table 1, Nuclear Powered Naval Ships, 144.

3. Willis C. Barnes, "Korea and Vietnam (1950–1972)," in *Naval Engineering and American Seapower*, ed. Randolph W. King (Baltimore: Nautical and Aviation Company of America, 1989), 280–81.

4. AEC, *Twenty-second Semiannual Report of the Atomic Energy Commission, July 1957* (Washington, D.C.: GPO, July 1957), 60; Hewlett and Duncan, *Nuclear Navy*, 272.

5. Friedman, *U.S. Submarines Since 1945*, 109–10, 128, 130.

6. Hewlett and Duncan, *Nuclear Navy*, 282–87.

7. Duncan, *Rickover and the Nuclear Navy*, 106–7.

8. Ibid., 111–14.

Chapter 12. Breakthrough on Nuclear Carriers

1. Oral History Interview with Vice Admiral H. G. Rickover, USN, 17 August 1964, Rickover Papers. The interview was carried out by Arthur Schlesinger Jr., for the John F. Kennedy Library.

2. Seaborg interview, 20 February 1979, CA; *Journal of Glenn T. Seaborg*, PUB-635 (Berkeley: Lawrence Berkeley Laboratory, 1989), 1:110, 18 March 1961 (hereafter cited as *Seaborg Journal*, followed by volume number, page number, and date).

3. For a very useful table on the shipbuilding programs during these years, see JCAE, *Naval Nuclear Propulsion Program—1970*, 91st Cong., 2d sess., 19 and 20 March 1970 (Washington, D.C.: GPO, 1970), Appendix 9, "New Construction Major Surface Warships and Submarines Authorized Since World War II," 228–35.

4. The above paragraphs are based on Duncan, *Rickover and the Nuclear Navy*, 117–20. The *Truxtun* was built by the New York Shipbuilding Corporation and commissioned by the Navy on 27 May 1967.

5. Duncan, *Rickover and the Nuclear Navy*, 121–22.

6. Polmar and Allen, *Rickover*, 260–61.

7. Report of Board of Medical Survey U.S. Naval Hospital, NMHC, Bethesda, Maryland, 18 October 1961, Rickover Papers; *Washington Evening Star*, 1 August 1961; *New York Times*, 21 August 1961.

8. For sea trials and catapult controversy, see Duncan, *Rickover and the Nuclear Navy*, 109–11, 122–24.

9. JCAE, *Naval Nuclear Propulsion Program—1970*, Appendix 9.

10. JCAE, *Tour of the U.S.S. "Enterprise" and Report on Joint AEC–Naval Reactor Program*, 87th Cong., 2d sess. (Washington, D.C.: GPO, 1962). For de Poix, see 3–8; for Rickover quotation, see 23.

11. Duncan, *Rickover and the Nuclear Navy*, 131.

12. Ibid., 129–36; memoranda and letters are in JCAE, *Nuclear Propulsion for Naval Surface Vessels*, 88th Cong., 1st sess., 30, 31 October, 13 November (Washington, D.C., GPO, 1964), 81, 102–7, 230–44.

13. JCAE, *Nuclear Propulsion for Naval Surface Vessels*. For Brown's testimony, 33–42; for Rickover, 61–62, 86, 99.

14. John F. Kennedy, President's News Conference of 31 October 1963, *Public Papers of the Presidents of the United States: John F. Kennedy, 1963* (Washington, D.C.: GPO, 1964), 381.

15. McNamara's testimony is in JCAE, *Nuclear Propulsion for Surface Vessels*, 151–96. Quotations are on 171, 192, 196. For comparative costs, see 188–89, and U.S. Congress, JCAE, *Report of the JCAE, Nuclear Propulsion for Naval Surface Vessels*, December 1963 (Washington, D.C.: GPO, 1963), 34.

16. Deborah Shapley, *Promise and Power: The Life and Times of Robert McNamara* (Boston: Little, Brown, 1993), 230.

17. Duncan, *Rickover and the Nuclear Navy*, 140–44, 145–46.

Chapter 13. Meeting with Kennedy

1. This chapter is heavily based on Duncan, *Rickover and the Nuclear Navy*, 170–85.

2. *Seaborg Journal* 5:098, 127; 4, 8 February 1963.

3. Description of the meeting is from Oral History Interview with Vice Admiral H. G. Rickover, USN, 1 August 17, 1964, and from *Seaborg Journal* 5:146, 11 February 1963. The *Journal* entry has nothing on education. I cannot be sure from either document that the events were discussed in the order I give them.

Chapter 14. *Thresher*

1. This chapter is based heavily on Duncan, *Rickover and the Nuclear Navy*, 52–98.

2. *Hartford Courant*, 16 April 1963.

3. JCAE, *Loss of the U.S.S. "Thresher,"* 88th Cong., 1st and 2d sess. (Washington, D.C.: GPO, 1965), 1963–64.

4. Quote is from *Record of Proceedings of a Court of Inquiry* 3:698 and is reproduced in Duncan, *Rickover and the Nuclear Navy*, 85.

5. JCAE, *Loss of the U.S.S. "Thresher,"* 17.

6. Ibid., 95.

Chapter 15. Every Two Years

1. The provisions of the code are more complicated. An officer (unless he was a fleet admiral) had to retire at sixty-two. The president could defer his retirement until he became sixty-four. In 1961 Kennedy had extended Rickover's active duty until 1964.

2. JCAE, *Tour of the U.S.S. "Enterprise,"* 44–45.

3. Shepard to McGeorge Bundy, 7 February 1963, President's Office Files, Departments and Agencies, Navy, 5/62–7/62, Box 84a, Folder 1/63–6/63, JFK.

4. *Seaborg Journal* 5:171, 174, 184; 14, 25 February 1963.

5. Ibid. 5:289, 20 March 1963.

6. The *Seaborg Journal* contains a copy of the Pastore letter. *Saturday Evening Post* 236 (16 March 1963): 80.

7. Brown, Memorandum for the Files, *Seaborg Journal* 5:308–10, 22 March 1963.

8. Seaborg to President, 25 March 1963, Seaborg Papers, AEC.

9. *New York Times*, 9 April 1963.

10. *Seaborg Journal* 5:619, 654; 11, 21 June 1963.

11. *New York Times*, 22 June 1963.

12. Seaborg to Korth, *Seaborg Journal* 6:102–3, 25 July 1963.

13. JCAE, *Management of the Naval Reactor Program*, 88th Cong., 1st sess. (Washington, D.C.: GPO, 1964). The hearing was never published and hence is rare. Quotations are on 6 and 10.

14. Alex A. Kerr, "As I Recall . . . The Korth Resignation," *Naval Review 1985* (Annapolis: Naval Institute, 1986), 168–69.

15. Pastore, Holifield, Anderson, and Price to the President, 13 December 1963, "Exec. ND 9/R National Defense, Military Personnel" Folder, Box 13, WHCF–Subject File, LBJ.

16. *Seaborg Journal* 7:075, 078, 090; 14 December 1963.

17. Ibid. Anderson statement is on 078.

18. Nitze, Memorandum for Vice Admiral H. G. Rickover, USN, *Seaborg Journal* 7:280, 27 December 1963.

19. Unsigned Memorandum for Record, lent to the author by Capt. John W. Crawford, USN (Ret.), JWC.

20. Rockwell, *Rickover Effect*, 334–36.

Chapter 16. New Classes of Surface Ships and Submarines

1. For the carrier schedule, see Duncan, *Rickover and the Nuclear Navy*, 146. For

authorization and appropriation of nuclear surface ships, see JCAE, *Naval Nuclear Propulsion Program—1970*, Appendix 9, 228–31.

2. HASC, *Hearings on Military Posture . . . to Authorize Appropriations During the Fiscal Year 1967 . . .* , 89th Cong., 2d sess., 8–31 March 1967 (Washington, D.C.: GPO, 1966), 7577.

3. Senate, *Committee Authorizing Appropriations During Fiscal Year 1967 for Procurement of . . . Naval Vessels . . .* , 89th Cong., 2d sess., 25 April 1966, Report No. 1136, pp. 5–6.

4. Memorandum of Telephone Conversation with Secretary Nitze Last Night, 2 May 1966, Rickover Papers.

5. HASC, *Hearings on Military Posture . . . Fiscal Year 1967*, 8124, 8127–36.

6. House, *Authorizing Defense Procurement and Research and Development, and Military Pay*, 89th Cong., 2d sess., 16 May 1966, H. Rept. 1536, 17–18. Reference to the destroyers is on 26.

7. Press Release, Honorable L. Mendel Rivers, HASC, 17 May 1966, Rickover Papers.

8. John W. Finney, "House Challenges M'Namara's Stand On Nuclear Ships," *New York Times*, 15 June 1966; "Capitol Stuff," *Washington Daily News*, 11 June 1966, and "Now It's Rivers vs McNamara," *U.S. News and World Report*, 27 June 1966, 3–6.

9. Document is in Rickover Papers.

10. House, *Authorizing Appropriations for Defense Procurement and Research and Development for Fiscal Year 1967; Military Pay Increase*, 89th Cong., 2d sess., 30 June 1966, H. Rept. 1679, 2.

11. Nitze, Memorandum for Vice Admiral H. G. Rickover, 9 July 1966; Rickover, Memorandum for the Secretary of the Navy, 12, 20 July 1966, Rickover Papers.

12. Memorandum of Telephone Conversation Between Representatives Chet Holifield, Chairman of the Joint Committee on Atomic Emery, Representative Melvin Price, and Vice Adm. H. G. Rickover, USN, 20 July 1966, Rickover Papers.

13. Rickover, Memorandum for File, 28 July 1966, Rickover Papers.

14. Rickover, Memorandum of Meeting Held at 1600, Wednesday, 3 August 1966, Rickover Papers. Nitze's understanding of the agreement is in *Seaborg Journal* 13:164, 22 August 1966. Nitze refers briefly to a meeting in his "Politics, Politics," *Naval History* 4, no. 2 (Spring 1990): 42–45.

15. Memorandum of Meeting held at 1430, Tuesday, 9 August 1966, Between Secretary of the Navy, the Chief of Naval Operations, and Vice Adm. H. G. Rickover, Rickover Papers. There is no evidence aside from the title that Admiral McDonald was present.

16. Friedman, *U.S. Submarines Since 1945*, 5–6.

17. JCAE, *Nuclear Submarines of Advanced Design*, 90th Cong., 2d sess., 21 June 1968 (Washington, D.C.: GPO, 1966), Appendix 1, "High Speed Chronology," 44

(hereafter cited as JCAE, *Advanced Design*, Appendix and page). Elmo R. Zumwalt Jr., *On Watch: A Personal Memoir* (New York: Quadrangle, 1976), 72.

18. Philip A. Beshany, "As I Recall . . . Selling the *Los Angeles*," U.S. Naval Institute *Proceedings* 110 (October 1987): 109–10.

19. In *Rickover and the Nuclear Navy*, 31, I dated the meeting 7 March. The correct date is 4 March; see JCAE, *Advanced Design*, Appendix 1, 46.

20. JCAE, *Naval Nuclear Propulsion Program—1967–68*, 90th Cong., 1st and 2d sess., 16, 28 March 1967, 8 February 1968 (Washington, D.C.: GPO, 1968).

21. Patrick Tyler, *Running Critical: The Silent War, Rickover, and General Dynamics* (New York: Harper and Row, 1986), 53, 59–60; Friedman, *U.S. Submarines Since 1945*, 164–65. In *Rickover and the Nuclear Navy*, 37, I incorrectly stated that the conform would use two S5Gs.

22. Tyler, *Running Critical*, 53.

23. For reference to the study, see Friedman, *U.S. Submarines Since 1945*, 164; for McNamara, Enthoven, Nunan, and Ignatius, see JCAE, *Advanced Design*, Appendix 1, 49, 50, 51.

24. Tyler, *Running Critical*, 17–18, 25, 26–28, 30–35, 38–44; Friedman, *U.S. Submarines Since 1945*, 165–66.

25. JCAE, *Advanced Design*, Appendix 1, 50, 54.

26. *Seaborg Journal* 16:190, 8 March 1968; Beshany, "As I Recall," 109.

27. JCAE, *Advanced Design*, Appendix 1, 63.

28. Arguments are in JCAE, *Advanced Design*, 1–42.

29. Duncan, *Rickover and the Nuclear Navy*, 39–40.

30. Memorandum of Discussion Between Mr. L. Mendel Rivers . . . and VADM H. G. Rickover, USN (David T. Leighton was present), 14 November 1967, Rickover Papers.

Chapter 17. Troubles, Sadness, and Happiness

1. Nixon to Rickover, 2 August 1961, Rickover to Nixon, 18 August 1961, NARA–Pacific Region.

2. Duncan, *Rickover and the Nuclear Navy*, 45.

3. Friedman, *U.S. Submarines Since 1945*, 165, 169, 170–71.

4. Undersea long-range missile system paragraphs are heavily dependent upon "Submarine Launched Ballistic Missile United States Nuclear Forces Guide," which contains a directory to various missiles and submarines and is maintained by John Pike. It is found on the Internet under the title "Nuclear Forces Guide." I have also used a draft of a "Historical Summary of the Trident Program" prepared in Naval Reactors as part of Rickover's sea trial letter for the *Ohio*, the first Trident submarine.

5. Duncan, *Rickover and the Nuclear Navy*, 41–43.

6. The estimate for the *Nimitz* is in Statement of Rear Admiral James L.

Holloway III . . . ," 10 April 1970, in Joint Hearings before the Joint Senate and House Armed Services Committees, *CVN-70 Aircraft Carrier*, 91st Cong., 2d sess., 7, 8, 10, 13, 15, 16 April 1970 (Washington, D.C.: GPO, 1970), 273.

7. Duncan, *Rickover and the Nuclear Navy*, 163–65.

8. JCAE, *Nuclear Propulsion for Naval Warships*, 92d Cong., 1st and 2d sess., 5 May 1971, 30 September 1972 (Washington, D.C.: GPO, 1972), 223–26. Quotation from the president's budget is on 224.

9. Joint Senate and House Armed Services Committees, *CVN-70 Aircraft Carrier*. For Stennis, 1–2; for Holloway's remark, 299; for Mondale's statement, 146–75; for Rickover's statement and remarks, 634–742 (but especially 646–48 on long-lead-time funds).

10. House, *Authorizing Appropriations, Fiscal Year 1971, for Military Procurement, Research and Development, and Reserve Strength, and for Other Purposes*, 91st Cong., 2d sess., 24 April 1970, H. Rept. 91-1022, 1. For excerpts from *Congressional Record*, see JCAE, *Nuclear Propulsion for Naval Warships*, 235–36, 238.

11. *Seaborg Journal*, introduction, 1:3.

12. Polmar and Allen, *Rickover*, 278–85; on interviews, see John W. Crawford Jr., "Passing Rickover's Muster," *Naval History* (Spring 1992): 35–38.

13. In chapter 5, "The Rickover Complication," in his *On Watch*, Zumwalt describes his relationship with Rickover. See also Thomas J. Cutler, "Elmo R. Zumwalt, Jr.: Hero or Heretic," in *Quarterdeck and Bridge, Two Centuries of American Naval Leadership*, ed. James C. Bradford (Annapolis: Naval Institute Press, 1997), 415–32; and Norman Friedman, "Elmo Russell Zumwalt, Jr., 1 July 1970–1 July 1974," in *The Chief of Naval Operations*, ed. Robert William Love Jr. (Annapolis: Naval Institute Press, 1980), 365–79.

14. Zumwalt, *On Watch*, 154–56; Historical Summary of the Trident Submarine—June 1981, WMH.

15. Friedman, *U.S. Submarines Since 1945*, 204–5.

16. Historical Summary of the Trident Submarine—June 1981, WMH.

17. Ruth D. Masters, *International Law in National Courts: A Study of the Enforcement of International Law in German, Swiss, French, and Belgian Courts* (New York: Columbia University Press, 1932), and "International Organization of European Rail Transport," *International Conciliation* 330 (May 1937): 487–544.

18. H. G. Rickover, *Eminent Americans: Namesakes of the Polaris Submarine Fleet*, 92d Cong., 1st sess., H. Doc. 92-345 (Washington, D.C.: GPO, 1972).

19. McIntyre, and others who shared his views, gave a concise statement in Senate, *Authorizing Appropriations for Fiscal Year 1974 for Military Procurement . . .* , 93d Cong., 1st sess., 6 September 1973, S. Rept. 93-385, 181; Duncan, *Rickover and the Nuclear Navy*, 46–48.

20. Frederick H. Hartmann, *Naval Renaissance: The U.S. Navy in the 1980s* (Annapolis: Naval Institute Press, 1990), 89–90.

21. "Exchange of Remarks Between the President and Admiral Hyman G. Rick-

over . . . ," 3 December 1973, Office of the White House Press Secretary, White House Press Releases, 26 November 1973 to 31 December 1973, Nixon Presidential Materials Project, Box 42, NARA.

22. Seapower Subcommittee, *Hearings on Military Posture and H.R 12564 . . .* , 92d Cong., 2d sess., 16, 17 January, 5, 15, 21 March, 9 April 1974 (Washington, D.C.: GPO, 1974), pt. 2, 1026, 1028–29, 1036, 1435–36.

23. For text, see JCAE, *Naval Nuclear Propulsion Program—1975*, 94th Cong., 1st sess., 5 March 1975 (Washington, D.C.: GPO, 1975), 16.

24. Richard M. Nixon, *Public Papers of the Presidents of the United States: Richard M. Nixon, 1975* (Washington, D.C.: GPO, 1975), 620.

25. Quotation is from a conversation he had with me on that date.

26. JCAE, *Naval Nuclear Propulsion Program—1974*, 93d Cong., 2d sess., 25 February 1974 (Washington, D.C.: GPO, 1975), 9.

Chapter 18. The Bitter Battle: Shipbuilding Claims

1. Testimony of Rear Adm. Jamie Adair, deputy for ship acquisition, and Rear Adm. Edward J. Fahy, both of the naval ship systems command, on 15 May 1969. Subcommittee of the House Committee on Appropriations, *Department of Defense Appropriations*, pt. 3, *Procurement*, 91st Cong., 1st sess. (Washington, D.C.: GPO, 1969), 523–27.

2. Because of the extensive documentation in the Proxmire hearings, I have used them more than those of other committees. See Subcommittee on Priorities and Economy in Government of the Joint Economic Committee, *Economics of Defense Procurement: Shipbuilding Claims*, 94th Cong., 2d sess., and 95th Cong., 1st sess. (Washington, D.C.: GPO, 1978). Part 1 contains testimony, and part 2 contains documents (hereafter cited as *Defense Procurement*, followed by part number). *Defense Policy*, pt. 1.

3. For the Todd claim and general accounting office comments, see Opening Remarks of Admiral H. G. Rickover Before Subcommittee on Priorities and Economy in Government, *Defense Policy*, pt. 2, 215–17; for May 1971 figures, see Chafee to Proxmire, 28 May 1971, *Defense Procurement*, pt. 2, 594–95.

4. HGR to RMR, 14 July 1935, Rickover Papers.

5. Seapower Subcommittee, *Hearings on Current Status of Shipyards, 1974*, pt. 3, *Governmental Actions*, 93d Cong., 2d sess., HASC 93-82 (Washington, D.C.: GPO, 1974), 1475–77.

6. Seapower Subcommittee, *Hearings on Current Status of Shipyards, 1974*, pt. 2, *Private Shipyards*, 93d Cong., 2d sess. (Washington, D.C.: GPO, 1974). For Pierce, see 727–85; for Diesel, 911–42 in part 2. For Rickover, see pt. 3, 1262–1329 and 1401–12.

7. For a critical appraisals of the Trident contract, see John F. Lehman Jr., *Command of the Seas: Building the 600 Ship Navy* (New York: Scribner's, 1988), 200–203, and Tyler, *Running Critical*, 134–35.

8. Seapower Subcommittee, *Current Status of Shipyards, 1974*, pt. 3, 1267, 1296.

9. For Electric Boat, see Tyler, *Running Critical*, 144–48; for Electric Boat and Newport News, see Statement of Deputy Secretary of Defense William P. Clements, *Defense Procurement*, pt. 1, 48; for Diesel letter, see *Defense Procurement*, pt. 2, 238–39.

10. From three tables under the general title "Statistical Summary, Navy Shipbuilding Program" included by Deputy Secretary of Defense William P. Clements in his testimony of 25 June 1976 in *Defense Procurement*, pt. 1, 52–54.

11. *Defense Procurement*, pt. 2, 257–59.

12. Ibid., 359–60.

13. Rickover, conversations with author, 14, 24 June 1976, CA.

14. Subcommittee on Priorities and Economy in Government of the Joint Economic Committee, *Economics of Defense Procurement: Shipbuilding Claims*, 94th Cong., 2d sess., 94th Cong. 1st sess., 7, 25 June 1976, 29 December 1977 (Washington, D.C.: GPO, 1977). For Rickover's testimony, see 1–26; for Clements and others with him, see 37–79. His quotation is on 43.

15. For establishing the board, see *Defense Procurement*, pt. 2, 386–87, 388–89, 394–96. For the $892 million, which was in ceiling price dollars, see *Defense Procurement*, pt. 1, 138.

16. Rickover, conversations with author, 30, 31 August 1976, CA.

17. For settlement of the claim, see *Defense Procurement*, pt. 1, 144–45; for reference to cost sharing, see Diesel's testimony in Subcommittee of the Committee of the House Committee on Appropriations, *Department of Defense Appropriations for 1978*, 95th Cong., 1st sess. (Washington, D.C.: GPO, 1977), 186–87.

18. Tyler, *Running Critical*, 148.

19. Ibid., 151.

20. Ibid., 167–83.

21. Ibid., 182, 204–5; Rickover, conversation with author, 25 November 1977.

22. For news stories, see *Defense Procurement*, pt. 2, 735–47; for Trident, see Tyler, *Running Critical*, 209, and the *New York Times*, 30 November 1977.

23. Proxmire to Claytor, 30 December 1977, *Defense Procurement*, pt. 2, 662.

24. Rickover spoke to me of his luncheon on 6 January 1978; his comments on returning the records to the board is based on my memory.

25. Excerpts of meeting are in House Appropriations Committee, *Department of Defense Appropriations for 1979*, pt. 6, 277–80.

26. Tyler, *Running Critical*, 225–26.

27. Ibid., 232–33.

28. For correspondence, see House Appropriations Committee, *Department of Defense Appropriations for 1979*, pt. 6, 173, 305–25.

29. Ibid., pt. 6. For Bryan, see 127–28; for Manganaro, 302; for Rickover, 470–71. For barge statement, see 484, and Tyler, *Running Critical*, 236.

30. Terms are in Claytor to Magnuson and attachments, *Defense Procurement*, pt. 2, 756–68; Tyler, *Running Critical*, 245–48.

31. James T. McIntyre Jr., Director, Office of Management and Budget, 30 June 1978, Folder 7/10/78, Handwriting File, Box 94, Office of Staff Secretary, Carter Presidential Papers, JCL.

Chapter 19. The Admiral and the President

1. Jimmy Carter, *Why Not the Best? Why One Man Is Optimistic About America's Third Century* (Nashville: Broadman Press, 1975), 11, 59.

2. Carter to Rickover, 23 October 1974; Rickover to Carter, 26 November 1974, Rickover Papers. For speech, see *Defense Policy*, pt. 2, 667–710.

3. Carter to Rickover, 11 August 1976, Rickover Papers.

4. Jimmy Carter, *Public Papers of the Presidents of the United States: Jimmy Carter, 1977* (Washington, D.C.: GPO, 1977), Remarks to the American People, 2 February 1977, bk. 1, 66 (hereafter cited as Carter, *Public Papers, 1977*, followed by book and page number).

5. Rickover, conversations with author, 5, 7, 18 February 1977, CA. He used the word "crest" on 18 February.

6. An excellent summary of Rickover's philosophy can be found in *Defense Policy*, pt. 2; Carter to Rickover, February 16, 1977, Staff Offices, Office of Staff Secretary, Folder 2/116/77, 2-16-77, Box 8, JCL.

7. Rickover, conversation on 17 February and paper given to me, CA.

8. Rickover to the President, 25 February 1977, Rickover Papers; Carter to Rickover, 28 February 1977, "Rickover, Hyman G. (Admiral), 1/20/77–12/31/77" Folder, WHCF–Name File, JCL.

9. Hartmann, *Naval Renaissance*, 24–25, 223; George W. Baer, *One Hundred Years of Sea Power: The U.S. Navy, 1890–1990* (Stanford, Calif.: Stanford University Press, 1994), 411–14.

10. The 8 April 1977 visit is from a conversation with me. The response to the request is Rickover to Carter, 9 April 77, Rickover Papers.

11. Rickover to President, 12 April 1977, Rickover Papers.

12. Address to the Nation, the Energy Problem, 18 April 1977, Carter, *Public Papers, 1977*, bk. 1, 656.

13. On the outing on the *Los Angeles*, see Rickover, Memorandum for the President, 9 March 1977, Rickover Papers; Rickover, conversation with author, 20 May 1977, CA; Question-and-Answer Session with Reporters . . . 27 May 1977; Carter, *Public Papers, 1977*, bk. 1, 1037, 1039; *New York Times*, 28 May 1977; Carter to Rickover, 1 June 1977, "Rickover, Hyman G. (Admiral), 1/20/77–12/31/77" Folder, WHCF–Name File, JCL. Tyler, *Running Critical*, 158–59.

14. Rickover talked about his views on abortion and other subjects in a conversation with me, 8 April, 25 July 1977, CA.

15. Carter to Rickover, 11 October 1977, "Rickover, Hyman G. (Admiral), 1/20/77–12/31/77" Folder, WHCF–Name File, JCL.

16. Duncan, *Rickover and the Nuclear Navy*, 190–91, 211–13, 219–23, 226; Carter, *Public Papers, 1977*, bk. 2, 2068–71.

17. For press conference and Wooten, see *New York Times*, 16 December 1977.

18. Telephoned to Susan Clough to give to President Carter, 16 December 1977. A copy of the note, handwritten and with his deletions and interlineation, was given by Rickover to me (CA).

19. Rickover, Memorandum of Telephone Conversation with President Carter, 1 February 1978, Rickover Papers.

20. House, *Department of Defense Appropriation Authorization Act, 1979*, 95th Cong., 2d sess., 6 May 1978, H. Rept. 95-1118, 17, 21–22; *New York Times*, 17 February 78.

21. Intelligence and Military Application of Nuclear Energy Subcommittee of the House Armed Services Committee, *Naval Nuclear Propulsion Program—1978*, 95th Cong., 2d sess., 1 March 1978 (Washington, D.C.: GPO, 1978), 18–22. Rickover gave sixty-three thousand tons for the CVV; on 31 May 1979 he gave the CVV as fifty-three thousand tons. Perhaps there were several designs of the CVV under consideration.

22. For Brown, see Senate Armed Services Committee, *Department of Defense Authorization for Fiscal Year 1979*, 95th Cong., 2d sess., 14, 16 March 1979, *General Procurement* (Washington, D.C.: GPO, 1979), pt. 5, 4261–69.

23. House, *Department of Defense Appropriation Authorization Act, 1979*, 16–17, 24, 51–52; Senate, *Authorizing Appropriations for the Fiscal Year 1979 for Military Procurement, Research and Development, Active Duty, Selected Reserve, and Civilian Personnel Strengths, and for Other Purposes*, 95th Cong., 2d sess., 15 May 1978, S. Rept. 95-826, 50–52; *Washington Post*, 18 May 1978.

24. Congressional actions are from the *Congressional Digest*, 95th Cong., 2d sess.

25. Press conference of the President of the United States, 4:00 P.M. August 17, 1978, Old Executive Office Building, Rickover Papers.

26. *Face the Nation*, CBS Television and CBS Radio, 3 September 1979. Copyright 1978 CBS, Inc., All Rights Reserved, CA.

27. Procurement and Military Nuclear Systems Subcommittee and the Seapower and Strategic and Critical Materials Subcommittee of the House Committee on Armed Services, *Naval Nuclear Propulsion Program—1979*, 96th Cong., 1st sess., 1 March 1979 (Washington, D.C.: GPO, 1979), 56–57.

28. The following account of Rickover's participation is based on Duncan, *Rickover and the Nuclear Navy*, 273–78. For accounts of the accident, I have used Scott Johnson, *Inside TMI: Minute by Minute* (Copyright Scott Johnson, 1998; web site: http://www.wowpage.com/tmi/ [2 February 2000]) and Mark Stephens, *Three Mile Island: The Hour-by-Hour Account of What Really Happened* (New York: Random House, 1980).

29. For further treatment of this subject, see chapter 22, "Engineering Legacy."

30. Unpublished remarks prepared by Rickover titled "Differences Between Naval Reactor and Commercial Nuclear Plants, August 1979"; quotation on 12–13, CA.

31. The following paragraphs are based on Rickover to the President, 1 December 1979, Folder 12/5/79, Handwriting File, Box 158, Office of the Staff Secretary, Carter Presidential Papers, JCL.

32. Jimmy Carter, "President's Commission on the Accident at Three Mile Island," *Public Papers of the President of the United States: Jimmy Carter, 1979* (Washington, D.C.: GPO, 1980), bk. 2, 2202–4.

33. For an excellent study, see Joseph V. Rees, *Hostages of Each Other: The Transformation of Nuclear Safety Since Three Mile Island* (Chicago: University of Chicago Press, 1988).

34. Rickover, Memorandum of Conversation with President Carter at My Apartment on 31 May 1979, Rickover Papers.

35. *Congressional Record*, 96th Cong., 1st sess., 26 October 1979, vol. 125, pt. 23, p. 29771.

36. Jimmy Carter, State of the Union Address, January 23, 1980, *Public Papers of the Presidents of the United States: Jimmy Carter, 1980–81* (Washington, D.C.: GPO, 1981), bk. 1, 197; Hartmann, *Naval Renaissance*, 25; *New York Times*, 4 March 1980; Rickover, Memorandum of Telephone Conversation . . . with Cyrus Vance, Secretary of State, 11 March 1980, Rickover Papers.

37. Rickover to Mr. President, 1 September 1980, JCL; for the post-election letters, see Peter G. Bourne, *Jimmy Carter: A Comprehensive Biography from Plains to Post Presidency* (New York: Lisa Drew/Scribner's, 1997), 474–75.

38. *Public Papers, 1980–81*, bk. 2, 1057–60.

Chapter 20. End of a Career

1. Norman Polmar and Thomas B. Allen, "The Plot to Get Rickover," *Washingtonian* 17 (April 1982): 140.

2. Lehman, *Command of the Seas*, 115–21, 171.

3. Statement of Vice Admiral Earl B. Fowler., Jr. . . . Before the Subcommittee on Seapower . . . of the House Armed Services Committee on Trident and SSN 688, 12 March 1981, CA.

4. Press statement by the Secretary of the Navy, John Lehman, Concerning SSN-688 Class Submarine Procurement, 17 March 1981, and Lehman to Lewis, 17 March 1981, CA.

5. *New London (Conn.) Day*, 26 March 1981; Tyler, *Running Critical*, 287–89.

6. Memorandum for Correspondents, 1 April 1981, Rickover Papers.

7. Lehman, *Command of the Seas*, 36; Rickover's remark to me, undated but around this time.

8. Discussion of Meeting this Date of 1630 at the CNO's Office . . . 26 March 1981, Rickover Papers.

9. Rickover, Memorandum of Visit with John F. Lehman Jr., Secretary of the Navy (At His Office) This Date, 1 May 1981, Rickover Papers. In *Command of the Seas*, 14–15, Lehman states that he had been told he would be "honored" by a direct communication. Because the Notes were unsigned, unaddressed, and unclassified, he knew he was not the only person who was to receive the memorandum.

10. Lehman, *Command of the Seas*, 1; Lehman, "Retiring a Legend," U.S. Naval Institute *Proceedings* 115/1/1031 (January 1989), 60–61.

11. Edwards to Weinberger, 6 May 1981; Thurmond to the President, 25 May 1981, Rickover Papers.

12. Remarks by Admiral Rickover on Completion of USS Ohio First Sea Trials, 20 June 1981, CA.

13. Polmar and Allen, "Plot to Get Rickover," 143; Tyler, *Running Critical*, 297–300. *New London (Conn.) Day*, 19 August 1981; *Providence (R.I.) Journal, Norwich (Conn.) Bulletin, Boston Herald American*, all 20 August 1981.

14. Rickover to Eleonore B. Rickover, 27 July 1981, Rickover Papers. I inserted the words in brackets to make the sentence complete.

15. C. A. Hansen, Memorandum to Adm. H. G. Rickover, 26 February 1981, CA.

16. Lehman, *Command of the Seas*, 33. Rickover, Memorandum of Telephone Conversation This Date Between Mr. Lehman . . . and Admiral Rickover at 1700, 20 August 1981, Rickover Papers.

17. Lehman, *Command of the Seas*, 30, 220–22.

18. John Lehman, Secretary of the Navy, transcript of interview with ABC *20/20* correspondent Tom Jarrel, Washington, D.C., 22 September 1981, Rickover Papers.

19. Transcript titled "John Lehman, News Conference at the Pentagon, Thursday, October 22, 1981, 10:00 A.M.," Rickover Papers. For other terms, see Lehman, *Command of the Seas*, 221–23.

20. Lehman, *Command of the Seas*, 31; Hartmann, *Naval Renaissance*, 90–91.

21. *Bremerton (Wash.) Sun*, 11 November 1981.

22. White, Introduction of Adm H. G. Rickover, USN, 11 November 1981, Rickover Papers.

23. My notes, CA.

24. News Conference by Secretary of the Navy . . . 13 November 1981, CA.

25. Memorandum of a Telephone Conversation . . . between Admiral Hayward, CNO, and Admiral Rickover, Rickover Papers.

26. Details of what transpired are not clear. This account is based on my notes and on Rickover to Senator Jackson, 7 December, and Rickover to Scoop, 15 December 1981, Box 18/9, Jackson Papers, Acc. 3560-5, University of Washington Libraries.

27. *Defense Policy*, pt. 1, 43–34, 61–62.

28. Remarks by Admiral H. G. Rickover on the Occasion of His Leaving Naval Reactors, 29 January 1982, CA.

29. For transition, see Hartmann, *Naval Renaissance*, 85–94; Lehman, *Command*

of the Seas, 1–8, 29–35; and Kinnaird McKee, "Relieving Admiral Rickover," *Shipmate* (April 2000): 9–12.

30. Two telephone calls to the author, n.d., but shortly after 30 January 1982, CA.

31. Executive Order 12344, 1 February 1982, and McKee to Distribution, 1 February 1982, are in Subcommittee on Strategic and Theater Nuclear Forces of the Senate Committee on Armed Services, *Nomination of Kinnaird R. McKee to be Admiral and Director of the Office of Naval Nuclear Propulsion, Department of Energy,* 97th Cong., 2d sess., 23 February 1982 (Washington, D.C.: GPO, 1982), 8–9, 4–6, respectively. The executive order also provides for a civilian director, presumably because the program was a joint program of the Navy and Energy Departments. There was never serious consideration that a civilian head the program.

Chapter 21. Death

1. Senate Committee on Appropriations, *Supplemental Appropriations Bill, 1982,* 97th Cong., 2d sess., 3 August 1982, S. Rept. 97-516, 58–59.

2. William F. Halsey, Ernest J. King, William D. Leahy, and Chester W. Nimitz each received five stars for service in World War II.

3. H. Rept. 4977 [Rept. 97-437], 97th Cong., 2d sess. The bill was introduced on 16 November 1981 and 1 March 1982 and placed upon the House Calendar No. 96 but got no further. Kane's remarks are in *Charleston (S.C.) News & Courier,* 3 February 1982.

4. Congress, *A Bill to Authorize Presentation of a . . . Gold Medal to Admiral Hyman George Rickover,* 97th Cong., 2d sess., 3 February 1982, H. Rept. 5432; *Congressional Record,* 97th Cong., 2d sess., vol. 128, pt. 5, S. 6494-6497.

5. Brochures from the H. G. Rickover Foundation, CA.

6. Program, Speakers's Remarks, and newspaper clippings are in CA.

7. *Washington Dossier* 8, no. 11 (April 1983): 15.

8. Program and papers in CA.

9. Papers in CA.

10. Rickover, *An Assessment of the GPU Nuclear Corporation Organization and Senior Management and Its Competence to Operate TMI-1,* 19 November 1983, and Rickover, *Follow-up Report of Assessment of the GPU Nuclear Corporation Organization and Senior Management and Its Competence to Operate TMI-1,* 19 April 1984, CA.

11. The following paragraphs are based on frequent conversations with Rickover and his staff.

12. Tyler, *Running Critical,* 4.

13. Secretary of the Navy to Adm. Hyman Rickover, 21 May 1985, Rickover to Secretary of the Navy, 7 June 1985, Rickover Papers.

14. *Congressional Record,* 99th Cong., 1st sess., 11 July 1985, vol. 131, pt. 7, pp. 18734–35.

15. Rockwell, *Rickover Effect,* 385–87.

16. *New York Times,* 11 July 1998. Jane Rickover in an authorized statement dated

18 July 1985 declared that Rickover used his "enormous personal influence with President Carter" to weaken the report on Three Mile Island to the president because of the effect the original report would have destroyed the nuclear power industry. See http://www.nonviolence.org/noflyby/ref/rick-st.htm (29 September 1999). Her charge has not been substantiated.

Chapter 22. Engineering Legacy

1. Rickover to Distribution, 20 August 1979, Principles of the Naval Nuclear Propulsion Program, lent to me by William M. Hewitt.
2. Rickover, conversation with author, 24 May 1978, CA.
3. J. M. Maloney to author, 10 September 1999.

Chapter 23. In Memoriam

1. "A Lifetime Commitment to Teaching Us Excellence"; quotation used with permission of Adm. James D. Watkins, USN (Ret.).
2. H. G. Rickover, *How the Battleship Maine Was Destroyed* (Annapolis: Naval Institute Press, 1976), 106.

SOURCES

Constructing an outline of Rickover's life is not hard; it is bringing life to that outline that is challenging. It is difficult because he drew a sharp line between his role as a public figure and his life as a private citizen. For that reason, this essay emphasizes primary sources. These consist of his papers, interviews with those who knew him, and official records that shed light on some of his assignments. The secondary sources include only those publications that give background or technical information. Listing all the books and articles on Rickover would have resulted in an extremely long essay.

Primary Sources
Rickover Papers

Admiral Rickover's papers, held by Eleonore B. Rickover, the admiral's second wife, was by far my most valuable source. It contains his official papers, such as Naval Academy records, fitness reports, and orders, as well as drafts of a history of the ship repair base at Okinawa, speeches, and other miscellaneous documents. The admiral also kept scrapbooks that show the press reaction to certain events in his career. His letters and those of his first wife, Ruth Masters Rickover, provide a superb portrait of life in the Navy between 1929 and 1939, and give revealing insights into his character. Because the admiral deleted some names and observations before having them typed, the letters are not holograph.

Eleonore B. Rickover's own papers are exceedingly important in understanding events in the latter part of the admiral's career and at the end of his life. Through her own service as a Navy nurse, she could assess the events she witnessed.

Interviews

Those individuals whom I interviewed or with whom I have corresponded about Admiral Rickover are as follows (the list does not necessarily include those already mentioned in the preface):

For the pre-atomic energy years I talked with Mrs. I. Berman (the admiral's sister Augusta); Rabbi Bruce E. Kahn; Rear Adm. Benton W. Decker; Clayton B.

Garvey; Rear Adm. Edgar H. Batcheller; Rear Adm. William A. Brockett; Chief Machinist's Mate Paul E. Dignan; Capt. Frederic S. Steinke; Capt. James S. Bethea; John F. O'Grady.

For the atomic energy years I listened to Capt. Edward L. Beach; Rear Adm. Albert G. Mumma; Rear Adm. Willis C. Barnes; Philip R. Clark; Capt. John W. Crawford Jr.; Capt. James M. Dunford; G. Wesley Faurot; Donald E. Fry; Jack C. Grigg; Souren Hanessian; Charles A. Hansen; Tom A. Hendrickson; Edwin E. Kintner; I. Harry Mandil; Theodore Rockwell; Louis H. Roddis Jr.; and Milton Shaw.

Some interviews do not fall into a particular category. Rep. Melvin R. Price talked about the Joint Committee on Atomic Energy, Chester L. Burns described the initial sea trials of the *Enterprise*, and Raymond L. Garthoff discussed the inspection of the *Lenin*. Melvin R. Laird, longtime member of the House Committee on Appropriations and former secretary of defense, viewed Rickover from both perspectives. Other officials who took time to talk to me were Glenn T. Seaborg, chairman of the AEC; John F. Lehman Jr., secretary of the navy; Robert P. Pirie Jr., assistant secretary of the navy; James T. Ramey, AEC commissioner; Vice Adm. Lando Zech, chairman of the Nuclear Regulatory Commission; and Adm. Elmo R. Zumwalt Jr., chief of naval operations.

For the post-atomic energy years, Joan Barnes, one of the admiral's nurses, recalled his final days, and Joann P. DiGennaro discussed the origins of the Rickover Foundation.

Oral Histories

I found the interviews conducted by the Naval Institute for its oral histories very helpful. They are in the Naval Historical Center in the Washington Navy Yard, or in the offices of the U. S. Naval Institute at Annapolis, Maryland. Because the histories span an entire career, they cannot deal with any subject in great detail. They are valuable, however, in providing clues on subjects for further research. Because Admiral Rickover figures in so many of them, I give here only those I found particularly useful: Capt. Slade D. Cutter, Rear Adm. William D. Irvin, Rear Adm. Charles E. Loughlin, Vice Adm. William Paden Mack, Rear Adm. Ralph K. James, Rear Adm. Ruthven E. Libby, Adm. Stuart S. (Sunshine) Murray, John C. Niedermair (naval architect), Rear Adm. Schuyler N. Pyne, Adm. James S. Russell, Carleton Shugg, Vice Adm. William R. Smedberg III, Capt. Henri Smith-Hutton, and Rear Adm. Charles C. Wheeler. *U.S. Naval Institute Oral History Collection, Catalog of Transcripts: 2000–2001* is an indispensable guide to other transcripts.

Documents Made Available with Permission

It is a pleasure to acknowledge those who gave me permission to use documents in their possession. Those individuals are Mrs. William A. Brockett, for Rear Adm. William A. Brockett's correspondence with Admiral Rickover; Capt. John W.

Crawford Jr., for his memorandum on the problem of establishing a deputy director; Donald E. Fry, for his meticulous statistics recording the dates of service of
Naval Reactors personnel; Theodore Rockwell, for quotations from his writings;
and Glenn T. Seaborg, for his multivolume journal.

Two organizations gave me permission to use material drawn from their records. They are the CBS Corporation, for portions of its copyrighted transcript of
CBS Television and CBS Radio Network interview with Admiral Rickover on
3 September 1978, and The Estate of Richard M. Nixon, for selected documents
from the deeded portion of the Richard M. Nixon Pre-Presidential Papers housed
at the National Archives Pacific Region, Laguna Niguel, California.

Documents from Other Published Collections

The *Journal of Glenn T. Seaborg*, printed by the Lawrence Berkeley Laboratory at
Berkeley, California, is a superb multivolume source for information on the history of atomic energy. Permission is no longer required to use the journals, for they
are now available in the Manuscript Division of the Library of Congress.

The diary of Maj. Gen. K. D. Nichols, general manager of the Atomic Energy
Commission from November 1953 to April 1955, has some enlightening entries on
Rickover's relationship with the commissioners. No permission is needed to use
the diary, which is held by the Research Collections, Office of History, HQ, U.S.
Army Corps of Engineers, in Alexandria, Virginia.

Official Documents

The National Archives and Records Administration (NARA) has several collections of official documents that provide background and context to events
described in the biography. I have identified them by the NARA Record Group
(RG) number and, where applicable, Entry (E) number.

RG 19, Records of the Bureau of Ships, E 993, has the records of the battery fire
on the *S-48*.

RG 19, Records of the Bureau of Ships, General Correspondence, 1925–1940,
E 115, contains the report of the erratic behavior of the submarine.

RG 19, Records of the Bureau of Ships, E 1266, contains much material on Pearl
Harbor and the work of the electrical section.

RG 24, Records of the Bureau of Naval Personnel, has the logs of the ships in
which Rickover served.

RG 46, Records of the United States Senate, Sars-T.13, has the hearing of the
Senate Committee on Armed Services on Rickover's promotion.

RG 80, General Records of the Department of the Navy, General Correspondence, deals with the condition of the *Finch*.

RG 80, General Records of the Department of the Navy, General Correspondence, General Board Subject File, 1950–January 1951 documents, places the *Nautilus* in the fiscal year 1952 building program.

RG 85, Records of the Immigration and Naturalization Service, Microfilm 682, establishes the date on which Rickover entered the United States and the year of his birth.

RG 128, Records of the Joint Committees of Congress, includes those of the Joint Committee on Atomic Energy. In general the quality of material is low. Searching the Outgoing Mail Files after the approximate date of an event may give clues to other material.

Microfilm M964, Records Relating to United States Fleet Problems I to XXII, makes it possible to trace the parts played by the ship in which Rickover served.

The NARA Presidential Libraries, through unclassified official papers, furnish some light on the relationships between Admiral Rickover and the officials in the administrations of Carter, Eisenhower, Kennedy, and Johnson. The Carter library has some correspondence between Admiral Rickover and President Carter that illustrates the personal ties between them. The President has donated his presidential and pre-presidential papers to the Jimmy Carter Library and has relinquished the literary rights to all his material except that published in books.

The Naval Historical Center, located in the Washington Navy Yard, contains an excellent library and archives.

Secondary Sources

Books

I have arranged the titles in a roughly chronological order. Except for a biography, those books covering his early life come first and are followed by works dealing with the later periods.

There are no good biographies of Rickover. That by Norman Polmar and Thomas B. Allen, *Rickover* (New York: Simon and Schuster, 1982), suffers because Rickover refused to have anything to do with it and discouraged others from helping the authors. Although short on biographical information, it has some material not easily found elsewhere.

The *Electrical Section History*, NAVSHIPS 250-660-24 (Washington, D.C.: Bureau of Ships, 1946), and W. P. Welch, *Mechanical Shock on Naval Vessels* (Washington, D.C.: GPO, 1946), which are official works, cover the electrical section years. The first is most important for understanding functions and growth of the organization under Rickover; the second describes a technical area on which Rickover had great influence. Capt. Edward L. Beach, *Salt and Steel: Reflections of a Submariner* (Annapolis: Naval Institute Press, 1999) is a valuable firsthand account of working with Rickover to establish the nuclear propulsion program. His treatment of Rickover in the *S-48* is weakened by the lack of access to reliable sources in Rickover's papers. Clay Blair Jr.'s *Admiral Rickover and the Atomic Submarine* (New York: Henry Holt, 1954) is a highly partisan account of Rickover as of the date of its publication but nonetheless useful. Because the book is hard to find, I have used the edition published in London by Odhams in 1957. The editions are not identical; nonetheless, both contain some biographical information. Ruth Masters Rickover in *Pepper, Rice, and Elephants* (Annapolis: Naval Institute Press, 1975) relates the travels she and her husband made in the Far East. Theodore Rockwell's *The Rickover Effect: How One Man Made a Difference* (Annapolis: Naval Institute Press, 1992) contains a great deal of biographical material. A senior engineer in Naval Reactors from 1949 to 1964, he witnessed many of the events he describes. He also writes of the Rickover Foundation and Rickover's final days. In addition, he placed a detailed chronology in the endpapers that is an exceedingly helpful reference. Adm. Elmo R. Zumwalt, *On Watch: A Personal Memoir* (New York: Quadrangle, 1976) details his clashes with Rickover. Patrick Tyler, *Running Critical: The Silent War, Rickover, and General Dynamics* (New York: Harper and Row, 1986) is a highly dramatic account of one part of the struggles over shipbuilding claims. Possibly the author exaggerates the influence of the conflict on the end of Rickover's career. Secretary of the Navy John F. Lehman Jr., in his *Command of the Seas* (New York: Charles Scribner's Sons, 1988), relates almost with a sense of personal triumph his moves to force Rickover out of the program. Frederick H. Hartmann, *Naval Renaissance: The U.S. Navy in the 1980s* (Annapolis: Naval Institute Press, 1990), summarizes the transition of program leadership from Rickover to McKee.

For Rickover's part in the development of civilian nuclear power, *The Shippingport Pressurized Water Reactor* (Reading, Mass.: Addison-Wesley, 1958) is an excellent source on the technical problems and the design philosophy with which he undertook the project. A brief summary of the later history of the station, including its part in investigating the feasibility of breeding with light water reactors, is in Francis Duncan and Jack M. Holl, *Shippingport: The Nation's First Atomic Power Station* (Washington, D.C.: History Division, Department of Energy, 1983). Richard W. Dyke and Francis X. Gannon in *Chet Holifield, Master Legislator and Nuclear Statesman* (Lanham, Md.: University Press of America, 1996) describe the role of the congressman in that area and his conviction that the safe application of the technology depended upon adopting Rickover's standards of technical excellence. Because the endnotes are numerous and meticulous, the biography is valuable for research on several activities of the committee. Joseph V. Rees, *Hostages of Each Other: The Transformation of Nuclear Safety Since Three Mile Island* (Chicago: University of Chicago Press, 1988) is an important study of the influence of Rickover standards on the operation of American nuclear power plants.

For background on the program, I used Richard G. Hewlett and Francis Duncan, *Nuclear Navy, 1946–1962* (Chicago: University of Chicago Press, 1974) and Duncan, *Rickover and the Nuclear Navy: The Discipline of Technology* (Annapolis: Naval Institute Press, 1989). For technical information on submarines, I have relied heavily on Norman Friedman's *U.S Submarines Since 1945: An Illustrated Design History* (Annapolis: Naval Institute Press, 1994) and Gary E. Weir's *Building American Submarines, 1914–1940* and *Forged in War: The Naval-Industrial Complex and American Submarine Construction*, both published in Washington, D.C., by the

Naval Historical Center, Department of the Navy, the first in 1991, the second in 1993. For surface ships, I used Friedman's *U.S. Aircraft Carriers: An Illustrated Design History* and *U.S. Cruisers: An Illustrated Design History*, published by the Naval Institute Press, the first c. 1983, the second c. 1984.

Rickover wrote several books, many with the aid of Ruth M. Rickover, herself an author of works on international law. Three of his books deal with education: *Education and Freedom* (New York: E. P. Dutton, 1959), *Swiss Schools and Ours: Why Theirs are Better* (Boston: Little, Brown, 1962), and *American Education, A National Failure: The Problem of Our Schools and What We Can Learn from England* (New York: E. P. Dutton, 1963). The first sees education as part of national defense, a not unexpected viewpoint considering the Soviet space achievements that had taken place a little earlier. The other books find the American educational system lacks the academic standards set by the Swiss and English. Two books deal with history. *Eminent Americans: Namesakes of the Polaris Submarine Fleet* (Washington, D.C.: GPO, 1972) is a series of biographical essays which are drawn from secondary sources. *How The Battleship Maine Was Destroyed* (Washington, D.C.: GPO, 1976 but copyrighted in 1975) was reprinted with some new material added by the Naval Institute Press in 1995. By its engineering analysis of the wreckage of the ship, the book makes a great contribution to understanding the event that precipitated the Spanish-American War.

Congressional Hearings

Rickover testified each year before the Senate and House authorization and appropriations committees as well as other congressional committees having different responsibilities. In the hearings he often incorporated documents, correspondence, and chronologies that cannot be found elsewhere. The very number of hearings makes them difficult to use.

The Joint Economic Committee, *Economics of Defense Policy: Adm. H. G. Rickover*, 97th Cong., 2d sess., 28 January 1982 (Washington, D.C.: GPO, 1982) is one guide into the hearings. It consists of six parts. Part 1 contains Rickover's last testimony before a congressional committee and, among other material, a very comprehensive summary of the basic organization and functions of the naval propulsion program as it existed at the end of Rickover's leadership. Part 1 also has a valuable several-page list of official published sources on the program beginning in 1953 and ending in 1981. The list includes a few references to the Shippingport Atomic Power Station. Part 2 contains a selected list of testimony and speeches on several subjects, among them accounting, government contracting practices, and education. Part 3 focuses on Navy contracts and government policies, Part 4 on shipbuilding claims, Part 5 on lawyers and legal ethics, and Part 6 on cost accounting standards and miscellaneous matters.

Appendix 9, "New Construction Major Surface Warships and Submarines Authorized since World War II," in Joint Committee on Atomic Energy, *Naval*

Nuclear Propulsion Program—1970, 19 and 20 March 1970 (Washington, D.C.: GPO, 1970), 226–35, has a most helpful table and notes showing by fiscal year the types of ships requested by the department of defense and the congressional actions. Unfortunately, the appendix does not go beyond fiscal year 1970.

Articles

John W. Crawford Jr., "Get 'em Young and Train 'em Right," U.S. Naval Institute, *Proceedings* 113/10/1016 (October 1987): 103–8, and his "Passing Rickover's Muster," *Naval History* (Spring 1992): 35–38, are excellent distillations of Rickover's philosophy.

Edwin E. Kintner, "Admiral Rickover's Gamble: The Landlocked Submarine," *Atlantic Monthly* 203 (January 1959): 31–35, and "The First Days of the Mark I," *Journal of the American Society of Naval Engineers* 72 (February 1960): 9–13, are graphic descriptions of the first achievement of nuclear propulsion. Kinnaird McKee, "Relieving Admiral Rickover," *Shipmate* (April 2000): 9–12, is his own account of the transition of program leadership.

I also want to thank colleagues and friends. They are not "sources" in the bibliographic sense of the word, but they were essential sources of assistance and encouragement. They are Annette D. Barnes, for critically scanning many chapters; Morris Cobern, for guiding me through the arcane ways of the personal computer; Evan M. Duncan of the Historians Office in the Department of State, for locating published official documents on the admiral's trip to the Soviet Union; John M. Duncan, for listening to me whenever our schedules allowed lunching together; Dr. Benjamin S. Loeb, for commenting on the early chapters; Gregory K. Myers, for information on electrical engineering; Dana M. Wegner, for providing invaluable advice in planning the biography; and Dr. Gary E. Weir, for his counsel and for describing the technology of pre–World War II submarines.

Jonathan Kiell, director of communications and external affairs, Naval Reactors, guided my way in locating others in the program for information.

INDEX

ABOUT THE AUTHOR

Francis Duncan earned his M.A. and Ph.D degrees in history from the University of Chicago. He was a historian for the Atomic Energy Commission (AEC) and its successor agency, the Department of Energy, from 1962 to 1982. During these years, he and Richard G. Hewlett coauthored *Atomic Shield*, the second volume of the history of the AEC. At Admiral Rickover's request, they also collaborated on *Nuclear Navy, 1946–1962*, a study of the naval nuclear propulsion program. Dr. Duncan later wrote *Rickover and the Nuclear Navy*, which won the 1991 Theodore and Franklin D. Roosevelt Naval History Prize. He and his wife reside in Bethesda, Maryland.